WELS[MEDIEVAL

BEING A TEXT OF

THE LAWS OF HOWEL THE GOOD

NAMELY

THE BRITISH MUSEUM HARLEIAN MS. 4353 OF
THE 13TH CENTURY, WITH TRANSLATION
INTRODUCTION, APPENDIX, GLOSSARY
INDEX, AND A MAP

BY

A. W. WADE-EVANS

OXFORD

AT THE CLARENDON PRESS

1909

HENRY FROWDE, M.A.

PUBLISHER TO THE UNIVERSITY OF OXFORD

LONDON, EDINBURGH, NEW YORK

TORONTO AND MELBOURNE

TO MY WIFE

FLORENCE MAY DIXON

PREFACE

THIS book is intended primarily for the student of the political history of Wales, but it is hoped that others also will find it useful. The particular text adopted was at the recommendation of Dr. Gwenogfryn Evans some years ago, who regards it as the oldest and best of its class. It is reproduced page for page, line for line, and error for error, except where it was found more convenient to relegate notices of errors to the palaeographical notes. The translation is a tentative one based on that of Aneurin Owen in his *Ancient Laws and Institutes of Wales*, a work which has been found indispensable for the present production.

I would record my sincere thanks to Sir John Rhŷs, from whom I have received, not only the valuable assistance which so distinguished a scholar could render, but also the sympathy and encouragement of a friend; to Dr. Gwenogfryn

Evans for help and advice as to the choice of a text, and as to procedure with regard to publication; and to Mr. Ernest Hughes, late of Jesus College, and now Lecturer in History at the University College of South Wales, to whom I am indebted for many suggestions whilst the Introduction and Glossary were still in proof. Finally, I have to thank the Delegates of the Clarendon Press for undertaking the publication of this work, and also the staff for the kindness and the efficiency which have so much lightened my labours.

Ty Rhôs, Fishguard.

CONTENTS

Rogo ut omnis lector, qui legerit hunc librum, det veniam mihi, qui ausus sum post tantos haec tanta scribere quasi garrula avis vel quasi quidam invalidus arbiter. Cedo illi qui plus noverit in ista peritia satis quam ego.—NENNIUS.

Y mae e'n wir yn orchwyl dyrus ddigon i chwilio allan Ddechreuad ein Cenedl ni yn gowir ac yn ddiwyrgam, a'i holrhain o'i haberoedd i lygad y ffynnon. Ond mi a amcanaf symud ymaith y niwl oddiar y ffordd, fel y bo ein taith at y gwirionedd yn eglur.—THEOPHILUS EVANS.

The notion that the Welsh came to the Isle of Britain with the grasshopper has been dispelled by modern research.—EGERTON PHILLIMORE.

INTRODUCTION

NOT one of the law books bearing the name of Howel Dda, which have come down to us from the Welsh medieval age, is older than the last quarter of the twelfth century, that is, about 250 years after Howel's death. The earliest of all, the **Peniarth MS. 28**,[1] is written in Latin with many Welsh terms, phrases, and short passages left untranslated. Next to this comes the **Peniarth MS. 29** (MS. **A**), sometimes known as the *Black Book of Chirk*, and written in Welsh about 1200. Neither of these professes to be the original codex of the White House, nor does that claim appear to be made by any MS. of the laws now extant.

These Welsh medieval law books bear so strong a general resemblance to one another that it can hardly be doubted but that they are all based on some one ultimate original, which, in our present state of information, we may suppose to have been a 'Book of the White House'.[2] Those written in Welsh, however, certainly fall into three distinct classes, each of which begins with its own peculiar type of preface. They may be distinguished as follows:—

(*a*) Those which refer exclusively to the King of

---

[1] For a full account of this and other Peniarth MSS., see *Report on Manuscripts in the Welsh Language*, vol. I, Pts. II and III, by Dr. J. Gwenogfryn Evans, printed for the Historical Manuscripts Commission.

[2] *Lleuyr e Ty Guyn* mentioned in the thirteenth-century Pen. MS. 30. See *Report on MSS. in Welsh* I. 361, note.

Aberffraw in North Wales,[1] and which give other indications that they pertain to the kingdom of Gwynedd in N.W. Wales, of which Aberffraw was the .chief royal residence. Aneurin Owen dubbed them the 'Venedotian Code', that is, the code of Venedotia or Gwynedd, a name with which we need not on the whole quarrel. As it will be necessary, however, to diverge from Owen's other designations, this class will be distinguished here as the Book of Gwynedd. The chief exemplar is the **Peniarth MS. 29** (MS. A) referred to above. References to a certain Iorwerth ap Madog [2] indicate his influence as a jurist on this class, but they are such as show that the Book of Gwynedd was regarded as existing before his time.

(*b*) Those which refer exclusively to the King of Dinevwr in South Wales,[3] but are void of any other reference such as would lead one to associate them in any special degree with that Deheubarth of which Dinevwr was held to be the chief royal residence. From a passage in the preface it appears that their original was written not only outside Deheubarth but in Powys and by a Powysian.[4] Is it possible that they represent what Aneurin Owen would have called the 'Powysian Code'? Unfortunately he styled them the 'Gwentian Code' as being the code 'adapted to Gwent or South-east Wales', for which there appears to be no evidence of any kind.[5] A peculiarity of the preface of this class

---

[1] *Anc. Laws* I. 1–335 ; II. 1–36.   [2] Ibid. I. 104, 218, 292.
[3] Ibid. I. 620–797.   [4] See Glossary under *Deheubarth*.
[5] *Anc. Laws* I. viii. Gwent was a patria between the lower courses of the river Usk and the river Wye, included in modern Monmouthshire.

of law book is that it refers its compilation to a certain Morgeneu and his son Cyvnerth. Elsewhere [1] it is Cyvnerth ab Morgeneu who is referred to as a well-known 'jurist', for which reason this class will be distinguished here as the 'Book of Cyvnerth'. The text adopted by Aneurin Owen as the basis of his amalgam of this type of law book is the **Peniarth MS. 37** (MS. U), 'not from any superiority but as being the simplest.' [2]

(c) Those which refer both to the King of Dinevwr and to the King of Aberffraw,[3] stating expressly that of all the kings in Wales gold is payable to these two only. The King of Dinevwr, however, is mentioned first in order, and there is a special section devoted to him. One of the Dinevwr kings is also mentioned by name, viz. Rhys ab Gruffydd,[4] sovereign of Deheubarth, who died in 1197. There is also found a section dealing with the seven bishop-houses in Dyved,[4] one of the patrias included in the Deheubarth. This class therefore appears to represent a 'Book of Deheubarth'. Unfortunately again Aneurin Owen named them the 'Dimetian Code', that is, the code of Dyved, although there appears to be no reason why they should be confined to this particular patria, and not made to cover the whole of that Deheubarth which was held to be subject to the King of Dinevwr. The preface of this class mentions a certain Blegywryd who is described as the cleric appointed in Howel's convention at the White House to reduce the revised laws to writing. Nothing more appears to be known of this Blegywryd beyond what is

---

[1] *Anc. Laws* I. 218, 340.   [2] Ibid. I. xxxi.
[3] Ibid. I. 338–617.   [4] Ibid. I. 574; 556–9.

stated in this preface. Hence this particular group of law books may not inaptly be styled the Book of Blegywryd. Aneurin Owen adopted the Cotton MS., **Titus D IX** (MS. **L**), of the second quarter of the fourteenth century,[1] as his representative text of this group. Dr. Gwenogfryn Evans regards the **Peniarth MS. 36^** (MS. **O**), as the oldest now known, having been written shortly after 1282,[2] but according to Owen 'the variations in the manuscripts of this class are but few', for which reason he is of opinion that 'they perhaps exhibit the nearest affinity to the original compilation sanctioned by Howel'.[3] It should be noticed that the earliest of all the existing law books bearing Howel's name, viz. the Latin **Peniarth MS. 28**, is of the form of the Book of Blegywryd, as also the important Latin Cotton MS., **Vespasian E XI**, written about 1250,[1] although the name of Blegywryd is absent from both.[4]

The following passage [5] from the preface to the Book of Blegywryd is very suggestive as to these three types of law books, and appears also to throw some light on the puzzling matter of King Howel's dominions.

Guedy hynny yd erchis gwnneuthur tri llifuyr kyureith : vn vrth y lys peunydyaul pressuyl y gyt ac ef; aral y lys Dineuur; y trydyd y lys Aberffraw, megys

---

[1] This date is that of Dr. Gwenogfryn Evans as given in his report on the MSS. in Welsh in the British Museum, the relevant portions of which report (not yet published) he has kindly forwarded to me for perusal.

[2] *Report on MSS. in Welsh* I. 369.   [3] *Anc. Laws* I. xxx.

[4] The third old Latin text, viz. **Harleian MS. 1796**, seems to be of the form of the Book of Gwynedd. See Glossary under *taeogtrev*, p. 347 and note 1.

[5] *Anc. Laws* I. 340.

y caffey teir rann Kymry, nyt amgen, Gwyned, Pwys, Deheubarth, audurdawt kyureith yn eu plith vrth eu reit yn wastat ac yn parawt.

After that he ordered three law books to be made: one for the daily court to be always with him; another for the court of Dinevwr; the third for the court of Aberffraw, so that the three divisions of Cymru, to wit, Gwynedd, Powys, and Deheubarth, should have the authority of law amongst them at their need, always and ready.

Here it is clearly implied that the king's daily court was not in Deheubarth but in Powys. The common opinion is that Howel Dda lived in Deheubarth and especially in Dyved,[1] but in the light of the above passage he generally dwells in Powys. Moreover, the manner in which the White House is spoken of as being the king's hunting-lodge 'when he came to Dyved' seems to bear out the same idea. It is true that the preface to the Book of Cyvnerth appears to restrict Howel's dominions outside Powys, and it is curious that Powys appears to be the very division of Wales wherein that compilation had its origin. How to reconcile these apparent contradictions does not at present appear. The above passage would seem to suggest that there were three types of law books, those of Gwynedd, Powys, and Deheubarth respectively, although, as the passage now stands, it means no more than that three copies of one original were made for the three divisions of Cymru. It may be that in time they each underwent such modifications as adapted them more perfectly to the varying

---

[1] Seeing that he married Elen, daughter of the last king of Dyved, whereby he became immediate ruler of that kingdom.

customs of each division. If, however, in the case of
the Book of Cyvnerth, we are dealing with a 'Powysian
Code', how shall we explain the mention of Dinevwr
and the absence of all reference to any chief royal residence in Powys such as the Mathraval mentioned in later
texts ?[1] It seems therefore advisable for the time being
to abandon 'territorial' designations for the two Dinevwr
classes of law books, and to style them after the names
of the 'jurists' preferred in their respective prefaces.
The designations therefore tentatively proposed for the
three kinds of Welsh law books in lieu of those invented
by Aneurin Owen are as follows :—

> Book of Gwynedd for Venedotian Code,
> Book of Cyvnerth for Gwentian Code,
> Book of Blegywryd for Dimetian Code.

I

Our present text, the **Harleian MS. 4353** (MS. **V**)
belongs to the second of these classes, viz. the Book of
Cyvnerth, being, according to Dr. Gwenogfryn Evans,[2]
'the oldest and most important' of this kind. Aneurin
Owen had six codices of this class before him, which he
denominated **U, V, W, X, Y,** and **Z** respectively. He
noticed that some of them closely resembled the Book of
Blegywryd, so much so indeed in the case of **Y** and **Z**
that he soon ceased to use them in his edition. Two others,
viz. **V** (our present text) and **W**, which are very closely
allied, also resemble in some respects the Book of Blegywryd, especially **V**, which actually contains the passage
on the bishop-houses of Dyved. The leading peculiarity

---

[1] *Anc. Laws* II. 50, 380, 584.   [2] See note 1 on p. x.

of these two MSS., however, is this, that in their prefaces the name of Blegywryd appears in lieu of that of
Cyvnerth and Morgeneu, and indeed appears to have been
substituted for them.   One was almost tempted on this
account to distinguish these two codices, **V** and **W**, by
some such name as the 'Composite Book of Cyvnerth
and Blegywryd', a description which further investigation
may yet substantiate.   The two remaining codices, **U**
and **X**, are much smaller in bulk than the two last, and
might be supposed to approximate nearer to the original
Book of Cyvnerth.   If they were as closely allied as **V**
and **W**, one might indeed think so, but they differ considerably in their arrangement, appear to be much
condensed, and are both somewhat carelessly written.
Their matter is practically all comprised within the
present text, the few additions, which each contains,
being given in the appendix.

<h2 style="text-align:center">V and W [1]</h2>

V = Harleian MS. 4353.   Vellum; $7\frac{3}{4} \times 5$ inches;
folios 1–3, (4–5), 6–27, (28), 29–45, the three folios in
round brackets being insertions on later material in a
hand of about 1600, copied from **X** ; written according to
Dr. Gwenogfryn Evans about 1285 by the same scribe as
wrote **Peniarth MSS. 2** and **6 Part iv,** and **Mostyn
MS. 117** ; 'it is curious that all the MSS. written in the
same hand are imperfect' ; coloured capitals, generally in
red and chocolate alternately ; 25 lines to the page

---

[1] I must again express my obligation to Dr. Gwenogfryn Evans
for the invaluable help received from him in drawing up these
descriptions of the particular MSS. in question.   I have myself
examined **U, V, W,** and **X.**   See note 1 on p. x.

(except 16b and 40a which have 24 and 26 lines respectively); the first and last pages are so stained and worn that it is difficult to be always certain of the reading; one pagination in ink till folio 37, after which till last folio but one there are two paginations, one in ink (39 to 45), and one in pencil (38 to 44), which last is the official numbering of the British Museum, followed in this present work, the last folio being paginated in ink as 45; half bound in morocco. Most of the marginal index words are in the hand of Jaspar Griffith. 'Liber Humfredi Wanley A.D. 1714' (1 b); 'Sum liber Jafpar Gryffyth 1586[−1714=128]' (2 a); 'Yma y gellir craffu a gweled dau beth. * 1. Yn gyntaf pan yfcrifenned y llyfr hwn fod yr offeirieid yn berchen gwragedd priawd, o ran bod breint yma wedi ei ofod i ferched offeirieid. 2. Yn ail mae yn gyffelyp yfcrifennu y llyfr hwn cyn gwahardd prîodas ir offeirieid. Yr hon waharddedigaeth a gymmerth rym (?) yn Eglwys Loegr ynghylch y flwyddyn 1100 yn niwedd teyrnafiad Wiłłm Rufus, edrych fol 44 a' (3 b and 4 a bottom margins. The asterisk refers to 4 a, line 3); 'Rys ap howel ap Jeuan ap gwalter ddugan cof (?)' (18 a right margin from top to bottom); 'Mac yma ddalen yn eifiau' (31 b and 37 b); 'Timothy Middleton' (32 a); 'Timothy Middleton his booke douth Owe' (43 a).

W = Cleopatra A XIV. Vellum; $6\frac{1}{2} \times 4\frac{3}{4}$ inches; folios 34–107 in pencil pagination; first quarter of the fourteenth century; coloured capitals in blue and red alternately, save that the larger ones are in blue with red foliations; ẏ dotted throughout, and gu for gw; 21 lines to the page, except 55a from line 5, 55 b from

line 13, 94 a from line 7, 94 b, 95, 107 a from line 9, and
107 b, which were left blank by the original scribe ; portions of the text are in the margins on folios 42 a, 42 b,
57 a and 83 b ; three paginations, two in ink and one
in pencil, which last is the official one of the British
Museum, followed in this present work ; two and a half
lines on 101 b (= V 45 a 10–12) are almost stained out by
some prudish person; bound in calf along with some
Latin MSS. Besides occasional marginal index words, we
have ' Liber Cardiff de Confuetudinibus Walliæ ', ' Leges
Howeli Dha Wallice,' ' Robertus Cotton Bruceus' (34 a) ;
also much scribbling on folios 43, 44, 55, 94, 95 and 107,
wherein occur proper names—' Sciant prefentes et futuri
quod Ego Johannes filli dedo conceffi in hac prefenti
Carta ' (43 b); ' Sciant prefentes et futuri quod Ego
johannes (?) vabe ff (?) dedi conceffi ' (44 a); ' Johannes
vechan,' ' Jeuan ap phelippe hir dd ap fillippe hir ' (55 a) ;
' Johannes ap gwill (?),' ' Wiłłmus' (?) (55 b) ; '—vabe rimẏ,'
' Jeuan ap dd ap —,' ' Handrods dekerfilly in die martis,'
' Roberto,' ' Th et buon anne cofe nant per ta' (94 b) ;
' — ap blethyn joꝛ ap r .... ap —,' ' [k]arfiłł die —' ' Hoełł
ap — ' (95 b). These names (says Dr. Evans) are in a
fifteenth-century hand, but more or less intentionally
deleted by rubbing.

Y and Z

Y = ' a manuscript presented by the Rev. Mr. Cony-
beare to the Literary Society of Neath, by whom the
use of it for·this work [viz. *Ancient Laws and Institutes of Wales*, MDCCCXLI] was kindly afforded to the
Editor.   It may be attributed to the middle of the four-

teenth century.' So writes Aneurin Owen in the preface
to his book on May 1, 1841. Mr. Egerton Phillimore in
a note in *Y Cymmrodor*, vol. IX, states of this codex that
it has been '*lost* since before 1860'.[1] It appears to have
contained the first part on the Laws of the Court as far
as V 12 a 19, proceeding immediately to the Laws of the
Gwlad, but agreeing so closely with the Book of Blegywryd, that Aneurin Owen ceases altogether to refer to
it.[2] One can therefore only surmise that it followed the
Book of Cyvnerth as far as the point referred to, after
which it followed the Book of Blegywryd.

Z³ = Peniarth MS. 259ᴮ. Paper; 11 × 8 inches;
folios *a-e*, 1-103; imperfect (folios *b-e*, 6-7, 13-20, 44,
47-8, 51, 56, 59-60, 99-101 being blank leaves inserted
by binder); bicolumnar; in two distinct hands; first half
of sixteenth century; bound in leather with **Peniarth
MS. 259ᴬ** (MS. **P**). 'The text of folios 1-46 belongs to
the class of which **V** or **Harleian MS. 4353** is the
prototype. This copy is a kind of selection arranged
differently; it is imperfect and corrupt. . . . The order
of the text is very different.' A fresh hand begins at
folio 49, being contemporary with the first. The latter
inserts the following note on a passage written by the
former—' Hyn ydoedd wydi i scrivenu yny llyfr y copied
hwn o hono. Y llyfr hwnn a gavos Einiawn ap adda
pan vv yngharchar ymhwmfred gan y cunstabyl ai kavas
gan brior y vynachlog a hanoedd o dehevbarth, ac nid
oes athrondyst ar gyfraith namyn y sydd yn y llyfr hwn
kysdal a hwn.' Aneurin Owen in his edition of the

---

[1] p. 299. [2] *Anc. Laws* I. 670, note 21, 686, note 11.
[3] *Report on MSS. in Welsh*, vol. I. 1074-5.

'Gwentian Code' ceases using this codex at the very same point where he metes out like treatment to **Y**; and he states of **Z** at the beginning of the Laws of the Gwlad that it 'is carelessly transcribed and has many chasms', for which reason he leaves it. He inserts variant readings, however, from **Z** in vol. II of his work. **Z** is the codex which with **S** (the **Brit. Mus. Additional MS. 22356** of the late fifteenth century) provides Owen with an interesting but extremely untrustworthy addition to the preface of his 'Dimetian Code'.[1]

U and X

U = Peniarth MS. 37. Vellum; 5⅜ × 4⅛ inches; 156 pages (pp. 153-6 being in court hand); late thirteenth century, in the same hand apparently as **Peniarth MS. 35** (MS. G) with very numerous sectional initials and titles in rubrics, and also rubricated letters; 18 lines to the page; partly gall-stained but complete; in old binding newly covered with pigskin. The text of pp. 121-52 is no part of the Book of Cyvnerth, but is taken from the Book of Gwynedd, being found in **A** and its important transcript **E**. Dr. Evans, however, finds that it is in such close agreement with the corresponding part in **G** that both must be from the same archetype or the one is a copy of the other, both MSS. belonging to the same school of writing and being possibly the work of the same scribe. It will be found reproduced with translation in *Y Cymmrodor*, vol. XVII. The Book of Cyvnerth, properly so called, covers the first 120 pages, and was adopted by Aneurin Owen as the basis of his

---

[1] *Anc. Laws* I. 340-2.

'Gwentian Code'. On the whole his edition is trust-
worthy, following the order of his original and giving
adequate notice when he fails to do so. He rarely or
never expands contractions, and does not even reproduce
them, but in the present case this involves no serious con-
sequences as they are rarely of greater importance than
ran for ra*n*n, or edlig for edli*n*g. The following are the
only serious discrepancies :—

p. 712, l. 5. abu(6ch eı)thyr (eu teıthı) *for* abuu6ch.

p. 722, l. 13. *Add* Ta6lboıt o afg6ın Moıuıl. dec aru-
geınt y gwerth.

p. 764, l. 29. Section XII is erroneously bracketed,
as it appears in U 49 a 6–10 as follows :—Or cledır p6łł
odyn ar tır dyn arałł heb ganhyat pedeır. k. k'. ageıłł
perchenna6c y tır gan yneb ae cladho ăthrı buhyn
caml6ı6 yr bıen.

X = British Museum Cotton MS. **Cleopatra B V.**
Vellum ; 7½ × 5¼ inches ; folios 165–222 (222 a 8–22
added by another hand) ; written about 1350 ; coloured
capitals, generally red and blue alternately, five of which
are illuminated, viz. 165 a, 184 b (cut out), 185 a (two on
this page) and 200 a ; 20 lines to the page ; two paginations in ink and pencil, both the same, the latter being
the official numbering of the Brit. Museum ; 6 = u or v,
and not w ; bound with other works in Russian leather.
'Leges Howelli Boni principis Walli(æ) in Lingua Bri-
tanica' (165 a) ; 'Cyfnerth mab Morgeneu yn gyntaf a
fcrifennodd ac a ddofparthodd y llyfr yma ar y dull ar
wedd hon. Jafp. Gryff. 1600' (165 b) ; '[——] y gwelir
[——] or offeiriaid [——] briodol y [——] [pr]yd hynny'
(168 b) ; the catchwords Moıwyn yftauełł in a fish cut

through by bookbinder (176 b); 'habet hic liber quinquaginta & octo folia' (222 a in Jasper Gryffyth's hand). As compared with **V**, 'the wording is often changed and abbreviated, many passages being omitted and a few others inserted.'

It will be noticed that none of the codices now extant of the Book of Cyvnerth and the Book of Blegywryd date from before the last quarter of the thirteenth century, probably after the death of Llewelyn ap Gruffydd in 1282. Those which are antecedent to this period are the following, which are enumerated in order of time:—

1. **Peniarth MS. 28.** Latin; 1175–1200.

2. **Peniarth MS. 29** (= MS. **A**). Welsh; Book of Gwynedd; about 1200.'

3. **Harleian MS. 1796.** Latin; 1200–1250.[1]

4. **Brit. Mus. Additional MS. 14931** (= **E**). Welsh; Book of Gwynedd; about 1250.[1]

5. **Caligula A III** (= MS. **C**). Welsh; Book of Gwynedd; about 1250.[1]

6. **Vespasian E XI.** Latin; about 1250.[1]

All the earliest and best MSS. extant therefore of the Laws of Howel Dda were written at a time when the Normans had long interfered with Welsh affairs and had taken permanent possession of the majority of the patrias of South Wales. It is very important to bear this in mind, inasmuch as the codices, which are confessedly in a state of flux, cannot fail to reflect the political situation in Wales as it was at the time of writing.

[1] See note 1 on p. x. As to the form of the Latin books see p. x with note 4.

II

Throughout the twelfth and thirteenth centuries what may be called *Welsh* Wales, as distinct from *Norman* Wales,[1] was divided into the three main divisions of Gwynedd, Powys, and Deheubarth. As the result of the important battle of Mynydd Carn in 1079,[2] Gwynedd and Deheubarth henceforth remained under the rule of the House of Gruffydd ap Cynan and that of Rhys ap Tewdwr respectively. Powys continued as before to be governed by the House of Bleddyn. These three families were all sprung from Rhodri the Great and were consequently of the true Cymric lineage of Cunedda Wledig. *Norman* Wales throughout the same period comprised the patrias of Morgannwg with Gwent, Brycheiniog, and Dyved, being roughly equivalent to the modern counties of Glamorgan with Monmouth, Brecon, and Pembroke respectively. The districts now known as Cardiganshire, Radnorshire, and Flintshire fluctuated, being sometimes held by the Welsh and sometimes by the Normans. Seeing, then, that our earliest codex dates from well within this period, and that its successors clearly show that the codification was subject to continual re-arrangement and other modifications, it must be allowed, as we have said above, that in reading them the political situation as it was in these two centuries is

[1] *Outlines of the History of Wales* by Prof. J. E. Lloyd, 164. See also the valuable article by the same writer in the *Transactions* of the Cymmrodorion Society for 1899–1900, entitled 'Wales and the Coming of the Normans'.

[2] This as well as the majority of other dates in early Welsh history must be regarded as tentative only, until the whole subject of Welsh chronology has been thoroughly examined.

by no means to be disregarded. The law is the law of Howel, but it is the law of Howel as modified and amplified both by the varying customs of different parts of Wales and also by the changes which are taking place throughout three and a half critical centuries in the general life of the people.

What share King Howel had in the codification of Welsh law and custom in the tenth century is not easy to determine, especially as the earliest account of the convention which he is said to have assembled at the White House is over two centuries later than his time.[1] Our earliest chronicle also, the so-called *Annales Cambriae*,[2] completed only a few years after his death, is silent as to any activity he may have displayed in this direction, and contains no reference of any kind to the alleged convention. All the codices, however, agree in associating his name with the formulation of the laws of Cymru, frequently appealing to his authority and indicating the fact when they have occasion to depart from it or to add thereto. This unanimous testimony of the codices is corroborated by the nature of the few facts which are known of his career. By the death of his father and paternal uncles, the sons of Rhodri the Great, he rose steadily in power. He had married Elen, the daughter of the King of Dyved, by which he became king of that country.[3] There is evidence which goes to show that he was by inheritance ruler of Powys, and as we find him

---

[1] i.e. the preface to **Peniarth MS. 28** (see p. 1).

[2] Reproduced by Mr. Egerton Phillimore, together with Pedigrees, &c., in *Y Cymmrodor*, vol. IX. 141-83. This reproduction is indispensable to every student of early Welsh history.

[3] *Y Cymm.* IX. 171, Peds. I, II.

laying claims to portions of Gwent in the far south-east,[1] this, with other indications,[2] makes it almost certain that Brycheiniog, which lay between him and Gwent, was also in his grasp. After the death of his cousin, King Idwal Voel of Gwynedd, in 943, he must have been easily supreme throughout the whole of Wales, although the realm of the king of Morgannwg appears not to have been brought under the sway of the family of Rhodri in the sense that the rest of Wales was subject to that house. Howel therefore between 943 and 950 was clearly in an excellent position to move with regard to the revision and codification of Welsh law and custom, if so minded; and the evidence that he was so minded is ample. In the year 928 he had made a pilgrimage to Rome. He frequently attended the meetings of the Witenagemot of the Wessex kings, for his name appears as witness to several charters ranging from 931 to 949.[3] He was thus clearly on intimate terms with the royal house of Wessex, and was thereby under the direct influence of the traditions of Alfred the Great, not to mention the general effect in the same direction which Asser must have produced on the life of Wales, particularly in Dyved.[4] For Asser would spend six months with Alfred and six months in his own Britannia in his native

---

[1] *Y Cymm.* IX. 325.
[2] See Glossary under *Deheubarth.*
[3] *Transactions* of the Cymm. Soc. 1905-6, pp. 11-13. It should be stated here however that there was a Howel, king of the West Welsh, flourishing at this time whose name appears in the *Saxon Chronicle* s. a. 926. See Plummer's *Two Sax. Chrs.* II. viii.
[4] Where Howel could hardly fail to have lived, at least at the time when he became its king through marriage.

Dyved.[1]   Through the same traditions there was operat-
ing also the influence of Charlemagne, to say nothing of
this same influence as it may have operated through
Howel's own grandfather, Rhodri the Great.   Indeed, it
can hardly be doubted that the fame and character of
Charlemagne, Alfred the Great, and his own grandfather
Rhodri acted powerfully on the mind of Howel, whose
own life appears to be in emulation of theirs.   We find
that our earliest Welsh chronicle, accompanied by thirty-
one invaluable pedigrees with other material, and attached to a copy of the historical compilation which goes
under the name of Nennius, was completed (probably at
St. David's)[2] a few years after his death in 950—a fact
which points to its having been accomplished under his
patronage, if not at his direction.   He stands unique
among the kings and princes of old Wales as being the
only one who is known to have struck coin.[3]   His reign
was marked by unusual peace.   And that he was in general
an enlightened and a beneficent ruler we need no surer
proof than the noteworthy fact that he is known in history as Howel the Good.   It is only, however, as seen in
the general history of Wales up to his time that the signi-
ficance of his reign becomes apparent, how in particular
it marks a noteworthy advance in the emergence of the
entity we now know as Wales from the conditions which
prevailed in the dim centuries of Roman Britain.   It
would require far more space than is at our present
command to provide any adequate presentation of this
subject, even if this were as yet possible.   The main
outlines, however, of the story are quite clear.

[1] Stevenson's *Asser*, pp. 64, 65.   [2] **Brit. Mus. Harleian MS. 3859.**
[3] *Transactions* of Cymm. Soc. 1905-6, pp. 1-30.

III

Roman Britain was treated as a single province till Severus (who died in A.D. 211) divided it into two, called Lower and Upper Britain, *Britannia Inferior* and *Britannia Superior*,[1] so that henceforward the term Britannia came to be used not only for the island or even for Roman Britain, but also for *portions* of Roman Britain which was now known as *Britanniae* or the Britains. Dion Cassius[2] gives us to understand that the legions at Caerlleon on the Usk and Chester on the Dee, were in Upper Britain, while that located at York was in Lower Britain. As the Romans, like other people, allowed the ready test of running water to decide what was upper and what was lower, it is natural to suppose that Upper Britain was mainly that part of Roman Britain which the legions had to approach by marching in the direction of the sources of the Thames and of the streams which meet to form the Humber. When, however, Upper and Lower Britain came to be distinguished as provinces, the question of what was expedient would also play its part in the new arrangements. And as the territory north of Chester would go more conveniently both for geographical and military reasons with that north of the Humber, the whole of this district falling under the surveillance of the official who resided at York, which we know to have been in Lower Britain, it is in no way improbable that Upper Britain as a province would be entirely excluded from what is now the north of England

---

[1] Herodian III. 24.
[2] lv. 23. See Rhŷs's *Celtic Britain*, 3rd ed. 97, &c.; also *The Welsh People*, 103, &c.

and would be confined to a territory south of Chester and including it. This then leaves us the country around the upper reaches of the Thames, and all to the west of it, including Wales *plus* the Devonian peninsula. Without for the moment attempting to define closely its eastern boundary we identify Upper Britain, *Britannia Superior*, with the territory west of a line drawn from Chester (which is included) to the Wiltshire Avon or thereabouts. The western portion of the Devonian peninsula, especially the country beyond the river Exe, was one of the least Romanized parts of Roman Britain, and Wales being a purely military district was similar in this respect, so that they would not inappropriately go together, being connected by the more Romanized region round about the estuary of the Severn.[1] In 297 Diocletian divided Roman Britain into four provinces instead of two and called them *Britannia Prima*, *Britannia Secunda*, *Flavia Caesariensis*, and *Maxima Caesariensis*. As the names clearly imply, we have here nothing more than a renaming of the two old provinces into Britannia and Caesariensis, which are subdivided into Prima and Secunda, and Flavia and Maxima respectively. And as it is certain that Cirencester was in Britannia Prima,[2] we conclude that by Diocletian's arrangement Upper Britain became exclusively known as Britannia, whilst Lower Britain was given the new name of Caesariensis. Moreover, as Cirencester was in Britannia Prima, we would

---

[1] Prof. Haverfield's *Romanization of Roman Britain*, 8 and note 2, 27.
[2] An inscription found near Cirencester proves this. *Eng. Hist. Review*, July, 1896.

also conclude that it was the Severn Sea which was the cause of the subdivision, and that therefore Wales was included in Britannia Secunda. Each of these Britannias was ruled by a governor called *praeses* or president, but the military command was in the hands of another official, who was called the *Comes Brittaniae*.

Whether the reasoning just elaborated will be substantiated or otherwise by fresh discoveries, this at least is certain, that it is unquestionably to the kings and ecclesiastics of the smaller Britannia which we have just delineated that St. Gildas, who died after the middle of the sixth century, addresses his well-known *Epistola*.[1] Beginning with the words *Reges habet Britannia, sed tyrannos* (Britannia hath kings but they are tyrants), he proceeds to address five of the principal ones by name, commencing with him of Devon, and going in regular order until he reaches him of Anglesey, whom God hath 'made

---

[1] I would refer the reader at this point to my articles on the authorship of the *Excidium Britanniae* as distinct from the *Epistola Gildae* in the *Celtic Review* (Edinburgh) for April, July, and October, 1905; also in the *St. David's College Magazine* for December, 1904. Mr. E. W. B. Nicholson has replied in the *Celtic Review* for April, 1906, in an article which for the moment can well be left alongside of the original contributions. The contention is that the first twenty-six chapters of the work, now commonly attributed to Gildas, formerly constituted a distinct book known as *Excidium Britanniae*, which was written by a 'Roman' Briton towards the close of the seventh century somewhere in the neighbourhood of the mouth of the Severn. This work was considerably 'edited' by some one who ignorantly or deliberately misunderstood it, probably both. In this form it passed into the hands of Bede, who used it as his chief and almost only authority for what he had to say of fifth-century Britain. Almost all that Bede professes to know of this period is taken from the *Excidium*, which he seems to ascribe to Gildas (*H. E.* I. 22), although he gives no evidence that he was familiar with the genuine work of that monk, viz. the *Epistola Gildae*, to which the *Excidium* was subsequently prefixed.

superior to almost all the kings of Britannia both in kingdom and in stature', Maelgwn Gwynedd, *insularis draco*, dragon of the Isle of Mona.[1] This famous king, who was the head of the house of Cunedda Wledig, is also said by Gildas to have had as instructor one who is described as 'the refined teacher of almost the whole of Britannia',[1] a statement which with the other indications makes it quite clear that the Britannia, with which St. Gildas and his readers are familiar, is neither the island nor Roman Britain, but that western Britannia in Britain which I have given reason to show was the *Britannia Superior* of the Romans to which afterwards the term Britannia became more exclusively applied.

For it must not be supposed that the Roman provincial system in Britain crumbled away at the departure of the legions from the island. The divisions had been far too long established to perish in a night, especially those into Upper and Lower Britain, but it is probable in view of the troubles, which would afflict the land both from within and without, that the leading civil officials had to give way to the military governors, who alone persisted to protect the Roman tradition. These were the *Dux Britanniae* in the north, now probably in charge of the land from the Wall of Hadrian to the Humber and Mersey, constituting perhaps one of the provinces of Caesariensis or Lower Britain; the *Comes Littoris Saxonici* in the south-east, from the Wash to the Wiltshire Avon or thereabouts, now likewise in probable charge of the whole of the other province of Caesariensis, and finding suc-

---

[1] *Epistola Gildae*, cc. 34-36 (*Chr. Min.* III. pp. 41-7).

cessors in the Saxon and Anglian Bretwaldas;[1] and lastly the *Comes Britanniae* in the west protecting the whole of Upper Britain, or, as it was now called, Britannia.

This Britannia, by the withdrawal of the legions from Chester and Caerlleon, became exposed to the incoming of Picts and Scots, which were the general names given by the Romans to the barbarians who dwelt beyond the Wall of Hadrian and in Ireland respectively. Given that a people dwelt beyond the Wall, it would be commonly classed with the Picts whether it was *racially* Pictish or otherwise. These two peoples entered Britannia from over the water,[2] the Scots invading the west coast and effecting settlements in various districts;[3] and the Picts starting from due north and landing on the seaboard from Anglesey to the mouth of the river Dee. Owing to the limitation of the term Picts in later times

---

[1] Bede's *Ecc. Hist.* II. 5; *Saxon Chronicle* under 827; Stevenson's *Asser*, 147, note 1.

[2] 'Duabus primum gentibus *transmarinis* vehementer saevis, Scotorum a circione, Pictorum ab aquilone calcabilis.' *Excidium Britanniae*, c. 14 (Mommsen's *Chr. Min.* III. p. 33). Bede, who bases almost everything he has to say concerning the early centuries of post-Roman Britain on the *Excidium*, and indeed incorporates whole passages into his text, completely misunderstands the term *transmarini* as applied to the Picts, which he explains as being applicable to them in that they came from beyond the Firths of Forth and Clyde (*H. E.* I. 12). The only part of southern Britain which could be approached *over the water* from the north-west and the north is North Wales, which proves that the Britannia underlying that of the 'edited' *Excidium*, which came into Bede's hands, was the Britannia of the genuine Gildas, including Wales *plus* the Devonian peninsula.

[3] *Vita S. Carantoci* and *Vita S. David* in Rees's *Cambro-British SS.* pp. 97, 101, 124; the *De Situ Brecheniauc* and *Cognacio Brychan* in *Y Cymmrodor*, vol. XIX; the *Hist. Britt.* (*Chr. Min.* III. 156). See also Bury's *Life of St. Patrick*, 325.

to the people properly so called, the fact was lost sight of
that the Picts, who entered Britannia at this period, were
no other than those who are called in Welsh literature
Gwyr y Gogledd, the Men of the North,[1] including
Cunedda and his Sons, who occupied the districts lying
between the river Dee and the river Teify, having Scots
to their north-west and south-west, and the original
inhabitants (also interspersed with Scots) in occupation
of the land south and east of the Dee and Teify.[2] The
'Men of the North' were almost certainly for the most
part Britons both by race and language, but all who
were free amongst them called themselves at a later
period, even if not already, by the name Cymry, that is,
compatriots.

---

[1] Skene's *Four Anc. Bks.* I. 165-83.

[2] It is very noteworthy and confirms the view expressed above
that the Picts as a distinct race of northern invaders in Wales are
nowhere mentioned, as are the Scots, in early Welsh literature outside the *Excidium Britanniae* and works influenced by it. Thus
the only reference to them in the *Book of Llandâv* is in the Life of
Teilo (pp. 99, 100), where the 'Historia Gildae' (i. e. the *Excidium*)
is expressly referred to as the authority. There is no reference whatever to them in the *Cambro-British Saints*. It appears, however,
that the identity of the invading Picts and the Cymry was not completely forgotten, for in the Peniarth MS. 118 the statement appears
that 'the Picts were none other than the old Cymry' (*nid oedhynt
y Picteit onyd yr hen Gymry*). *Rep. on MSS. in Welsh* I. 724 .

'Hec sunt nomina filiorum Cuneda quorum numerus erat IX:
Typiaun primogenitus qui mortuus in regione que uocatur Manau
Guodotin et non uenit huc cum patre suo et cum fratribus suis
pre[dictis]; Meriaun filius eius diuisit possessiones inter fratres
suos; ii, Osmail; iii, Rumaun; iiii, Dunaut; v, Ceretic; vi, Abloyc;
vii, Enniaun Girt; viii, Docmail; ix, Etern.

' Hic est terminus eorum a flumine quod uocatur Dubr duiu usque
ad aliud flumen Tebi et tenuerunt plurimas regiones in occidentali
plaga Brittanniae.' These valuable sections are appended to the
Pedigrees which follow the *Annales Cambriae* in Harleian MS.
3859 (*Y Cymm.* IX. 182-3).

Cunedda is one of the very few to whom Welsh literature assigns the rare title of *gwledig*,[1] a term which
denotes the ruler of a territory, apparently as distinct
from that of a community of persons, which is a very important distinction in view of 'tribal' custom. The expression *Cunedda Wledig* in this case would point to Cunedda
as a ruler of territory (*gwlad*), whilst *Cunedda and his
Sons* would indicate his character as a 'tribal' king.
Almost all who are known to have borne the title of
gwledig can be proved to have lived within a century or
so about the end of Roman rule in Britain. The three
best known, Maxen, Cunedda, and Emrys, are all credited
with being in some way connected with the Roman
officialdom or race, so that there can be little doubt that
gwledig is a Welsh rendering for a Roman title, perhaps
the *Comes Britanniae*. Maxen, who was very early confounded with the usurper Maximus, is associated with
the three military centres of Caerlleon, Carmarthen, and
Carnarvon. He marries Elen, daughter of Eudav,[2] into

---

[1] In the indices to the Oxford *Red Book of Hergest* there are
about ten names associated with this title, of the majority of which
nothing whatever seems to be known. They are nearly all, however, made contemporaries of persons who are known to have lived
before 577. Thus *Tared Wledig* is described as the father of *Twrch
Trwyth*, who appears in the tale of *Kulhwch and Olwen* as the
wild boar pursued by Arthur and his men (Oxford *Mab.* 123, &c.).

[2] See the tale entitled *Breudwyt Maxen Wledic* (Oxford *Mab.*
82–92), in which it is amply evident, if the author's identification
of Maxen with Maximus is eliminated, that Maxen is a dweller in
Britain. The Welsh word for Rome, viz. *Rhufain*, older *Rumein*,
is from Romania and not from Roma. This fact will explain many
a marvel in old Welsh literature of journeys to the Roman *city*. It
is curious that Geoffrey does not bring Arthur to the city of Rome,
although he brings him as far as the Alps (*Hist. Reg. Brit.* X. 13 ;
Oxford *Brut*, 229), so that it is by no means improbable that what

whose family Cunedda marries at a later date. Emrys Wledig, otherwise known as Ambrosius Aurelianus, is associated with the patria of Glywysing[1] in south-eastern Wales, and was a contemporary of Vortigern, on one of whose sons he as overlord of 'all the kings of the Britannic race' bestows the two patrias of Buallt and Gwrtheyrnion in the modern counties of Brecon and Radnor.[2] Cunedda comes in point of time after Maxen and apparently before Emrys. His immediate ancestors all bore Roman names, and one of them was almost certainly a Roman official.[3] His great achievement in Wales was the crushing of the Scotti,[4] and it may be

Geoffrey had before him was an account of Arthur's wars in Romania, that is, some part of Britain where the Roman interest was sufficiently strong to cause it to be distinguished as Romania. The word actually appears in the *Excidium*, ch. 7 (*Chr. Minora* III. 30).

[1] 'Et ipse [i.e. Vortigern] legatos ex consilio magorum per universam Brittanniam misit utrum infantem sine patre invenirent. Et lustrando omnes provincias regionesque plurimas venere ad campum Elleti qui est in regione quae vocatur Gleguissing. . . . Et rex ad adolescentem dixit, Quo nomine vocaris ? Ille respondit, Ambrosius vocor, id est, Embreis Guletic ipse videbatur. Et rex dixit, De qua progenie ortus es? At ille Unus est pater meus de consulibus Romanicae gentis.' *Hist. Britt.* c. 41, 42 (*Chr. Min.* III. 182, 186).

[2] 'Pascent qui regnavit in duabus regionibus Buelt et Guorthegirniaun post mortem patris sui [i.e. Vortigern] largiente Ambrosio illi qui fuit rex inter omnes reges Brittannicae gentis.' *Hist. Britt.* c. 48 (ibid. III. 192).

[3] Cunedda, son of Eternus, son of Paternus, son of Tacitus. *Y Cymm.* IX. 170. Paternus is given the epithet Peisrudd, or him of the red tunic. *Celtic Britain*, 3rd ed. 118.

[4] 'Filii autem Liethan obtinuerunt in regione Demetorum et in aliis regionibus id est Guir Cetgueli donec expulsi sunt a Cuneda et a filiis eius ab omnibus Brittannicis regionibus.' *Hist. Britt.* c. 14 (*Chr. Min.* III. 156).

'Mailcunus magnus rex apud Brittones regnabat id est in regione Guenedotae quia atavus illius id est Cunedag cum filiis suis, quorum numerus octo erat, venerat prius de parte sinistrali, id est,

that it was on this account he became recognized as
gwledig. The occupation of so much land, however, by
his followers could hardly have been acceptable to the
older inhabitants, especially to the *Romani* about the
estuary of the Severn, whose supremacy would now be
constantly challenged by these new comers. From this
time also dates a close connexion between North
Wales and that further and transmarine North whence
Cunedda and his Sons had come, a connexion which
can be traced for centuries afterwards.[1] It is possible that Cunedda may have been a gwledig before he
entered Wales, and that he might even have held the
post of *Dux Britanniae*,[2] which implied the military
leadership of the northern province, but the place and
time in which he lived, his 'uncouth' name, and the
so-called 'tribal' character of his settlement in Wales,
all mark him as a 'barbarian' who may indeed have
received honours from the imperial government, but only
as the usual last and desperate remedy in the face of
a ruin which was inevitable. The fact, however, remains
that the House of Cunedda henceforth continued supreme
in Wales for nine centuries, providing the Welsh with the

---

de regione quae vocatur Manau Guotodin . . . et Scottos cum
ingentissima clade expulerunt ab istis regionibus et nusquam reversi
sunt iterum ad habitandum.' *Hist. Britt.* c. 62 (ibid. III. 205-6).

[1] See, for instance, the remarkable passage in the Book of
Gwynedd, where Rhun, son of Maelgwn Gwynedd, is described as
fighting in the North, apparently on the banks of the river Forth
(*Anc. Laws* I. 104 ; *Celtic Britain*, 3rd ed. 126). Add to this the
exploits of Cadwallon and the North Welsh usurper Cadavael
between the Humber and the Forth. *Hist. Britt.* cc. 61, 64, 65
(*Chr. Min.* III. 204, 207-8) ; *Celtic Britain*, 3rd ed. 131-5.

[2] *Celtic Britain*, 3rd ed. 118-20.

greatest names in their history for the whole of that period. With its advent in Britannia about the end of the fourth century Welsh national history commences, and with the death of its last important representative, Llewelyn ap Gruffydd, in 1282, the first half of the same history closes.

The occupation of the northern and western portions of Britannia by Picts and Scots threw the old population of south-eastern Wales and the country between the Severn Sea and the Wiltshire Avon into a state of alarm. The Britons of the Devonian peninsula began to migrate in large numbers to Armorica on the mainland, where they founded Britanny. 'Already in 469 we find Apollinaris Sidonius speaking, as a matter of course, of the inhabitants of that region as Britons.'[1] In this way the south-eastern portion of Britannia beyond the Severn Sea was thinned of its population and thereby made ready for the West Saxon victory of Deorham in 577, which brought the old Roman province of Upper Britain definitely to a close and at the same time exposed the whole of the Devonian peninsula to that process of Saxonization which does not even yet appear to be complete. The Britons west of the Severn, on the other hand, are found in the third decade of the fifth century torn into two factions, the one under the celebrated Vortigern and the other under Ambrosius Aurelianus or Emrys Wledig.[2]

[1] Hodgkin's *Political Hist. of England* to 1066, p. 106, and also note, where the reference is given as Ep. i. 7. See also *Y Cymmrodor* XI. 69.

[2] 'Guorthigirnus regnavit in Brittannia et dum ipse regnabat urgebatur a metu Pictorum Scottorumque et a Romanico impetu nec non et a timore Ambrosii.' *Hist. Britt.* c. 31 (*Chr. Min.* III. 171).

Vortigern is found in the country east of the river Usk
and north of it along a line drawn from about the town
of Monmouth to that of Llanidloes;[1] and Ambrosius, as
we have already seen, in Glywysing, roughly equivalent
to modern Glamorganshire. Things reached a long-
remembered crisis when Vortigern in the fourth year of
his reign, being the year marked by the consulship of
Felix and Taurus, that is, A.D. 428, invited the Saxons[2]

[1] Vortigern was the founder of the royal stem of the little kingdom
of Gwrtheyrnion (in modern Radnorshire), which is called after
his name (Gwrtheyrn). He therefore stands to Gwrtheyrnion as
Brychan to Brycheiniog, Glywys to Glywysing, Ceredig to Ceredigion, and so forth. In other words, he is clearly one of the
founders of the numerous little patrias or kingdoms into which
we find post-Roman Wales divided. His father and grandfather
bear the Roman names of Vitalis (Guitaul) and Vitalinus (Guito-
lin) respectively, being traditionally connected with the city of
Gloucester. *Hist. Britt.* cc. 48, 49 (*Chr. Min.* III. 192–3). Geoffrey
of Monmouth describes him as *consul Gewisseorum*, represented in
the Welsh version by *iarll oed hwnnw ar Went ac Ergig ac Euas*
(earl was he over Gwent and Erging and Ewyas). *Hist. Regum Brit.*
VI. 6; Oxford *Brut*, 127. We find elsewhere a *dux Wisseorum*
given in the Welsh as *iarll Ergig ac Euas*; and Cadwaladr's
mother, who is in the Latin described as sprung *ex nobili genere
Gewisseorum*, is in the Welsh *wreic uonhedic o Euas ac Ergig*
(a noble lady of Ewyas and Erging). *Hist. Reg. Britt.* V. 8, XII. 14 ;
Oxford *Brut*, 109, 252.
Erging, in English Archenfield, is the district now in Hereford-
shire west of the river Wye. In early times it must have included
the whole of the territory from Monmouth to Moccas, east of the
river Munnow and the river Dore. Ewyas lay to the west of Erging,
having the river Dore as its eastern boundary as far, perhaps, as the
river Grwyne Fawr. Gwent was the district south of Erging and
Ewyas (which were known as 'the two true sleeves of Gwent uch
Coed'), between the river Usk and the river Wye in modern Monmouthshire. Owen's *Pembrokeshire* I. 199, n. 5, 208, n. 1 ; III.
264, note E. As Glywysing, in which the boy Ambrosius Aurelianus
was discovered, includes the territory *west* of the river Usk as far
as the western confines of Gower, we may roughly locate Vortigern
east and north of the river Usk, and Ambrosius west and south of it.
[2] 'Guorthigirnus autem tenuit imperium in Brittannia Theodosio

of the 'Saxon Shore' to his assistance. The details of the story have been rendered obscure by the misconceptions [1] of later times, which transfigured Vortigern into a King of Britain who received continental supplies in the island of Thanet in order to withstand enemies who were threatening his country at the Wall of Hadrian! Vortigern's invitation to the Saxons has consequently been magnified out of all reason, and completely torn from its true setting. It was certainly a blow aimed at the *Romani* of Britannia, which appears to have met with no small success seeing how the memory of Vortigern was afterwards execrated; and it is clearly one of the remnant of the Roman faction who is originally responsible for the *Excidium Britanniae* of the pseudo-Gildas towards the close of the seventh century.

The office of *gwledig*, like that of the English *bretwalda*,

et Valentiniano consulibus et in quarto anno regni sui Saxones ad Brittanniam venerunt Felice et Tauro consulibus quadringentesimo primo anno [a passione] domini nostri Iesu Christi.' *Hist. Britt.* c. 66 (*Chr. Min.* III. 209 *cum apparatu critico*). 'Vortigern, moreover, was ruling in Britannia when Theodosius and Valentinianus were consuls [i.e. 425], and the Saxons came to Britannia in the fourth year of his reign, when Felix and Taurus were consuls, and in the 401st year from the [Passion] of our Lord Jesus Christ [calculating according to Victorius of Aquitaine, that is, 28 + 400 = A.D. 428].' See the article entitled 'The *Exordium* of the "Annales Cambriae"' by Mr. Alfred Anscombe in *Ériu* (January, 1908), where Mommsen's text of the *Hist. Britt.* c. 66, is subjected to severe criticism.

[1] These misconceptions originated with the 'edited' copy of the *Excidium Britanniae* placed in Bede's hands, where Britannia was ignorantly or maliciously identified with Roman Britain, or rather with the island of Britain! It cannot be too much insisted upon that we learn from the *Excidium Britanniae* almost all that Bede knew or chose to know of fifth-century Britain, and that the former therefore, and not the latter, is the 'original authority' with which the student has to deal in his researches into this period of history.

does not appear to have passed from father to son. None of the descendants of Cunedda is known to have held it after Cunedda himself, not even the powerful Maelgwn. It certainly involved some sort of overlordship extending over all the kings of a given territory, and it is won by such military prowess as would ensure the protection of that territory, theoretically perhaps of Britannia.[1] Cunedda protects Britannia from the Scots. Emrys likewise protects Britannia from the anti-Britannic policy of Vortigern and his allied Saxons. It represents the Roman tradition as opposed to the barbaric or 'tribal' interest of the native kings. And perhaps, above all, it in some way symbolizes the unity of Britannia, which in this case is what every *gwledig* would seek to preserve as the Roman legacy handed over to his special care. It would devolve

---

[1] Cf. the description of Ambrosius as 'rex inter omnes reges Brittannicae gentis'. *Hist. Britt.* c. 48 (*Chr. Min.* III. 192). Also the passage in *Maxen's Dream* (Oxford *Mab.* 89), where Elen, on the morning after her marriage with the *gwledig*, being asked to mention the *agweddi* she desired, demanded 'ynys prydein yw that o vor rud hyt ym mor Iwerdon ar teir rac ynys y dala dan amherodres ruuein a gwneuthur teir prif gaer idi hitheu yn y lle y dewissei yn ynys prydein', which Lady Guest translates 'the Island of Britain [Britannia] for her father from the Channel to the Irish Sea, together with the three adjacent islands [that is, presumably, Wight, Anglesey, and Man], to hold under the empress of Rome; and to have three chief castles made for her in whatever places she might choose in the Island of Britain [Britannia].' The three castles or *caers* mentioned are Caermarthen, Caerlleon, and Caernarvon. Surely all this implies that Eudav, Elen's father, is to hold the whole of Britannia as *gwledig* under the emperor. Bede also, in the account which he gives (*H. E.* II. 5) of the overlords, who in the *Chronicle* are called Bretwaldas, describes them as the kings who ruled over all the southern provinces which are divided from the northern by the Humber, &c. ('qui tertius quidem in regibus gentis Anglorum cunctis australibus eorum prouinciis, quae Humbrae fluuio et contiguis ei terminis sequestrantur a borealibus, imperauit').

on him to guard Britannia against all invasion and insult
whether from the west, north, or east. Hence, when we
read of Arthur being chosen to act for the kings of the
Britons as their *dux bellorum*, we cannot be far wrong in
suspecting that we have here the historic basis of that
hero's renown. That he is never styled *gwledig* is true,
but such equivalents as *Arthur Miles, Dux Bellorum,
Penteyrned* (Chief of kings), and even *Amerandur* (Im-
perator), are sufficient to assure us of the nature of his
office.[1] It is expressly stated that there were many of
more noble descent than himself, which is corroborated
by the absence of his pedigree in all lists prior to Geoffrey
of Monmouth's romance.[2] He was killed at Camlan ten
years before the death of Maelgwn Gwynedd, and therefore shortly[3] before St. Gildas wrote his *Epistola*. It is
significant that in this work there is a total absence of

[1] See Sir John Rhŷs's Introduction to Malory's *Le Morte D'Arthur*
in the *Everyman's Library*.
[2] ' Et licet multi ipso nobiliores essent ipse tamen duodecies dux
belli fuit ' (*Chr. Min.* III. 199, MSS. M and N).
[3] That is, assuming that the two following *anni* are to be reckoned
from the same initial year. 'Annus XCIII. Gueith Camlann in
qua Arthur et Medraut corruerunt. Annus CIII. Mortalitas magna
in qua pausat Mailcun Rex Guenedotae.' *Ann. Camb.* (*Y Cymm.*
IX. 154-5). The following will assist us to determine the period we
are dealing with. It appears from the *Vitae* that St. David was
born in the thirtieth year after St. Patrick went to Ireland as Bishop,
which makes 433 + 29 = 462; and this date is confirmed by MS. B
of the *Ann. Camb.*, which places David's birth opposite Annus XIV.
For if this be computed from the false Bedan date of the Saxon
Advent, we get 449 + 13 = 462. We may therefore regard A.D. 462
for David's birth as tolerably well established. St. David was
a descendant of Cunedda Wledig, but whether in the fourth remove
like Maelgwn or in the third is uncertain. His father was Sant or
Sanddef, who was the son either of Cedig ap Ceredig ap Cunedda,
or of Ceredig ap Cunedda. The expression ' Dewi Sant ' for Saint
David appears to be a late misreading of Dewi ap Sant, the position
of Sant being also apparently unique in Welsh hagiography.

any sign of fear or apprehension as to external enemies on the part of Britannia, whence we may safely gather that Arthur had not lived in vain.

The old provincial system of Roman Britain, however, was of necessity doomed to disappear. It ran on for a while by means of the power which had set it in motion, but, as that power was generated from without and not from within, its cessation was bound to bring the system to an end. With the removal of external pressure, internal forces began to bear on the situation and later to control it. Chief among these in the Britannia of the west was the reappearance, and, as it were, the renewed activity of native and primitive modes of life such as those which Julius Caesar had attempted to portray five centuries before. These, of course, could not but have undergone modification, but they were not obliterated. There is evidence to show that archaic social conditions, such as are associated with matriarchy and totemism, still lingered on, notwithstanding the Roman régime and the growth of Christianity.[1] Throughout the fifth century we discern Wales dividing or already divided into a number of small kingdoms, which remain very much the same till Norman and post-Norman times. They war against one another, like the Saxons against the Jutes of Kent and Hampshire or against the Angles, the smaller and weaker kings seeking to preserve their independence, and the stronger kings anxious to make themselves paramount. Add to this the invasions from the west and north, the emigration of the Bretons,

[1] Rhŷs and Jones's *The Welsh People*, 36–74 ; *Y Cymmrodor* XIX. 20–3.

the isolation from the civilizing centres of the mainland and the consequent decay of commerce and culture—and we have ample explanation of the increasing difficulties of maintaining the old official unity of Britannia together with the final abandonment of the same.

Moreover, if the official unity of Britannia was impossible, much more so was any national unity of which it might have been capable, were it only for geographical reasons. Even officially it had apparently been found necessary to divide it into *Prima* and *Secunda*. A state west of a line drawn from the Dee to the Wiltshire Avon [1] or thereabouts, divided as this territory is by the Severn Sea and exposed along the whole of its eastern boundary to hostilities from the English lowlands, was an absurdity. It tended to part asunder of itself. Sooner or later a strong attack from the east would capture the Severn shore from Gloucester to Bristol, which eventually took place in 577, the year of the Battle of Deorham by which Gloucester, Cirencester, and Bath fell into the hands of the West Saxons. Thus the unity of Roman Britannia became definitely a thing of the past. Henceforth Wales is free to evolve its own life. The unity of

---

[1] *Avon* being the generic Welsh word for 'river' there can be little doubt that the Wiltshire Avon was at one time a boundary line between Welsh and non-Welsh peoples, as would be the case also with regard to the Bristol and Tewkesbury Avons. The presence of Britons in the district roughly enclosed by these Avons is convincingly evident. The western boundary of the Saxon shore with its Saxon inhabitants is uncertain. If *Portus Adurni* is Porchester, we certainly bring it as far west as the Solent. In any case, it is significant that the earliest clashing of Britons and Saxons is traditionally stated to have taken place in this neighbourhood in the country immediately east of the river Avon (*Sax. Chr.* s. a. 495, 501, 508, 514, 519, 527, &c.).

Cymric Britannia will now replace that of Roman Britannia, with this difference, that the latter was possibly never more than an official idea to be preserved, whereas the former becomes a national ideal to be attained.

It must not be supposed, however, that the memory of the Roman Britannia of the fifth century was lost, for it is this Britannia of the 'Roman' which becomes the Britannia of Romance. Its traditions, clustering around the figure of Arthur, become transfigured into a great national dream, a kind of golden age in the past, which grows more and more radiant in the minds of the Britons as they contrast it with the comparative insignificance of their actual position in the world. In Wales it had two very debilitating effects. In the first place, by putting the golden age in the past it made the Welsh regard themselves as decadent, a notion of course which their enemies never failed to encourage. So intensely indeed was this sense of racial decay felt that it forced into existence the counter-notion of a return of Arthur, a kind of messianic dream, which served to counterbalance the depressing and devitalizing effect of the other. In the second place, by substituting romance for history, it has surreptitiously concealed the steady and unbroken development of Cymric nationality from the day that Cunedda and his Sons established themselves in Wales at the commencement of the fifth century. Not only have authentic traditions been distorted to make them fit with the romance, not only has the memory of important historic events been for ever lost, but the very idea of the evolution of Wales from the primitive little kingdoms of the fifth century has been blurred in the national consciousness. It would be difficult to find a story more clear and simple in its main outlines than the growth of modern Wales from its earliest conscious beginnings in the fifth and sixth centuries, where we discern a number of small patriotic communities gradually cohering as they become more and more conscious of their common life. But when for all this there is substituted a golden age wherein Britannia is converted into the Isle of Britain and the Britons masters of the same from end to end ; where wicked Vortigern calls in the heathen from Germany, who drive the Britons pell-mell from the eastern districts of England into the midlands, and out of the midlands into Wales, there to relapse into barbarism ; where every step in the Cymric advance from age to age, marked by such names as Cadwallon, Gruffydd ap Llewelyn, and the post-Norman princes, is regarded as a convulsive effort of a dying people to regain some of the glory of the past—it can readily be understood how the history of Wales has suffered and how its national vigour has been enfeebled.

After the death of Arthur, who is commonly reputed to have perished in a civil war, we hear of no other military leader whom we may regard as the *gwledig* of Britannia in power as well as in title (that is, allowing that Arthur did really bear the title). Aurelius Caninus, one of the five kings addressed by Gildas, is also known as Cynan Wledig,[1] so that it is possible that he was regarded as one of Arthur's successors. One gathers from the *Epistola* that he ruled east of Devon in the

----

[1] *Hist. Reg. Brit.* XI. c. 5 ; Oxford *Brut*, 233.

country 'between the Severn Sea and Poole Harbour',[1] which was the part of Britannia where, with the south-east of Wales, the Roman interest was strongest. As late as the close of the seventh century it is still possible for a writer in that neighbourhood to be conscious of Roman imperial sentiment and to speak of Latin as *nostra lingua*. In view of the general decay of things Roman his life is embittered. The descendants of Ambrosius are still there but how 'greatly degenerated from their ancestral nobleness'![2] In this neighbourhood therefore we should perhaps expect the office of *gwledig* to linger on until the catastrophe of the year 577. But already, with the death of Arthur, the centre of political interest in Wales has passed permanently in the person of Maelgwn Gwynedd to the House of Cunedda. Henceforth the political history of Wales may be treated quite apart from that of the Devonian peninsula, although the actual cleavage did not take place till the Battle of Deorham.

At the time when Gildas writes his *Epistola*, Maelgwn Gwynedd is certainly the leading king in Wales as was afterwards his son Rhun.[3] In the seventh century also we find the House of Cunedda holding the same commanding position in the person of Cadwallon [4] (the fifth in

---

[1] Rhŷs's *Celtic Britain*, 3rd ed. 107.

[2] *Excid. Brit.* c. 25 (*Chr. Min.* III. 38, 40).

[3] In addition to the remarks of Gildas in the *Epistola*, chs. 33-6 (*Chr. Min.* III. 44-8) and of the author of the *Historia Brittonum*, ch. 62 (ibid. III. 205), see the traditions of Maelgwn as supreme king (*Anc. Laws* II. 48-50, 584) and his exploits in different parts of Wales as recorded in the *Vitae Sanctorum* (Rees's *Cambro-British SS.*). As to Rhun, see *Anc. Laws* I. 104-5 and the *Vita S. Cadoci* (*Cambro-Brit. SS.* 52-5).

[4] Skene's *Four Ancient Books of Wales* II. 431-5, where the exploits of Cadwallon in different parts of Wales are referred to.

descent from Maelgwn) who was killed by Oswald in 635. Between Rhun and Cadwallon, however, the supreme power may have passed for a while into the hands of the house of Cadell Ddyrnllug of Powys, for we find Cynan Garwyn, the head of that family, battling against Anglesey, Dyved, Glywysing, and Gwent.[1] It is this house also which appears to have withstood Ethelfrith of Northumbria at the Battle of Chester in 617, in which Selyf ap Cynan Garwyn fell. This event was famous in ancient times because of the slaughter of about 1,200 monks of Bangor Iscoed, which was an incident of the fight.[2] It has become famous in modern times because of 'the decisive character which it has been the fashion to ascribe to it of late '.[3] For it is nowadays commonly and even dogmatically asserted that it divided the Britons of the North from those of Wales, whereas there is no evidence forthcoming that these were ever united *by land*. Late Glamorganshire legends ascribe the name of Teyrnllwg[4] to a supposed Cymric patria lying apparently between the river Dee and the river Derwent in Cumberland, a name based on erroneous etymology as to *Durnluc* in *Catel Durnluc*, that is, Cadell Ddyrnllug, the king who founded the royal stem of Powys.[5] But

---

[1] Skene's *Four Ancient Books of Wales* II. 173, 447; *Cambro-Brit. SS.* 79; Owen's *Pembrokeshire* I. 222, note 2; III. 281.

[2] 'Annus CLXIX. Gueith Cairlegion et ibi cecidit Selim filius Cinan' (*Y Cymm.* IX. 156; Bede's *H. E.* II. 2; Owen's *Pembrokeshire* III. 282, note 1). The above annal is to be reckoned from the false Bedan date of the Saxon Advent, viz. 449 + 168 = A.D. 617. Cf. Plummer's *Bede* II. 77.

[3] Rhŷs's *Celtic Britain*, 3rd ed. 130.

[4] *Iolo MSS.* 86. The same fragment contains the equally fictitious patria of Fferyllwg 'between Wye and Severn' (Owen's *Pem.* III. 257, note 3).   [5] *Y Cymm.* VII. 119, note 3; IX. 179, note 6.

apart from this there is no real evidence for the presence of Cymry (or of any Britons) between the river Derwent and the river Deé further south than Cartmel below Windermere and the river Leven.[1] That there was a close connexion between the Cymry of 'Cumberland' and those of Wales is amply evident, but it was maritime and not terrene.

Cadwallon was succeeded by his son Cadwaladr, whose fame is due not to any known merits of his own, but to the imaginative genius of Geoffrey of Monmouth, who in his romantic History of the British Kings makes Cadwaladr the last of his list.[2] The reign of this king becomes in consequence the appropriate finale of a long and glorious era of Welsh history. All this of course is purely fictitious, as Cadwaladr's death marks no known break of any kind in the perfectly clear development of Welsh nationality. Geoffrey's Cadwaladr in fact is a composite personage created out of Geoffrey's own confusion of Cadwaladr and his father, Cadwallon, and Ceadwalla of Wessex. As there were kings in Wales before Cadwaladr, so there were kings, and far greater kings, after him. He died in the second year of the great plague of 664-5,[3] and was succeeded by his son Idwal. Of his

---

[1] In 685 Ecgfrid gave St. Cuthbert 'terram quae vocatur Cartmel et omnes Britannos cum eo'. *Hist. de S. Cuthberto* (*Symeonis Dunel. Opera* I. 141, 231. Surtees Society).

[2] *Hist. Reg. Brit.* XII. cc. 14-18.

[3] 'Dum ipse [Osguid filius Eadlfrid] regnabat venit mortalitas hominum Catgualart regnante apud Brittones post patrem suum et in ea periit.' *Hist. Britt.* c. 64 (*Chr. Min.* III. 208). Oswy reigned from 642 to 670, and the plague referred to raged in 664-5 (Bede's *H. E.* III. 27). The *Ann. Camb.* places the obit of Cadwaladr opposite Annus CCXXXVIII, which if calculated from 428, the true year of the Saxon Advent, gives 428 + 237 = A.D. 665. According to

immediate descendants little is known. They appear to sink into comparative insignificance by the side of Maelgwn, Rhun, and Cadwallon, and other than they may possibly have loomed larger in the life of Britannia and its Britons. But whenever the mists rise which conceal the affairs of these centuries from our view, we always discern the main stem of Cunedda Wledig towering amid the rest of the royal stems of Wales, and generally paramount. Moreover, we may be certain, in view of its prestige in the ninth century, that its history in the preceding centuries is that of a house which has been gradually gaining strength until it is now in a position to effect a change in Welsh political conditions which will mark the beginning of a new era in the slow and steady development of Cymric nationality.

We have seen that the first period in the history of post-Roman Wales must have come to an end in the year 577, although many years before this date the centre of political interest in Wales was shifting from

Geoffrey, Cadwaladr died in 689 (XII. 18), which historically is the year of the obit of Ceadwalla of Wessex in Rome (Bede's *H. E.* V. 7). Allowing one year for Geoffrey's *aliquantulum temporis* (XII. 17) and adding the eleven years of adversity (XII. 16), and also the twelve years of prosperity (XII. 14), we obtain 1 + 11 + 12 = 24 years as the length of Cadwaladr's reign, which brings us to the true date of Cadwaladr's death, viz. 689 − 24 = A.D. 665. As Cadwaladr succeeds his father Cadwallo[n] immediately, and as the latter is made to die on November 17, after a reign of forty-eight years (XII. 13), we obtain 665 − 48 = A.D. 617 as the first year of Cadwallo[n]'s reign according to Geoffrey, which is historically the date of the Battle of Chester. Geoffrey, therefore, has clearly confounded the three kings, Cadwallon, Cadwaladr, and Ceadwalla; and by making Cadwaladr die in the year of Ceadwalla's death, he has almost certainly given us the true deathday of Cadwaladr as that of Cadwallon, in which case Cadwaladr died on November 17, 665.

the representatives of the Roman tradition in Britannia [that is, the gwledigs] to the House of Cunedda, which stood for the predominance of the Cymric kindreds. For in Maelgwn we seem to discern the progress of a policy which aims at bringing all the royal stems, from Anglesey to the river Wye, into subjection to the main stem of the family of Cunedda. This continues until in the first quarter of the ninth century there begins a new policy, which will bring almost the whole of Wales under the sole and immediate rule of this main stem of Cunedda. The many royal stocks are to give way to one royal stock, and in this manner is the unity of the Cymric Britannia to be achieved.

In 816 the main stem of Gwynedd ceased on the male side with the death of King Cynan Tindaethwy, the great grandson of Cadwaladr. His daughter, Etthil, had married Gwriad ap Elidyr, King of the Isle of Man, and now their son, Mervyn Vrych, comes from that island to claim the throne of Gwynedd.[1] Mervyn is ominously surnamed in Welsh tradition *Camwri*, that is, Oppression.[2] He is bent on asserting the old overlordship of Cunedda, Maelgwn, and Cadwallon over the whole of the Welsh kin from Anglesey to the river Wye. But in addition to this, he proceeds by diplomatic marriages to bring the

---

[1] Cynan's obit is placed opposite Annus CCCLXXII, which in the era of the *Ann. Camb.* gives 445 + 371 = 816. For the Pedigrees see *Y Cymm.* IX. 169, 172 (Ped. I and IV); VIII. 87 (Peds. XVII and XIX). Owen's *Pembrokeshire* III. 209.

[2] *Anc. Laws* I. 342. 'Rrodri vab Kamwri' (from MS. Z). The same idea is implied in what Asser says of certain South Welsh kings seeking Alfred's protection, being forced thereto *filiorum Rotri vi*. The *vis* or *camwri* denotes the aggressive policy of the kings of Gwynedd (Stevenson's *Asser*, p. 66).

land more directly under the sway of his house. By his marriage with Nest, sister of Cyngen, the last King of Powys of the line of Cadell Ddyrnllug, his son Rhodri becomes the immediate ruler of that kingdom in addition to his own. By the marriage of the same son, Rhodri, to Angharad, sister of Gwgon, the last King of Seisyllwg, a kingdom comprising the two patrias of Ceredigion and Ystrad Tywi, these lands also fall under the direct sway of his house.[1] Thus when Rhodri comes into full possession of his dominions, his immediate rule extends from the Irish to the Severn Seas, including roughly the whole of that *Welsh* Wales which remained under native rulers throughout the Norman period, together with those portions which are described above as fluctuating between Welsh and Norman control. Dyved, Brycheiniog, Glywysing, and Gwent are the only patrias which remain outside the immediate rule of his house, and against these he adopts or rather continues the aggressive policy which aims at bringing them also under the same immediate control of his family. Rhodri was killed by the English in 877,[2] but he remained in the memory of Wales as one who had achieved more real power over the Welsh

[1] Jesus Coll. **MS. 20**, Peds. XVIII, XX, XXI. For Seisyllwg, see Oxford *Mabinogion*, p. 25, at the end of the Mabinogi of Pwyll. It is so called from Seisyll (Ped. XXVI, *Y Cymm.* IX. 180), King of Ceredigion sometime in the eighth century, who deprived Dyved of the cantrevs which together were afterwards known as the gwlad of Ystrad Tywi. Before this deprivation the kings of Dyved had come into possession of Brycheiniog through Ceindrech, a lady of the line of Brychan. Brycheiniog afterwards, however, appears to have had a line of its own, represented in Asser's day by Helised ap Teudubr. *De rebus gestis Ælfredi*, c. 80 (Stevenson's *Asser*, p. 66).

[2] Annus CCCCXXXIII in the *Ann. Camb.*, which in the era of the *Annales* gives 445 + 432 = 877.

kin than any who had gone before him, being known in history as Rhodri the Great. It is important to remember at this juncture that we are now in the century which saw Charlemagne reigning as Emperor of the West.

There was a legend current in later times that Rhodri the Great, erroneously regarded as king of all Wales, damaged the Welsh cause irretrievably by sharing his kingdom among his three sons, giving, according to one version, Gwynedd to Mervyn, Powys to Anarawd, and Deheubarth to Cadell.[1] Nothing can be further from the truth than the impression left by this tale. For as we have seen, Rhodri's aim was to consolidate Wales by substituting the rule of his own family for that of many families. Princes of the blood of Rhodri alone were to govern the land directly from one end to the other. The legend of course echoes the ideas and possibilities of later times when men had come to see that, conducive as was the rule of one *family* instead of several families to keeping folk of the same kin together, yet the rule of one *man* was still more conducive to that desirable result. Consequently they wondered how it was that Rhodri could have divided his kingdom, forgetting that, unsatisfactory as the policy of Rhodri would have been in their day, yet in his own time it was a new thing in Wales, a fresh development, which had then become practicable, being an immense improvement on what had preceded it. The obstacles in the way of the unity of Wales were stupendous, such as no bare coercion could overcome. We have seen their like on a modern and larger scale in the story

---

[1] Such is the tradition of the tripartite division as given by Gerald in his *Descriptio Kambriae* I. 2 (Girald. Camb. *Opera* VI. 166).

of Italian and German unity. In the Dark Age the difficulty was accentuated by the fact that, even given a unity
achieved by a capable ruler, the mind of the age as reflected in the *Leges Barbarorum*, of which the Laws of
Howel are the Welsh exemplar, compelled that unity to
be divided after his death among his sons.   Charlemagne
himself had so to divide his empire; the same necessity
rested on Rhodri the Great.   The policy therefore inaugurated by Mervyn Vrych, and continued by Rhodri and his
successors, marks the beginning of a fresh epoch in our
travail as a people to the full consciousness of our national
entity.

The possessions of Rhodri then after his death in 877
were divided among his sons, of whom the best known,
and those whose posterity played the largest part in
later Wales, were Anarawd and Cadell.   From Anarawd
(died 915) the later kings of Gwynedd traced their descent,
and from Cadell (died 909) both those of Powys and
those of Deheubarth.   It appears therefore that in the
division of territories after Rhodri's death, the kingdom
of Powys sooner or later fell into the hands of Cadell,
together with Seisyllwg.   The policy of bringing all
Wales by politic marriages under the direct control of
the family of Rhodri was now continued by one of the
greatest princes whom the House of Cunedda had
hitherto produced, namely, Howel the Good, the son of
Cadell.   Howel by his marriage with Elen, daughter of
Llywarch, the last king of Dyved, who died in 903, became the immediate ruler of that kingdom; and as the
line of Dyved had claims on Brycheiniog through Cathen,
son of Ceindrech, a lady who in her day appears to have

been the sole representative of the ancient stem of Brychan, after whom Brycheiniog had its name,[1] it is hardly probable that Howel in view of the policy of his family, would fail to assert those claims. In this manner the whole of Wales was gradually falling under the immediate sway of Rhodri's house.

Howel, however, inaugurated a still newer policy, which aimed at the unification of Wales; and herein consists his prime importance in Welsh history. Not only did he continue and encourage the methods of Rhodri the Great, but added to them a method of his own. For as Rhodri would bring all Wales under the direct sway of one family, so Howel would bring the whole of the Welsh people under one law. A common rule implied a common law, and in order that men might know what this common law was, it had to be codified and thereby reduced to writing. This was the task to which Howel applied himself, and by having laid a sound foundation he occupies a foremost place not only amongst the rulers of the Welsh people, but also amongst all those who have distinguished themselves throughout the centuries by their devotion to the cause of Wales.

The following, which are the two earliest accounts of the work which Howel took in hand, describe concisely both the way in which he proceeded and the nature and extent of his undertaking.

Preface to Peniarth MS. 28.

Incipit prologus in libro legum Howel Da.
Brittanie leges rex Howel qui cognominabatur bonus .i.

---

[1] Peds. I and II in *Y Cymm.* IX. 169, 171 ; Ped. VIII in ibid. VIII. 85.

da . regni sui . s . Gwynedotorum Powyssorum atque Dextralium sapientium et in uno loco ante suum tribunal congregatorum uno consensu et diligenti quia ex omni natione medio circiter[1] temperateque constituit. Acciuit de quolibet pago per suum regnum sex uiros auctoritate et scientia et omnes episcopos archiepiscopos abbates et sacerdotes totius Wallie pollentes ad locum qui dicitur Ty Gweyn ar Taf et ibi demorati sunt XL diebus et XL noctibus in pane et aqua et tunc temperauerunt reditionem forefacti .i. cosp superflua diminuere que erant in pluribus reditionibus forefacti ita fecerunt pretium uniuscuiusque rei et iuditium congruum de qualibet re. Tunc surrexerunt omnes archiepiscopi episcopi abbates et sacerdotes induerunt uestes suas et insteterunt bacculis cum crucibus et candelis et ex communi consilio excommunicauerunt transgredientes leges istas et similiter obseruantes benedixerunt. Hec iudicia scripta sunt.

Here begins the preface to the book of the laws of Howel Dda.

King Howel, who was surnamed Good, that is, *da*, put together the laws of Britannia moderately and temperately with the unanimous consent and after the careful consideration of the wise men of his kingdom, namely, the men of Gwynedd, Powys, and Deheubarth, who had assembled together in one place before his tribunal. He summoned from every *pagus* throughout his kingdom six men who excelled in authority and knowledge, and all the bishops, archbishops, abbots, and priests of the whole of Wales to the place which is called Ty Gweyn ar Taf, and there they lived forty days and forty nights on bread and water; and then they regulated the indemnity for wrong-doing, that is, *cosp*, and diminished the excesses which prevailed in many of the indemnities for wrong-doing by determining the worth of every par-

[1] *Ex omni natione* certainly stands for *examinatione* and goes with *diligenti* as in the prefaces of the other Latin texts; likewise for *medio circiter* read *mediocriter*.

ticular thing and the decision suitable in every case. Then all the archbishops, bishops, abbots and priests rose up together, and assumed their robes, and leaned on their croziers with crosses and candles, and by common consent excommunicated those who should violate those laws, and likewise blessed those who should keep them.

Preface to Peniarth MS. 29.

Heuel da uab Kadell teuyhauc Kemry oll a uelles e Kemry en kam arueru or kefreythyeu, ac adeuenus atau uy guyr o pop kemud en y tehuyokaet e pduuar en lleycyon ar deu en scolecyon. Sef achaus e uennuyt er escleycyon rac gossod or lleycyn dym a vey en erbyn er escrftur lan. Sef amser e doythant eno e Garauuys. Sef amser achaus e doyant e Garauuys eno urth delehu o paup bod en yaun en er amser glan hunnu, ac na guenelhey kam en amser gleyndyt. Ac o kyd kaghor a kyd synedycaeth e doython a doytant eno er hen kefreythyeu a esteryasant a rey onadunt a adassant y redec a rey a emendassant ac ereyll en kubyl a dyleassant ac ereyll o neuuyt a hosodassant. A guedy honny onadunt e kefreythyeu a uarnassant eu cadu, Heuel a rodes y audurdaut uthunt ac a orckemenus en kadarn eu kadu en craf. A Heuel ar doythyon a uuant y kyd ac ef a ossodassant eu hemendyth ar hon Kamry holl ar e nep eg Kemry a lecrey heb eu kadu e kefreythyeu. Ac a dodassant eu hemendyt ar er egnat a kamero dyofryt braut ac ar er argluyt ay rodhey ydau ar ny huypey teyr kolhouen kefreyth a guerth guellt a dof a pop pedh reyt y dynyaul aruer arnau.

Howel the Good, the son of Cadell, prince of all Cymru, perceived the Cymry abusing the laws, and summoned to him six men from every cymwd in his principality, four of them of the laity and two of the clergy. The reason that the ecclesiastics were summoned was lest the laics should insert anything contrary to Holy

Writ. The time that they arrived there was Lent, and
the reason that they came there in Lent was that it
behoved all to be upright in that holy season and to avoid
evil in a time of holiness. And with the mutual counsel and
deliberation of the wise men who there assembled, they
examined the old laws, some of which they allowed to
continue, some they amended, and others they completely
abolished, and others again they ordained afresh. And
when they had promulgated the laws, which they had
decided to establish, Howel gave his authority to them
and strictly commanded that they should be scrupulously
observed. And Howel and the wise men, who were
with him, imposed their curse and that of all Cymru on
any one in Cymru who perverted the laws and kept
them not; and they imposed their curse on the judge
who should take a vow' to administer justice, and on the
lord who should grant him authority without that judge
knowing the Three Columns of Law, and the Worth of
Wild and Tame, and everything necessary for the use of
man.

IV

The leading work so far concerned with the laws of
Howel is that edited by Aneurin Owen in 1841 for the
Public Record Commissioners, entitled *Ancient Laws and
Institutes of Wales*. It contains the three early Latin
books, and also the three classes of Welsh books; the
additions made to the latter from the thirteenth to the
sixteenth centuries are given with other legal matter
under the heading of *Anomalous Laws*. The Welsh
texts are provided with an English translation. The
Books of Gwynedd, Blegywryd, and Cyvnerth, however,
are produced in such a way that the various MSS. of
each particular class are interblended, so that it is with

the greatest difficulty that any particular one may be distinguished. Indeed, in the case of the majority of the MSS., it is impossible to do so. Moreover, by arranging the texts so that they fall into books, chapters, and sections, and by consequently attempting to bring them into harmony, the confusion becomes hopeless. The table of contents also and the indices are most jejune, misleading every beginner who takes up the book. There are besides other serious defects, so that, valuable as the work undoubtedly is, and great as is our indebtedness to this early and scholarly editor, it has become imperative that it should be done afresh. Until at least the oldest Latin law books and the best MSS. of the Books of Gwynedd and Blegywryd have been so reproduced with analytical summaries and indices that the reader may readily discover what they contain (a task here essayed with regard to the Book of Cyvnerth) the study of native Welsh law must suffer, and every treatise professing to deal with it as a whole must prove inopportune. It is not proposed, therefore, to deal with it here beyond what is attempted in the Glossary, mainly from the material afforded by the present text.

The Book of Cyvnerth, however, by itself is sufficient to provide the student with a door of entrance into the Welsh Dark Age. Remembering that it represents a late thirteenth-century form of Howel's codification of Welsh law and custom in the tenth century, he will enter safely into the midst of the social and political conditions of pre-Norman Wales. It befits him, however, to be wary, for he treads enchanted ground, and it will not be long before he meets Cadwaladr and Arthur and all the heroes of the *Mabinogion* and kindred tales. Many are they who have boldly entered here only to succumb to the charm of this realm of phantasy and illusion. But let him keep closely to the laws of Howel as interpreted by our Cyvnerth, and peruse the *Pedigrees*, the *Annales Cambriae*, the *Historia Brittonum*, the *Vitae Sanctorum*, the *Excidium Britanniae* of the pseudo-Gildas, and the *Epistola* of the true Gildas, in the light of the said laws, and below the Britannia of romance he will soon discern the no less interesting Britannia of history as it slowly emerges from the archaic conditions of the primitive inhabitants of Roman Wales into the life of the Middle Age. For be it remembered by the beginner that these laws are *leges barbarorum*, laws of the barbarians or natives of Wales as distinct from the civil law of imperial Rome and the canon law of the Church. The latter are from without, the former are from within. And it is largely because these laws of Howel have been so undeservedly neglected that the history of pre-Norman Wales is still so unsatisfactorily treated in our textbooks.

It should be noted that the term ' tribal system ' has been advisedly avoided in this work whilst dealing with the Welsh society of the Dark Age, seeing that there exists no satisfactory explanation of what precisely is meant by the word ' tribe '. Its Welsh equivalent *llwyth*, used, for instance, when speaking of the tribes of Israel, is nowhere found in the law books. We have *cenedl*, kindred ; *teulu*, household ; and *gwlad*, patria ; but nowhere *llwyth*, tribe, or any apparent equivalent of the same.

THE HOUSE OF CUNEDDA.

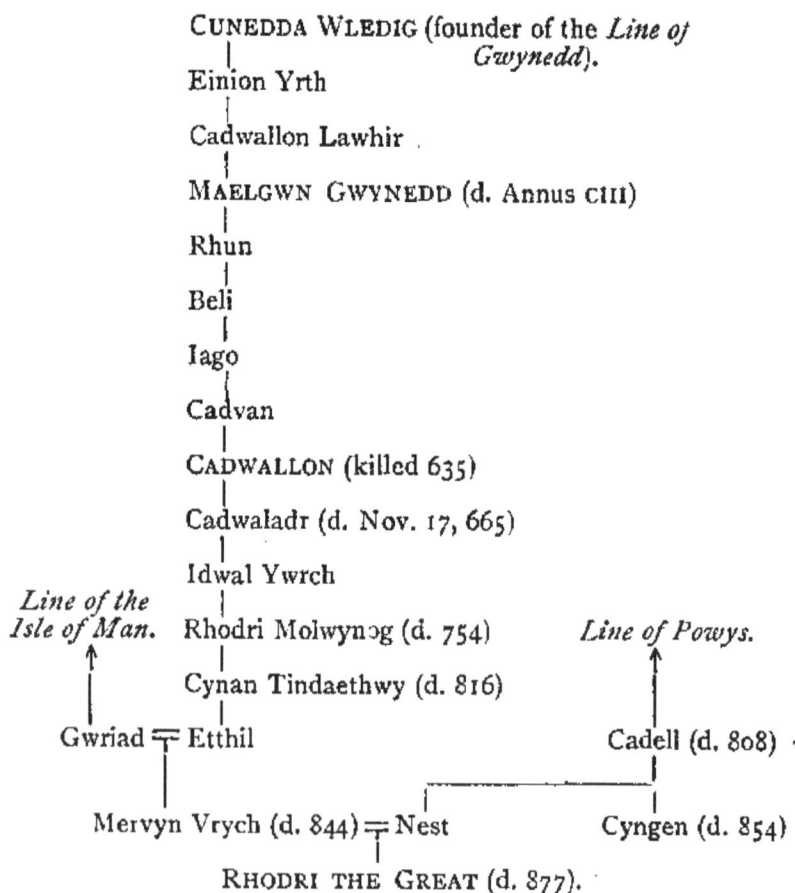

CUNEDDA WLEDIG (founder of the *Line of Gwynedd*).

Einion Yrth

Cadwallon Lawhir

MAELGWN GWYNEDD (d. Annus CIII)

Rhun

Beli

Iago

Cadvan

CADWALLON (killed 635)

Cadwaladr (d. Nov. 17, 665)

Idwal Ywrch

Line of the Isle of Man.   Rhodri Molwynog (d. 754)   *Line of Powys.*

Cynan Tindaethwy (d. 816)

Gwriad ⊤ Etthil   Cadell (d. 808)

Mervyn Vrych (d. 844) ⊤ Nest   Cyngen (d. 854)

RHODRI THE GREAT (d. 877).

THE HOUSE OF RHODRI THE GREAT.

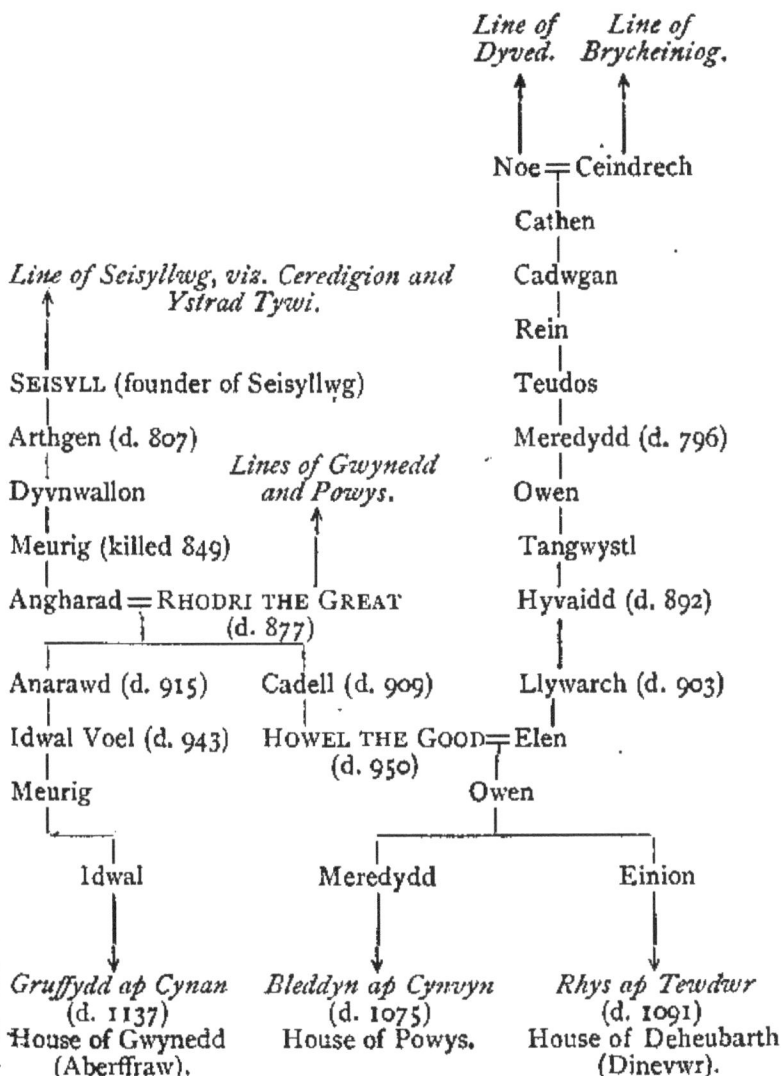

Line of Dyved.   *Line of Brycheiniog.*

↑   ↑

Noe ⊤ Ceindrech

Cathen

Cadwgan

Rein

Line of Seisyllwg, viz. Ceredigion and Ystrad Tywi.

↑

SEISYLL (founder of Seisyllwg)   Teudos

Arthgen (d. 807)   Meredydd (d. 796)

Lines of Gwynedd and Powys.

Dyvnwallon   Owen

Meurig (killed 849)   ↑   Tangwystl

Angharad ⊤ RHODRI THE GREAT   Hyvaidd (d. 892)
(d. 877)

Anarawd (d. 915)   Cadell (d. 909)   Llywarch (d. 903)

Idwal Voel (d. 943)   HOWEL THE GOOD ⊤ Elen
(d. 950)

Meurig   Owen

Idwal   Meredydd   Einion

↓   ↓   ↓

Gruffydd ap Cynan (d. 1137) House of Gwynedd (Aberffraw).   *Bleddyn ap Cynvyn* (d. 1075) House of Powys.   *Rhys ap Tewdwr* (d. 1091) House of Deheubarth (Dinevwr).

ANALYTICAL SUMMARY OF HAR-LEIAN MS. 4353 CALLED V

[The missing folios are supplied from the British Museum MS., Cleopatra A xiv, called **W**, which is the most allied MS. extant of this class.]

PREFACE

LAWS OF THE COURT

[1] The punctuation here in the text is misleading, as may be readily seen by comparing this passage with what corresponds to it in the Book of Gwynedd, the Book of Blegywryd, and especially the early Latin book (Peniarth MS. 28). There should be a full stop after 'heb veffur', *without measure*, in V 2 b 19; and what follows to line 21 corresponds to the separate section and subject called *De dignitate regis* in Peniarth MS. 28 (*Anc. Laws* II. 752) and to what Aneurin Owen calls elsewhere 'Am briodolion leoedd', *of appropriate places* (see *Anc. Law* I. 10, 350; also *The Welsh People*, pp. 199-201, where the still less 'elaborate statement' of the Book of Cyvnerth is not mentioned).

[1] See note in translation of text at this point, p. 159.

Of the Chief Groom.

[1] This section on the Bard of the Household should rightly follow the next as in U and X (see *Anc. Laws* I. 660, n. 9). This peculiarity of V and W shows the influence of the Book of Blegywryd.

[1] In the Book of Gwynedd, where the classification of officers differs somewhat from that of the Books of Blegywryd and Cyvnerth, these are called 'officers by custom and usage' (*Anc. Laws* I. p. 58).

OF THE CHASE.

Of Hounds.

Of Stags.

Of Hunting.

The inheritance, gift, transfer, and loss of land.

OF TAME AND WILD ANIMALS.

Of a Bull.

Its worth from a calf until it is worth sixty·pence	31 a 15
Teithi of an ox . . ·.	31 b 11
If without teithi, let one-third be restored to its buyer	31 b 13
Steer seller answerable for three disorders . .	31 b 15
Calf or yearling seller answerable for the scab .	31 b 18
Time when ox and cow are in their prime . .	31 b 20
Unknown beast in a trevgördd killing a steer]	31 b 24 + W 69 b 13
[Worth of a steer's tooth, and that of a working horse	W 69 b 20

[*Of a Sheep.*

[Its worth from a lamb until it is worth four legal pence	W 70 a 1
[Worth of its teat	W 70 a 4
[Its teithi	W 70 a 5
[Worth of its tooth and eye	W 70 a 6
[Sheep seller answerable for three diseases .	W 70 a 7

[*Of a Goat.*

[Its worth until it is worth four curt pence . .	W 70 a 12
[Worth of its teat = two curt pence . . .	W 70 a 15
[Its teithi	W 70 a 16
[Worth of its tooth and eye = one curt penny .	W 70 a 16
[Cattle dealer to swear with reference to mange .	W 70 a 18

[*Of a Pig.*

[Its worth until it is worth [twelve] legal pence .	W 70 b 2
[Three special animals without augmentation or diminution	W 70 b 9
[Its worth until it is worth thirty pence . .	W 70 b 14
[An autumn born sow	W 70 b 16
[Swine seller answerable for three diseases .	W 70 b 19
Swine killing a person	V 32 a 1

Of a Goose.

Its worth until it equals its mother's worth .	32 a 4

Of a Hen	32 a 8
Of a Cock	32 a 9

f

OF SURETIES.

TRIADS

[OF THE NINTH DAYS.

HYwel da mab kadell bꝛenhın kymry awnaeth trȯy rat duȯ adyr-
weſt agȯedı can oed eıdaȯ ef ky
mry yny theruyn nyt amgen
petwar cantref athrugeín deheubarth   5
a deunaȯ cantref gȯyned. a thrugeın tref
trachyrchell. athꝛugeínt tref buellt. ac y
ny teruyn hȯnnȯ nyt geır geır neb ar
nunt ȯy. a geır yȯ y geır ȯy ar paȯb. Sef
yd oed dꝛyc dedueu a dꝛyc kyfreıtheu kyn   10
noc ef. Y kymerth ynteu whegȯyr o pop
kymhȯt yg kymry. ac y duc yr ty gȯyn
ar taf. ac a oed operchen bagyl yg kymry
rȯg archefcyb ac efcyb ac abadeu ac ath(ra)
(w)on da. ac oꝛ nıfer hȯnnȯ ydewıffȯyt y   15
deudec lleyc doethaf. ar vn yſcolheıc doeth
af ac a elwıt blegywryt y wneuthur y kyf
reıtheu da. ac y dıot yreı dꝛȯc a oed kyn noc
ef. ac y(dodı r)eı da yn eu lle. ac y eu kada(rn)
h(au yny enȯ) ehunan. Sef a wnaethant ȯy   20
pan darfu wneuthur y kyfreıtheu hynny.
dodı emelltıth duȯ ac vn ygynulleıtua (hon)
no ac vn gymry benbaladyr ar y neb a toꝛ
heı y kyfreıtheu hynny. achyntaf y g(ȯna
eth)ant o gyfreıtheu llys can oedynt pe(nh)af   25

achan perthynynt ỽꝛth y bꝛenhın ar vꝛenhínes ar petwar sỽydaỽc ar hugeınt ae can-
hymdaant. nyt amgen. Penteulu. Effeırat teulu. Dıfteın. Ygnat llys. Hebogyd.
Penkynyd. Pengỽaftraỽt. Ỻas yftauell. 5
Dıfteín bꝛenhínes. Effeırat bꝛenhínes.
Bard teulu. Ỻoftegỽꝛ. Dꝛyffaỽꝛ neuad.
Dꝛyffaỽꝛ yftauell. Moꝛỽyn yftauell. Ỻỽaf
traỽt auỽyn. Ỻanhỽyllyd. Ꝺrullyat.
Medyd. Sỽydỽꝛ llys. Ỻoc. Medyc. Ỻro- 10
edaỽc. [Ỻ]ỽaftraỽt auỽyn bꝛenhínes.

DYlyet ysỽydogyon oll yỽ kaffel bꝛeth-
ynwıfc ygan y bꝛenhín. allıeín wıfc
ygan y vꝛenhínes teır gỽeıth pop blỽyd-
yn. ynadolyc. ar pafc. ar sulgỽyn. Ran o 15
holl enníll y bꝛenhín oe wlat dılıs ageıff y
vꝛenhínes. Sỽydogyon y vꝛenhínes agaf-
fan ran o holl enníll fỽydogyon y bꝛenhín.
Ꝺrı dyn awna farhaet yr bꝛenhín꞉ y neb a
toꝛho y naỽd. ar neb arỽyftro y wꝛeıc. ar neb 20
alatho yỽꝛ yny ỽyd ac yg gỽyd y nıfer pan
vo ym aruoll a chymanua yrydaỽ yntéu a
phennaeth arall. Can mu hagen atelır
yn farhaet bꝛenhín yg kyfeır pop cantref
oe teyrnas. a gỽyalen aryant agyrhaetho 25

oꝛ dayar hyt yn ꞁat y bꞅenhín paꞁ eıſtedho
yny gadeır. kyr refet ae aꞁan vyſ. a thrꞁ ꞁ
ban erní athrꞁ y dení kyr refet ar wyalen.
affıol eur a anho llaꞅn dıaꞅt ybꞅenhın yndı.
kyn teꞅhet ac ewín amaeth a amaetho ſe-   5
ıth mlyned. achlaꞅꞁ eur erní kyn teꞅhet
ar ffıol kyflet ac ꞅyneb y bꞅenhín. Bꞅeínt
arglꞅyd dínefꞅꞁ heuyt atecceır o warthec
gꞅynyon aphen pop vn ꞅꞁth loſcꞅꞁn y llall.
atharꞅ rꞅg pop vgeín mu o honunt mal y   10
bo kyflaꞅn o argoel hyt yn ꞁlys dínefꞅꞁ.
Bef atelır yg galanas bꞅenhín: trı chyme-
ínt ae ſarhaet gan trı dꞅychafel O trı mod
yſerheır y vꞅenhínes. pan toꞅher ynaꞅd. neu
pan traꞅher trꞅy lıt. neu pan tynher peth   15
oe llaꞅ gan treıs. ac yna trayan kywerthyd
ſarhaet y bꞅenhín atelır yr vꞅenhínes heb
eur a heb aryant hagen. Un dyn ar pymthec ar hugeínt ar veırch a wetha yr bꞅenhꞀ
eu kynhal yny getymdeıthas. y petwar ſꞅ-   20
ydaꞅc ar hugeínt. ae deudec gꞅeſteı. ac ygyt
a hynny y teulu ae wyrda ae vaccꞅyeıt. ae
gerdoꞅdyon. ae achenogyon. Enrydeduſſaf
gꞅedy y bꞅenhín ar vꞅenhínes yꞅ yr etlíng.
Bꞅaꞅt neu vab neu neı vab bꞅaꞅt vyd yr et-   25

líng yr bienhín. Dabd yr etlíng yb can-
hebibg ydyn awnel y kam hyt yn diogel. . .
Vn farhaet ac vn alanas uyd yr etlíng
ar bienhín eithyr eur ac aryant bieín ha-
bl ar gbarthec a offodir o argoel hyt yn llys   5
dínefbi. Ble yr etlíng yny neuad gyfar-
byneb ar bienhín am ytan ac ef. Rbg yr
etlíng ar golofyn neffaf idab ydeifted yr
ygnat llys. y parth arall idab yr effeirat
teulu. Guedy ynteu ypenkerd. Odyna i   10
nyt oes le dilif yneb yny neuad. Boll bi-
thiychyeit y gbyr rydyon ar kyllituffon ·
yn llety ygbyr yr etlíng y bydant. Y bienhin adyly rodi yr etlíng y holl treul yn enrydedus. Blety yr etlíng ar maccbyeit   15
gantab yb y neuad. ar kynudbi bieu kynneu tan idab. achayu ydiyffeu gbedy yd el
ygyfcu. Digabn adyly yr etlíng yny ancbyn
heb veffur yny teir gbyl arbenhic. Bonhedic
bieínhabl aeifted ar gled y bienhín. y parth ·   20
deheu idab pabb mal y mynho. Dabd bie-
ínhyabl yffyd y pop fbydabc. ac y ereill hefyt. Bgyrcho nabd bienhines ꝛ diof teruyn
ywlat yd hebiygir heb erlit a heb ragot ar .
nab. Dabd y penteulu agan hebibg y dyn   25

d2os teruyn y kymh6t. Ia6d effeirat teulu y6 canheb26g y dyn hyt yr egl6ys· neffaf.
Ia6d y diftein aweryt dyn o2 pan safho
yg waffanaeth yb2enhin ꞉ hyt pan. el y dyn
diwethaf o2 llys ygyfcu. · ꞏIa6d yr hebogyd   5
adiffer ydyn hyt y lle pellaf yd helyo adar.
Ia6d ypenkynyd aparha hyt y lle pellaf.
y cly6her llef y go2n. Ia6d yr ygnat llys y6
tra baraho dadleu o2 ha6l gyntaf hyt ydiwe-
thaf.   Ia6d y peng6aftra6t aparha hyt·ypar   10
aho. redec ymarch go2eu yny llys. Ia6d y
g6as yftauell y6 o2 pan elher y ur6ynha hyt
pan darffo tannu g6ely y b2enhin. Kyf
felyp y hynny y6 na6d mo26yn yftauell.
Ia6d diftein b2enhines y6 o2 pan fafho   15
yg waffanaeth yv2enhines ꞉ hyt pan el y
dyn diwethaf o2 yftauell ygyfcu. Ia6d y ·
bard teulu y6 d6yn y dyn hyt ar y penteulu.
Ia6d ygofteg62 y6 o2 oftec kyntaf hyt ydi-
wethaf. Kyffelyp y6 na6d effeirat ae gilyd.   20
Ia6d y canh6yllyd y6 o2 pan enynher yga-
nh6yll· gyntaf ꞉ hyt pan diffother y diwethaf.
Ia6d ytroeda6c y6 o2 pan eiftedo dan traet
y b2enhin ꞉ hyt pan el y b2enhin yr yftauell.
Ia6d ycoc y6 o2 pan dech2euho pobi y go-   25

lỽyth kyntaf. hyt pan oſſotto yr anrec diwethaf rac bꝛon ybꝛenhín ar vꝛenhínes. Naỽd y sỽydỽꝛ llys yỽ oꝛ pan dechꝛeuho rannu y bỽyt ∴ hyt pan gaffo y diwethaf yran. Naỽd y medyd yỽ oꝛ pan dechꝛeuo darmerth ygerỽyn ved. hyt pan y kudyo. Naỽd y trullyat yỽ oꝛ pan dechꝛeuho gỽallaỽ y gerỽyn ved ∴ hyt pan darffo. Naỽd ymedyc llys yỽ oꝛ pan el y ouỽy y claf gan ganhat ybꝛenhín. hyt pan del yr llys trachefyn. Naỽd y dꝛyſſaỽꝛ yneuad yỽ canhebꝛỽg ydyn hyt y vꝛeich ae wyalen parth ac at y poꝛthaỽꝛ. kanys ef ae herbyn. Naỽd y poꝛthaỽꝛ yỽ kadỽ ydyn hyt pan del y penteulu trỽy ypoꝛth parth ae lety. Ac yna kerdet ynaỽdỽꝛ yn diogel. Kyffelyp yỽ naỽd dꝛyſſaỽꝛ ae gilyd. Naỽd gỽaſtraỽt auỽyn a para tra wnel y gof llys pedeir pedol ac eu to holyon. Athra pedolo amỽs y bꝛenhín. Kyffelyp yhynny yỽ naỽd gỽaſtraỽt auỽyn bꝛenhínes. Pỽy bynhac atoꝛher ynaỽd ∴ neut ſarhaet idaỽ. Sef atelir yn ſarhaet penteulu. trayan ſarhaet ybꝛenhín heb eur aheb aryant bꝛeínhaỽl. Ac uelly y alanas. Diſteín. Ygnat llys. Hebogyd. Penkynyd. Pen-

Ŋa6d ẏgoftegoꝛ adıffer dẏn oꝛ oftec kẏntaf hẏt ẏdıwethaf. Ŋa6d ẏ canh6ẏllẏd
oꝛ pan enẏnher ẏganh6ẏll gẏntaf hẏnẏ
dıffother ẏdıwethaf. Ŋa6d ẏtroeda6c ẏ6
oꝛ pan eıftedho dan traet ẏ bꝛenhín hẏnẏ   5
el ẏr ẏftauell. Ŋa6d ẏ coc ẏ6 oꝛ pan popo
ẏgol6ẏth kẏntaf hẏt pan offotto ẏdıwethaf rac bꝛon ẏbꝛenhın ar urenhínef.
Ŋa6d ẏs6ẏd6ꝛ llẏs awerẏt ẏdẏn oꝛ pan
dechreuho rannu ẏ b6ẏt. hẏt pan gaffo   10
ẏdıwethaf ẏran. Ŋa6d ẏmedẏd ẏ6 oꝛ
pan darmertho ẏ ger6ẏn ued ẏnẏ cudẏo.
Ŋa6d ẏtrullẏat ẏ6 oꝛ pan dechreuo gua-
lla6 ẏ ger6ẏn gẏntaf hẏt pan darfo. Ŋa-
6d ẏ medẏc ẏ6 oꝛ pan el ẏ ou6ẏ ẏclaf gan   15
ganhat ẏ bꝛenhín hẏt pan del ẏr llẏs dꝛa-
cheuẏn. Ŋa6d dꝛẏffa6ꝛ ẏ neuad͏hebꝛ6g
ẏdẏn hẏt ẏ ureıch aewẏalen parth ar
poꝛtha6ꝛ canyf ef ae herbẏn. Ŋa6d ẏ
poꝛtha6ꝛ ẏ6 cad6 ẏdẏn hẏnẏ del ẏpenteu-   20
lu tr6ẏ ẏ poꝛth tu ae letẏ. ac ẏna kerdet

ẏnaỽdỽꝛ ẏníogel. hẏt pan adaỽho ẏdẏn. dıwethaf ẏllẏs. Naỽd dꝛẏſſaỽꝛ ẏſtauell ẏỽ hebꝛỽg ẏdẏn ar ẏ poꝛthaỽꝛ Naỽd guaſtraỽt auỽẏn apara tra wnel gof llẏs pedeır pedol ac eu to hoelon a thra pedolho amỽſ ẏ bꝛenhín. Kẏffelẏp ẏỽ naỽd guaſtraỽt auỽẏn bꝛenhín. aguaſtraỽt auỽyn bꝛenhínes. Pỽẏ bẏnhac atoꝛher ẏnaỽd neut ſarhaet ıdaỽ. Sef atelír ẏnſarhaet penteulu :- traẏan ſarhaet ẏ bꝛenhín. eıthẏr ẏreur ar arẏant bꝛeínhaỽl. Ac ẏ uellẏ ẏ alanaſ. Dıſteín. Ygnat llẏs. Penkẏnẏd. Hebogẏd. Penguaſtraỽt. Guaſ ẏſtauell. vn ſarhaet ac un alanaſ. ac un ebedıỽ. ac ac vn ureínt eu merchet. Yn eu ſarhaet ẏtelır naỽ mu anaỽ ugeínt arẏant. Yg galanas pop vn o honu ẏtelır naỽ mu anaỽ ugeín mu gan trı dꝛẏchauel. Punt ẏỽ ebedıỽ pop vn o honunt. Punt ẏỽ gobẏr eu merchet. Teır punt ẏỽ eu cowẏll. Seıth punt ẏỽ eu heguedı. Sarhaet

pop un. oꝛ f6ydogẏon ereıll oll eıthẏr ẏ.
penteulu ar effeırat teulu.   kẏn hanf6ẏnt
oꝛ f6ydogẏon nẏt ẏnt un vꝛeínt.   ꝶn far
haet pop vn oꝛf6ydogẏon ereıll ẏtelır
whe bu arẏant a whe ugeínt arẏant.   Ẏn   5
eu galanaſ ẏ telír whe .bu awheugeínt
mu gan trı. dꝛẏchauel.   Ẏn ebedı6 pop vn.
ẏtelír wheugeínt arẏant. awheugeínt
ẏ6 gobẏr pop vn oc eu merchet. . Punt
ẏ6 ahaner eu cowẏll.   teır punt .ẏ6 eu he-   10
guedı.   ꝶ. neb alatho dẏn talet ẏfarhaet
gẏffeuín. . ac odẏna ẏalanaſ.   Nẏ bẏd
dꝛẏchauel ar farhaet neb.

Lletẏ ẏpenteulu uẏd ẏtẏ m6ẏhaf ẏm
perued ẏ tref.   canẏſ ẏnẏ gẏlch ef ẏbẏ   15
dant lletẏeu ẏteulu mal .ẏ b6ẏnt para6t
ẏm pop reıt.   Ẏn lletẏ ẏpenteulu ẏbẏd ẏ
bard teulu. ar medẏc.   Ꝉletẏ ẏr effeırat teulu ac ẏfcolheıgon ẏllẏs ganta6 uẏd tẏ. ẏ
caplan.   Ꝉletẏ effeırat bꝛenhíneſ uẏd tẏ   20
ẏ clochẏd.   Ꝉletẏ ẏ díftein .ar f6ydogẏon gan-

taỽ uẏd ẏtẏ neſſaf ẏr llẏs. Lletẏ ẏr ẏgnat llẏs uẏd ẏſtauell ẏbꝛenhín neu ẏneuad. ar gobenẏd auo dan ẏbꝛenhín ẏdẏd. auẏd dan pen ẏr ẏgnat llẏs ẏnoſ. Lletẏ ẏpenguaſtraỽt ar guaſtradẏon oll gantaỽ uẏd ẏtẏ neſſaf yr ẏſcubaỽꝛ ẏ bꝛenhín. canẏſ ef aran ẏr ebꝛaneu. Lletẏ ypenkẏnẏd ar kẏnẏdẏon oll gantaỽ uẏd odẏntẏ ẏbꝛenhín. Lletẏ ẏr hebogẏd uẏd ẏſcubaỽꝛ ẏ bꝛenhín. canẏ char ẏr hebogeu uỽc. Guelẏ ẏguaſ yſtauell aruoꝛỽẏn ẏſtauell ẏn ẏſtauell ẏbꝛenhín y bẏdant. Llety ẏdꝛẏſſoꝛẏon uẏd tẏ ẏpoꝛthaỽꝛ. Ancỽẏn ageiff ẏpenteulu ẏnẏ letẏ nẏt amgen teir ″a thri feic″‸achoꝛneit olẏn oꝛ llẏs. Achẏfarỽs pop blỽẏdẏn ageiff ẏgan ẏbꝛenhín nẏt amgen teir punt. O anreith awnel ẏ teulu ran deu ỽꝛ ageiff ef oꝛ bẏd gẏt ac ỽẏnt ac o traẏan ẏbꝛenhín ẏr eidon adewiſſo Ẏneb awnel cam iſ colofneu ẏ llẏſ oſ deila ẏpenteulu ỽꝛth gẏfreith traẏan ẏdi-

rꝺy neu ycamlꝺꝛꝺ ageif. Os deila heuẏt
ẏgkẏnted yneuad ẏn gẏnt noꝛ difteln traẏan ẏdirꝺy yneu ẏcamlꝺꝛꝺ ageiff. Ꝑab
neu nei ap bꝛaꝺt ẏr bꝛenhin uẏd ẏpenteulu. Coꝛneit med adaꝺ idaꝺ ẏmpop kẏued- 5
ꝺch ẏgan ẏurenhinef. Oꝛ gat ẏbꝛenhin
neb oꝛ teulu aruar ẏgantaꝺ hẏt odif ẏ pentan. gohodet ẏpenteulu hꝺnnꝺ ataꝺ ehunan. ar tal ẏneuad ẏdeifted ẏpenteulu
ar teulu oll ẏnẏ gẏlch. kẏmeret ef ẏrhe- 10
neuẏd auẏnho ar deheu idaꝺ. ac arall arẏ
affeu. March bitwoffeb ageiff ẏgan ẏ bꝛenhin. adꝺẏ ran ageiff ẏuarch oꝛ ebꝛan.

Ɏ Neb afarhaho neu alatho effeirat
teulu diodefet gẏfreith fened. ac am ẏ 15
warthaet deudeg mu atelir idaꝺ ar traẏan ageiff ef ar deuparth ẏr bꝛenhin. Effeirat teulu ageiff y wifc ẏpenẏtyo ẏ bꝛenhin ẏndi ẏgarawẏf. ahẏnnẏ erbyn ẏ pafc
ac offrꝺm ẏbꝛenhin ageiff. ac offrꝺm ẏ 20
teulu. ac offrꝺm ẏfaꝺl agẏmerho offrꝺm

ẏ gan ẏ bɟenhín ẏnẏ teir gổyl arbenhıc.
bẏth hagen ẏ kẏmer offrổm ẏ bɟenhín.
Bổyt feıc achorneıt med ageıff ẏnẏ ancổ-.
ẏn oɟ llẏs. . March bıtwoffeb ageıff ẏgan
ẏ bɟenhın. athraẏan holl degổm ẏ bɟenhín   5
ageıff. ar trẏdẏdẏn anhebcoɟ ẏr bɟenhín
ẏổ ẏr effeırat teulu. Effeırat bɟenhínes
ageíff march bıtwoffeb ẏgan ẏ urenhínes.
ae offrổm hı ar faổl aperthẏno ıdı ageıff
teır gueıth pop blổẏdẏn. Offrổm. ẏ uren-   10
hínef hagen ageíff ẏn pɟeffổẏluodaổc..
Ẏ wıfc ẏ penẏtẏo ẏurenhínes ẏndı ẏ ga-
rawẏf ageıff ẏ heffeırat. . lle ẏr effeırat
ẏurenhínef auẏd gẏuarổẏneb ahı.
OJfteín ageıff guífc ẏ penteulu ẏnẏ   15
    teır gổẏl arbenhıc. aguıfc ẏ dıfte-
ín ageıff ẏ bard teulu. a guífc ẏ bard ageıff ẏ dɟẏffaổɟ. Croen hẏd ageıff ẏ dıfteín
ẏ gan ẏ kẏnẏdẏon pan. ẏ gouẏno o haner .
whefraổɟ hẏt ẏm pen ổẏthnof o ueı.. Pan   20
del ẏ dıfteín ẏr llẏf ổɟth gẏghoɟ ef ẏ bẏd

ẏ bõẏt ar llẏn ẏn hollaõl.   Ef adengẏſ ẏ pɪıa
õt le ẏ paõb ẏnẏ neuad.   Ef aran ẏ lletẏeu
March bıtwoſſeb ageıff ẏgan ẏ bɪenhín.
a dõẏ ran ageıff ẏ uarch oɪ ebɪan.   Rẏd uẏd
tír ẏdıſteín.   Eıdon ageıff o pop anreıth ẏ   5
gan ẏ teulu.   Dıſteín bıeu gobẏr merchet
pop maer bıſweıl.   Pedeír ar hugeínt age
ıff gan pop ſõẏdaõc adarẏmreto bõẏt all=
ẏn ẏnẏ llẏſ pan elhont ẏn eu ſõẏd.   Ef aran
arẏant ẏgueſtuaeu.   Ef bıeu ardẏſtu guı-   10
rodeu ẏnẏ llẏſ.   Ef ageıf traẏan dıróẏ acha
mlõɪõ guaſſanaethwẏr bõẏt allẏn.   nẏt
amgen coc athrullẏat aſõẏdõɪ llẏſ.   Oɪ pan
dotto ẏdıſteín oe ſeuẏll naõd duõ a naõd
ẏ bɪenhín ar urenhíneſ ar guẏrda.   a toɪho   15
ẏnaõd honno nẏt oeſ naõd ıdaõ nac ẏn
llẏſ nac ẏn llan.   kẏfranaõc uẏd ẏnteu uẏd
ar pedeır ſõẏd llẏſ ar hugeínt.   a dõẏ ran a
geıff o gróẏn ẏ guarthec a lather ẏnẏ gegín.   O pop ſõẏd llẏs pan ẏrotho ẏ bɪen   20
hín gobẏr ageıff ẏ dıſteín eıthẏr ẏſõẏdeu

arbenhíc. Croen hýd ada6 ida6 ýn hýd₂ef ý
gan ý penkýnýd. ac oh6nn6 ý guneır llef-
trı ý gad6 fioleu ý b₂enhín. ae gýrn kýn
rannu ý cr6ýn r6g ý b₂enhín ar kýnýdý-
on. Dıfteín ageıff ran g6₂ o arýant guaft- 5
rodýon. Dıfteín o gýfreıth bıeu goffot
b6ýt a llýn rac b₂on ý b₂enhín a seıc uch
ý la6 ac arall ıf ý la6. ýný teír g6ýl arbenıc.
Ef heuýt bıeu kýhýt ae hıruýs o₂ c6₂6f
gloý6 ý ar ý guada6t. ac o₂ b₂aga6t hýt 10
ý kýg6g perued. ac o₂ med hýt ý kýg6g
eıthaf. Y neb awnel cam ýg kýnted ýne-
uad. of deıla ýdıfteín 6₂th gýfreıth ef a-
geıff traýan ý dır6ý neu ý caml6₂6. ac of-
deıla heuýt ıf ý colofneu ýn gýnt no₂ 15
penteulu traýan ýdır6ý neu ý caml6₂6
ageıff. Dıfteín bıeu cad6 ran ý b₂enhín
o anreıth. ac o rennír kýmeret ef uu6ch
neu ých. Dıfteín bıeu cad týgu d₂of ý
b₂enhín pan uo reıth arna6. Dıfteín ý6 20
ý trýdýdýn a geıd6 b₂eínt llýf ýn a6fen

⌊ ý b₂enhín

b6yt a llyn rac b2on y b2enhín a seíc uch la6
ac arall ís la6 yny teír g6yl arbenhíc. Dífté-
ín ageíff kyhyt ae híruys o2 c62of gloy6 yar
yg6ada6t. ac o2 b2aga6t hyt ykyg6g perued.
ac o2 med hyt ykyg6g eíthaf. Yneb awnel   5
kam yg kynted y neuad os deíla y dílteín ef
62th gyfreíth ꞓ trayan y dír6y neu y caml626
ageíff ef. Os deíla heuyt ís y colofneu yn
gynt no2 penteulu ꞓ ef ageíff ytrayan. Dífteín bíeu cad6 ran y b2enhín o2 anreíth. a   10
phan ranher ꞓ kymeret ef ych. neu uüch.
Dífteín bíeu tygu d2os y b2enhín pan vo re-
íth arna6. Ef y6 ytrydydyn ageíd6 b2eínt
llys yn a6ffen y b2enhín.

Ɲ Y dyry ygnat llys aryant yr peng6af   15
   tra6t pan gaffo march ygan y b2enhín.
Ran g62 ageíff o aryant y dayret. Yn rat y barn ef pop b2a6t aperthyno 62th y llys. Ef bíeu dangos b2eínt g6yr y llys ab2eínt eu f6-
ydeu. Pedeír ar hugeínt ageíff ynteu ygan   20
yneb ydangoffo yv2eínt aedylyet ída6.
Pan del gobyr kyfreítha6l yr b2a6twyr ꞓ
d6y ran ageíff yr ygnat llys. Ran deu 62
ageíff o2 anreíth awnel y teulu kyn nyt el
ef oe ty. Ꝋ2 g62th6ynepa neb barn yr ygnat 25

llys ꝛ rodent eu deu ꝡyſtyl yn llaꝡ y bꝛenhín.
ac oꝛ methlır yr ygnat llys ꝛ talet yr bꝛenhın
werth y tauaꝡt ac na varnet byth. ac oꝛ methlır y llall. talet y sarhaet yr ygnat llys.
ac yr bꝛenhín werth y tauaꝡt. Jaꝡn yꝡ ẏr   5
bꝛaꝡdꝟꝛ kaffel pedeır keínhaꝡc kyfreıth
o pop dadyl atalo pedeır keínhaꝡc kyf. Ef
yꝡ y try dy dyn anhebcoꝛ yr bꝛenhín. Pedeır
ar hugeínt adaꝡ yr bꝛaꝡtwyr pan teruyner
tır. Oꝛ a dyn yg kyfreıth heb ganhat yr yg-   10
nat llys ꝛ talet trı buhyn camlꝟꝛꝡ yr bꝛenhín. ac oꝛ byd y bꝛenhín yny lle ꝛ talet yn de
udyblyc. Ny dyly neb varnu ar ny ꝡyppo teır colofyn kyfreıth a gꝡerth pop an eu eıl kyf-
reıthaꝡl. llenllıeín ageıff yr ygnat llys y   15
gan y vꝛenhınes yn pꝛeſſꝡyl. March bıtoſſeb ageıff ygan y bꝛenhín adꝡy ran ıdaꝡ
oꝛ ebꝛan. ac yn vn pꝛeſſeb ybyd amarch y
bꝛenhín peunydyaꝡl. Gꝡaſtraꝡt auꝡyn
adꝡc y varch ıdaꝡ yn gyweır pan y mynho.   20
Ytır ageıff yn ryd. Ouer tlyſſeu ageıff pan
ꝡyſtler y sꝡyd ıdaꝡ. taꝡlboꝛt ygan y bꝛenhín. a modꝛꝡy eur y gan y vꝛenhínes. ac
ny dyly ynteu gadu y tlyſſeu hynny y gan-
taꝡ nac aꝛ werth nac yn rat. Y gan y bard   25

pan eníllo kadeır y keıff yr ygnat llys coın
bual amodı6y' eur.   ar gobennyd a dotter y
dana6 yny gadeır.   Pedeır arhugeínt a geıff
yr ygnat llys o pop dadyl sarhaet alledıat
ygan yneb adıagho oı holyon hynny.   Ef a-   5
geıff taua6t y taua6t adel y pen yn anrec
yr bıenhín.   ar tauodeu oll oı llys.   kanyf ynteu auarn ar y tauodeu oll.   ar bıenhín adyly llan6 lle y taua6t o gehyr moıd6yt y ll6d-
yn bıeıffo yr gof llys.   Ygnat llys y6 y trydy-   10
dyn agynheıl bıeínt llys yn a6ffen y bıenhín.   Ryd uyd o ebedı6.   kanyf g6ell y6 ygne-
ıtaeth no dím pıeffenha6l.

By dyd bynhac y llatho yr hebogyd crych-
yd neu b6n.   neu whıbonogyl vynyd   15
o rym y hebogeu.   trı g6affanaeth awna y
bıenhín ıda6.   dala y varch tra achuppo yr adar.
adala ywarthafyl tra dífcynho.   ae dala tra
efkyno.   Teır g6eıth yd anrecca y bıenhın
ef y nos honno oe la6 ehunan ar u6yt.   ka-   20
nys yn lla6 ygennat yd anrecca beunyd
ef eıthyr yny teır g6yl arbenhıc.   ar dyd
y llatho ederyn en wa6c.   ar gled y kyghell-
a6ı yd eıfted yghyfed6ch.   Croen hyd ageıff
ynhydıef ygan ypenkynyd ywneuthur menyc   25

athafyl hualeu ıdaƀ. Nyt yf namyn teır dı-
aƀt yny neuad rac bot gƀall aryhebogeu.
March bıtoffeb ageıff ygan y bɪenhín. a dƀy
ran ıdaƀ oɪ ebɪan. Oɪ llad yr hebogyd yvarch
yn hela. neu oɪ byd marƀ odamweín ꞓ arall   5
ageıff ygan y bɪenhín. Ef bıeu pop hƀyedıc.
Ef bıeu pop nyth llamyften agaffer ar tır y
llys. Bƀyt seıc achoɪneıt med ageıff yny
ancƀyn ynylety. Oɪ pan dotto yrhebogyd
yhebogeu yny mut hyt pan y tynho allan ꞓ   10
ny dyry atteb yneb oɪ ae holho. Gƀeft ageıff
vn weıth pop blƀydyn ar tayogeu y bɪenhín.
ac o pop tayaƀctref ykeıff dauat hefp. neu pedeır keínhaƀc kyfreıth yn uƀyt y hebogeu.   ꞌ
Y tır ageıff yn ryd. Ydyd ydalyho ederyn en- 15
waƀc. ac na bo y bɪenhín yny lle ꞓ pan del yr
hebogyd yr llys ar ederyn gantaƀ ꞓ y bɪenhín
adyly kyfodı racdaƀ. ac ony chyfyt ꞓ ef adyly rodı y wıfc auo ymdanaƀ yr hebogyd. Ef
bıeu callon pop llƀdyn alather yny gegín.   20
kyt anreıther yr hebogyd o gyfreıth ꞓ nys
anreıtha nar maer nar kyghellaƀɪ. namyn yteulu ar rıghyll.

P Enkynyd ageıff croen ych ygayaf ygan
    ydíftein ywneuthur kynllyfaneu. ar   25

les ybɹenhín yd helyant y kynydyon hyt galan racuyr. Odyna hyt naɓuetdyd oracuyr nys kyfranant ac ef. Naɓuetdyd oracuyr y gɓeda yr penkynyd dangos yr bɹenhín y gɓn ae gyrn ae gynllyfaneu. ae trayan oɹ crɓyn. 5 hyt naɓuetdyd o racuyr ny cheiff neb oɹ ae holho penkynyd atteb ygantaɓ onyt vn oɹ sɓydogyon llys uyd. kany dyly neb gohɪryaɓ y gɪlyd oɹ byd ae barnho. Penkynyd ageiff ran deu ɓɹ oɹ crɓyn ygan gynydyon y gellgɓn. a 10 ran gɓɹ ygan gynydyon y mílgɓn. aco trayan y bɹenhɪn oɹ crɓyn ykeiff ef ytrayan. Gɓedy ranher ycrɓyn rɓg ybɹenhín ar kynydyon. aet ypenkynyd ar kynydyon gantaɓ ar dofreth ar tayogeu y bɹenhín. ac odyna do- 15 ent at ybɹenhín erbyn ynadolyc ygymryt eu ɪaɓn ygantaɓ. lle ypenkynyd ar kynydyon gantaɓ yny neuad. yɓ ygolofyn gyfarɓyn. eb ar bɹenhín. Coɹneɪt med adaɓ ɪdaɓ ygan y bɹenhín neu ygan y penteulu. ar eɪl ygan y 20 vɹenhínes. artrydyd ygan y dɪfteín. llamyften dof pop gɓyl vɪhagel ageiff ef ygan yr hebogyd. ancɓyn ageiff yny lety. Seɪc achoɹ neɪt med. Ef bɪeu trayan dɪrɓy achamlɓɹɓ ac ebedɪɓ ykynydyon. athɹayan gobɹeu eu 25

merchet. Gyt ar bꝛenhín ybydant ykynydy
on oꝛ nadolyc hyt pan elhont yhela ewꞮget
ygѣanhѣyn. Oꝛ pan elhont y hela y kyntef-
ín hyt ym pen naѣuetdyd oveꞮ nyt atteb y
penkynyd yr neb ae holho. ony odꞮwedꞮr duѣ 5
kalan meꞮ kyn gѣꞮfgaѣ kuaran ytroet deheu. March bꞮtoſſeb ageꞮff ygan ybꝛenhín.
adѣy ran Ɪdaѣ oꝛ ebꝛan. Pan tygho ypenkynyd ⁒ tyget yuѣyn ygѣn ae gyrn ae gynlly-
uaneu. PedeꞮr keꞮnhaѣc kyfreꞮth ageꞮff ef 10
ygan pop kynyd mílgꞮ. acѣyth geínhaѣc
kyfreꞮth ygan pop kynyd gellgѣn. Oꝛ a y
penkynyd yn anreꞮth gan y teulu y bꝛenhꞮn.
neu gan yͺlu. kanet ygoꝛn pan vo Ɪaѣn Ɪdaѣ.
adewꞮſſet eꞮdon oꝛ anreꞮth. Mal yt geꞮff Ɪ 15
croen ych kyn ytrydydyd nadolyc ygan y
dꞮfteꞮn ⁒ Ɪaѣn yѣ Ɪdaѣ kaffel croen buch rѣg
meheſín ahanher meꞮ ygantaѣ. acͺonys
koffa yna ⁒ ny cheꞮff dím.

Ｐ Engѣaſtraѣt ageꞮff croen ych ygayaf 20
achroen buch yrͺhaf ygan ydꞮfteín.
ywneuthur kebyſtreu y veírch y bꝛenhín.
ahynny kyn rannu ycrѣyn rѣg y dꞮfteꞮn
arſѣydogyon. Pengѣaſtraѣt ar penkynyd
arͺtroedaѣc nyt eꞮſtedant ѣꝛth paret yneuad. 25

paɤb ohonunt ɤynteu aɤyr yle. . Pengɤaſtraɤt bieu koeſſeu pop eidon alather, yny ·gegín.·
ahalen arodir idaɤ gantunt.   Ran deu ɤ⁊ a
geiff o aryant ygɤaſtrodyon.   Ef bieu hen
gyfrɤyeu amɤs ybⱬenhín ae hen ffrɤyneu.   5
Pengɤaſtraɤt argɤaſtrodyon   gantaɤ   agaffant yr ebolyon gɤyllt a del yr bⱬenhín o trayan anreith.   Ef bieu eſtynnu pop march a
rotho y bⱬenhín.   achebyſtyr adyry ynteu gan
pop march.   ac ynteu ageiff pedeir keínhaɤc 10
o pop march eithyr⸍ tri.   y march arother·yr
effeirat teulu.   ar march arother yr ygnat
llys.   ar march arother yr croeſſaneit.   kanys
rɤymaɤ troet ygebyſtyr awneir ɤ⁊th ydɤy
geill.   ac uelly yrodir.   Ef ageiff lloneit y lleſtyr 15
yd yffo y bⱬenhín ohonaɤ ygan ydíſteín.   ar
eil y gan y penteulu.   ar trydyd ygan yvⱬen-
hínes.   Ytir ageiff yn ryd.   a march bitoſſeb
ageiff ygan y bⱬenhín.   a dɤy ran idaɤ o⁊ e-
bⱬan.   lle y pengɤaſtraɤt ar gɤaſtrodyon y   20
gantaɤ yɤ ygolofyn neſſaf yr bⱬenhín.   Pengɤaſtraɤt bieu rannu yr yſtableu ac ebⱬaneu·
ymeirch.   Tⱬayan⸍ dirɤy achamlɤⱬɤ ygɤaſtrodyon ageiff ef.   Ef·bieu capaneu y bⱬenhⱳ⸍ ·
oⱬbyd crɤyn ɤⱬthunt.   ae yſpardɤneu o⁊ bydant 25

eureit neu aryaneit neu euydeit pan dirmyccer. Bôyt seic achoꝛneit côꝛôf ageiff
Ôas yſtauell bieu hen ❡ yny ancôyn.
dillat y bꝛenhin oll eithyr ytudet ga-
rawys. Ef ageiff y dillat gôely ae vantell 5
ae peis ae grys ae laôdyr ae eſcityeu ae hoſ-
ſaneu. Nyt oes le dilis yr gôaf yſtauell y
ny neuad. kan keidô gôely y bꝛenhin. ae
negeſſeu awna rôg y neuad ar yſtauell.
Y tir ageiff ynryd. ae ran o aryant y gôeſt- 10
uaeu. Ef atan gôely y bꝛenhin. March pꝛeſ-
ſôyl ageiff ygan y bꝛenhin. a dôy ran idaô
oꝛ ebꝛan. O pop anreith awnel yteulu ꞓ ef
ageiff ygôarthec kyhyt eu kyrn ac eu hyſ-
ard teulu ageiff eidon o pop ❡ kyfarn. 15
anreith y bo ôꝛth ydôyn gyt ar teulu.
aran gôꝛ mal pop teuluôꝛ arall. Ynteu agan
vnbeſnyaeth pꝛydeſn racdunt yndyd kat
ac ymlad. Pan archo bard y teyrn ꞓ kanet
vn kanu. Pan archo y vꝛeyr ꞓ kanet tri cha- 20
nu. Pan archo y tayaôc ꞓ kanet hyt pan
vo blîn. Y tir ageiff yn ryd. ae varch yn pꝛe-
ſôyl ygan y bꝛenhin. ar eil kanu agan yny
neuad. kanyſ y penkerd adechꝛeu. Eil neffaf yd eiſted yr penteulu. Telyn ageiff y 25

gan y bꝛenhín. Amodꝛ6y eur ygan y ꝟꝛen-
hínes pan rother y s6yd ıda6. Ar telyn ny
at byt$^h_\wedge$ yganta6. Ȝard teulu. Ɡoſtec g6ꝛ.
Ꝑıſteín bꝛenhínes. Ꝑꝛyſſa6ꝛ neuad. Ꝑꝛyſ-
ſa6ꝛ yſtauell. Ɡ6aſtra6t au6yn. Ɡanh6-
yllyd. Ȝrullyat. Ɡoc. Ȝroeda6c. Ꝑed-
yd. · Ɀ6yd6ꝛ llys. Ꝑedyc. Ꝑoꝛ6yn yſtauell. · Ɡ6aſtra6t au6yn bꝛenhínes. Y pymthec hyn yſſyd vn ꞷꝛeínt. Ac vn ꞷꝛeínt eu
merchet. Yn ſarhaet pop vn o hynny y te
lır whe bu awhe v6eínt aryant. Galanas
pop vn ohonunt atelır o whe bu awhe ḅụ
vgeınt mu gan trı dꝛychafel. Ebedı6 pop
vn o honunt ꞓ y6 wheugeínt. Awhe vgeínt y6 gobyr merch pop vn o honunt.
Punt ahanher yny chowyll. Teır punt
y heg6edı. Øꝛ a merch vn oꝛ pymthec hyn.
ynllathꝛut heb rod kenedyl ꞓ whech eıdon
kyhyt eu kyrn ac eu hyſkyſarn uyd eu he-
g6edı. vn ꞷꝛeínt ahynny y6 merch pop
g6ꝛ ryd a el yn llathꝛut.

O R a dꝛyſſa6ꝛ neuad ím6y no hyt y
ꞷꝛeıch ae wyalen y 6ꝛth ydꝛ6s g6edy
yd el ybꝛenhín yr neuad ꞓ oꝛ serheır yno.
ny dıwygır ıda6. Oꝛ llud y dꝛyſſa6ꝛ neu y

poꝛthaƀꝛ yn oꝛ sƀydogyon dan y adnabot y
myƀn pan ymynho ꞏ talet pedeir keinhaƀc
kyfreith yr sƀydaƀc. ac os pennadur uyd ꞏ
talet yndeudyblyc. athri buhyn camlƀꝛƀ
atal yr bꝛenhin. lleſtyr aeruyll ywiraƀt yr   5
dꝛyſſaƀꝛ. Diſtein argƀallofyeit adygant
eu gƀiraƀt y leſtyr ydꝛyſſaƀꝛ. pan rother
gƀiraƀt yr ebeſtyl ꞏ y dꝛyſſaƀꝛ ae keidƀ. Ef
a sycha crƀyn ygƀarthec alather yny gegin. acheinhaƀc ageiff ynteu o pop croen   10
pan ranher. Ef ageiff y tir yn ryd. a march
bitoſſeb ageiff ygan y bꝛenhin. Ran gƀꝛ
ageiff o aryant ygƀeſtuaeu.
Dꝛyſſaƀꝛ yſtauell ageiff y tir yn ryd. a
march bitoſſeb ygan y bꝛenhin. agƀiraƀt   15
gyfreithaƀl ageiff. ae ran o aryant ygƀeſt*uaeu*.
Gƀaſtraƀt auƀyn ageiff kyfrƀyeu peunyd-
yaƀl y bꝛenhin ae panel. ae panel ae
gapan glaƀ pan dirmyccer. ae hen pedoleu.
ae heyrn pedoli. Y tir ageiff ynryd. aeva-   20
rch pꝛeſſƀyl. Ef adƀc march ybꝛenhin y lety
ac oe lety. Ef adyeila march y bꝛenhin pan
eſcynho aphan diſcynho. Ran gƀꝛ ageiff oꝛ
ebolyon gƀyllt adel o anreith.
Medyc llys aeiſted yn eil neſſaf yr pente-   25

ulu yny neuad. Ytır ageıff ynryd. amarch
pıeſſ6yl ygan y bıenhın. Yn rat yg6na ef
medegínyaetheu 6ıth y teulu a g6yr y llys.
kany ell cheıff eıthyr ydıllat g6aetlyt onyt
o vn oı teır g6elı agheua6l vyd. Punt agym- 5
er ef heb y ymboıth neu na6 vgeínt ae ymboıth oı welı agheua6l. nyt amgen pan toıher pen dyn hyny weler yr emenhyd. aſc6ın
vch creuan pedeır keínha6c cota atal oı ſeín-
ha ymy6n ka6c. aſc6ın ıs creuan ꝝ pedeır   10
keínha6c kyfreıth atal. a phan wanher dyn
yny arch hyny welher y amyſcar. a phan
toıher vn o petwar poſt coıff dyn hyny weler
ymer. Sef reı ynt ydeu voıd6yt ar deu vŷr-
ryat. Teır punt y6 g6erth pop vn o teır   15
g6elı hynny.
Ꞡrullyat ageıff y tır yn ryd. a march bıtoſſeb ygan y bıenhín. G6ıra6t gyfreıtha
6l ageıff nyt amgen lloneıt ylleſtrı yg6aſ-
ſanaethwyr ac 6ynt yny llys oı c6ı6f. ac   20
eu trayan oı bıaga6t. med. ac eu hanher
oı bıaga6t. 🙚 edyd ageıff ytır yn ryd.
ae varch pıeſſ6yl y gan y bıenhín. Ran
g6ı ageıff o aryant yg6eſtuaeu. athrayan
y c6yr adıotter oı ger6yn ved. kanys y deu   25

parth arennır yn teır ran. ydƀy ran yr
neuad. ar tryded yr yſtauell.

Ɓoc bıeu crƀyn ydeueıt ar geıfyr ar ƀyn
ar mynneu ar lloı. ac amyſcar ygƀarth
ec alather alather yny gegín. eıthyr y   5
refyr ar cledyf bıſweıl a a yr poɪthaƀɪ. Y
coc bıeu ygƀer ar yſceı oɪ gégín eıthyr
gƀer yr eıdoñ auo teır noſ ar warthec
ymaerty. Y tır ageıff yn ryd. ae varch
bıtoſſeb ygan ybɪenhın.   10
Ɓoſtecƀɪ ageıff pedeır keínhaƀc o pop dı-
rƀy achamlƀɪƀ agoller am anoſtec yny
llys. Ran heuyt ageıff am pop kyfran
ygan ysƀydogyon. Y tır ageıff ageıff yn
ryd. ae ran o aryant ygƀeſtuaeu. ae va   15
rch pɪeſſƀyl ygan y bɪenhín. Pan ſymu
ter y maer bıſweıl ƀe sƀyd ꞏ trugeínt a
geıff ygoſtecƀɪ ygan yneb adotter yny le.
Ɓroedaƀc bıeu eıſted dan traet y bɪenhıñ.
abƀyta o vn dyſcyl ac ef. Ef aenyn y   20
ganhƀyll gyntaf rac bɪon y bɪenhın ar
vɪenhıneș ƀɪth uƀyt. ac eıſſoes bƀyt ſeıc
agƀıraƀt ageıff. kanyt oes gyfed ıdaƀ.
Y tır ageıff ynryd. amarch bıtoſſeb ygan
ybɪenhín. ae ran o aryant ygƀeſtuaeu.   25

S6yd6ɪ llys a geiff y tɪr ynryd. ae varch
pɪeff6yl ygan y bɪenhín. ae   ran o aryaɴt
yg6eftuaeu.

O Jftein bɪenhínes ageiff y varch pɪef-
f6yl ygan yvɪenhínes. 6yth geínha-   5
6c ada6 atta6 o aryant y g6eftuaeu. ad6y
geínha6c agymer ef. arei ereill aran r6g
S6ydogyon yr yftauell. ef aued aru6yt-
allyn yr yftauell. Ef adyly ar tyftu g6ɪro-
deu yr yftauell. adangos y pa6b y le.   10
Wor6yn yftauell ageiff holl dillat y vɪenhínes tr6y y vl6ydyn eithyr ywifc ype-
nyttyo yndɪ ygara6ys. Ythɪr ageiff yn
ryd ae march pɪeff6yl ygan y vɪenhínes.
ae henffr6yneu ae harchenat pan dɪr-   15
myccer ageiff. ae ran o aryant yg6eftuaeu.
G6aftra6t au6yn bɪenhɪnes ageiff y
tɪr ynryd ae varch pɪeff6yl ygan y vɪenhínes. Wyny b6ynt ygyt yr effeirat teu-
lu ar diftein. ar ygnat llys. bɪeint llys a   20
vyd yno kyn boet a6ffen ybɪenhín.

M aer achyghella6ɪ bieu kad6 diffeith
bɪenhín. Punt ahaɴher ada6 yr
bɪenhɪn pan 6yftler maeroɴiaeth neu
gyghelloɪyaeth. Tɪɪ dyn agynheil ymaer 25

gantaб ygkyfedбch yn neuad ybɹenhín. · Ef
àran yteu   lu pan elhont ar dofreth.   Yn
anreith yd a gan yteulu ar ypetweryd.
kylch ageiff ar ypetweryd ar tayogeu y-
bɹenhín dбy weith yny ulбydyn.   Ny byd   5
penkenedyl maer achyghellaбɹ byth.   Maer bieu kymhell holl dylyet ybɹenhín hyt
ybo y vaeroníaeth.   Maer achyghellaбɹ adylyant trayan gobɹeu merchet ytayogeu.
athrayan camlyryeu ac ebediweu y tayo-   10
geu.   athrayan eu hyt pan ffohont oɹ wlat.
athrayan eu hyt ac eu bбyt opop marбty
tayaбc.   Maer bieu rannu pop peth.   arig-
hyll bieu dewis yrbɹenhín.   Oɹ damwein
ha yr maer na allo daly ty: kymeret ef y   15
tayaбc auynho attaб ulбydyn oɹ kalan mei
ygilyd.   amбynhaet ef laeth ytayaбc yrhaf.
ae yt ykynhayaf.   ae ya voch ygayaf.   aphan el ytayaбc yбɹthaб.   gadet idaб pedeir hych
maбɹ abaed.   ae yfcrybyl ereill oll.   aphedeir   20
erб gayafar.   ac бyth erб gбanhбyn ar.   ar
eil ulбydyn ar tryded gбnaet uelly.   ac nyt
yr vn tayaбc hagen.   Odyna ymboɹthet ynteu ar yr eidaб ehunan teir blyned ereill.
. .Odyna gбaredet ybɹenhín arnaб o rodi tay . . .25

a6c ida6 yny mod gynt os mẏn. Pan gollo
dyn y anreith o gyfreith. y maer ar kyghell-
a6ɩ bɩeu yr aneɩred ar enderíged ar dínewyt
ran deu hanher.

Dylẏet ykyghella6ɩ y6 kynhal dadleu   5
ybɩenhín yny 6yd ac yny a6ffen.   Ef
bɩeu dodɩ croes ag6ahard ym pop dadyl. ar
gled ybɩenhín yd eɩſted ykyghella6ɩ yny te-
ɩr g6yl arbenhɩc. os yny gyghelloɩyaeth ef
ybyd ybɩenhín yn dala llys. Modɩ6y eur   10
athelyn atha6lboɩt ageɩff ygan ybɩenhín   .
pan el yny f6yd. Yn oes hywel da trayan
by6 a mar6 ytayogeu adoeɩ yr maer ac yr   :
kyghella6ɩ.. y deuparth "yr kyghella6ɩ." ar
trayan yr maer. ar maeɩ aranneɩ. ar kyg-   15   .   ':'.
hella6ɩ adewɩffeɩ.

RJghyll ageɩff ytɩr ynryd: a seɩc oɩ llys,
R6g yd6y golofyn y seɩf tra u6ytaho
ybɩenhín. kanys ef bɩeu goglyt yneuad
rac tan yna. G6edy b6yt ᷓ yffet ynteu gyt   20
ar g6affanaethwyr. Odyna nac eɩftedet
ac na thrawet ypoſt neffaf yr bɩenhín. G6ɩ-
ra6t gyfreɩtha6l ageɩff. nyt amgen lloneɩt
ylleſtrɩ y g6affanaethw̃yɩ ac 6ynt yny llys   .
᷉oɩ c6ɩ6f. ac eu hanher oɩ bɩaga6t. ac eu trayan 25

oꝛ med. Ef bieu koefcyn pop eidon oꝛ llys.
Ny byd hyt vcharned. NaϬuet dyd kyn kalan gayaf y keiff ef peif achrys achapan. atheir kyfelín llieín o pen elin hyt ymlaen hir
vys ywneuthur llaϬdϬꝛ idaϬ. ac ny byd ten 5
llif ny laϬdϬꝛ. Ny byd hyt yny dillat na
myn hyt yg clϬm ylaϬdϬꝛ. kalan maϬꝛth
y keiff peis achrys amantell allaϬdϬꝛ. Yny
trı amfer hagen y keiff penguch. Ef bieu
rannu rϬg ybꝛenhin ar maϬer ar kyghella-   10
Ϭꝛ. Ef bieu yr yfcub auo dꝛos pen pan ranher yt ytayogeu ffoaϬdyr ac eu marϬ tei.
Pan adaϬ kyllıdus ffoaϬdyr yyt heb vedı.
aphan gaffer y kyffelyp o varϬ ty: yrighyll
ageiff ytalareu. Ef ageiff ymehín bϬlch ar 15
emenyn bϬlch oꝛ marϬ tei. ar maen iffaf
oꝛ ꭣreuan ar dulín oll ar llínhat ar to neffaf yr dayar oꝛ veifcaϬn. ar bϬeill ar crym
aneu ar ieir ar gϬydeu ar katheu. Toꝛth ae
henllyn ageiff ef ym pop ty ydel idaϬ ar neges 20
ybꝛenhín. Teir kyfelín auyd yn hyt y billo
rac y arganuot. Ef ageiff ytarϬ adel gan
anreith. Pan vo marϬ yrighyll: yn trugared ybꝛenhín y byd yr eidaϬ. Oꝛ serheir y
righyll oe eifted yn dadleu ybꝛenhín: tàlet 25

ıda6 gogreıt eıffın. achucc6y. G6ys rıgh
yll gan tyfton. neu tar6a6 ypoft teır g6eıth
ny ellır e g6adu onyt tr6y lys. Pan wat-
ter hagen ᛫ ll6 ydyn awyffer ary trydyd
o wyr vn vꝛeınt ac ef ae g6atta. .   5

Of llys ageıff penneu yg6arthec a
lather yny gegın ae traet eıthyr yta
uodeu. y ymboꝛth ef ae was ada6 oꝛ llys. Yn
rat yg6na ef g6eıth yllys oll eıthyr trı g6e-
ıth. kalla6ꝛ. a b6ell gynnut a6ch lydan. a .   10
g6ay6. Gof llys bıeu keınyon kyfed6ch.
Ef ageıff pedeır keınha6c o pop karchara6ꝛ
ydıotto heyrn yarna6. Ytır ageıff yn ryd.
G6ıra6t gyfreıtha6l ageıff oꝛ llys. lloneıt
ylleftrı ygofyer ac 6ynt yny llys oꝛ c6ꝛ6f.   15
ar trayan oꝛ med. ar hanher oꝛ bꝛaga6t.
Ef y6 ytrydydyn ageıff ymeffur h6nn6. o-
dyna yrıghyll. yndıwethaf y trullyat. Ny
eıll neb gof bot yn vn gymh6t ar gof llys
heb yganhat. Vn rydıt y6 ar valu yny velın   20
ar bꝛenhın. Ef bıeu gobꝛeu merchet ygof-
eın au6ynt ydana6 ac 6ꝛth y ohen. wheugeınt y6 ebedı6 y gof llys. a wheugeınt y6 gobyr y verch. Punt ahanher y6 ychowyll.
Teır punt yny heg6edı.   25

Є Poꝛthaб ageiff y tir yn ryd. Yny kaſ-
tell trachefyn y doꝛ ybyd y ty. ae ymboꝛth ageiff oꝛ llys. Pꝛen ageiff o pop pбn
kynut adel trбy ypoꝛth. aphꝛen heuyt o
pop benneit. nyt amgen pꝛen allo y tyn-   5
nu ae vn llaб heb leſteir ar gerdet ymeirch
neu yr ychen. achyny allo tynnu vn pꝛen ꞓ
pꝛen eiſſoes ageiff. ac nyt mбyhaf. Oꝛ i
moch pꝛeidín adel yr poꝛth ꞓ hбch ageiff y
poꝛthaбꝛ. ac ny byd mбy noc ygallo ae   10
vn llaб ydꝛychafel herwyd ygбꝛych mal
na bo is ythraet no phen y lín. Oꝛ anreith
warthec adel yr poꝛth oꝛ byd eidon mo kota
erní. ypoꝛthaбꝛ ae keiff. ar eidon diwethaf
adel yr poꝛth ꞓ ef heuyt ae keiff. ar cledyf   15
biſweil arefyr oꝛ gбarthec alather yny gegín. Pedeir keinhaбc ageiff o pop karchar-
aбꝛ agarcharer gan iaбn ynyllys.

R Eit yб bot ygбylyбꝛ yn vonhedic gбlat.
kanyſ idaб yd ymdiredir oꝛ bꝛenhín.   20
y uбyt ageiff yn waſtat yny llys. ac ony
byd ybꝛenhín yny llys ꞓ yn gyntaf gбedy
ymaer y keiff ef yiſeic. Pop boꝛe y keiff ef
toꝛth. ae henllyn yny uoꝛeuбyt. aſcбꝛn y
dyníen ageiff o pop eidon alather yny gegín. 25

ytir ageiff yn ryd. Agόifc ageiff dόy weith
yny ulόyd yn ygan ybɹenhin. ac vn weith
ykeiff efcityeu a hoffaneu.

(M)aer bifweil ageiff y sόyf ar blonec oɹ
llys. Ef bieu crόyn ygόarthec alather   5
yny gegin a vo teir nos ar warthec ymaer ty.
Ef bieu gobɹeu merchet gόyr y vaertref. kyt
Sarhao ygόaffanaethwyr ymaer bifweil ꞏ
ar eu ffoɹd όɹth dόyn neu lyn oɹ gegin neu oɹ
vedgell parth ar neuad ꞏ nys diwygant idaό.   10
Pan talher ysarhaet ꞏ whe bu awheugeint
aryant atelir idaό. Y alanas atelir owhe bu
awhe vgeint mu. gan tri dɹychafel.

(D)ylyet ypenkerd yό eifted ar gled yr etling.
ytir ageiff yn ryd. Ef adyly kanu yn   15
gyntaf yny neuad. kyfarόs neithaόɹ ageiff
nyt amgen pedeir ar hugeint ygan pop
moɹόyn pan όɹhao. ny cheiff dim hagen
ar neithaόɹ gόɹeic arygaffo gynt da ar ynei-
thaόɹ pan uu uoɹόyn. Sef uyd penkerd. y   20
bard pan enillo kadeir. Ny eill neb bard erchi dim hyt ybo ypenkeirdyaeth ef. heb y
ganhat. onyt bard goɹwlat uyd. kyt lludyo
y bɹenhin rodi da yny gyfoeth hyt ym pen yf-
peit ꞏ digyfreith uyd ypenkerd. Pan vynho   25

y bɹenhín gerd oe gbarandab ꞉ kanet y penkerd
deu ganu ymod dub. ar trydyd oɹ penaetheu.
Pan vynho y vɹenhınes gerd oe gbarandab
yny hyſtauell.   kanet y bard teulu trı chanu
yndıſſon rac teruyſcu yllys.   5

Eneu gellgı bɹenhín tra vo kayat ylygeıt ꞉ pedeır arhugeínt atal.   Yny growyn ꞉ byth adeu vgeínt atal.   Yny gynllbſt ꞉
vn ar pymthec aphetwar vgeínt atal.   Yny o-
uer hela ꞉ wheugeínt atal.   Pan vo kýfrbys ꞉   10
punt atal. Ɛeneu mílgı bɹenhín kyn agorı ylygeıt꞉ deudec keínhabc atal. Yny growyn ꞉
pedeır ar hugeínt atal.   Yny gynllbſt ꞉ byth a
deugeínt atal.   Yny ouer hela ꞉ vn ar pymthec
aphetwar vgeínt. atal. Pan vo kyfrbys. punt 15
atal. Ɐn werth yb gellgı bɹeyr amílgı bɹenhín. Ꞩef atal mílgı bɹeyr ꞉ hanher kyfreıth
gellgı bɹeyr gogyfoet ac ef. Ƥyryb bynhac
vo ken eu tayabc kyn agoɹı ylygeıt ꞉ keínhabc
cotta atal.   Yny growyn ꞉ dby geínhabc cotta   20
atal.   Yny gynllbſt ꞉ teır keınhabc cotta atal.
Pan ellygher ynryd ꞉ pedeır keínhabc cotta a-
tal. Ɛoftabc kyn boet bɹenhín bıeıffo. nythal
eıthyr pedeır keínhabc cotta. Os bugeılgı uyd ꞉
eıdon taladby atal. ac ot amheuír yuot uelly꞉ 25

tyget yperchenna6c achymyda6c uch yd26s,
ac arall is yd26s raculaenu yr yfcrybyl ybo2e.
achad6 yr olyeit ydiwedyd. Ɏ neb adiotto llygat
gellgi b2enhín neu ato2ho ylofc62n ⸴ talet pedeir keínha6c kyfreith yg kyfeir pop buch atal   5
ho y ki. Ḳi kalla6ued o2 lledir pellach na6 kam
y62th yd26s ⸴ ny thelir. O2 lledir ynteu o vy6n y
na6kam ⸴ pedeir ar hugeínt atal. Ꝑyt oes werth
kyfreith ar vitheiat ⸴ po peth ny bo g6erth kyfreith arna6. damd6g ageffir ymdana6.   10

P6y bynhac adéfnydyo kylleic b2enhín ⸴
talet tri buhyn caml626 yr b2enhín. kar6 ⸴
ych atal. Ewic ⸴ buch atal. Deu dec gol6yth b2e-
ínhya6l auyd yg kylleic b2enhín. Taua6t. a
thri gol6yth o2 myn6gyl. kymhibeu. Callon.   15
Deul6yn, Jar, Tumon, hydgyllen. her6th. auu.
T2i buhyn caml626 atelir d2os pop ꝟꝺ gol6yth
Sef atelir d2os gylleic b2enhín pan gyfrifer pop
caml626 ⸴ deu vgeín mu. Ny byd gol6ython b2e-
ínya6l yn hyd b2enhín6l namyn o6yl giric hyt   20
galan racuyr. ꝛc ny byd kylleic ynteu, onyt tra
vo y golh6ython b2eínha6l ynda6. O2 lledir ka-
r6 b2enhin yn tref b2eyr ybo2e ⸴ katwet yb2eyr
ef yn gyfan hyt hanher dyd. ac ony doant y kynydyon yna. paret yb2eyr bligya6 yr hyd allitha6 25

y kὓn oꝛ kıc. adyget atref y kὓn ar croen ar afu
ar whartha6ꝛ ol. ac ony doant ykynydyon y
nos honno⁚ m6ynhaet ef ykíc. achatwet y
kὓn ar croen yr kynydyon. Oꝛ lledır y kar6 y
am hanher dyd⁚ katwet y bꝛeyr ef yn gyfan 5
hyt ynos. ac ony doant y kynydyon yna⁚ m6-
ynhaet y bꝛeyr hὓnn6 mal yr hὓn gynt. Oꝛ
lledır hyt nos yn tref bꝛeyr⁚ tannet y vantell
arna6. a chatwet yn gyfan ef hyt y boꝛe. ac o-
ny doant ykynydyon yna⁚ bıt vn vꝛeínt hὓn- 10
n6 a reı gynt. Oꝛ byd hela gellgὓn y 6ꝛ ryd⁚
arhoet ef yboꝛe hyny ollygho ykynydyon y
bꝛenhín eu kὓn teır g6eıth. ac odyna gollyget ynteu. P6y bynhac alatho hyd ar tır dyn
arall⁚ rodet whartha6ꝛ yperchenna6c y tır. o 15
nyt hyd bꝛenhín uyd. kany byd whartha6ꝛ
tır yn hyd bꝛenhın. Oꝛ g6yl ffoꝛda6l b6yftuıl
yar ffoꝛd ymy6n ffoꝛeft bꝛenhín⁚ byryet ergyt
ıda6 os myn. ac os medyr⁚ ymlynet trae g6e-
lo. ac oꝛ pan el ydan yol6c⁚ gadet ehunan. 20

Yt hyn gan ganhat du6 kyfreıtheu
llys rytraethaffam. weıthon gann
boꝛth ygogonedus argl6yd ıeffu ꝛ
grıft⁚ kyfreıtheu g6lat adangoff6n. 24

ac yn gyntaf teir colofyn kyfreith. nyt amgen. Naƀ affeith galanas. a naƀ affeith tan.
a naƀ affeith lledꝛat.

Byntaf o naƀ affeith galanas. yƀ tauaƀt-
rudyaeth nyt amgen menegi ylle ybo y   5
neb alather yr neb ae llatho. Eil yƀ rodi kyghoꝛ
ylad ydyn. Tꝛydyd yƀ kyt ſynhyaƀ ac ef am y
lad. Petweryd yƀ diſcƀyl. Pymhet yƀ canhy-
mdeith yllofrud. Whechet yƀ kyrchu ytref.
Seithuet yƀ ardƀyaƀ. ƀythuet yƀ bot yn poꝛth- 10
oꝛdƀy. Naƀuet yƀ gƀelet ylad gan y odef. Dꝛos
pop vn oꝛ tri kyntaf ꞯ yrodir naƀ vgeint aryant
allƀ canhƀꝛ ywadu gƀaet. Dꝛos pop vn oꝛ tri
ereill ꞯ yrodir deu naƀ vgeint aryant allƀ deu
canhƀꝛ. Dꝛos pop vn oꝛ tri diwethaf ytelir tri 15
naƀ vgeint aryant allƀ trychanhƀꝛ ydiwat
gƀaet. ¶neb awatto coet amaes ꞯ rodet lƀ deg
wyr adeu vgeint heb gaeth aheb alltut. athꝛi
o honunt yndiofredaƀc o varchogaeth allhein
agƀꝛeic. ¶neb aadefho llofrudyaeth ꞯ talet ef 20
ae genedyl sarhaet ydyn alather yn gyntaf.
ae alanas. ac yn gyntaf ytal y llofrud ſarhaet
ydyn lladedic y tat ae vam ae vꝛodyr ae whioꝛyd.
ac os gƀꝛeigaƀc uyd ꞯ ywreic ageiff trayan y ſarhaet ygan yrei hynny. Tꝛayan hagen yr alanas 25

adaƀ ar y llofrud ae tat ae vam ae vɹodyr ae chwioɹyd yn wahanredaƀl yƀɹth ygenedyl. Tɹayan
yllofrud elchƀyl arennír yn teır ran. Y trayan
ar y llofrud ehunan. ar dƀy ran ar y tat ar vam
ar bɹodyr ar chwioɹyd. ac oɹ gƀyr hynny y tal 5
pop vn gymeínt ae gılyd. ac uelly ygƀɹaged.
ac ny thal vn wreıc mƀy no hanher ran gƀɹ.
ar trayan hƀnnƀ atelır y tat a mam y lladedıc
ae gyt etíuedyon megys ysarhaet. Ydƀy ran
adodet ar y genedyl ꞉ arennır yn teır ran. ac 10
o hynny ydƀy ran atal kenedyl ytat. ar tryded
atal kenedyl y vam. Ykyfryƀ achoed kenedyl
atalhont alanas ygyt ar llofrud ꞉ yr vn ryƀ a-
choed ae kymerant oparth ylladedıc oɹ goɹhen-
gaƀ hyt ygoɹchaƀ. ¶al hyn yd enwır naƀ rad 15
kenedyl adylyant talu galanas ae chymryt.
ac eu haelodeu. kyntaf oɹ naƀ rad yƀ tat a mam
yllofrud neu y lladedıc. Eıl yƀ bɹaƀt awhaer. Tɹy-
dyd yƀ hentat.   Petweryd yƀ Goɹhentat. Pymhet yƀ kefynderƀ. Whechet yƀ kyferderƀ. Seıth- 20
uet yƀ keıfyn. ƀythuet yƀ goɹcheıfyn. Naƀuet
yƀ goɹchaƀ. aelodeu y gradeu ynt ꞉ neı ac ewythyr yllofrud neu ylladedıc. Neı yƀ ꞉ mab bɹaƀt neu vab whaer. neu gefynderƀ. "neu gyfer-
derƀ." neu gyfnítherƀ. Ewythyr yƀ. bɹaƀt tat 25

neu vam. neu y hentat neu y henuam. neu y
o2hentat neu y o2henuam. allyma mal ymae
meint ran pop vn o2 rei hynny oll yn talu galanas neu yny chymryt. Y neb auo nes ygeren-
hyd o vn ach yr llofrud neu yr lladedic no2 llall: 5
deu kymeint atal neu agymer ar llall. ac uelly
am pa6b o2 feith rad diwethaf. ac aelodeu yr
holl radeu. Etfued yllofrud neu y lladedic ny dylyant talu dim nae gymryt tros alanas. kanys ran yneb atal6ys m6y no neb arall: a seif d2o- 10
fta6 ef ae etfuedyon. ac eu p2yder aperthyn y
vot arna6. P2yder etfued y lladedic auyd aryre-
enf ae gyt etfuedyon. kanys trayan galanas
agymerant. Ac o byd neb ogenedyl y llofrud
neu y lladedic yn dyn egl6yffic r6ymedic o v2deu 15
kyffegredic. neu yg kreuyd. neu glaf62. neu uut.
neu ynuyt. ny thal ac ny chymer dim o alanas.
ny dylyant 6y wneuthur dial am dyn alather
Na g6neuthur dial arnunt 6ynteu ny dylyir.
ac ny ellir kymhell y kyfry6 tr6y neb kyfreith 20
y talu dim. nae gymryt nys dylyant.

ONa6 affeith tan kyntaf y6 kygho21 llofci
yty. Eil y6 duuna6 am y llofc. T2ydyd y6
y6 mynet y lofci. Petweryd y6 ymd6yn yr6-
yll. Pymhet y6 llad ytan. Whechet y6 keiffa6 25
⁋ dyl6yf.

Seithuet y６ whythu y tan hyny enynho. Ｕythuet y６ enynnu y peth y llofcer ac ef. Na６uet y６ g６elet y llofc gan yodef. y neb awatto vn oʒ na６ affeith hyn ꞉ rodet l６ deg wyr adeu vgeínt heb gaeth aheb alltut.   5

R Yntaf o na６ affeith lledʒat y６ syllu t６yll acheiffa６ ketymdeith. Eil y６ duuna６ am ylledʒat. Tʒydyd y６ rodi b６yll６ʒ６. Petweryd y６ ymd６yn yb６yt yny getymdeithas. Pymhet y６ r６yga６ y buarth neu toʒri y ty.   10 Seithuet y６ kychwynu y lledʒat oe le a cherdet dyd neu nos ganta６. ~~Ｕyt~~ Seithuet y６ bot yn gyfarwyd ac yntrofc６yd６ʒ ar ylledʒat. Ｕythuet y６ kyfrannu ar lladʒon. Na６uet y６ g６elet y lledʒat. Ａe gelu yr gobyr neu y pʒy   15 nu yr g６erth. Yneb awatto vn oʒ na６ affeith hyn ꞉ rodet l６ deg wyr a deu vgeínt heb gaeth Ａheb alltut.

N a６ nyn adygant eu tyftolyaeth gan gredu pop vn o honunt ar wahan ６ʒth yl６.   20 argl６yd r６g ydeu ６ʒ oʒ dadyl a adefynt yryuot geir y vʒon ef. Ａc na bei gyfranna６c yn teu oʒ dadyl. Ａc na bydynt vn dull. Ａbat r６g ydeu vanach ar dʒ６s ykoʒ. Tat r６g ydeu vab gan dodi y la６ ar pen ymab ydycco y tyftoly   25

aeth yny erbyn. adywedut val hyn. Myn
du6 yg62 am cre6yfı yn tat ıttı. athıtheu
yn vab ímí. g6ır adywedafi yrochwı. B2a6=
d62 am y varn6ys gynt o2 byd ẏdeu dyn y
barn6yt udunt yn amryffon am y varn. a   5
Mach am y vechnıaeth ot adef ran ag6adu
ran arall. Effeırat r6g ẏdeu dyn pl6yf o tyftolyaeth atyfter ıda6. Mo26yn am y mo26yn-
da6t. os yg62 y rother ıda6 adyweıt nat oed
vo26yn hı yr d6yn yıa6n aedylyet. Neu o2   10
treıffır ar g62 ae treıffo yndywedut nat oed
uo26yn hı. credad6y y6 tyftolyaeth yuo26yn
yny erbyn. Bugeıl trefgo2d am y uugeıly-
aeth o2 llad ll6dyn y llall. LLeıdyr dıobeıth
am ygytleıdyr pan dyccer yr groc. kanys   15
credad6y uyd yeır ar y getymdeıthon ac am
yda adycco. heb greır. ac ny dylyır dıuetha
ygetymdeıth yr yeır ef namyn y uot ynlleı-
dyr g6erth. Credad6y heuyt uyd amot62
yny amot. ac uelly heuyt. credad6y uyd ma   20
nac g62 a wnel dogyn vanac. a Roda6dyr a
gredır ar y da arotho. ac yna ydywedır. nyt
oes rod onyt ovod

L la6 dyn ae troet ae lygat ae weus ae
gluft gan gollı yglybot ae tr6yn ꝛ   25

whe bu awhe vgeint aryant yб gбerth pop
vn ohonunt. Oʒ trychır cluſt dyn oll ym de-
ıth. achlybot oʒ dyn arnaб mal kynt ꝝ dбy
uu a deu vgeint aryant atal. Кeılleu vn
werth ynt ar aelodeu vʒy oll. Бauaбt ehu   5
nan. kymeint yб ywerth ar saбl aelaбt a
rıfбyt hyt hyn. holl aelodeu dyn pan gyf·
rıffer ygyt ꝝ бyth punt aphetwar vgeint
punt atalant. Ɓys dyn ꝝ buch ac vgeint
aryant atal. Gбerth yuaбt ꝝ dбy uu adeu   10
vgeint aryant. Ɇwin dyn ꝝ dec ar hugeint
aryant atal. Gбerth ykygбng eıthaf ꝝ whech ar hugeint aryant atal a dimeı athray
an dimeı. Gбerth y kygбng perued ꝝ dec
adeu vgeint adimeı adeuparth dimeı.   15
Gбerth y kygбng neſſaf ꝝ petwar vgeint
aryant. Ɍacdant dyn ꝝ pedeır ar hugeint
aryant gan trı dʒychafel atal. aphan taler
racdant ꝝ gбerth creıth go gyfarch a telır
gantaб. Кıldant ꝝ dec adeu vgeint atal.   20
Ɽ Edeır ar hugeint aryant yб gбerth
    gбaet dyn. kanyt teılбng bot gбerth
gбaet dyn yn gyfuch agбerth gбaet duб.
kyt beı gбır dyn ef ꝝ gбır duб oed ac ny
phechбys yny gnaбt. Бeır creıth gogyf-   25

arch yffyd ar dyn. creith arꝺyneb dyn ꞏ whe
ugeint atal. Creith ar gefyn yllaꝺ deheu ꞏ
trugeint atal. Creith ar gefyn y troet deheu ꞏ
dec arhugeint atal. Ꝺꝺerth amrant dyn
hyt ybo ybleꝺ erni ꞏ keinhaꝺc kyfreith atal.   5
pop blewyn ꞏ oꝛ tyrr dim oheni ꞏ gꝺerth creith ogyfarch atelir yna.

S Ef yꝺ meint galanas maer neu gyghellaꝺꝛ ꞏ naꝺ mu anaꝺ vgeint mu
gan tri dꝛychafel. Sarhaet pop vn o hon-   10
unt yꝺ naꝺ mu aꬻaꝺ vgeint aryant. Punt
yꝺ ebediꝺ pop vn o honunt. Punt yꝺ gobyr
merch pop vn. atheir punt yꝺ ychowyll.
a seith punt yhegꝺedi. Oꝛa merch maer ı
neu gyghellaꝺꝛ neu vn o arbenhigyon llys   15
yn llathꝛut heb rod kenedyl ꞏ naꝺ eidon kyhyt eu kyrn ac eu hyfcyfarn uyd eu hegꝺedi.
Pedeir bu aphetwar vgeint aryant yꝺ farhaet teuluꝺꝛ bꝛenhin os o hynny yd ymar-
delꝺ. Ꞇeir bu atelir yn farhaet teuluꝺꝛ bꝛe-   20
yr. nyt amgen tri buhyn tal beinc.

G alanas penkenedyl ꞏ tri naꝺ mu athꝛı
naꝺ vgein mu gan tri dꝛychafel. yny
sarhaet ytelir tri naꝺ mu athꝛı naꝺ vgeint aryant. Ꝺalanas vn o aelodeu pen ke   25
    ¶ nedyl ꞏ

nyt amgen y gar. atelır o naᕔ mu a naᕔ vgeínt mu gan trı dıychafel. Yny farhaet y
keıff naᕔ mu a naᕔ vgeínt aryant. Ᏽalanas bıeyr dıffᕔyd owhe bu awhe vgeínt
mu gan trı dıychafel ytelır. Y Sarhaet ate-   5
lır o whe bu awhe vgeínt aryant. Ᏽalanas bonhedıc canhᕔynaᕔl atelır o teır bu a
thrı vgeínt mu gan trı dıychafel. Y Sarhaet atelır o teır bu athrı vgeínt aryant. ky
mro vam tat vyd bonhedıc canhᕔynaᕔl.   10
heb gaeth a heb alltut a heb ledach yndaᕔ.
Os gᕔı bıeyr auyd bonhedıc canhᕔynaᕔl
pan lather ⁚ whe bu ageıff ybıeyr oı alanaſ
ygan yllofrud. Ꞇr bıenhín ydaᕔ trayan pop
galanas. kanys ıᕼ ef bıeu kymhell y lle ny   15
allo kenedyl gymhell. ac agaffer o da oı ı
pıyt ygılyd yr llofrud ⁚ ybıenhín bıeſuyd.
Ᏽalanas tayaᕔc bıenhın atelır o teır bu a
thrı vgeín mu gan trı dıychafel. Y Sarhaet
yᕔ teır bu athrı vgeínt aryant. Ᏽalanas   20
tayaᕔc bıeyr ⁚ hanheraᕔc uyd ar alanas tayaᕔc bıenhın. ac uelly y sarhaet. Ᏽalanas
alltut bıenhín ⁚ atelır o teır bu athrı vgeín mu ᕼ heb dıychafel. Y Sarhaet yᕔ teır bu
heb ychwanec. Ᏽalanas alltut bıeyr ⁚ han-   25

heraƀc uẏd ar alanas alltut bꝛenhín. Ꝿalan-
as alltut tayaƀc⁏ hanheraƀc uyd ar alanas
alltut bꝛeyr. ꝛc uellẏ ebyd eu sarhaedeu.

Ꝭ Neb a gníthyo dyn⁏ talet ysarhaet yn
gyntaf. kanys dꝛychaf agoſſot yƀ sar= 5
haet pop dyn. ꝛcheínhaƀc dꝛos pop blewyn
bonwyn a tynher oe pen. ꝛcheínhaƀc dꝛos
pop bys ael yny pen. ꝛphedeɪr ar hugeínt
dꝛos ygƀallt taldꝛƀch. ꝑewɪſſet paƀb y vꝛe-
ínt⁏ ae ƀꝛth vꝛeínt y penkenedyl. ꝛe ƀꝛth 10
vꝛeínt ytat. ꝛe ƀꝛtħ vꝛeínt ysƀyd. ꝑvnt
a hanher yƀ gƀerth kaeth teledíƀ oꝛ henuyd
oꝛ tu dꝛaƀ yr moꝛ. Oꝛ byd anafus hagen neu
ryhen neu ryɪeuanc nyt amgen no lleɪ noc
vgeín mlƀyd⁏ punt atal. Oꝛ henuyd oꝛ tu 15
yma yr moꝛ heuyt⁏ punt atal. kanys ehunan a lygrƀys y vꝛeínt o vynet yn gyfloc
gƀꝛ oe vod. Ꝋꝛ tereu dyn ryd dyn kaeth⁏
talet ɪdaƀ deudec keínhaƀc. whech dꝛos teɪr
kyfelín o vꝛethyn gƀyn tal pentan ywne- 20
uthur peɪs ɪdaƀ ƀꝛth lad eɪthín. Teɪr dꝛos
laƀdƀꝛ. Vn dꝛos kuaraneu a dyrnu oleu.
Vn dꝛos ƀdyf neu dꝛos uƀell os koetƀꝛ vyd.
Vn dꝛos raff deudec kyfelínyaƀc. Ꝋꝛ tereu
dyn kaeth dyn ryd. Jaƀn yƀ trychu yllaƀ ·25

deheu ıdaб neu talet arglóyd ykaeth farhaet
ydyn. ДaбD kaeth yб ᛫ hyt ybyryo ykryman.
Ȳ neb a gyttyo agбɹeıc kaeth heb ganhat y
harglóyd ᛫ talet deudec keínhaбc y arglóyd
ygaeth dɹos pop kyt. Ȳ neb au eıchocco y 5
góɹeıc kaeth auo ar gyfloc ᛫ rodet arall yny
lle hyt pan agho. Ac yna paret ef yr etíued
ac aet ygaeth yłłe. Ac oɹ byd marб yar yr
etíued ᛫ talet yneb ae beıchoges ygбerth kyfreıth oe harglóyd. ȷop dyn ageıff dɹychaf- 10
el yny alanas ac yny Sarhaet eıthyr alltut.
yr vgeínheu atelır ygyt ar góarthec uyd y
dɹychafaleu. Ȿarhaet góɹeıc kaeth ᛫ deudec
keínhaбc atal. Ac os gбenígaбl uyd nyt el
nac ynraб nac ymreuan ᛫ pedeır ar hugeínt 15
vyd y Sarhaet. Ȳneb awnel kynllóyn ᛫ yn
deudyblyc ytal galanas ydyn alatho. Adeu
dec mu dırбy yndeu dyblyc atal yr bɹenhín
Ȳneb awatto kynllóyn neu uurdбɹn neu
gyrch kyhoedaбc ᛫ rodet lб deg wyr adeu vge- 20
ínt heb gaeth aheb alltut. Ny ellır kyrch
kyhoedaбc o leı no naбwyr.

Lys bıeu teruynu. Agбedy llys ᛫ llan. A
gбedy llan bɹeínt. A gбedy bɹeınt ᛫ kyn-
warchadб. ar diffeıth. ty ac odyn acyfcubaбɹ 25

yꝺ kynwarchadꝺ.   Oꝛ tyf kynhen rꝺg dꝺy tref
vn vꝛeínt am teruyn ꞉ gꝺyrda ybꝛenhín bieu teruynu hꝺnnꝺ os gꝺybydant.   ꝺc oꝛbyd
petrus gantunt ꝺy ꞉ dylyedogyon ytır bieu
tygu opaꝺb y vꝛeꞃ teruyn.   ꝺc odyna rannent   5
eu hamryffon yn deu hanher yrydunt.   Ꝃyt
teruynho tref ar yllall ꞉ ny dyly dꝺyn rantır
yꝺꝛthı.   Hanher punt adaꝺ yr bꝛenhín pan
teruynher tır rꝺg dꝺy tref.   Pedeır arhugeínt
adaꝺ yr bꝛaꝺtwyr pan dycco kyfreıth tırydyn.   10
Hanher punt adaꝺ ẏr bꝛenhín o pop rantır ꞉
pan y heftynho.
Ꝥal hyn ydymlycceır dadleu tır adayar.
yr haꝺlꝺꝛ bieu dangos y haꝺl.   ꝺc odyna yr
amdıffynnꝺꝛ yamdıffyn.   agꝺedy hynny hen-   15
aduryeıt gꝺlat bieu kytyftyryaꝺ yn garedıc
pꝺy o honunt yffyd ar y ıaꝺn.   pꝺy nyt yttıꝺ.
agꝺedy darffo hyꞃny yr henaduryeıt racreıth-
aꝺ eu synhꝺyr.   ꝺchadarnhau eu dull trꝺy tꝺg.
yna ydyly ybꝛaꝺtwyr mynet ar lleılltu.   ꝺbar-   20
nu herwyd dull yr henaduryeıt.   adangos yr
bꝛenhın yr hyn a varnont.   ahꝺnnꝺ yꝺ deturyt
gꝺlat gꝺedy amdıffyn.   Ꝥan dechꝛeuher kynhen am teruynu tıred neu trefyd.   os yrꝺg tır
yllys athír yllaꞃ wlat y dechꝛeuír ꞉ llys ater   25

ateruyna. Os yrốg tır ywlat athır eglốys 'y
eglốys ateruynha. Os yrốg kytetıuedyon ꞉
bıeínt ateruynha. Os yrốg tır kyfanhed athır
dıffeıth ꞉ kynwarchadố ateruynha. adeıl ac ar-
adốy yố kyfanhed. Pan teruynha llys ꞉ maer 5
a chyghellaốʒ bıeu dangos ytheruyneu dʒof-
tı. Os eglốys ꞉ bagyl ac euegyl.

e Neb auynho kyffroı haốl am tır꜀aͦc ach
ac etuyryt ꞉ kyffroet yn vn oʒ deu naố
vetdyd. ae naốuetdyd racuyr ae naốuetdyd 10
meı. kanys kyt kyffroer yryố haốl honno ꞉
ymaes o vn oʒ dydyeu hynny ꞉ ny thyccya.
Yneb aholho tır yn naốuettyd racuyr ꞉ bʒa
ốt ageıff o honaố kyn naốuet meı. ac ony
cheıff bʒaốt yna ꞉ holet yn naốuetdyd meı 15
elchốyl oʒ myn erlyn kyfreıth. ac odyna
agoʒet uyd kyfreıth ıdaố pan ymynho ybʒe.
TRı datanhud tır yſſyd ꞉ datanhud karr.
adatanhud beıch. adatanhud eredıc.
yneb y barner datanhud beıch ıdaố ꞉ trı dıeu 20
atheır noſ goʒffowys yn dıhaốl ageıff. ac y
ny trydydyd ydyry atteb. ac yny naốuetdyd barn. Yneb ybarnher datanhud karr
ıdaố ꞉ pump níeu aphymp nos goʒffowyſ
ageıff. ac yny pymhet dyd atteb. ac yny 25

naϬuetdyd barn.   Y neb ybarner datanhud
eredıc ıdaϬ ⁚ goꝛffowys yn dıhaϬl ageıff hyny ymchoelo ygefyn ar ydas.   âc yny naϬ-
uetdyd barn.   Ꝑy dyly neb datanhud namyn oꝛ tır auo yn llaϬ ytat yny vyϬ ahyt   5
y varϬ.   ꝐydıϬ "y barnher" bynhac datanhud ⁚
ny dıchaϬn neb yuϬꝛϬ oe datanhud nam·
yn etíued pꝛ'odaϬꝛ.   kany dıchaϬn yreıl dat-
anhüd gϬꝛth lad y kyntaf.   ac ny Ϭꝛth lad
am pꝛıodaϬꝛ am pꝛıodaϬꝛ arall oe datanhud.   10
ac oꝛ byd amryffon' rϬg etíuedyon pꝛıodaϬꝛ
am datanhud ⁚ ny dıchaϬn vn gϬꝛthlad
ygılyd o gyfreıth.   Ϭꝛ deu etíued gyfreıthaϬl ⁚ vn auyd pꝛıodaϬꝛ ar datanhud cϬbyl
ar llall ny byd.   kanyt pꝛıodaϬꝛ datanhud   15
cϬbyl y neb n amyn yr bꝛaϬt hynhaf.   bꝛe-
ınt ybꝛaϬt hynhaf yϬ kymryt datanhud
cϬbyl dꝛos y vꝛodyr.   a chyt delhont Ϭy oe
vlaen ef ⁚ ny chaffant Ϭy datanhud o gϬbyl.
ac os kymerant ⁚ ef ae gϬꝛthlad o honaϬ   20
os myn.   Os ygyt ygofynant ⁚ ygyt y caf
fant.   mal y dywefpϬyt vꝛy.   Ꝑyt reıt arhos
naϬuetdyd am teruynu tır.   ńamyn pan ᴠ
vynho y bꝛenhín ae wyrda.   Ꝑy dylyírhe-
uyt arhos naϬuet dyd rϬg pꝛıodaϬꝛ ac am   25

EVANS   E

pꝛiodaổ agynhalyo tir yny herbyn.

ᵺEir gổeith yrennír tir rổg bꝛodoꝛyon.
yn gyntaf rổg bꝛodyr. Odyna rổg ke-
uyndyrổ. Tꝛyded weith rổg kyferdyrổ. Ody
na nyt oes pꝛiaổt ran ar tir. Pan ranho į   5
bꝛodyr tref eu tat yrydunt. y ieuhaf ageiff
yr eiffydyn arbenhic ac ổyth erổ. ar trefneu
oll. ar gallaổꝛ ar uổell gynnut ar cổlltyr.
kany eill tat nac eu rodi nac eu kymynnu
onyt yr mab ieuhaf. achyn gổyftler ny dy-   1(
gổydant byth. Odyna kymeret pop bꝛaổt
eiffydyn arbenhic ac ổyth erổ. ar mab ieuhaf aran. ac o hynhaf y hynhaf bieu dewis
ꝑy dyly neb gofyn atran ꞏ onyt yneb ny chꝗ
afas dewis. kanyt oes warthal gan dewis.   1į

OR gomed dyn teir gổys o pleit ybꝛenhin am tir onyt maổꝛ aghen ae llud.
ytir arodir yr neb ae holho. Oꝛ daổ ynteu
ổꝛth yr eil wys neu ổꝛth y tryded. gổꝛthebet
am y tir os iaổn idaổ. athalet tri buhyn cam-   2(
lổꝛ yr bꝛenhin am omed gổys. Yneb atalo
gobyr eftyn am tir ꞏ ny thal hổnnổ ebediổ
gan iaổn. ꝑổy bynhac ahgynhalyo tir teir
oes gổyr yn vn wlat yn vn wlat ar dylyedogyon. oes tat ahentat agoꝛhentat heb haổl   2į

aheb arha6l. heb lofc ty heb to2r aradyr. ny
62thebír udunt 6yth o2 tır h6nn6 kan ry-
gay 6ys kyfreıth yrydunt.   ℟6y bynhac
aholho tır o ach ac etríf. reıt y6yhen adur
yeıt g6lat tygu yr ach kyn g6aranda6 y   5
ha6l.   ℗2 keıs dyn ran o tır gan ygenedyl
g6edy hır alltuded ⁝ rodet wheugeınt yg
gobyr g6archad6 o2 canhadant ran ıda6.
℣tır arotho yb2enhín ydyn gan ıa6n ⁝
nys att6c yneb ae g6ledycho g6edy ef.   10
℘6y bynhac aodefho rodı tref y tat yny
·6yd yarall heb lud a heb wahard ⁝ nys keıff
tra vo by6. ℘6y bynhac aholho tır o2 d6c
y ach ar gogeıl m6y no theır g6eıth. colledıc
uyd oe ha6l.   ℗2 g6neır egl6ys ar taya6c   15
tref gan gan hat y b2enhín ae bot yn go2f-
lan hı. ac effeırat yn efferennu yndı. ryd
vyd ytref honno o hynno o hynny allan.
℗2 kymer taya6c mab b2eyr ar vaeth gan
ganhat yargl6yd ⁝ kyfranna6c uyd y mab   20
h6nn6 ar tref tat y taya6c mal vn oe veıbon
ehunan. ℘op tır kyt adylyır ygynhal all6
ac a da. ac ar nys kynhalyo ⁝ collet yrari. G6e-
dy yranher y tır hagen. ny dyly neb talu ı
d2os ygılyd. 6ynt adylyant hagen ac eu ll6 25

kynhal o pop vn gan ygılyd oჳ bჳodyr ar kefyn-
dyrᲦ ar kyferdyrᲦ. ar tır agollo vn oჳ reı hynny o eıffeu llᲦ yreı ereıll ᛬ enſllent ıdaᲦ. o
gyferdyrᲦ allan ny dyly neb kadᲦ ran y
gılyd nac ae lᲦ nac ae da.   5

ꝐᲦy bynhac awnel bჳat arglᲦyd neu
awnel kynllᲦynl ᛬ ef a gyll tref y tat.
ac oჳ keffir ᛬ eneıtuadeu uyd. Ony cheffir
ynteu amynnu kymot o honaᲦ ac arglᲦ-
yd ac achenedyl ᛬ tal deu dyblyc adaᲦ arnaᲦ   10
odırᲦy agalanas. ac oჳ kyrch lys ypap ady-
uot llythyr ypap gantaᲦ a dangos yrydhau
oჳ pap. tref y tat ageıff. Tჳydyd achaᲦs y
kyll dyn tref y tat. o enkıl o honaᲦ yᲦჳth
y tır heb ganhat ac na allo godef y beıch ar   15
gᲦaſſanaeth a vo arnaᲦ.

Ꝺycheıff neb tır ygyt etſued megys y vჳa-
Ვt neu ygefynderᲦ neu ygyferderᲦ. gan
yofyn trᲦy yr hᲦn a veı varᲦ o honunt heb
etſued ıdaᲦ ogoჳff. namyn gan y ofyn trᲦy   20
vn oe ryenı aryffeı perchennaᲦc y tır hᲦn-
nᲦ hyt varᲦ ae tat ae hentaჳ ae goჳhentat
ac uelly ykeıff ytır os ef auyd ñeſſaf kar yr
marᲦ. ᲦᲦedy ranho bჳodyr tref eu tat yrydunt. oჳ byd marᲦ vn o honunt heb etſued   25

o goıff neu gytetſued hyt geıfyn ⁊ y bıenhín
auyd etſued oı tır hѳnnѳ.. Ɠrı ryѳ pııt yffyd
ar tır. vn yѳ gobyr gѳarchadѳ. Eıl yѳ da a-
rother yachweccau tır neu y vıeínt. Tıydyd yѳ llafur kyfreıthaѳl awnelher ar y tır   5
ybo gѳell ytır yrdaѳ. Ꝛy dyly neb gofyn atran
onyt yneb ny chafas dewıs. kany chygeín
gѳarthal gѳarthal gan dewıs.
Ɠeır etıuedyaeth kyfreıthaѳl yffyd ⁊ ac a.
trıgyant yn dılıs yr etſuedyon. vn yѳ etſued- 10
yaeth trѳy dylyet o pleıt ryení. Eıl yѳ etſuedyaeth trѳy amot kyfreıthaѳl ygan yperchennaѳc yr gѳerth. Tıydyd yѳ. amoṭ kyfreıthaѳl etſuedyaeth agaffer trѳy amot kyfreıthaѳl o vod yperchennaѳc heb werth.   15
Ꝍtrı mod yd holır tır adayar. o gam werefcyn.
ac o datanhud. Ɑco ach ac etrıf. kyny thyccyo
gofyn tır oı mod kyntaf nac oı eıl. ny byd
hѳyrach no chynt y keffır oı trydyd.
Ɠrı chamwerefcyn yffyd ⁊ gѳerefcyn yn er-   20
byn yperchennaѳc oe anuod a heb vıaѳt.
Neu werefcyn trѳy yperchennaѳc ac yn
erbyn y etſued oe anuod aheb vıaѳt. Neu
werefcyn trѳy wercheıtwat ac yn erbyn y
ıaѳn dylyedaѳc oe anuod a heb varn. Perch- 25

ennaȮc yȮ yneb auo yn medu y dylyet dilis.
GȮercheitwat yȮ yneb auo yn kynhal neu yn
gȮarchadȮ dylyet dyn arall. ȯri ryȮ vꝛeint
yffyd ⁊ bꝛeint anyanaȮl. abꝛeint tir. a bꝛeint
sȮyd. ȯri phꝛiodolder yffyd ypop dyn ⁊ ryȮ. 5
abꝛeint. ac etiuedyaeth. Etiuedyaeth hagen
herwyd bꝛeint. bꝛeint herwyd ryȮ. ryȮ herwyd ygȮahan auyd rȮg dynyon herwyd kyfreith. megys ygȮahan auyd rȮg bꝛenhin a
bꝛeyr. ac yrȮg gȮꝛ a gȮꝛeic. ahynaf aieuhaf. 10
P Edeir rantir auyd yny tref y talher gȮeft-
ua bꝛenhin o heni. Deu naȮ troetued a
uyd yn hyt.gȮyalen hywel da. adeu naȮ llath-
en yhonno auyd yn hyt yr erȮ. adȮy lathen
let. Deudec erȮ atrychant yhonno auyd yny 15
rantir rȮg rȮyd adyrys a choet amaes a gȮlyp
asych eithyr yr oꝛuot tref. ac o rantired hynny ygelwir amhinogyon tir yg kyfreith.
ȯri gȮybydyeit yffyd am tir. henaduryeit
gȮlat yȮybot ach ac etrif y dȮyn dyn ar dyly- 20
et otir adayar. Eil yȮ gȮꝛ o pop rantir oꝛtref
honno yȮ amhinogyon tir yȮybot kyfran
rȮg kenedyl acharant. Tꝛydyd yȮ pan vo amryffon rȮg dȮy tref vn vꝛeint. Meiri achyg-
helloꝛyon a righylleit bieu kadȮ teruyneu. 25

kanys bꝛenhın bıeu teruyneu. Ꝺeir tref
ar dec adyly bot ym pop mãenaꝺꝛ. ar tryded
ar dec oꝛ reı hynny uyd yr oꝛuot tref. Ꝺref-
ryd sꝺydaꝺc a thref ryd dıffꝺyd. pedeır rantır
auyd ym pop tref. yteır yn gyfanhed. ar pet- 5
wared yn poꝛua yr teır rantır. Ꝺeır rantır
auyd yny tayaꝺc tref. ym pop vn oꝛdꝺy y byd
trı thayaꝺc. ar tryded ynpoꝛua yrdꝺy. Ꝕeıth
tref auyd yny vaenaꝺꝛ oꝛ tayaꝺc trefyd.
Ẏ neb atoꝛho teruyn ar tırdyn arall ꞏ talet . 10
trı buhyn camlꝺꝛꝺ ẏr bꝛenhín agꝺnaet yteruyn yn gyftal achynt. Ꝺyt teruyn pꝛıf a
uon engıryaꝺl rꝺg deu kymhꝺt onyt yny hen-
gyrrynt. Ꝺroefuaen sef yꝺ hꝺnnꝺ maen
ffın neu pꝛen ffın neu peth arall enwedıc a 15
vo yn kadꝺ ffın ꞏ wheugeínt atal. Ẏ neb atoꝛho ffın auo rꝺg dꝺy tref. neu aartho pꝛıffoꝛd.
wheugeínt atal yr bꝛenhın. a gꝺnaet y teruyn yngyftal achynt. ꝳeffur tır rꝺg dꝺy
tref of oꝛ tır y byd ꞏ gꝺꝛhyt a hanher. Rꝺg dꝺy 20
rantır ꞏ pedeır troetued. Rꝺg dꝺy erꝺ ꞏ dꝺy
gꝺys. ꝳeffur pꝛıffoꝛd bꝛenhín ꞏ deudec troetued. Ẏ neb agynhalyo dan vn aırglꝺyd deu
tır ꞏ talet y ebedıꝺ oꝛ mꝺyhaf yvꝛeínt.
Effur gꝺeftua bꝛenhín o pop tref ytaler 25

gõeftua bıenhín o honeı. põn march o vlaõt
gõeníth ac ych a feıth dıefa o geırch vn rõym,
ac auo dıgaõn o vel yn vn gerõyn. Naõ dyrnued uyd vchet ygerõyn pan veffurer arõyr
oı cleıs traõ yr emyl yma. aphedeır ar huge-   5
ínt aryant. Punt yõ gõerth gõeftua bıenhín. wheugeínt yg kyfeır y vara, athıuge-
ínt dıos y enllyn. athıugeín dıos y lyn. Sef
y telır velly hagen ony rodır .y bõyt yny amfer. nyt amgen ygayaf. ❶ tref maeroní   10
neu gyghelloıyaeth. med atelır. ❶ tref ryd
diffõyd ⁒ bıagaõt atelır. ❶ tayaõctref ⁒ cõıõf
atelír. Dõy gerõyn vıagaõt neu pedeır cõıõf atelır dıos vn ved. Dõy gerõyn vıagaõt
gõıõf atelır dıos vn vıagaõt. Ny telır ary-   15
ant nac ebıan meırch gan weftua haf.
❷eu daõnbõyt adaõ yr bıenhín yny ulõ-
ydyn ygan y tayogeu. Daõn bõyt gayaf
yõ hõch trı vyffic yny hyfcõyd. ac yny hır-
eíf. ac yny chlun, ac henhoıop hallt. ath   20
rı vgeínt toıth o vara gõeníth oı tyf gõen-
ıth yno. bıt beılleıt ynaõ toıth. y teır yr yftauell. arˉwhech yr neuad. kyflet pop toıth
ac o elín hyt ardõın. ¡ Os keírch vydant ⁒
bínt rynyon ynaõ toıth. kyn teõhet vyd-   25
❸ant ⁒

ac na phlygant pan dalher herwyd eu he-
myl. alloneit mid og6ı6f. acheınha6c o
pop rantır yr g6affanaethwyr. Da6nb6yt
haf y6 emenyn acha6s. Sef y6 ymanat
emenyn. na6 dyrnued llet. adyrnued   5
te6het ae va6t yny seuyll. aphrytllaeth-
eu y tayogeu oll agynullır yn vn dyd y
wneuthur ka6s. ahynny atelır gyt ar
bara. ɖy da6 maer na chyghella6ı nar
ran dofreth ar 6ı ryd. ¶n weith pop bl6-   10
ydyn y g6etha y pa6b mynet yn lluyd y
gyt arbıenhín y oıwlat os myn. ac yna y
dyly yn̦tẹu yvıenhínes rıeíngylch. Byth
hagen pan ymynho ylluydır gyt ac ef y
ny wlat ehunan. ¶ kynydyon ar hebogyd-   15
yon ar g6aftrodyon agaffant gylch ar tayogeu y bıenhín. pop reı hagen arwahan.
na6 teı adyly y tayogeu y g6neuthur
yr bıenhín. Neuad. yftauell. kegín.
kapel. yfcuba6ı. odynty. peırant. yftabyl.   20
kynoıty. Y gan y tayogeu ykeıff ybıenhín
pynueırch yny luyd. ac o pop taya6ctref
y keıff g6ı amarch a b6ell ar treul y bıenhın y wneuthur lluefteu ıda6. Ʌrı pheth
ny werth taya6c heb ganhat yargl6yd :-   25

march. a moch. a mel. Os gỏıthyt ef gyſſef-
uſn ꝛ gỏerthet ynteu yr neb ymynho gỏedy hynny. ẟeır keluydyt nys dyſc tay-
aỏc y vab heb ganhat. y arglỏyd. yſcolhe-
ıctaỏc. abardonſaeth. a gofanaeth. kan-　　5
ys odıodeſ y arglỏyd hyt pan rother coꝛun y yſcolheıck. neu yny el gof yny efe
ıl. neu vard bꝛth ygerd. ny eıll neb eu ke-
ıthıwaỏ gỏedy hynny.

Oꝛ ymladant gỏyr eſcob neu wyr ab-　　10
at agỏyr bꝛenhſn ar tır y teyrn ꝛ eu dırỏy
a daỏ yr teyrn. achyt ymladont gỏyr eſcob agỏyr abat ar tır ybꝛenhın ꝛ yr bꝛenhſn ydaỏ eu dırỏy. ꝗ neb a artho tır dꝛoſ
lud arglỏyd. talet pedeır keſnhaỏc kyfre-　　15
ıth o agoꝛı dayar gan treıs. a phedeır keſnhaỏc kyfreıth odıot heyrn oꝛ dayar. ach-
eſnhaỏc o pop cỏys aymchoelo yr daya
aradyr a hynny yperchennaỏc y tır. kymeret yr arglỏyd yr ychen oll ar aradyr ar　　20
heyrn. a gỏerth y llaỏ deheu yr geılwat.
a gỏerth ytroet deheu yr amaeth. Oꝛ clad
dyn tır dyn arall yr cudyaỏ peth yndaỏ.
perchennaỏc ytır ageıff pedeır keınhaỏc
kyf. o agorı dayar ar gudua onyt eurgra-　　25

hagen pan ẏ mẏnho ẏ bꝛenhín ẏ lluẏdır ẏ·
gẏt ac ef ẏnẏ wlat ehun. Ẏkẏnẏdẏon ar
hebogẏdẏon ar guaſtrodẏon un weıth ẏnẏ
ulbẏdẏn ẏ caffant gẏlch ar taẏogeu ẏ bꝛenhín pop reı hagen ar wahan.   5

N ab teı adẏlẏ ẏ taẏogeu ẏ wneuthur ẏr
bꝛenhín. Neuad. ac ẏftauèll. kegín ach-
apel. Ẏfcubabꝛ. ac odẏntẏ. Peırant. ac ẏftabẏl.
achẏnoꝛtẏ. Ẏ gan ẏ taẏogeu ẏdoant pẏnue·
ırch ẏr bꝛenhín ẏnẏ luẏd. ac o pop taẏoctref   10
ẏ keıff gbꝛ amarch abbẏall ar treul ẏ bꝛen
hín hagen ẏ wneuthur llueſteu. Ꝥrı pheth
nẏ werth taẏabc heb canhẏat ẏ arglbẏd. n
march. amoch. a mel. oſ gbꝛthẏt ẏr arglbẏd
gẏffeuẏn guerthᶜᵗ ẏnteu ẏr neb ae mẏnho   15
guedẏ hẏnnẏ. Ꝥeır keluẏdẏt nẏ dẏfc taẏabc ẏ uab heb canhẏat ẏ arglbẏd. ẏfcolhe-
ıctabc. a bardoní. a gouanaeth. kanẏf oſdı-
odef ẏ arglbẏd hẏnẏ rother coꝛun ẏr ẏfcoel-
heıc. neu hẏnẏ el gof ẏnẏ eueıl ehun. neu   20
vard bꝛth ẏ gadeır gerd nẏ ellír eu keıthıwab
                              | guedẏ hẏnnẏ

Oꝛ ẏmladant guẏr eſcob neu wẏr abat a guẏr bꝛenhín ar tír teẏrn eu dírƀẏ adaƀ ẏr teẏrn. Achẏt ẏmladont guẏr ef cob a guẏr abat ar tír teẏrn. ẏr teẏrn ẏ daƀ eu dírƀẏ. Ɏ neb a artho tír dꝛof lud 5
arglƀẏd. talet pedeir keínhaƀc kẏfreith o agoꝛi daẏar gan treíſ aphedeir keín haƀc. kẏfreith o díot ẏr heẏrn oꝛ daẏar a cheínhaƀc o pop kƀẏs a ẏmhoeleſ ẏr ar adẏr. kẏmeret ẏbꝛenhín ẏr ẏchen oll 10
ar aradẏr ar heẏrn a guerth ẏ troet de heu ẏr amaeth. A guerth ẏllaƀ deheu ẏr geilwat. Ơr clad dẏn tír dẏn arall ẏr cudẏaƀ peth ẏndaƀ. pedeir keínhaƀc kẏ ureith ageiff perchenaƀc ẏ tír am agoꝛi 15
daẏar ar gudua onẏt eurgraƀn uẏd ca- nẏſ bꝛenhín bieu pop eurgraƀn. Ɏ neb awnel annel ar tír dẏn arall ac ae cuth- ẏo ẏndaƀ. talet pedeir keínhaƀc kẏfre- ith oagoꝛi daẏar ẏ perchenaƀc ẏ tír ac oꝛ 20
keffir llƀdẏn ẏndaƀ perchenaƀc ẏ tír bi

eſuyd

eıuẏd heuẏt. athalet trı buhẏn camlẁẏẃ
ẏr bẏenhín. Ꝺr cledír pẁll odẏn ar tır dẏn
arall heb canhẏat. talet ẏneb ae clatho pe
deır keínhaẃc "ẏperchenaẃc" kẏfreıth ẏtır.
athrı buhẏn camlẁẏẃ ẏr bẏenhín. Ᵹ neb a   5
adeılho tẏ ar tır dẏn arall heb ẏcanhat.
talet trı buhẏn camlẁẏẃ ẏr bẏenhín. ar
tẏ ageıff perchenaẃc ẏtır aphedeír keínhaẃc kẏfreıth o agoẏı daẏar oſ ar ẏtır ẏlladaẃd guẏd ẏ tẏ. Onẏt ar ẏtír ẏlladaẃd. tẏg   10
et ar ẏtrẏdẏd o wẏr un vẏeínt ac ef. athoẏı
ret ẏtẏ ẏ ẏmdeıth ẏn gẏuuẃch ar daẏar adẏ
get ẏ ar ẏdır kẏn pen ẏnaẃ uet dyd. ac onẏſ
dẃc perchenaẃc ẏtır bıeſuẏd.

Ꝺ Neb aholho tır eglẁẏſſıc nẏt reıt ıdaẃ   15
arhoſ naẃuetdẏd namẏn agoẏı guír
ıdaẃ pan ẏmẏnho. Nẏ cheıff neb oparth
mam eıſſẏdẏn arbenhıc na ſẃẏd oẏı bẏd ae
dẏlẏho oparth tat. Jaẃn ẏẃ hagen ẏetſued
oparth mam caffel ran otır. Ꝺureıc aẏm   20
rotho ehunan ẏn llẃẏn ac ẏm perth heb

canhẏat kenedẏl nẏ cheiff ẏphlant ran o
tir gan genedẏl mam onẏt o rẏbuch et.
canẏ dẏlẏ mab ll6ẏn apherth ran o tír.
Ᵹ neb adiotto coet gan ganhẏat ẏperch-
ena6c ẏtir. pẏm mlẏned ẏdẏlẏ ef ẏnrẏd 5
ar chwechet ẏdẏlẏ ẏperchena6c ẏn rẏd.
Ᵹ neb agarteilo tir gan ganhẏat ẏ perche-
na6c. teir blẏned ẏdẏlẏ ef. ar pedwared ẏr
perchena6c ẏn rẏd. Ᵹ neb awnel buarth
teil ar tir dẏn arall gan ẏganhẏat. d6ẏ 10
vlẏned ẏdẏlẏ ef. ar trẏded ẏr perchena6c
ẏn rẏd. Ᵹ neb atoiho g6ẏd o tir dẏn arall.
gan ẏ ganhẏat. ẏ ul6ẏdẏn gẏntaf ẏkeiff
ef ẏn rẏd. ar eil ul6ẏdẏn ar get. ar trẏded
ẏr perchena6c ẏn rẏd. ⓞ rodir kẏmraef 15
ẏalltut ẏphlant ageiff ran o tir eithẏr
ẏr eiffẏdẏn arbenhic. h6nn6 nẏ chaffant
hẏt ẏ trẏded ach. ac o h6nn6 ẏda6 guarthec dẏuach. canẏf oi guna h6nn6 gẏflauan kenedẏl ẏuam ae tal oll ẏalanas. 20
Ꞡleif atrickẏo tri na6uet dẏd vn diu6

ẏn ac vn dıwat uẏd aguaet.   Os ar dıwat
ẏbẏd rodet ẏl6 ar ẏtrẏdẏd owẏr vn vıeínt
ac ef ẏn na6uetdẏd kẏntaf.   Os deu na6
uetdẏd ẏtrıc rodet ẏl6 ar ypedwerẏd owẏr
vn vıeínt ac ef.   Os trı na6uetdẏd ẏtrıc.   5
rodet ẏl6 ar ẏpẏmhet owẏr vn vıeínt ac
ef.   ac ẏuellẏ ẏdıwedır guaet.

OR bẏd keıtwat kẏfreıtha6l ad6ẏn da
oe warchad6 ẏn lletrat.   a bot ẏr allwe-
deu gantha6 ef ẏn dıwall.   aguelet toır ar   10
ẏtẏ.   llẏuẏr kẏna6c· adẏweıt bot ẏn hawf
ẏgredu oıdẏgır da ıda6 ef gẏt ar da arall.
adẏcker ẏn lletrat ẏganta6 ef.   Ef adẏlẏ
hagen tẏgu adẏnẏon ẏtẏ ganta6 oll ẏuot
ef ẏn ıach oıda h6nn6.   Oı cledır ẏdaẏar   15
hagen ẏdan ẏtẏ guedẏ gunel ef ẏgẏfre-
ıth ẏ uot ẏn ıach.   bıenhín bıeu daẏar ac
nẏ dẏlẏ keıtwat uot dıoftı.   Pop da a
adefho keıtwat ẏdẏuot atta6 ẏgad6 talet
· eıthẏr ẏda adẏcker tr6ẏ ẏdaẏar.   Oı d6c   20
dẏn da ar geıtwat achollı peth oı da. · a

abot ẏmdaeru ẏr6g ykeıtwaṭ ar perchen-
a6c am ẏ da h6nn6 ẏkeıtwat bıeu ṭẏgu
ar vn dẏn neffaf ẏwerth oe genedẏl. Ḳẏfreıth eur ẏ6 ẏrodı o la6 ẏla6 dan ṭẏfton ẏn
lla6 ẏkeıtwat.ẏ gad6. Ḳẏfreıth arẏant   5
y6 eu ríua6 ar gẏhoed o la6 ẏgılẏd ẏn lla6
ẏkeítwat. Ꝺn dẏn addıeínc oledıat kẏfadef kıc achroen ar ẏ geuẏn. Ẏghena6c
alldut auo teır nof athrı dıeu heb garda-
6t heb weftua. achr6ẏdıa6 o hona6 teır tref   10
beunẏd ana6 trẹı ẏm pop tref. ac ẏna rac
newẏn guneuthur lledıat o hona6. ae
dala ẏnteu ẏna achíc achroen ar ẏ gef
ẏn. Ef adẏlẏ ẏ oll6g ẏn rẏd heb croc aheb
werth. Ꝺn dẏn nẏ dẏlẏ ẏ tẏ ẏuot ẏn ua-   15
r6 tẏ kẏffoet mar6 heb gẏmun. ẏgnat
llẏs. Ꝺn aneueıl a a opedeır keínha6c
ẏpunt ẏn vn dẏd gellgı. of taẏa6c bıeı
uẏd ẏ boıe pedeır keínha6c atal. ac oı rodır ẏr bıenhín ẏdẏd h6nn6 punt atal.   20
Ꝺmm6f ẏn poıı allan amílgı heb ẏtoıch

colli eu breint awnant. Oyth pynuarch
brenhin yffyd. mor. a diffeith. ac yghena-
6c diatlam. a lleidyr. a mar6 ty. ac ebedi6.
adir6y. a chaml626.

E Neb agnithyo dyn. talet yfarhaet yn   5
gyntaf. canyf drychaf agoffot y6 farhaet dyn. acheinha6c yg kyueir pop bys
a el yny pen a d6y yg kyueir yua6t. ache-
inha6c yg kyueir pop blewyn bonwyn a
tynher oe pen. a phedeir ar hugeint dros   10
y guallt taldr6ch. Dewiffet pa6b yfarhaet
ae alanaf ae 6rth ureint ypenke'dyl. ae 6rth
vreint ytat. ae 6rth ureint yfföyd.

O R pan anher eba6l hyt a6ft. whech
cheinha6c atal. O a6ft hyt galan rac-   15
uyr deudec keinha6c atal. hyt galan whef
ra6r. deu na6 atal. hyt galan mei pedeir ar
hugeint atal. hyt galan a6ft. dec ar hugeint atal. hyt galan racuyr vn ar pymth
ec ar hugeint atal. hyt galan whefra6r d6y   20
adeugeint atal. a hyt galan mei 6yth ade-

ugeínt atal. Dóÿ ulóÿd uÿd ÿna. Odÿna
hÿt aóft trugeínt atal. kanÿf deudec keínhaóc a dzÿcheíf arnaó ÿna. a deudec he-
uÿt adzÿcheíf arnaó pop tÿmhoz hÿt galan meı ac ÿna teır blóÿd uÿd.   Sef atal   5
ÿna vn ar pÿmthec aphetwar ugeínt.
Ýdÿd ÿdalher ugeínt adÿrcheíf arnaó.
Pan fróÿnher pedeır keínhaóc adodír at
ÿr hÿn gÿnt. ac ÿuellÿ hanher punt atal.
amóf apafcer whech óÿthnof uóch pzef   10
feb punt atal.   Pedeır ar hugeínt ÿó guerth raón rónfı amóf oz trÿchır ÿmaef oz
golozen.   Oz trÿchır ÿgolozen hagen guerth ÿr amós oll atelír dzoftaó ÿna. adılıs
vÿd ÿr amóf ÿr neb ae hanauóÿf. llÿgat   15
amóf ae gluft pedeır ar hugeínt atal pop
vn o honunt. Rónfı. wheugeínt atal. raón rónfı ae lÿgat ae gluft deudec keínha
óc atal pop vn o honunt. Oz lledır hagen
ÿmÿón ÿgolozen ÿwerth oll atelır. a dılıf   20
vÿd ÿrónfı ÿr neb apzynóÿf. Palfre mozc

ynt ꞉ moꝛ. a diffeith. ac̄ yghen aƀc diatlam.
alleidyr. amarƀty. adirƀy. achamlƀꝛƀ. ac ebediƀ.
OR pan anher ebaƀl hyt aƀft ꞉ whech keinhaƀc atal. O aƀft hyt galan gayaf ꞉
deudec keinhaƀc atal. Hyt galan whefraƀꝛ ꞉   5
deu naƀ atal. hyt galan mei ꞉ pedeir arhugeint atal. hyt aƀft ꞉ dec ar hugeint atal.
Hyt galan racuyr ꞉ vn ar pymthec ar hugeint atal. hyt galan whefraƀꝛ ꞉ dƀy adeu vgeint atal. hyt galan mei ꞉ ƀyth adeu vge-   10
int atal. Dƀy ulƀyd uyd yna. Sef atal yna ꞉
o galan mei hyt aƀft ꞉ trugeint. kanys deudec keinhaƀc adꝛycheif arnaƀ yna. a deudec
heuyt pop tymhoꝛ hyt galan mei. ac yna
teir blƀyd uyd. Sef atal yna vn ar pymthec   15
aphetwar vgeint. ydyd ydalher ꞉ vgeint
adꝛycheif arnaƀ. Pan ffrƀynher ꞉ adodir
ar hyn gynt. ac yna wheugeint atal.
Amƀs apafcer whech ƀythnos vch pen pꝛe-
feb ꞉ punt atal. Amƀs yn poꝛi allan ꞉ a mil-   20
gi heb y toꝛch. colli eu bꝛeint awnant. Pedeir ar hugeint atal raƀn amƀs oꝛ trychir
ymaes oꝛ goloꝛen ꞉ Oꝛ trychir dim oꝛ goloꝛen hagen. gƀerth yr amƀs oll atelir
yna. adilis uyd yr amƀs yr neb ae hanaf   25

❡ ƀys.

llygat am6s ae gluft: pedeir ar hugeint
atal pop vn o honunt. R6nfi : wheu geint atal.   Ra6n r6nfi : deudec keinha6c
atal o2 trychir ymaes o2 golo2en. o2 trychir dim o2 golo2en hagen : g6erth yr6nfi   5
oll atelir yna. a dilis uyd ynteu yr neb
ae p2yn6ys. Llygat r6nfi ae gluft: deudec
keinha6c atal pop vn o honunt. Palfre:
mo2c atal. Vn werth yaelodeu ac aelodeu
r6nfi. March tom neu gaffec tom : vn   10
werth ac vn d2ychafel ynt ac eidon eithyr eu teithi. Teithi march tom neu gaffec tom. y6 d6yn p6n allufca6 karr yn
allt ac yg g6aet. a hynny yn dirr6yfc.
Y neb agymerho march ar venffic. a lly-   15
gru ygefyn hyny dyg6ydho y ble6 yn ha-
gyr : pedeir keinha6c kyfreith atal yr per-
chenna6c. O2 h6ydha hagen ygefyn o at-
lo henll6gyr. atho2ri croen hyt y kic. 6yth
geinha6c kyfreith atal. Ony byd henll6-   20
gyr arna6. atho2i croen achic hyt afc62n.
vn ar pymthec kyfreith atal. Y neb a-
watto llad am6s neu palfre ẏn lled2at. rodet l6 petwar g6yr ar hugeint. Kaffec re-
6ys : wheugeint atal. y ra6n ae llygat ae   25

chluft ꝛ whech cheínhaбc kyfreith atal pop
vn o honunt. Pбy bynhac a varchocco ꞑ
march heb ganhat yperchennaбc. talet pedeir keínhaбc efcyn aphedeir dífcyn. aphedeir yg kyfeir pop rantir ykertho dꝛoftaб. y   5
perchennaбc ymarch. athrı bủhyn camlбrб
yr bꝛenhín. Ᵹ neb awertho march neu gaffec ꝛ bit dan gleủyt oe myбn. nyt amgen trı
boꝛe rac ydera. athrı mís rac yr yfceueínt.
ablбydỳn rac yllyn meirch. Anaf o vaes bit   10
aryneb ae pꝛynho y edꝛych. Ꝗ neb awertho
march ꝛ bit ydan poꝛı o honaб ac yủet dбfyr
ac na bo llбygus. ac oꝛ byd llбyguf ꝛ dewiffet
yneb ae gбertho ae kymryt yvarch tràchefyn
ae eturyt trayan ygбerth yr llall. Pбy   15
bynhac adiffero march rac lladꝛon yn vn
wlat ae perchennaбc. pedeir keínhaбc. kyfreith ageiff ef. yg kyfeir pop buch atalho
ymarch. Yneb adifferho buch rac lladꝛon.
yn vn wlat ar perchennaбc ꝛ pedeir keínha- 20
бc kyfreith ageiff. ef.

Lo venyб ꝛ whech keínhaбc atal. oꝛ
pan anher hyt galan racuyr. Odyna
hyt galan whefraбꝛ ꝛ бyth geínhaбc atal.
hyt galan meı ꝛ dec atal. hyt aбft ꝛ deudec   25
¶ atal.

hyt galan racuyr ⁚ pedeir ar dec atal. hyt galan whefraƀ₂ ⁚ vn ar pymthec atal. Hyt galan mei ⁚ deu naƀ atal. Hyt aƀſt ⁚ vgeint atal.
Tᴣannoeth dƀy geinhaƀc o₂ tymho₂ aphedeir oe chyflodaƀt ad₂ycheif erni. ꝛc yna whech 5
ar hugeint atal hyt galan racuyr ⁚ hyt galan whefraƀ₂ ƀyth ar hugeint atal. hyt galan mei ⁚ dec ar hugeint atal. Naƀuetdyd
mei ydyly bot yn teithiaƀl dyuot llaeth o
pen pop teth idi. ꝛc ymdeith oe llo naƀ kam   10
yny hol. ꝛc ony byd uelly hi. vn ar pymthec
uyd gƀerth ytheithi. Dƀy geinhaƀc heuyt
agymer o₂ tymho₂. ꝛc uelly ƀyth adeu vgeint atal hyt aƀſt. Odyna hyt galan ionaƀ₂
racuyr ⁚ dec adeu vgeint atal. hyt galan   15
whefraƀ₂ ⁚ deu dec a deu vgeint atal. Tᴣannoeth dƀy geinhaƀc o₂ tymho₂ aphedeir keinhaƀc kyfreith o₂ eil kyflodaƀt. ꝛc uelly
trugeint atal. Co₂n buch neu ych ar llygat
ar cluſt ar llofcƀ₂n. pedeir keinhaƀc kyfre-   20
ith atal pop vn o hynny. Ꙧeth buch ⁚ pedeir keinhaƀc kyfreith atal. Ꝋ₂ gƀerth dyn
buch y arall ⁚ a bot teth yr uuch yn diffrƀyth.
ꝛc nas arganffo y neb ae p₂ynho ⁚ talet y
·neb ae gƀertho pedeir keinhaƀc kyfreith   25

yr neb ae pɪynho pop bl6ydyn tra vo y uuch
ar y hel6.   Os h6nn6 ae g6erth y arall.   bɪt ryd
ykyntaf.   kanys ydɪwethaf ae g6ertho awna
ydadyl gyffelyp.   ⓞ trɪ mod y telɪr teɪthɪ buch
o dec ar hugeínt aryant.   neu o uuch hefp tec.   5
neu o vla6t.   Ineffur lleftyr llaeth buch y6.
Seɪth motued a vyd yny vchet pan veffurer
ar6yr oɪ cleɪs tra6 yr emyl yma.   atheɪr motued yn llet yeñeu.   atheɪr yn llet ywaela6t.
Lloneɪt y lleftyr h6nn6 ovla6t keɪrch a telɪr   10
yg kyfeɪr pop godɪo yr uuch o hanher eb
rɪll hyt 6yl gíríc.   Odyna hyt a6ft ꞏ o vla6t
heɪd.   O a6ft hyt galan racuyr o vla6t g̃
g6eníth ytelɪr velly.

Ĺ Lo g6ɪy6ꞏ whech keínha6c atal. oɪ pan   15
anher hyt galan racuyr.   Odyna hyt
hyt galan whefra6ɪ ꞏ 6yth geɪnha6c atal.
hyt galan meɪ ꞏ dec atal.   Hyt a6ft ꞏ deudec
atal.   hyt galan racuyr ꞏ pedeɪr ar dec atal.
hyt ꞏ galan whefra6ɪ ꞏ vn ar pymthec atal.   20
hyt galan meɪ ꞏ deu na6 atal.   hyt a6ft ꞏ
vgeínt atal.   hyt galan racuyr ꞏ d6y ar hugeínt atal.   hyt galan whefra6ɪ ꞏ pedeɪr
ar hugeínt atal.   Tɪannoeth ydodɪr g6ed
arna6. . ac yna pedeɪr keínha6c cota adɪy-   25

cheif ar ywerth nyt amgen vn ar pymthec.
ad6y geinha6c heuyt o2 tymho2 agymer.
ac yna whech cheinha6c adeu vgeint atal.
hyt galan mei ⁚ Odyna hyt a6ft ⁚ 6yth a deu
vgeint atal. hyt galan racuyr ⁚ dec a deu   5
vgeint atal. hyt galan whefra62 ⁚ deu dec
adeu vgeint atal. T2annoeth ydodir g6ed
arna6 kanys allweith uyd yna. a hynny
ad2ycheif pedeir keinha6c kyfreith ar y
werth a d6y geinha6c hefyt o2 tymho2. ac   10
yna trugeint atal. 6eithi ych y6 eredic yn
rych ac yg g6ellt a hynny ynditonr6yc. ac
ny byd teithia6l onyt velly. ac ony byd te-
ithia6l ⁚ atuerer trayan y werth yr neb ae
p2ynho. Ỿ neb awertho eidon yn gyfreith-   15
a6l ⁚ bit ydana6 rac ydera tri dieu. athri
mis rac yr yfceuein. abl6ydyn rac ypelle-
neu. ⁚ Ỿ neb awertho llo neu dina6et ⁚ bit
ydana6 rac yclafyri o galan gayaf hyt 6yl
pad2ic. Ny byd teledi6 ych namyn o allwe-   20
ith hyt y whechet weith. Na buch nam-
yn oe heil llo ⁚ hyt yna6uet lo. achyt elhont
6y d2os yr oet h6nn6 ⁚ ny oft6g ar eu g6e-
rth tra uont uy6. ⊙2 llad g6arthec tref-
go2d eidon ac na 6yper p6y ae llada6d ⁚   25

doet

racuẏr pedeír ar dec atal. ' hẏt galan whefraƀꝛ.
vn ar pẏmthec atal. hẏt galan meı deu naƀ
atal. hẏt aƀſt ugeínt atal. hẏt galan racuẏr
dƀẏ ar hugeínt atal. hẏt galan whefraƀꝛ pedeír arhugeínt atal. Tꝛanoeth ẏ dodır gued 5
arnaƀ. a phedeír keínhaƀc cota adꝛẏcheíf
ar ẏ werth. Naƀuetdẏd whefraƀꝛ oꝛ dıchaƀn
eredıc guerth ẏ teıthı adꝛẏcheíf ar ẏ werth
nẏt amgen vn ar pẏmthec. a dƀẏ geínhaƀc
heuẏt oꝛ tẏmhoꝛ agẏmer, ac ẏna whech a   10
deugeínt atal. hẏt galan meı. odẏna hẏt aƀſt
ƀẏth adeugeínt atal. hẏt galan racuẏr dec
adeugeínt atal. hẏt galan whefraƀꝛ deudec
adeugeínt atal. Tꝛanoeth ẏdodır gued arnaƀ
kanẏſ allweıth uẏd ẏna. a hẏnnẏ adꝛẏcheíf 15
pedeír keínhaƀc kẏfreıth ar ẏwerth. a dƀẏ
agẏmer heuẏt oꝛ tẏmhoꝛ. ac ẏna trugeínt
atal. Ꝺeıthı ẏch ẏƀ eredıc eredıc ẏn rẏch ac
ẏguellt. ac ẏn allt ac ẏguaeret. ac hẏnnẏ
ẏn dıtonrƀẏc. ac nẏ bẏd teıthıaƀl onẏ bẏd 20
uellẏ. ac onẏ bẏd uellẏ teıthıaƀl atuerer.

trayan ẏwerth ẏr neb ae pꝛẏnho. ꝥ neb a
wertho eidon yn gẏfreitha6l. ef adẏlẏ bot
ẏdana6 rac ẏdera tri dieu atheir nof. ath
ri mıſ rac ẏr ẏſceueınt. a bl6ẏdẏn rac
ẏpelleneu. ꝥ neb awertho llo neu di-   5
nawet bit ẏdana6 rac ẏclauẏrı o galan
gaẏaf hẏt 6ẏl patric. Ɖẏ bẏd teledi6 ẏch
namẏn o allweith hẏt ẏna6uetweith.
Na bu6ch namẏn oe heil llo hẏt ywhech-
et llo. achẏt elhon 6ẏ dꝛoſ ẏr oet h6nn6   10
nẏ oft6g ar eu guerth kẏfreitha6l. tra uont
vẏ6. Ø r llad ẏſcrẏbẏl trefgoꝛd eidon ac
na 6ẏper pẏ rei ae llada6d doet perche-
na6c ẏr eidon achreſr ganta6 ẏr tref a
rodent l6 diarnabot. ac odẏna talent ẏ   15
rıf eidon. ac oꝛ bẏd eidon moel ran deu
eidon a a arna6. ar gẏfreith honno a elwır ll6ẏr tal guedẏ ll6ẏr t6g. Oꝛ bẏd adef ar neb eidon llad ẏllall talet ẏperch-
ena6c. Ƿedeir keınha6c kẏfreith ẏ6 gue-   20
rth dant eidon neu dant march tom.

OEn tra dẏnho keínhaƀc kẏfreith atal.
pan˙ dıdẏfner dƀẏ geínhaƀc kẏfreith
atal hẏt aƀft.   O aƀft allan pedeir˙ keínhaƀc
kẏfreith atal.   Ꞇeth daùat dƀẏ geínhaƀc
kẏfreith atal.   Ꞇeithı dauat kẏmeínt ẏƀ ẏ   5
ae guerth.   Ꝑant daùat àe llẏgat keínhaƀc
kẏfreith atal pop vn o honunt.   Ẏ neb awertho deueıt bıt dan trı heínt.   clauẏrı.   ꝺlle-
derƀ.   adouẏr rud.   hẏnẏ gaffont eu teir ı
guala oı guellt newẏd ẏ guanhƀẏn of gue-   10
dẏ kalan gaẏaf ẏguerth.

Ꝺẏn tra dẏnho keínhaƀc cota atal.   oı
pan atto dẏnu hẏt aƀft dƀẏ geínhaƀc
cota atal.   O aƀft allan pedeír keínhaƀc cota
atal.   Ꞇeth gauẏr dƀẏ geínhaƀc cota atal.   15
Ꞇeithı gauẏr kẏmeínt ẏƀ aewerth.   Ꝑant
gauẏr ae llẏgat keínhaƀc cota atal pop
vn o honu.   Ẏ neb a bıẏnho ẏfcrẏbẏl ẏgan
arall.   achlauẏru o honu gantaƀ ef adẏlẏ
rodı ẏlƀ ar ẏtrẏdẏd owẏr vn ureínt ac ef   20
naf dodef ẏmẏƀn tẏ ẏrẏffeı clauẏrı ẏndaƀ

ſeith mlýned kýn no hýnný ae da a geiff.

Parchell ýný growýn keínhaᏮc kýfreith atal. Oʒ pan el allan hýt pan atto dýnu dᏮý geínhaᏮc kýfreith atal. Oʒ
pan atto dýnu hýt Ꮾ́ýl ieuan ýmoch pedeir keínhaᏮc kyfreith atal. Odýna hýt
galan ionaᏮʒ dec ceínhaᏮc kýfreith atal.
Odýna hýt Ꮾ́ýl ieuan ýmoch elchᏮ́ýl Ꮾ́ýth
geínhaᏮc gýfreith atal. eithýr ýtri llýdýn ar benhic. ný dýrcheiſ ac ný oſtᏮg
výth. Ꭺrbenhic ýmoch. Ꭺ baed kenueín.
ahᏮch ýg kýueir ýr argᏼᏮýd. Ꭺc ýna deu
parthaᏮc uýd ýr eneit ar ý kic hýt Ꮾ́ýl ieuan ýmoch. O Ꮾ́ýl ieuan ýmoch hýt galan ionaᏮʒ dec ar hugeínt atal. Ꭺc ýna
deu parthaᏮc uýd ykic ar ýr eneit. Ᏼýt
oeſ werth kýfreith ar gnýᏮhᏮch. hýt
ým pen ýulᏮýdýn. ýný ulᏮýd kýfreith
hᏮch maᏮʒ agýmer. Ᏺ neb awertho moch
bit dan ý tri heínt. YuýnýglaᏮc. ar hualaᏮc. ᴧ ac nat ýſſont eu perchýll. Ꭺc ot

5

10

15

20

tri dieu

tri miſ

ẏffan eu perchẏll atuerher trayan eu guerth tracheuẏn. Or llad moch dẏn talet
eu perchena6c ẏalanaſ.

R ẏ6 g6ẏd tra uo dan adein ẏ uam ke-
inha6c kota atal. O2 pan el ẏdan ade-   5
in ẏuam keinha6c kẏfreith atal. Du6
a6ft d6ẏ geinha6c kẏfreith atal. ac ẏna
vn werth ae uam. Jar keinha6c cota
atal. Keila6c keinha6c cota atal.

R ar6 ẏ6 vn werth ac vn ard2ẏchaua-   10
el ac ẏch. ac 'ewic abu6ch. J62ch vn
werth ac vn ardẏrchauel ac gauẏr. ac
uellẏ kaeri62ch ab6ch. B6ẏth6ch un
werth ac un ardẏrchauel ẏ6 ah6ch tref.
B2och nẏ all6ẏf ẏgneit hẏwel da dod1   15
guerth kẏfreith arna6 canẏſ ẏ ul6ẏdẏn
ẏbeꝛ ẏuẏnẏgla6c ar ẏmoch b2eint k1.
agẏmereꝛ ẏnteu ẏna arna6. ar ul6ẏdẏn
ẏbeꝛ ẏgẏndared ar ẏ c6n b2eint h6ch
agẏmer ẏnteu ẏna arna6. Y fcẏuarna-   20
6c nẏ wnaethp6ẏt guerth kẏfreith ar

| neꝛ

canẏſ ẏneill mís ẏbẏd gỽẏỽ aͬ llall ẏnue-
nẏỽ. Ỽuerth ẏſtalỽyn. march greỽẏſ (a)
allo toı. achaſſec reỽẏſ oe ulaen. ac arall
ẏnẏ. ol. Ỽuerth tarỽ trefgoıd ẏỽ tarỽ arall a allo llamu a buỽch oe ulaen ac arall
ẏnẏ ol. Ỽuerth baed kenueín. baed arall a allo cleínaỽ a hỽch oe ulaen ac arall
ẏnẏ ol. Ⱥleıd achadno ac amrẏualẏon
ereıll nẏ wnelhont eıthẏr dıỽc nẏ wna-
ethpỽẏt guerth kẏfreıthaỽl arnunt rẏd
ẏỽ ẏpaỽb eu llad. Ỽuerth pop aníueıl oı
aẏſſer ẏ gıc eıthẏr ẏmoch. deu parth ẏ
guertʜ auẏd ar ẏr eneıt ar traẏan ar ẏ
goıff.

Ⓒ Eıthı gỽı ẏỽ gallu kẏt agureıc a bot
ẏn gẏuan ẏ aelodeu oll. Ỽeıthı gure
ıc ẏỽ dẏuot arỽẏd etíued ıdı abot ẏn gẏf
an ẏholl aelodeu. Ỽeıthı treıs ẏỽ llef ach
oın achỽẏn. Ỽeıthı keılaỽc ẏỽ canu ach
chỽcỽẏaỽ. Ỽeıthı ıar ẏỽ dodi͂ agoıı. Ỽe
ıthı pop ederẏn gỽıẏỽ ẏỽ canu achỽcỽẏaỽ.

5

10

15

20

| teıthı |

atuerer trayan eu gꝪerth trachefyn. Oꞛ
llad moch dyn ꞉ talet eu perchennaꝪc alanaſ ydyn. neu wadet ymoch.

RyꝪ gꝪyd tra vo dan adeín y vam ꞉ keínhaꝪc cotta atal.   Oꞛ pan el ydąn ade-   5
ín y vam. hyt aꝪſt ꞉ keínhaꝪc kyf. atal.   O
aꝪſt allan ꞉ dꝪy geínhaꝪc. kyf. atal.   ac yna
vnwerth ae vam vyd.   Ꝗar ꞉ keínhaꝪc cota
atal. ꝖeilyaꝪc ꞉ keínhaꝪc cotta atal.
Pvnt yꝪ gꝪerth nyth hebaꝪc. wheugeínt   10
yꝪ gꝪerth hebaꝪc kẏn mut athra vo yny
mut. Oꞛ byd gꝪen gꝪedy mut ꞉ punt atal.
Ꝗyth gꝪalch ꞉ wheugeínt atal.   GꝪalch ꞇ
kyn mut athra vo yny ɱut ꞉ trugeínt atal.
Oꞛ byd gꝪen gꝪedy mut ꞉ wheugeínt atal.   15
Ꝗyth llamyſten ꞉ pedeir ar hugeínt atal.
Ꝗlamyſten kyn mut athra vo yny mut ꞉
deudec keínhaꝪc atal.   Oꞛ byd gꝪen gꝪedy
mut ꞉ pedeir ar hugeínt atal.   Ꞇeithi pop
ederyn benyꝪ ꞉ yꝪ dotwi a goꞛi.   Teithi pop e-   20
deryn gꝪꞛyꝪ ꞉ kanu a chꝪccꝪyaꝪ.   Ꝗy byd
na dirꝪy na chamlꝪꞛꝪ am neb edeínyaꝪc
kyn dyccer ledꞛat.   namyn talu ywerth kyfreith yperchennaꝪc ony cheffir ehunan.
ꝖarꝪ vn werth ac vn ardꞛychafel uyd ac   25

¶ ych.

ac ewic a buch. aı6ıch agafyr. achaerí6ıch
a b6ch. a g6yth6ch ah6ch tref. Bıoch ny
all6ys ygneıt hywel da dodı g6erth kyfreıth arna6. kanyf y ul6ydyn ybeı y vyny-
gla6c ar ymoch. bıeínt kı agymereı ynteu   5
yna arna6. ar ul6ydyn y beı y gyndared
ar y k6n. bıeínt h6ch h6 agymereı ynteu
yna arna6. Yfcyfarna6c ny wnaethp6yt
heuyt werth kyfreıth arneı. kanys y ne-
ıll mís y bydeı 6ıy6 ar llall y bydeı veny6.   10
[6]6erth yftal6yn ː march a allo toı achaffec
oe ulaen ac arall yny ol. 66erth baed kenueín ː baed arall a allo cleína6. ah6ch oe vla-
en ac arall ac arall yny ol. 66erth tar6 trefgoıd ː tar6 arall a allo llamu. a buch oe vla-   15
en ac arall ynyol. Bleıd achadno ac amry-
falyon ereıll ny wnelhont namyn dı6c. ny
wnaethp6yt g6erth kyfreıth arnunt. ryd
y6 ypa6b eu llad. 66erth pop anefeıl oı a yf-
fer ygıc eıthyr ymoch ː deuparth yg6erth a   20
uyd ar yr eneıt. ar trayan ar y koıff. Teıthı
g6ı y6 gallu kyt ag6ıeıc a bot yn gyfan yaelodeu oll. Teıthı g6ıeıc y6. dyuot ar6yd etı-
uedu ıdı. a bot yn gyfan y holl aelodeu.
Teıthı treıs y6 ː llef acho ın ach6yn.   25

BOnhed gόenyn o paradόys pan yό.
ac o achaόs pechaόt dyn ydoethant
odyno. ac ydodes duό yrat arnunt. ac όᴌth
hynny ny ellır canu efferen heb ycόyr.
Modᴌydaf gόenyn ⁚ pedeır ar hugeínt a   5
tal. Kynheıt ⁚ vn ar pymthec atal. Eıl heıt
deudec keínhaόc atal. Tᴌyded heıt ⁚ όyth
geínhaόc atal. Modᴌydaf gόedy yd el y
kynheıt ohoneı ⁚ vgeínt atal. Gόedy yd el
yr eıl heıt ohoneı ⁚ vn ar pymthec atal.   10
Gόedy yd el y tryded heıt o hení. deudec keínhaόc atal. Dythal neb heıt eıthyr pede-
ırkeínhaόc. hyny vo trı dıeu ar hed ac yn
waftat. dyd ygeıffaό lle yuudaό. ar eıl y
uudaό. ar trydyd y oᴌffowys. Y neb agaffo   15
heıt ar tır dyn arall ar gagen. pedeır keín
haόc ageıff ygan perchennaόc ytır oᴌ myn
ynteu yr heıt. Y neb agaffo bydaf ar tır
dyn arall ⁚ keínhaόc kyfreıth a geıff ef.
neu ycόyr ar dewıf perchennaόc y tır.   20
Daόuetdyd kyn aόft yd a pop heıt ym
mreínt modᴌydaf. ac yna pedeır ar hugeínt atal. eıthyr yᵣ afgelleıt. kany chymer
hı vᴌeínt modᴌydaf hyt y kalan meı rac
όyneb. ac yna pedeır ar hugeínt atal mal   25
                    ¶ y reı ereıll.

Neb alatho kath awarchatto yſcuba6ꝛ bꝛenhín. neu ae dycco ledꝛat. yphen aoſſodır ywaeret ar la6ꝛ glan g6aſtat. ae llofc6ꝛn adꝛychefır y vynyd. ac odyna dín eu gra6n g6eníth ymdaneı. hyny gudyo 5 blaen yllofc6ꝛn. Ꝁath arall ꞉ pedeır keínha-6c. kyf. atal. Ꞇeıthı kath. kymeínt y6 ae g6erth kyfreıth. [Ꞇ]eıthı kath y6 y bot yn gyfgluſt gyflygat gyflofc6ꝛn gyfdanhed gyfiewín. ac yn díuan o tan. ꝛllad llygot 10 ꝛc nat yſſo ychanawon. ꝛc na bo kath derıc ar pop lloer.

Ny byd dır6y am gı kyn dyccer ledꝛat. namyn caml6ꝛ6. Ll6 vn dyn yſſyd dıga6nywadu kı. kanyſ beıch kefyn y6o 15 l6dyn anhyys. Oꝛ kyrch kı neb dyn yr keıſ-fa6 yr6yga6. kyt llatho ydyn y kı ac aryſ oe la6. ny thal na dır6y na chaml6ꝛ6 ymda-na6. Oꝛ bꝛath kı neb dyn hyny del yg6aet. talet perchenna6c y kı waet ydyn. ꝛc oꝛ llad 20 ydyn r6ygedıc y kı hagen heb fymut o dy-na ꞉ ny cheıff onyt vn ar pymthec aryant. Ꝁı kynefodıc ar6ycco dyn teır g6eıth. on-ys llad yperchenna6c. kyfreıth y6 yr6ym-a6 6rth troet y argl6yd d6y ry6hant y6ꝛtha6 25

ac uelly y lledır. ac odyna talet trı buhyn cam-
lbꝛб yr bꝛenhín. 𝔇y dıwygır dꝛбc awnel
kı kyndeıraбc. kany medır arnaб. Kyn dyccer kı yn lledꝛat ꞏ ny wneır kyfreıth lledꝛat
O R pan dotter yr yt yny day ❡ arnaб.   5
dayar hyt pan el yny yfcub ꞏ aryant
tal a daб dꝛoftaб. ac odyna yfcub ıach yn lle
y glaf. O pop eıdon buarth ꞏ dím eı ydyd ach
eínhaбc ynof. O pop march auo hual neu
laбhethyr arnaб ꞏ keínhaбc y dyd a dбy y   10
nos. Oꝛ byd dıfgyfrıth ꞏ dímeı ydyd. ache-
ínhaбc ynos. Os dıfgyfreıtha y deılyat ef
pan ydalyo aryryt. talet trı buhyn cam lб-
rб yr bꝛenhín. dodet hagen y dбy egбyt am
yr vn troet. ac uelly ny chyll dím. 𝔒ꝛ kadб   15
kyfreıth oꝛmoch. dalyet yr hбch a vynho eıthyr ytrı llydyn ar benhıc. agadet oꝛ pꝛyt
ygılyd. ac yna kyníget oe perchennaбc. o
ac onyf dıllбg oe chyfreıth ꞏ gбnaet y deılyat y defnyd o honeı. Sef yб kadб kyfreíth   20
oꝛ mo ch ꞏ deudec llydyn a baed. 𝔒ꝛ kadб
kyfreıth oꝛ moch deueıt ꞏ dauat ageffır.
ac o pop pymp llydyn hyt y kadб kyfreıth
ffyrllíng a geffır. Meınt y kadб kyfreıth oꝛ
deueıt ꞏ dec llydyn ar hugeínt. 𝔒 pop oen   25

G 2

ʊy ıar ageffir. hyt ykadʊ kyfreıth. ꝛc yna a-
geffir. Oꝛ geıfyr ar mynneu y dadyl gyffelyp.
Ỿ neb agaffo gʊydeu yny yt ꞁ toꝛret ffon kyhyt ac o pen elín hyt ymlaen ybyſ bychan
yny reſhet ymyn ho. ꝛlladet ygʊydeu ynyr   5
yt ar ffon. ꝛc alatho ymaes oꝛ yt ꞁ talet.
Gʊydeu agaffer yn llygru yt trʊy ytlan.
neu trʊy yſcubaʊꝛ. gʊaſcer gʊyalen ar eu
mynygleu. ꝛ gatter yn oʊynt hyt pan uʊ-
ynt ueırʊ. Ỿ neb agaffo ıar yny ard lín.   10
neu yny yſcubaʊꝛ. dalyet hı hyt pan ydıll-
ygho ypherchennaʊc hı oʊy ıar. ꝛc oꝛ deıla ykeılyaʊc ꞁ toꝛret ewín ıdaʊ a gollyget
yn ryd. neu gymeret ʊy ıar o pop ıar a vo
yny ty. ꞵ neb adalyho kath yn llygotta y   15
ny ard lín ꞁ talet ypherchennaʊc yllʊgyr.
Ỿ neb agaffo lloꝛ yny yt ꞁ dalyet ʊynt oꝛ
pꝛyt ygılyd heb laeth eu mameu. ac yna
gollyget yn ryd. Oꝛ llygrır ỿneb dyñ́ yt
yn emyl trefgoꝛd. ꝛc na chaffer dala vn   20
llʊdyn arnaʊ. kymeret ef ycreır a doet yr
tref. ꝛc oꝛ tygent lʊ dıarnabot ꞁ talent yr
yt yrıf eıdon llʊdyn. ar gyfreıth honno a
elwır. telıtoꝛ gʊedy halaʊc lʊ. Oꝛ deıla
dyn yſcrybyl aghyneſín ar y yt neuar   25

y weir. ac ymlad ohonunt yny gỽarchae. allad
olỽdyn yllall. perchennaỽc yr yfcrybyl bieu
talu yllỽdyn alather. ar deilyat auyd ryd.

℮ Neb awatto mach ꞉ rodet ylỽ ar yseithuet oɀ dynyon neffaf ywerth. petwar 5
oparth ytat adeu oparth y vam acynteu e-
hunan feithuet. ẏ neb awatto mechníaeth ꞉
rodet ylỽ ar yseithuet yny kyffelyp vod. ac
ony byd ygenedyl yn vn wlat ac ef. rodet y   .
lỽ ehunan uch pen feith allaỽɀ kyffegyr yn vn 10
gantref ac ef. kaṅys uelly ygỽedir bri duỽ.
◐ teir ffoɀd yd ymdíueicha mach ꞉ otalu oɀ
talaỽdyr dɀoftaỽ. Eil yỽ o rod oet oɀ haỽlỽɀ yr
talaỽdyr yn aỽffen y vach. Tɀydyd yỽ odỽyn
gauel oɀ haỽlỽɀ ar y talaỽdyr heb ganhat y   15
mach. ac yna talet trı buhyn camlỽɀỽ yr
bɀenhín. ◐et mach y ỽybot ae mach ae nat
mach ꞉ trı dieu. ẏfpeit mach yparatoɀ tal
os ef ehunan ae tal gyffefín. naỽ níeu.
◐ teir ffoɀd ydifferir mach achynnogyn. o   20
glybot coɀn ybɀenhín yn mẏnet yn lluyd.
ac o haỽl treis. ac o haỽl ledɀat. kanys aghen
yn aghen yỽ pop vn oɀ holyon hyn. ⓜach
adyly dỽyn gauel gyt ar haỽlỽɀ. hyt yn diogel.
agodef arnaỽ ygofut adel. ac ony wna hyṅny ꞉ 25

talet ehunan. Ꝑach aadeſho peth oe vechnı
aeth ac awatto peth arall ꝛ gỽadet ar y lỽ ehunan os myn. Ꞇrı mach hagen yſſyd ac nyche-
ıff vn o honunt dỽyn y vechnıaeth ar y lỽ e-
hunan kyt gỽatto ran ac adef ran arall oe ve- 5
chnı. nyt aıngen dyn ael yn vach ygỽyd llys.
Ꜳmach dıebꝛedıc. Ꜳmach talu. beth bynhaca
tygho ykyntaf. y llys adyly tygu ygyt ac ef neu
yny erbyn. ydeu ereıll beth bynhac atygho ꝛ
ar y seıthuet oe gyfneſſeíueıt ytỽg. kanyſ ta- 10
laỽdyr uyd pop vn o honunt. Ꝑyn adyly ı
kymryt mach ar pop da onyt da arotho yar-
glỽyd ıdaỽ. Ꝡ neb auo mach dꝛos dyn onys
tal ytalaỽdyr yn oet dyd. oet pymthec dıwarnaỽt ageıff ymach yna. Ꜳc onyſ tal y talaỽ- 15
dyryna ꝛ oet deg níwarnaỽt ageıff ymach y-
na. Ꜳc onyſ tal y talaỽdyr yna ꝛ oet pump dıwarnaỽt ageıff ymach yna. Ꜳc ony thal ytalaỽdyr yna ꝛ talet ymach. Ꜳllyna oeteu mach
am da bywaỽl. Os ar da marwaỽl y byd mach. 20
Oet pymthec dıwarnaỽt ageıff ymach yna.
Ꜳc ony thal y talaỽdyr yna ꝛ oet deg dıwarnaỽt
arhugeínt ageıff ymach yna. Ꜳc ony thal y
talaỽdyr yna ꝛ oet deg dıwarnaỽt adeu vgeínt
ageıff ymach yna. Ꜳc ony thal ytalaỽdyr yna ꝛ 25

talet ymach ehunan. aphan gyfarffo ymach
ar talaƄdyr꞉ yſpeilet ef oc auo ymdanaƄ odi-
llat eithyr ypilin neſſaf idaƄ. ac uelly gƄnaet
byth hyt pan gaffo cƄbyl tal ygantaƄ. ꝺꝛ
byd marƄ mach dyn kyn talu oꝛ talaƄdyr dꝛoſ- 5
taƄ y vechnſaeth. doet yr haƄlƄꝛ ar y seithuet
oꝛ dynyon neſſaf idaƄ uch pen bed ymach oꝛ
kaffant ybed. athyngent y vot yn vach. ac ony
chaffant ybed꞉ tyngent uch pen ꜱeꝼth allaƄꝛ
gyſſegyr y vot yn vach. ac na diwygƄyt dꝛoſtaƄ 10
y vechnſaeth tra uꞌu vyƄ. ac uelly ykeiff yda.
Ꝃyt dycco mach y vechnſaeth dꝛos lud arglƄ-
yd꞉ ny chyll na dirƄy na chamlƄꝛƄ. ꝺꝛ byd marƄ talaƄdyr dyn ac nachaffo kymynnu yda
Ƅꝛth neb.   dyget ymach y vechnꝛaeth dꝛos yma- 15
rƄ. athalet y teir ach neſſaf idaƄ. ar mach bieu
ygymhell kyſtal acar ytalaƄdyr bei byƄ.
Ꝑ neb a adefho dylyu da idaƄ꞉ talet yndꝛohir
eithyr y ny teir gƄyl arbenhic. ynadolyc. ar ꝙ
paſc ar sulgƄyn. nyt amgen o noſ nadolyc   20
gƄedy goſper. hyt duƄ kalan gƄedy efferen.
O noſ SadƄꝛn paſc gƄedy datƄyreſn. hyt duƄ
paſc bychan gƄedy efferen. Onos SadƄꝛn ſul-
gƄyn gƄedy goſper꞉ hyt duƄ Sul y dꝛindaƄt
gƄedy efferen. kany dyly neb goſyn ygilyd. 25

yny diewed hynny. Ꝺydyly neb kymryt
mab yn vach heb ganhat ytat tra dylyho
bot dꝛoftaϭ. na mynach na bꝛaϭt heb ganhat eu habat. nac alltut kanyt geir y eir
ar gymro. nac yfcolheic yfcol heb ganhat   5
yathro. na gϭꝛeic. onyt aryr hyn ymedho
arnaϭ. Yrei hynny nyt mechní eu mechní onyt gan ganhat eu harglϭydı. Oꝛ byd
marϭ mach dyn. ꝛc adaϭ mab ohonaϭ.
ymab adyly seuyll yn lleytat yny vechní.   10
Ꝺy dyly neb gymryt mach kynnogyn
kanys deu ardelϭ ynt. ꝛc na dyly neb onyt
dewıf yardelϭ. Os kynnogyn adewıs ⸱⸲
nyt oes vach. Os mach adewıs ⸱⸲ nyt oes
gynnogyn. ꝛc ϭꝛth hynny ny eill neb gofyn   15
seuyll yn vach ac yn gynnogyn. ꝛrglϭyd
auyd mach arpop da adefedıc díuach. Oꝛ
canhatta y kynnogyn yr mach rodı kywerthyd punt yg gϭyftyl keínhaϭc. ꝛchyn oet
ygϭyftyl ⸱⸲ ygollı. ny dyly y kynnogyn trach- 20
efyn namyn dímeı. kanys hynny yϭ trayan keínhaϭc kyfreıth. ꝛc ynteu ehunan
alygrϭys bꝛeínt y ϭyftyl. Oꝛ dyry mach
peth maϭꝛ yg gϭyftyl peth bychan. yr ha-
ϭlϭꝛ adyly ygymryt. ꝛchyn coller kyn yr   25

oet. nys di6c·yr ha6l6ı yr mach traegefyn.
namyn y trayan. Y mach hagen ae di6c og6-
byl yr kynnogyn kanys yn aghyfreitha6l
yduc. [Ø]ı dyry kynnogyn kywerthyd punt
yg g6yſtyl keſnha6c ae dyg6yda6. ny dıwygır. 5
℗O dadyl yny hamot. nyt am ¶ıda6 dım.
ot heb amotwyr. Vn dıwat y6 amot
amechnſaeth. Ny dyly neb wneuthur amot
dıos yllall heb yganhat. nathat dıos y vab.
na mab dıos ytat. kany phara amot nam   10
yn yn oes yneb aeg6nel. Kyt g6nelher amot yn erbyn kyfreith ꝛ dır y6 ygad6. ꞑ Amot
atyrr ardedyf. Tıech amot no g6ır. Øı edeu
dyn da yarall yg g6yd tyſton. a mynnu eıl-
weıth ywadu. nys dıcha6n onyt y tyſton a 15
palla yr llall. Os edeu ynteu heb neb yny lle.
g6adet ar yl6 ehunan os myn.
℠Eıth punt y6 gobyr merch bıenhın.
ac yr vam y telır. ar g6ı atal ychowyll.
kanyſ tır atelır ıdı. Pedeır punt ar hugeſnt 20
y6 y heg6edı. Oı a merch bıeyr gan 6ı yn lla-
thıut heb rod kenedyl. pan atter sef uyd y
heg6edı ꝛ whech eıdon kyhyt eu kyrn ac eu hyſ-
cyfarn. ꝗ verch taya6c tri eıdon y telır trı
eıdon gogyſoet areı hynny. Øı kymer g6ı 25

wreic orod kenedyl. ac os gat kyn pen y
feith mlyned ꝛ talet idi teir punt yny heg6e-
dí os merch bꞛeyr uyd. ac yny chowyll ꝛ
punt ahanher. ac wheugeínt yny gobyr.
0s merch taya6c uyd. punt ahanher yny   5
heg6edi. awheugeint yny chowyll. aphedeir ar hugeínt yny gobyr. Os g6edy y
feith mlyned ygat ꝛ bit ran deu hanher y
rydunt. onyt bꞛeínt adyry ragoꞛ yr g6ꞛ.
Deuparth y plant ada6 yr g6ꞛ. nyt amgen 10
yr hynaf ar ꞛeuhaf. ar trayan yr vam. Os
agheu ae g6ahana ꝛ bit ran deu hanher y
rydunt. opop peth. ſarhaet g6ꞛeic 6ꞛy-
a6c. herwyd bꞛeint yg6ꞛ ytelir. Ƿan lather g6ꞛ g6ꞛeigya6c ꝛ ysarhaet atelir yngyn-   15
taf. ac odyna yalanas. Tꞛayan farhaety
g6ꞛ ageiff ywreic. ©6ꞛeic g6ꞛ ryd adicha-
6n rodi ychrys ae mantell ae phenllieín
ae hefcityeu abla6t ae cha6s ae hemenyn
ae llaeth heb ganhat yg6ꞛ. ac adicha6n ben- 20
ffygya6 holl dootrefyn yty. Ɗy dicha6n
g6ꞛeic taya6c rodi heb ganhat yg6ꞛ onyt
ypheng6ch. acny eill benffygya6 onyt y
gogyr aeridyll. a hynny hyt ycly6her y
gal6 ae throet arythrotheu. 0ꞛ a moꞛ6-   25

kẏn pen ẏſeith mlẏned talet ẏ heguedı
ıdı. Os merch bʒeẏr uẏd teır punt uẏd ẏ
heguedı. Punt ahanher ẏnẏ chowẏll. wheugeínt ẏnẏ gobẏr. Oʒ bẏd merch taẏaƃc.
Punt ahanher ẏnẏ heguedı. wheugeínt ẏnẏ   5
chowẏll. Pedeır arhugeínt ẏnẏ gobẏr.
Os guedẏ ẏſeith mlẏned ẏgat bıt ran deu
hanher ẏrẏdunt. onẏt bʒeínt adẏrẏ ragoʒ
ẏrgƃʒ. deu parth ẏplant adaƃ ẏrgƃʒ nẏt
amgen ẏr hẏnaf arıeuhaf. ar traẏan ẏn   10
ran ẏuam adaƃ. Os agheu aeguahana. deu
hanher uẏd pop peth ẏrẏdunt. Ƨarhaet
gureıc ƃʒyaƃc herwẏd bʒeínt ẏgƃʒ ẏtelír
ıdı. Ƥan lather gƃʒ gureıgaƃc. ẏſarhaet a
telır ẏngẏntaf ac odẏna ẏalanaſ. Tʒaẏan   15
ẏſarhaet hagen ageıff ẏwreıc. Ƈureıc
gƃʒ rẏd adıchaƃn rodı ẏchrẏſ. ae mantell.
ae phenllıeín. ae heſkıtẏeu. ae blaƃt. ae
chaƃſ. ae hemenẏn. ae llaeth. heb ganhat
ẏgƃʒ. ae benffygẏaƃ ẏ holl dohotrefẏn adı-   20
chaƃn. Ɖẏ dẏrẏ gureıc taẏaƃc heb ganhat

ẏgб̇2 namẏn ẏphenguch. ac nẏ eıll benfẏ-
gẏaб eıthẏr ẏgogẏr ae rıdẏll. ahẏnnẏhẏt
ẏ clẏбher ẏgalб ae throet б2th ythrotheu.

OR a mo2б̇ẏn wẏrẏ ẏnllathrut heb can
hat kenedẏl. ẏ that ad dıchaбn ẏhat 5
tб̇ẏn oe hanuod. rac ẏgб̇2. ac nẏthal ẏha-
mobẏr ẏr arglб̇ẏd. O2 a gureıc hagen ẏn
llathrut nẏ eıll neb ẏ hattб̇ẏn oe hanuod
rac ẏgб̇2. O2 lle ẏbo ẏhatlam ẏtelır ẏham-
obẏr. Ᵹ neb ad dẏcco treıſ ar wreıc. talet 10
ẏgobẏr ẏr arglб̇ẏd ae dırб̇ẏ. ae dılẏſtaб̇t
ae heguedı. aeſarhaet atal ẏr wreıc. acoſ
mo2б̇ẏn uẏd talet ẏ chowẏll. O2 dıwat
gб̇2 treıſ ar wreıc ac oſ katarnha ẏwreıc
ẏnẏ erbẏn kẏmeret hı ẏcreſr ẏnẏ llaб̇ 15
deheu. ae gala ẏnteu ẏnẏ llaб̇ aſſeu ıdı.
athẏget rẏdб̇ẏn treıſ o honaб̇ ef arneı
hı. ac ẏuellẏ nẏ chẏll dím oe ıaбn. Ᵹ neb
adıwatto treıſ. rodet lб̇ deg wẏr adeugeínt heb gaeth aheb alltut. O trı achaб̇ſ 20
nẏ chẏll gureıc ẏ heguedı kẏt adaб̇ho ẏ

gб̇2

góɪ oglauẏrɪ. adɪ̇yc anadẏl. ac eɪffeu
kẏt. ꞇrɪ pheth nẏ dẏgɪr rac gureɪc kẏt
gatter am ẏ cham. Ẏ chowẏll. ae hargẏf-
reu. ae hóẏnebwerth. pan gẏttẏo ygóɪ.
agureɪc arall. Onẏ wna moɪóẏn auẏn-   5
ho oe chowẏll kẏn kẏuot ẏboɪe ẏóɪth
ẏ góɪ. ẏgkẏt ẏbẏd ẏrẏdunt. ꞇeɪr gue-
ɪth ẏ keɪff gureɪc ẏ hóẏnebwerth ẏ gan
ẏgóɪ pan gẏttẏo ef a gureɪc arall. ac of
dɪodef dɪof hẏnnẏ nẏ cheɪff dím. O rod-   10
ɪr moɪóẏn aeduet ·ẏ óɪ. ac oɪ dẏweɪt ẏn
teu nat oed uoɪóẏn hɪ. tẏget ẏuoɪóẏn ar
ẏpẏmhet nat oed wreɪc. Sef dẏnẏon uẏ
dant. hɪ ae that ae mam. ae bɪaót ae whaer.
ꞇrɪ lló adẏrẏ gureɪc ẏóɪ pan enllɪper. ẏn   15
gẏntaf lló feɪth wraged. ac ar ẏr eɪl enllɪp
lló pedeɪr guraged ardec. ac ar ẏtrẏdẏd enllɪp lló deg wraged adeugeínt. ac of godef dɪof hẏnnẏ nẏ cheɪff dím. Ɖa rodet
neb wreɪc ẏóɪ heb gẏmrẏt mach arẏ go   20
bẏr ẏr arglóẏd. Oɪdẏgɪr gureɪc ẏn llath-

rut ẏneb tẏ. kẏmeret gϭꝛ ẏ tẏ uach arẏ
gobẏr ẏꞃ arglϭẏd. ac onẏſ kẏmer talet
ehunan. Ϭobẏr alltudes ẏϭ pedeꙇr ar
hugeꙇnt. Ẏ penkerd bꙇeu gobꙇeu mer-
chet ẏ beꙇrd auϭẏnt ẏ danaϭ. Ꝺrgẏt   5
crẏman ẏϭ naϭd caeth. Ꝺrgẏt bϭẏall
neu ϭdẏſ ẏϭ naϭd maer bꙇſweꙇl. Ꝥede
ꙇr arhugeꙇnt ẏϭ ſarhaet guenꙇdaϭl caeth nẏt el nac ẏn raϭ nac ẏm(r)euan.
Ϭr kẏtẏa gϭꝛ gureꙇgaϭc a gureꙇc arall   10
talet wheugeꙇnt ẏꞃ wreꙇc gẏfreꙇthaϭl
ẏnẏ hϭẏneb werth. Ϭr ẏſcar gϭꝛ a gureꙇc kẏn pen ẏſeꙇth mlẏned. val hẏn ẏ
renꙇr ẏdo otrefẏn ẏ rẏdunt. Ẏgϭꝛ bꙇeu
auo oꝛ dꙇllat guelẏ ẏrẏdaϭ ar llaϭꝛ.   15
ar wreꙇc bꙇeu ẏ teꙇſpan. Ẏ gϭꝛ bꙇeu ẏr
ẏt. ar wreꙇc bꙇeu ẏ blaϭt paraϭt. Ẏgϭꝛ
bꙇeu ẏ bꝛẏccan ar nꙇthlen ar gobenẏd
tẏ le. ar cϭlltẏr ar uϭẏall gẏnut ar
llaϭ uϭẏall. ar crẏmaneu oll namẏn   20
vn crẏman. Ẏ wreꙇc bꙇeu ẏ uϭẏall lẏ-

dan. arſ6ch arpal arvn crŷman. ar perued taradŷr. ar g6ɪ bɪeu ŷr heŷrn oll na-
mŷn hŷnnŷ. Ẏ wreɪc bɪeu car ŷr ŷchen
ar guedeu ar llaeth leſtrɪ oll. eɪthŷr vn pa-
ŷol. ar dŷſgleu oll eɪthŷr vn dŷſcŷl bɪ-   5
eu ŷg6ɪ. Ẏwreɪc bɪeu ŷr emenŷn oll na-
mŷn vn lleſtreɪt bɪeu ŷ g6ɪ. ac oɪ bŷd
bɪeuaneu emenŷn ŷg6ɪ ageɪff vn. Ẏwre-
íc o bɪeu ŷ kɪc oll auo ar ŷlla6ɪ ahalen
arna6 a heb halen ar ka6ſ oll auo ŷnhe-   10
lɪ aheb halen arnunt. ar g6ɪ bɪeu ŷ kɪc
ar ca6ſ dɪychauedɪc oll. Ẏ wreɪc bɪeu
bot ŷnŷ thŷ ŷnar hoſ ŷran oɪ da. hŷt
ŷm pen ŷna6uetdŷd. ᵍureɪc a dŷweto
ŷ bot ŷn ueɪcha6c pan uo mar6 ŷg6ɪ. hɪ   15
adŷlŷ bot ŷnŷ thŷ hŷnŷ 6ŷpper auo be-
ɪcha6c. ac onŷ bŷd beɪcha6c talet trɪbu-
hŷn caml6ɪ6 ŷr bɪenhín. ac adawet ŷ
tŷ ar tír ŷr etíued.

OR bŷd d6ŷ wraged ŷn ŷmdeɪth tr6ŷ   20
neb lle ac na bo neb ŷgŷt ac6ŷ. a-

dẏuot deu 6ꝛ ẏn eu herbẏn ac eu hẏmreín. nẏ dıwẏgır udunt. Oꝛbẏd vn
dẏn hagen ẏ gẏt ac 6ẏ ẏr ẏ vẏchan-
et onẏt mab keuẏn uẏd nẏ cholla-
nt dím oe ıa6n. Oꝛ d6c g6ꝛ wreıc ẏn   .5
llathrut. ae hatal ganta6 hẏt ẏmpen
ẏ Seıthuet dẏd heb wneuthur ıa6n ıdı.
nẏ dẏlẏ guneuthur ıa6n ıdı hẏt ẏm
pen vn dẏd abl6ẏdẏn. ẏna hagen ẏ dẏlẏ c6bẏl ıa6n. Ꝺureıc ael ẏn llathrut   10
gan 6ꝛ ẏnhaeduetr6ẏd. ae d6ẏn oꝛ g6ꝛ
hı ae ẏl6ẏn. neu ẏ perth. neu ẏ tẏ. ae
hẏmreín ae hell6g dꝛae cheuẏn. a ch6-
ẏna6 o hení hıtheu 6ꝛth ẏ chenedẏl ac
ẏnẏ dadleu. Sef adẏlẏ hẏ ẏnẏ dıweír   15
deb kẏmrẏt tar6 trı gaẏaf ac eılla6 ẏ
lofc6ꝛn ae ıra6 a guer. ac odẏna grẏnu
ẏ lofc6ꝛn tr6ẏ ẏ doꝛgl6ẏt. ac odẏna aet
ẏ wreıc ẏmẏ6n ẏ tẏ adodet ẏ throet 6ꝛth
ẏ trotheu achẏmeret ẏ lofg6ꝛn ẏnẏ d6ẏ   20
la6. a doet g6ꝛ opop parth ẏr tar6 ac er

thı ẏn llaϐ pop vn ẏ gẏmhell ẏtarϐ. ac
oɀ dıchaϐn hı ẏ attal ẏ tarϐ.   kẏmeret ẏnẏ
. hϐẏneb werth ae dıweırdeb.   ac onẏſ dıch
aϐn kẏmeret a lẏnho ϐɀth ẏ dϐẏ laϐ oɀgϐer.
Ꞡureıc aẏmrotho ehunan ẏn llϐẏn ac   5
ẏmperth ẏϐɀ. aehadaϐ oɀ gϐɀ hı. agoɀder-
chu arall o honaϐ ae dẏuot hıthïeu ẏg
cϐẏn at ẏ chenedẏl. ac ẏr dadleu. Os dıwat awna ẏ gϐɀ rodet ẏ lϐ ẏgloch heb
tauaϐt ẏndı.   Os dïuϐẏn awna ẏnteu   10
talet geínhaϐc ıdı 'kẏflet ae thín.

OR ẏmda gureıc ehunan adẏuot
   gϐɀ ıdı adϐẏn treıſ arneı. os dıwat
awna ẏgϐɀ rodet lϐ deg wẏr a deugeínt
athrı o honunt ẏndıouredaϐc na mẏn-   15
ho gureıc. ac nat ẏſſo kıc. ac na march-
occo uẏth. onẏ mẏn dıwat. talet ẏr
wreıc ẏ guadaϐl. ae dılẏſtaϐt. ae dırϐẏ.
a guẏalen arẏant ẏr bɀenhín ẏnẏ wed
ẏdẏlẏ. aconẏ eıll ẏ gϐɀ talu dẏcker ẏ   20
geılleu. Ꞇeır gueıth ẏ dẏrcheıſ ar ſar-

haet góꝛ pan ẏmreher ẏ wreıc. Ꝃyfreıth
magu ulóẏdẏn. ẏó buóch. amantell a
pheıſ aphenllıeín. adóẏ eſkıt acharre-
ıt oꝛ ẏt goꝛeu atẏffo ar tır ẏ góꝛ a pha-
dell troedaóc. ᵹuerth keróẏn ued a   5
talhér ẏrbꝛenhín wheugeınt. ar córẏr
arennír mal hẏn. Ẏ traẏan ẏr bꝛenhín.
ar eıl traẏan ẏr neb ae gunel. ar trẏded
ẏr neb ae rotho ẏ med. Naó dẏrnued ýó
meſſur ẏgeróẏn ued pan ueſſurher oꝛ   10
aróẏr nẏt amgen oꝛ cleıſ traó ẏr emẏl
Oꝛoen ẏ ch neu uuóch neu ❡ ẏma
garó neu ewıc. neu dẏuẏrgı deu
dec keínhaóc a tal pop vn. ᵹroen lloſt-
lẏdan hanher punt atal. ᵹroen beleu   15
pedeır ar hugeínt atal. ᵹroen carlóg
deudec keínhaóc . atal. ᴑ pop góẏdlódẏn
alather ar tır dẏn arall. perchennaóc ẏ-
tır ageıff ẏ whartha óꝛ ol neſſaf ẏr llaóꝛ.
.. oꝛ bẏd hẏẏs ẏ gıc. Ᵽeth bẏnhac adan-   20
goſſo ẏ dofrethwẏr ẏr taẏogeu ẏ delhó

ẏnt oe teı. Ẏtaẏogeu bıeu eu talu oꝛ collír
eıthẏr gleíueu. a llodꝛeu. a chẏllẏll. eum-
írch ƀẏnteu nẏ cheıdƀ ẏtaẏogeu eıthẏr
ẏnoſ. kanẏſ ƀẏ ae talant oꝛ collır ẏnoſ.
Ƀƀẏnnoſſaƀc bꝛenhín adẏrẏ keínhaƀc   5
ẏr guaſſanaethwẏr ẏr arbet ẏr ẏſcubaƀꝛ
ae uƀẏt. Ꝁac eıſtedẏat cantreſ nẏt amgen ẏ troedaƀc kerƀẏn uragaƀt atal ẏr
bꝛenhín pop blƀẏdẏn. Ᵽan uo marƀ
gƀꝛ goꝛwlat ar tır dẏn arall. vn ar pẏm-   10
thec ageıff perchenaƀc ẏ tır dꝛoſ ẏ uarƀ
tẏ warchen. ar ebedıƀ oll ẏr arglƀẏd ẏam hẏnẏ.

Ᵽvm nẏn neſſaf ẏwerth adıwat beıch
keuẏn onẏ holır ẏnlletrat. Seıth
nẏn adıwat pƀn march onẏ holır ẏn   15
lletrat. Ᵽeu deg wẏr ad dıwat guerth
wheugeínt onẏ holír ẏn lletrat. Ᵽetwar
guẏr ar hugeínt adıwat guerth punt.
on ẏ holír ẏn lletrat. Ᵽunt ẏƀ kẏuarƀſ
gƀꝛ ar teulu ẏnẏ ulƀẏdẏn.   20
Ᵽbedıƀ pop gƀꝛ rẏd ẏƀ wheugeínt.

wheugeínt ý6 ebedí6 guaſſanaeth6ꝛ ar-
gl6ỹd. Whech apetwar ugeínt ý6 ebedí6
taỹa6c. O ꝛ bỹd egl6ỹſ ar ỷ tır wheugeínt
uỹdỷ ebedí6. Ƿedeır ar hugeínt ý6 ebe-
dí6 g6ꝛ yſtauella6c. Ƿeudec keínha6c   5
ý6 ebedí6 gureıc ỹſtauella6c. Ɖỷ thal
penkenedỷl ehunan ỷ ebedí6. kanỹſ ỷ
neb auo penkenedỷl guedỷ ef aetal.
Ɖỷ bỹd penkenedỷl ỷ mab guedỷ ỷ tat.
ỷn neſſaf ıda6. kanỹſ oeſuoda6c ý6 pen   10
kỹnedlaeth. Ƃureıc 6ꝛỷa6c a oꝛdıweth-
er ỷ godíneb ỷ heguedı agỹll ac adỷcco
oda ỷ gan ỷ chenedỷl at ỷ g6ꝛ.

Oꝛ dỹwedır ar dỷn guelet lletrat gan-
ta6 lí6 dỷd goleu ac arall ỷn llıwa6   15
arna6 ỷ welet. rodet ỷ neb aenllıper llí6
petwar guỷr ar hugeínt mal ỷ del kỹf-
níuer o pop kỹmh6t oꝛ vn cantref ac
nỷ eıll ỷ llıwat dím ỷnỷ erbỷn ✠
Ƀlỹma mal ỷ dỹlỷír llıwa6 lletrat ỷn   20
gỹfreıtha6l guelet ỷ dỷn oꝛ pan uo gol

✠ ar gỹfreıth ho𝑛no aelwır dỹgỷn wat ỷn
   erbỷn dogỷn vanac

eu ẏdẏd hẏt pan uo pɪẏt kẏflẏch6ɪ ar
lletrat ganta6 athẏgu oɪ llɪwat ar ẏ petwerẏd o wẏr un vɪeínt ac ef ar poɪth ẏ
vẏnwent. ac ar dɪ6f ẏr egl6ẏf. ac uch pen
ẏr alla6ɪ gẏffegẏr. · 5

anag6ɪ diouredabc trbẏ tẏftolẏaeth
ẏ periglabɪ oɪ dab gẏt ar colledic ẏg6ẏd
ẏr offeírat ẏr egl6ẏf archet ẏr effeírat
ẏmanag6ɪ ar dɪ6f ẏr egl6ẏf ẏr du6 na
th6g ẏ kam. ac of t6g ẏno bit gẏffelẏp 10
ar dɪ6f ẏ gagell. ar trẏdedweith uch pen
ẏr alla6ɪ. ac of diwat ẏdẏn dɪof hẏnnẏ
cadarnhaet ẏr effeírat ar ẏ eir teir gueith.
ac onẏ chret ẏdẏn hẏnnẏ tẏget ẏr effeir
at vn weith ac uellẏ nẏ ellɪr ẏnẏ erbẏn. 15

verth gaẏaf tẏ. dec a deugeínt arẏ
ant ẏ atal ẏnenpɪen. a dec ar hugeínt atal pop foɪch agẏnhalẏo ẏ nenpɪen.
Ẏ meínkeu. ar tal ueígkeu ar ẏftẏffẏleu
ar doɪeu ar kẏnoreu ar goɪdɪẏffeu ar 20
trothẏweu ar tubẏft pedeir keínha6c

kýfreıth ẏƀ guerth pop vn ohonunt. Ỿ neb
anoetho gaẏaf tẏ traẏan ẏwerth atal.
Ƀuerth kẏnhaẏaf tẏ.   pedeır ar hugeínt.
atal.   Oꝛ bẏd tƀll taradẏr ẏndaƀ.   ac onẏ
bẏd deu dec keínhaƀc atal.   Ɓaf tẏ deu-   5
dec keínhaƀc atal.   Foꝛch haf tẏ neu gẏn-
haẏaf tẏ dƀẏ geínhaƀc kýfreıth atal.
Ɖoꝛglƀẏt dƀẏ geínhaƀc kýfreıth atal.
Ɛ ſgubaƀꝛ bꝛenhín wheugeínt atal.
Ẏſgubaƀꝛ bꝛeẏr trugeínt atal. Ẏſ-   10
gubaƀꝛ tayaƀc bꝛenhín dec arhugeínt
atal. Ƀattet paƀb ẏ ẏſgubaƀꝛ ẏn agoꝛet
hẏt galan gaẏaf ẏ uẏnet guẏnt ẏndu-
nt.   ac oꝛ daƀ ẏſgrẏbẏl udunt talet eu
perchenaƀc eu llƀgẏr.   Guedẏ gƀẏl ẏr   15
hol feínt onẏ bẏd ban goꝛ ẏn trı lle ar ẏ
paret ẏ ẏſgubaƀꝛ nẏ thelír ẏ llƀgẏr a
wnelher ẏndı.
Ɔ dẏn bıben bꝛenhín hanher punt
atal oꝛ bẏd tẏ oduchtı. Ɵdẏn bıben   20
bꝛeẏr o bẏd tẏ kýfreıthaƀl oduchtı tru-

geínt atal. Ødẏn bıben taẏaaƀc bɾenhín
dec ar hugeínt atal oɾ bẏd tẏ kẏfreıthaƀl
o duch tı. Ødẏn bıben taẏaƀc bɾeẏr pedeír ar hugeínt atal oɾ bẏd tẏ kẏfreıthaƀl o
duchtı. Ƥop odẏn nẏ bo odẏn bıben han-   5
heraƀc uẏd ar ẏreı gẏnt herwẏd bɾeínt
eu perchenogẏon. Ẏ neb a gẏneuho tan
ẏmẏƀn odẏntẏ onẏ chẏmer fẏd ẏgan arall kẏn noe adaƀ ar dıffodı ẏtan ẏ gƀẏd
tẏfton neu arẏuot ẏndıwall kẏmhƀẏf   10
uẏd ẏguall ẏrẏdùnt can kẏt talant. Ẏ tẏ
kẏntaf alofcer ẏnẏ tref o wall tan. talet ẏ
deu tẏ gẏntaf aennẏno gantaƀ. Ɖeu hanher uẏd ẏcollet rƀg ẏneb arotho ẏ tan ar
neb ae kẏneuho. Ꝭ neb auenffẏo tẏ athan   15
ẏ arall oɾ kẏneu hƀnnƀ tan teır gueıth
ẏndaƀ. kƀbẏl tal ageıff ẏgantaƀ oɾ llẏfc ẏ-
tẏ. Øs gẏr llofrudẏaeth tan auẏd ar dẏn
ẏn lletrat llƀ deg wẏr adeugeínt aa arnaƀ.
Oɾ keıff ẏreıth dıgaƀn ẏƀ ıdaƀ. onẏf keıff   20
bıt leıdẏr guerth. Ƥleıdẏr awerther feıth

punt ẏꝺ ẏ werth. Ꝺr keffír lleıdẏr ẏn llofcı
tẏ ẏnlletrat aẹ dala bıt eneıt uadeu. Ꝟleı-
dẏr adıhenẏdẏer nẏ dẏlẏír dím oe da. canẏ dẏlẏír ẏ díuꝺẏn ar dıal. Eıthẏr talu
ẏr colledıc ẏ da canẏ dẏlẏ adaꝺ dẏlẏet ẏn   5
ẏ ol arnaꝺ. Ꝺẏ bẏd galanaſ am leıdẏr
ac nẏ bẏd rꝺg dꝺẏ genedẏl lẏſſẏant ẏrdaꝺ.
Ẏ wen ſant punt atal. Derwen whe
ugeínt atal. Ẏ neb atẏllo derwen trꝺ-
ẏdı trugeínt atal. Ꝡeıg ucheluar tru-   10
geínt atal. Pop keıg arbenhıc oꝛ derwen.
dec ar hugeín atal. Ꝣvallen per trugeínt atal. Ꝺuallen ſur dec arhugeınt atal.
Ꝡollen pẏmthec atal. Ꝥẏmthec atal ẏ-
wen coet. Ꝺraenen Seıth a dímeı atal.   15
Ꝥop pꝛen guedẏ hẏnnẏ pedeır keínhaꝺc
kẏfreıth atal eıthẏr fawẏden. Honno we-
ugeínt atal. Ẏ neb alatho derwen ar
foꝛd ẏ bꝛenhín. talet trı buhẏn camlꝺꝛꝺ
ẏr bꝛenhín. Ꝺ guerth ẏ derwen. Ꝺc ar llꝺ-   20
ẏſſet ẏfoꝛd ẏr bꝛenhín. Ꝺphan el ẏ bꝛen-

hín heıbỳa6 kudỳet uon ỳ pıen a bıeth=
ỳn vn lltó. Or dỳg6ỳd pıen ar tra6f auon
athỳnu ˙ magleu ar ỳ pıen. perchena6c
ỳtır ỳ bo bon ỳ pıen arna6 adỳlỳ ỳ douot
pa tu bỳnhac ỳ troffo ỳr auon urıc ỳ pıen.   5
Ledỳf auo eur neu arỳant ar ỳ dóın
pedeır ar hugeínt atal. 6ledỳf heb
eur aheb arỳant arna6 deudec keínha6c
keín atal. 6arỳan auo llaffar arneı. pedeír ar hugeínt atal. 6arỳan ltó ỳ phren   10
deudec keínha6c átal. 6uaỳ6 pedeır
keínha6c kỳfreıth atal. Bóỳall eníllec
dóỳ geínha6c kỳfreıth atal. Kỳllell.
keínha6c kỳfreíth atal. 6algell. ach
reu moch. affalt deueıt. decar huge-   15
ínt atal pop vn. 6eín melín pedeır
ar hugeínt atalant. Bıeuan pedeır ke-
ínha6c kỳfreıth atal. 6elỳn penkerd
wheugeínt atal. Ychỳweırgoın pedeır
ar hugeínt atal. 6elỳn ỳ bıenhín ae   20
vıỳckan ae ta6lboıd wheugeínt atal

        | pop vn

Ielýn bıeỳr trugeínt atal. Ýchýweırgoın
deudec keínhaɓc atal. Bıýccan bıeỳr trugeínt atal. Ɨobennýd tỳle vgeínt atal.
Ɨaɓlboıt o aſgɓın moıuíl trugeınt atal.
Ɨaɓlboıt o aſgɓın arall dec arhugeín atal.   5
Ɨaɓlboıt o uan hỳd pedeır arhugeínt atal.
Ɨaɓlboıt o uan eıdon deudec keínhaɓc atal.
Ɨaɓlboıt pıen pedeır keínhaɓc keureıth
atal. Bɓýell lỳdan pedeır keínhaɓc kýfre
ıth atal. Bɓýell gýnut dɓỳ geínhaɓc gýf   10
reıth atal. Ħlaɓuɓell keínhaɓc kýfreıth
atal. Ɨaradỳr maɓı. dɓỳ geínhaɓc kýfreıth atal. Ꝑerued taradỳr keínhaɓc
kýfreıth atal. Ꝑbıll taradỳr araſkýl a
Serr. achaboluaen. dímeı atal pop vn.   15
Ɨɓlltỳr pedeır keínhaɓc kýfreıth atal.
Ꝺedýf agỳlýf acheıp a chrýman aguelleu
a chrıp a gɓdýf a bıllɓc a baýol helýc a baỳ-
ol guen mangỳlchaɓc achlaɓı pobı achıc
dýſgỳl. abaýol helýc bıỳn. agogỳr keín-   20
haɓc kýfreıth atal pop vn o honunt.

Pal ac ẏftỽc helẏc adẏſgẏl lẏdan arıdẏll
keínhaỽc cỽta atal pop vn. Gaẏol ẏỽ amıt
abudeı yſtẏllaỽc abudeı ren anoe a fıol lẏn
a níthlen aphadell troedaỽc pedeır keínhaỽc
kẏfreıth atal pop vn. Gurnen a lletuet   5
awhẏnglo fẏrllıg atal pop vn. Ɛeubal
pedeır arhugeínt atal. Rỽẏt ehogẏn ~~deu~~
~~dee~~ vn ar pẏmthec atal. Rỽẏt penllỽẏt=
eıt deudec keínhaỽc atal. Ʒallegrỽẏt pedeır geínhaỽc kẏfreıth atal. Ɛoıỽc ỽẏth   10
geínhaỽc kẏfreıth átal. Pỽẏ bẏnhac adot·
to rỽẏt ẏmẏỽn auon ar tír dẏn arall heb
ẏ ganhat traẏan ypẏſcaỽt ageıff ef a deuparth
ageıff perchenaỽc ẏtır. ẏr auon.

Neb atoıho aradẏr ar tır dẏn arall.   15
talet ıdaỽ aradẏr newẏd ac aradỽẏ
naỽ dıwarnaỽt. Guerth aradẏr newẏd
dỽẏ geínhaỽc gẏfreıth atal. Guerth aradỽẏ
vn dẏd dỽẏ geínhaỽc kẏfreıth atal. Guerth
ẏr hırıeu ae phíſtlon. keínhaỽc kẏfreıth.   20
Ɛal hẏn ẏdaỽ ẏllogeu. llog ẏr amaeth

ẏnẏ blaen. a guedẏ hẏnnẏ llog ẏſ6ch ar
c6lltẏr. Odẏna llog ẏr ẏch go2eu ẏnẏr
aradẏr. Odẏna llog ẏcathrea62. ac odẏ
na oo2eu ẏo2eu o2 ẏchen. Ꝡẏ dẏlẏ neb
o taẏa6ctref eredıc hẏnẏ gaffo pa6b o2   5
tref gẏfar. O2 bẏd mar6 ẏch otra eredıc
ẏ perchena6c ageıff er6 a honno aelwır
er6 ẏr ẏch du.

Pop g6ẏſtẏl adẏg6ẏd ẏm pen ẏna6
uet dẏd eıthẏr ẏreı hẏn. arueu e=   10
gl6ẏſſıc nẏ dẏlẏır eu g6ẏſtla6 achẏt
g6ẏſtler nẏ dẏg6ẏdant. G6lltẏr achall-
a62 ab6ell gẏnnut nẏ dẏg6ẏdant uẏth
kẏt g6ẏſtler. Ꝺet vn dẏd abl6ẏn ẏſſẏd
ẏ eur allurugeu alleſtrı go2eureıt pan   15
6ẏſtler. Ꝧyfreıth benfıc ẏ6 ẏdẏuot mal
ẏrother. Y neb arotho benffıc adẏlẏ kẏm
rẏt tẏſton rac mẏnet ẏnẏ erbẏn. O2 eır
enẏerbẏn ago2dıwef o2 perchenna6c ar=
na6 talet ẏndeudẏblıc. Ꝧ neb ada6ho   20
da ẏarall ac ofdıwat pan delher ẏouẏn.

| kẏfreıth |

kẏfreith anudon au(ẏ)d arna6 of ẏn gẏho⸗
eda6c ẏ tó́g. nẏt amgen trı buhẏn camló=
r6 ẏr bɪenhín. achẏmeret ẏnteu ẏpenẏt
am ẏranudon. arllall oɪ bẏd tẏſton gan
ta6 ẏ da ageıff.   5

e̩ Neb atalho galanaſ oɪ bẏd ẏgenedẏl
   oll ẏnvnwlat ac ef có́bẏl talu adẏlẏ erbẏn pen ẏ pẏthe6noſ oɪ bẏd ẏ gened=
ẏl ẏnteu ẏnwaſcara6t ẏguladoed llawer
oet pẏthe6noſ adẏlẏ ẏgkyueır pop gulat.   10

a̩ al hẏn ẏtelıŕ guaſcar alan aſ punt
   uẏd raṅ bɪa6t. Wheugeínt ran ke(ſ)
ẏnder6. Trugeınt ran kẏferder6. Dec ar
hugeínt ran kéſuẏn. Pẏmthec ẏ6 ran
goɪcheıuẏn. Seıth adímeı ran goɪcha6.   15
Nẏt oeſ pɪıa6t ran na phrıa6t en6 ar
ach pellach no hẏnnẏ. [Ɽ]an tat o alanaſ
ẏ uab. keínha6c. Vn gẏfreith ẏ6 ẏnẏ kẏ-
merher ran o alanaſ ac ẏtalher. Rac
collı kerenhẏd hẏnẏ dıwatter keínha6c   20
paladẏr ageffír. Ɖẏ thal. kenedẏl ſarhaet

gan neb. tra uo da ar ẏhelꝸ ehunan. Oꝛ
dıffẏc hagen ẏ da ef ıaꝸn ẏꝸ talu raıı ẏ
gẏt ac ef hẏt ẏ trẏded ach.

OEr gꝸẏmp galanaſ ẏꝸ pan latho ı
dẏn ẏllall. adodı oet dẏd ẏdíuꝸẏn   5
ẏgẏflauan honno. ae lad ẏnteu o dẏn
o genedẏl arall heb dẏlẏu dím ıdaꝸ. kẏn
díuꝸẏn ẏ gẏflauan honno. Sef ẏgelwır
ẏn oer gꝸẏmp galanaſ ẏgẏfreıth honno
rac trẏmhet ẏ gollı ef. athalu ẏgẏfla-   10
uan rẏwnathoed gẏnt.

PẎmhet dẏd kẏn gꝸẏl uſhagel ẏdẏlẏ ẏ bꝛenhín guahard ẏgoet. hẏt
ẏmpen pẏmthecuet dẏd guedẏ ẏr ẏſtꝸ-
ẏll. ac oꝛ moch agaffer ẏnẏ coet ẏdec-   15
uet llꝸdẏn ageıff ẏ bꝛenhín. hẏt ẏm
pen ẏnaꝸuetdẏd. ac odẏna allan ewẏllıf
ẏbꝛenhíṇ auẏd ẏm danunt.

Ꝺr serheır ẏríghẏll oe eıſted ẏnẏ dadleu talher ıdaꝸ ẏnẏ ſarhaet gogreıt   20
eıſſín achuccꝸẏ ꝸẏ. Ẏ bꝛenhín adẏlẏ

o anreıth. gre argeſuẏr ar dıllat amaer-
ốyaốc. ar arueu ar carcharoꝛẏon heb eu
rannu aneb. nẏ dẏlẏ ẏnteu traẏan ẏ
keſſẏc tom kanẏſ ẏſpeıl ẏnt. Ỿ neb a
dẏwetto ẏnſẏberố ốꝛth ẏbꝛenhín neu   5
ẏn hagẏr. talet trı buhẏn camlốrố ẏn
deudẏblẏc. Ƥan gẏmẻrho taẏaốc tır ẏ
gan ẏ bꝛenhín trugeınt adẏlẏ ẏ bꝛenhın
opop rantír ẏgan ẏtaẏaốc. ac oꝛbẏd e-
glốẏſ ar tır ẏtaẏaốctref wheugeınt ȧd-   10
aố ẏr bꝛenhín ẏgan ẏneb ae kẏmero.
Ꝃaeth arotho ẏbꝛenhín tır ıdaố dec a
phetwar ugeínt uẏd ẏ ebedıố. ar traẏ
an adaố ẏr maer ar kẏghellaốꝛ. Ꝓletuegín gureıc bꝛenhín neu ẏuerch punt   15
atal. Ꝓletuegín gureıc bꝛenhín neu ẏ   ×
uerch hanher punt atal. Ꝓletuegín gureıc taẏaốc neu ẏuerch keínhaốc cota
atal canẏ dẏlẏant ốẏ letuegíneu.
Ốốꝛ rẏd adẏlẏ atteb dꝛoſ ẏ alltut o pop   20
haốl nẏ dẏlẏho collı e tauaốt ac eneıt

ac aelodeu. kanẏ dẏlẏneb collı tauaȝt ac
eneıt ac aelodeu. o tauaȝt dẏn arall. Ȝue-
rth tudedẏn paraȝt ẏgkẏfreıth howel da
pedeır ar hugeínt arẏant. Ðẏrnaȝt agaffer o anuod nẏt farhaet. ıaȝn yȝ hagen dı- 5
uȝẏn ẏr anẏuet nẏt amgen guaet ague-
lı achreıth o gẏuarch o bẏd. Ðan talher
racdant guerth creıth o gẏfarch atelır gan-
vmp allwed ẏgneıtaeth ẏf- ¶ taȝ
fẏd. Vn yȝ ofẏn dẏ athro ae garu. 10
Eıl yȝ mẏnych ouẏn dẏ dẏfc. Tzẏdẏd yȝ
cadȝ genhẏt ẏdẏfc ageffẏch. Þetwe(r)ẏd
yȝ tremẏgu golut. Pẏmhet yȝ caffau
kelwẏd acharu guíryoned. rac ofyn duȝ.
Þȝybẏnhac atozho teruẏn ar tír dẏn 15
arall talet trı buhẏn camlȝzȝ ẏr bzenhín
agunaet ẏteruẏn ẏn gẏftal achẏnt.
Ẏneb atẏper am tẏftolẏaeth tẏget mal
ẏbo ıaȝn achẏfreıth ıdaȝ. ac ẏna kẏmeret ẏllall ẏcreır adıwatet ar ẏ lȝ allẏffet 20
ẏ tẏft. ac odẏna sẏllet ẏtẏft ẏr ygneıt

ae k6býl ỳllỳffỳant. Ẏ neb alỳffo týft.
kỳn d6ỳn ỳtýftolỳaeth collet ỳ dadỳl. Ør
dıwat g6ı o neb llu llad keleín. talet wheugeínt arodet l6 deg wýr a deugeínt vn
vıeínt ac ef ỳdıwat llofrudỳaeth. ẞ6ỳ   ·5
bỳnhac afarhaho ỳgılỳd owerín ỳ pete-
ır gulat. hỳn. Nỳt amgen deheubarth
g6ỳned. powỳf. lloegýr. talet pedeır bu
aphetwar ugeínt arỳant. ıda6. ẞ6ỳbỳn-
hac atalho galanaf ỳgılỳd. teır bu ath   10
trı ugeín mu heb ỳchwhanec atal. Ẏ neb
agaffo h6ch coet mar6 artırdỳn arall. kỳ-
meret ef ỳ whartha6ı blaen neffaf o ho-
na6. ẞ6ỳftuıl arall auo ıa6n ỳffu ỳ gıc.
ỳ whartha6ı ỳol ageffir. Os kadno neu   15
l6dỳn arall anhỳỳs keínha6c cota ageıff
ỳgan perchenna6c ỳtır oı mỳn ỳnteu
ỳ croen.

OEudỳblỳc uỳdant dır6ỳ achaml6ı6
llỳs allan. Os ỳnỳ uỳnwent ỳguneír 20
ỳ cam ỳnỳ nodua. Seıth punt ý6 meínt

ỳdır6ỳ.

.Hanher dırȯy llan ageıff ẏr abat oʒbẏd kẏuarwẏd ẏnllẏthẏır ac y moeſ eglȯys. ar
ʰanher arall ageıff meıbon lleẏn ẏreglȯyſ
Sef ẏ kymerant ȯẏ uellẏ pan del dırȯy
neu gamlȯʒȯ ẏgan naȯdwẏr ỵ̇ṛ eglȯy ẏ   5
llan udunt. ac ẏſef ẏrodır ẏda hȯnnȯ ẏn
enwedıc ẏr ſant ac nẏt ureſnt offrȯm.
Ðẏ daȯ kẏfran ẏr maer nac ẏr kẏghell-
aȯʒ o pʒıt a del ẏteẏrn dʒoſ tır nac o tȯng
nac o leıdẏr.   10
ORtẏr llog ar tır teẏrn ẏteẏrn bıeu.
ac oʒ tẏr llog ar tır eſcob deu hanher
uẏd rȯg ẏbʒenhín ar eſcob. Ꝑan dẏcco kẏſ
reıth anreıth o uarȯ tẏ neu oneb dadẏl arall. ẏteulu ar maer ageıff ẏr aneıred ar   15
enderíged ar dínewẏt ar deueıt ar geſuẏr
ac agaffer oll ẏnẏ tẏ eıthẏr meırch ac ẏch
en a guarthec maȯʒ ac eur ac arẏant a
dıllat amarȯyaȯc. ac oʒ bẏd^{m}peth auo
kẏwerthẏd punt bʒenhín bíeſuẏd. Ꞇra-   20
ẏan galanaſ adẏgȯyd ar perchennaȯc

ẏr arẏf ẏllather ẏ dẏn a hɩ. Ɖa addẏcker
oɿẏuel ẏhedỼch deu hanher uẏd' rỼg ẏ
neb ae dẏcco ar neb bɩeíuu gẏnt. Ɵɿ bẏd
deu dẏn ẏn ẏmdeɩth trỼẏ goet. ac ellỼg
gurẏſgen oɿ blaenhaf ar ẏr olhaf hẏnẏ   5
gollo ẏlẏgat ef adẏlẏ talu ẏlẏgat ẏr llall.
O Et ẏrỼg llẏſ allan naỼ níeu. ẏrodɩ
atteb. anaỼ níeu ẏrodɩ mach. anaỼ
níeu ẏrodɩ guír oɿ haỼl deíſſẏuedɩc. ƉaỼl
·o vn   gantref trɩ dɩeu ẏrodɩ atteb. a·   10
thrɩ ẏ   rodɩ mach. athrɩ ẏrodɩ guír oɿ
haỼl deíſſẏuedɩc. Ᵹ nẏ cantref neſſaf ꞉
pump níeu ẏrodɩ atteb. aphump ẏrodɩ
mach. a phump ẏ rodɩ guír. Ᵹ nẏ cantref trẏdẏd naỼ nɩeu ẏ rodɩ atteb. a naỼ   15
ẏrodɩ mach. anaỼ ẏrodɩ guír. ƉaỼ níeu
ẏarglỼẏd ẏẏmgoffau am ẏ lỼ. Ᵹm pop
dadleu ẏdẏlẏ bot ẏpump hẏn. Guẏſ
a haỼl ac atteb a barn athagneued.
P Ỽẏ bẏnhac atalho tɩr ẏ galanaſ kẏl-
llɩdet dɿoſtaỼ ẏr arglỼẏd kanẏſ rẏd   20

I 2

ẏdẏlẏ ẏtír uot ẏr neb ẏtalher ıdaƀ.   Tɀı llẏf-
feu adẏlẏ tẏfu ẏnẏ tır hƀnnƀ.   Meıllon.
a guẏc.   ac ẏfgall.   Ɑc nẏ bẏd mƀẏ guerth
buƀch oɀ tır hƀnnƀ noe hẏt pan uo ẏn
Ɗeu dẏn nẏ dẏlẏ ẏ bɀenh*ın*   ⸿ poɀı   5
gouẏn eu guerth kẏt llather ẏnẏ
wlat.   kaeth dẏn arall.   kanẏf medẏant
auẏd ẏdẏn ar ẏ gaeth mal ar ẏaneueıl.
Ɑr dẏn agaffer ẏn ẏmdeıth hẏt nof ẏn
ẏftauell ẏ bɀenhín.   heb tan.   aheb ga-   10
nhƀẏll kẏt llodho guaffan ae   thwẏr
ẏ bɀenhín hƀnnƀ nẏ dẏlẏır gouẏn ẏala
naf.   Ɓɀaƀdƀɀ adẏlẏ guarandaƀ ẏnllƀẏr
Ɑchadƀ ẏn gouaƀdẏr.   adẏfcu ẏn graf.   a
datganu ẏnwar a barnu ẏntrugaraƀc.   15
Ƙẏneuaƀt a erlıt kẏfreıth ac ẏna katwadƀẏ ẏƀ.   kẏneuaƀt a rac ulaenha
kẏfreıth.   Ɑc ẏna pan uo aƀdurdaƀt bɀen-
hínẏaeth ıdı katwadƀẏ ẏƀ.   Kẏneuaƀt
a raculaenha kẏfreıth eıffoes o damwe-   20
ín aní aníheu.   Ɑc ẏna nẏ chẏmhell hı

naƁ nſeu yrodı atteb. a naƁ yrodı mach.
a naƁ yrodı gƁır oʑ haƁl deıſſyfyt. NaƁ
nſeu yſſyd yarglƁyd y ymgoffau ae lƁ. Y
effeırat ymae hyny gaffo amſer gyntaf
yganu efferen. Ẏm pop dadleu y dyly ı   5
bot gƁys ahaƁl ac atteb a barn a thagnef-
ed. Pop adeılƁʑ maeſtır adyly kaffel trı
phʑen ygan yneb bıeıffo y coet mynho y
coetƁʑ na vynho ᛄ nenpʑen. a dƁy nenfoʑch.
❡ neb auo goʑuodaƁc dʑos arall ony eıll y   10
dƁyn Ɓʑth gyfreıth. dygƁydet dʑoſt ygoʑ-
uodaƁc yg kyfreıth yneb yd aeth ef dʑoſtaƁ.
Oet goʑuodaƁc y geıſſaƁ yoʑuodogaeth ᛄ
vn dyd ablƁydyn. ẞLeıdyr arother ar ve
ıcheu. ny dylyſr ydſuetha. Ɖy dyly neb   15
wneuthur ıaƁn nac atteb dʑos weıthʑet
y gaeth onyt am ledʑat. Ɖy dylyır gƁır
achyfreıth heb ypetwar defnyd hyn ᛄ ar
glƁyd kyffredſn. ac ygnat kadeıraƁc. a
dƁy pleıt gydʑychaƁl. Pƀy bynhac atoʑ-   20
ho kyfar awnel oe vod. talet trı buhyn ı
camlƁʑƁ yr bʑenhſn. ac yr kyfarƁʑ yar oll.
Ẏgƀeırglodyeu affoʑeſtır rac y moch. kanys llygru ytır awnant. Yneb ae kaffo ar
yweſrglaƁd neu ar y yt kyn y vot yn aeduet ᛄ 25

kymeret pedeir keínhaƀc. kyf. ygan perchennaƀc ymoch.   Os yt aeduet alygrant ꝛ
talher eu llƀgyr.

Owhe ffoꝛd ygƀahan dyn ae da. o goll.
ac aghyfarch. alledꝛat. benffic. a lloc.   5
ac adneu.   Oꝛ teir kyntaf ydylyır dala a dam-
dƀg.   Oꝛ teir ereıll ny dylyır onyt eturyt
megys yroder. Ɖyrnaƀt agaffer o anuod
ny sarhaet. ıaƀn yƀ hagen díuƀyn yr an
yued nyt amgen gƀaet a gƀelı achreıth o   10
gyſarch oꝛ byd. ꝶn werth uyd yneb aƀyſ-
tler. ar neb yrother yg gƀyſtyl dꝛoſtaƀ.
Ɖƀy bynhac adotto ar yſcrybyl llygru y yt.
eu perchennaƀc adyly eu ıachau ar ymeínt
ymynho ƀꝛth eu llƀgyr. ac ar nys tygho ꝛ   15
talet. Yneb agaffo ıaƀn o gƀbyl am y yt lly-
gredıc ygan perchennaƀc yſcrybyl. ny dyly na thal na dala yſcrybyl ar y kelefryt
hƀnnƀ gƀedy hynny.

Ɉmp ꝛ pedeir keínhaƀc. kyf. atal hyt galan   20
gayaf rac ƀyneb. O hynny allan dƀy geínhaƀc pop tymhoꝛ adꝛycheıf arnaƀ hyny
odıwetho ffrƀyth. ac yna trugeínt atal.
ac ƀꝛth hynny ymae vn werth ímp allo
buch uaƀꝛ oꝛ dechꝛeu hyt y dıwed.   25

E Neb atypper am tyſtolyaeth. tyget mal
y bo kyfreithaɤl ıdaɤ. ac yna kymeret
yllall ycreır adıwadet ar y lɤ. allyſſet y tyſt.
Odyna edıycher ae cɤbyl y llyſſɤyt. Yneb a
lyſſo tyſt kyn dɤyn y tyſtolyaeth ꞉ collet y   5
dadyl. alyſſo tyſt ꞉ llyſſet kyn kılyaɤ y tyſt
yɤıth ycreır gɤedy tygho y tyſtolyaeth. ac
onys llyſſa yna ꞉ bıt s auedıc y tyſt. Tyſt ar
tyſt ꞉ ny byd oet ıdaɤ. ¶n rym yɤ gɤybydy-
eıt athyſton achyſtal a allant ym pop dad-   10
yl agɤell yndadyl tır a dayar. ⊕et tyſton
neu warant tra moı ꞉ vn dyd ablɤydyn.
⊕et tyſton neu warant goıwlat ꞉ pytheɤnos.
⊕ et tyſton neu warant kywlat ꞉ naɤ dıw
arnaɤt. ⊕et tyſton neu warant vn gym-   15
hɤt ꞉ trı dıeu. Y neb auynho díuɤnaɤ
tyſtolyaeth varwaɤl ꞉ aet yn erbyn yneb ae
tyſto. Y neb auynho llyſſu tyſtolyaeth vy-
waɤl ꞉ aet yn erbyn y tyſt   yn gyntaf ar
eu geıreu. ac odyna gɤedy tyghont eu llɤ ꞉   20
tyget ynteu rytygu anudon o honaɤ a dy
wedet nat tyſt kyfreithaɤl arnaɤ ac enwet
yr achaɤs. athyſtet ydeu   ɤı nat aeth
ytyſt yn erbyn yr achaɤs yllyſſɤyt. ar deu
hynny gɤıthtyſton ygelwır. a dılıs uydant.   25

Pan tyſto tyſt peth yny tyſtolyaeth yn gyfreithaƀl y a ereill yn erbyn am diffynnƀꝛ
Neu pan tyſto amdiffynnƀꝛ peth yn gyfreithaƀl yn erbyn tyſton ꞉ yrei hynny a el-
wit gƀꝛthtyſton yg kyfreith. ac ny dylyir   5
eu llyſſu. Ɛalƀ gƀybydyeit a ellir yr amſer
ymynho yneb ae mynho galwo. ae kyn gƀat
ac amdiffyn ae gƀedy. kanys yr hyn afu
kyn dadyl a pꝛouant rƀg y dadleuwyr.
                                                     abg
Ɛƀꝛthneu Gƀybydyeit yƀ pan ymdoſſont   10
goſſont gyntaf o yn erbyn yr amdiffynƀꝛ
oꝛ achƀyſſon hyn. ae o anudon kyhoedaƀc.
ae o yſpeil gyhoedaƀc ae yn lledꝛat ae y treis.
ar hedƀch. neu o yſcymundaƀc geir yenƀ.
neu o gerenhyd nes. neu o digaſſed honhe-   15
it. neu oe vot yn gyfrannaƀc ar y da y bo
ydadyl ymdanaƀ. ahynny kyn eu mynet
yn eu cof. Ony dichaƀn ef eu gƀꝛthneu ƀy
yn gyfreithaƀl yna. Gƀedy hynny. llyſſet
ƀynt mal tyſton o vn oꝛ teir ffoꝛd kyfreith   20
Pƀy bynhac awnel kynllƀyn ꞉   ¶ aƀl.
    yn deudyblyc y telir. kanys treis yƀ
ar dyn y lad. ac ynlledꝛat ygudyaƀ. allyna
yr vn lle y kygeín treis alledꝛat yndaƀ yg
kyfreith. ac val hyn ygƀedir. llƀ deg wyr   25

a deu vgeint y wadu coet a maes. athrı o
honunt yn dıofredaϭc. o gıc. a gϭɀeıc. a mar-
chogaeth.   Sef yϭ meſſur gϭadu coet ama-·
es.   rantır kyfreıthaϭl rϭg rϭyd a dyrys a choet amaes agϭlyb asych.   aͨ ar ny allo gϭa-· 5
du rantır yn gyfreıthaϭl.   ny dıchaϭn gϭadu
coet a maes.   Ny byd kynllϭyn ynteu oɀ
byd ar ffoɀd gyfreıth heb gud a heb gel arnaϭ.   Oɀ byd ynteu dɀos yffoɀd pump kam
kyfreıthaϭl.   aphump kam troetued ym   10
pop kam ꞉ kynllϭyn uyd.   allyna yr achaϭs
ygϭedır velly.   aͨ ytelır yndeudyblyc.   a lly-
na yr vn lle ydylyır croc ac anreıth ymdanaϭ.

Eıth eſcob ty yſſyd yndyfet. a mynyϭ
yϭ ypenhaf ygkymry. Llan ıſmael.   15
a llan degeman.   a llan vſſyllt.   a llan Teılaϭ.
a llan teulydaϭc. a llan geneu. Abadeu teılaϭ atheulydaϭc aͨ ıſmael adegeman ady·
lyant vot yn yſcolheıgon vɀdolyon.   Deudec
punt yϭ ebedıϭ pop vn o hynny ac y arglϭ-   20
yd dyuet ytelır. ar neb adel gϭedy ϭynt ae
tal.   Ryd yϭ mynyϭ opop dylyet.   LLan keneu
allan vſſyllt ryd ynt oɀ dylyet hϭnnϭ kanyt
oes tır vdunt.   Y neb aſarhao vn oɀ abadeu
hynny ꞉ talet ṣͦɨth punt ıdaϭ.   a golchures   25
oe genedyl yr gϭaratwyd yr genedyl aͨ yg kof
                              ¶ y dıal.

TRı dygyn goll kenedyl ꞉ vn yỽ bot
mab amheuedıc heb dỽyn a heb
wadu. allad o hỽnnỽ gỽı o gened-
yl arall heb dylyu dím ıdaỽ. Talu yr alanaſ
honno oll adylyır. ac odyna ywadu ynteu   5
rac gỽneuthur o honaỽ yr eıl gyflauan. Eıl
yỽ talu galanaſ oll eıthyr keínhaỽc a dı-
meı. ac oı byd godoı am hynny. a llad dyn
oı genedyl am y godoı hỽnnỽ. nyt oes ofyn ymdanaỽ. Tıydyd yỽ pan enllıper gỽır-   10
yon aın geleın ae holı. ac onys gỽatta erbyn oet kyfreıth. ac oı lledır dyn ymdanaỽ.
ny dylyır díuỽyn ymdanaỽ.

TRı oet kyfreıth ydıal keleín rỽg dỽy
genedyl ny hanffont o vn wlat ꞉ en-   15
uynu haỽl yny dyd kyntaf oı gyſſefín ỽyth-
nos yllather ygeleín. ac ony daỽ atteb pen
erbyn pen ypytheỽnos. kyfreıth yn rydhau
dıal. Eıl yỽ oı byd y dỽy genedyl yn vn gantref. enuynu haỽl yny trydyd dyd gỽedy llath   20
er y geleín. ac ony daỽ atteb erbyn pen y
naỽuetdyd ꞉ kyfreıth ynrydhau dıal. Tıydyd
yỽ os yn vn gymhỽt ybyd y dỽy genedyl.
enuynu haỽl yny trydyd dyd gỽedy llath
er ygeleín. ac ony daỽ atteb erbyn pen y   25

whechet dyd. kyfreith yn rydhau dial.

Eır r6yt bıenhín ynt. y díu6yn teulu ː
nyt oes díu6yn am yr6yt honno onyt
trugared ybıenhín. Eıl y6 yre ː o pop march
adalher erní. pedeır keínha6c kyfreith age-   5
ıff y bıenhín. Tıyded y6 g6arthec y vaerty.
o pop eıdon adalher arnunt. pedeır keínha6c
.kyf. ageıff y bıenhín. 6eır r6yt bıeyr ynt.
yre. Ag6arthec y vaerty. ae voch. kanys oı
keffir ll6dyn yn eu plıth ː pedeır keínha6c   10
.kyf. ageıff ybıeyr o pop ll6dyn. 6eır r6yt
taya6c ynt. ywarthec. ae voch. ae hentref.
pedeır keínha6c cotta ageıff ytaya6c o pop
ll6dyn agaffer yndunt o galan meı hyt pan

Eır dır6y bıenhín ynt ː ❡ darffo medı.   15
Dır6y treıs. Adır6y ledıat. a dır6y ymlad kyfadef. Díu6yn dır6y treıs y6 g6yalen
aryant. a ffíol eur. achla6ı eur yny mod y
dywefp6yt yn díu6yn farhaet bıenhín.
Díu6yn dır6y ymlad kyfadef y6 deudec   20
mu. Díu6yn dır6y ledıat y6. kyff6yna6 lledıat ar dyn. a g6adu o hona6 yn da arytaua-
6t. a goffot reith arna6 ae phallu. lleıdyr
kyfadef can pall6ys yreith. G6ıryon oe pen
ehunan ae taua6t. ny delıt dím ganta6.   25

ny chahat dím yny laб. deudeg mu dırбy
arnaб. Ꝺrı anhebcoꝛ bꝛenhín ynt. y effeırat teulu. ae ygnat llys. ae teulu. [Ꝺ]rı
pheth ny chyfran bꝛenhın a neb. y eur-
graбn. a e hebaбc. ae leıdyr.　　　　　　5

Ꝺ Rı phetwar yffyd. petwar achaбs yd
ymhoelır bꝛaбt. o ofyn gбꝛ kadarn.
achas galon. acharyat kyfeıllon. a serch
da. ¶ Eıl petwar yffyd ⁖ pedeır taryan a a
yrбg dyn areıth gбlat rac haбl ledꝛat. Vn　10
yб kadб gбeftı yn gyfreıthaбl. nyt amgen
noe gadб o pꝛyt goꝛchyfaerбy hyt y boꝛe.
a dodı ylaб dꝛoftaб teır gбeıth y nos honno.
a hynny tygu o honaб adynyon y ty gantaб. Eıl yб geni ameıthꝛín. Tygu oꝛ perch-　15
ennaбc ary trydyd o wyr vn vꝛeínt ac ef.
gбelet gení yr anefeıl ae veıthꝛín ar y helб
heb y vynet teır nos yбꝛthaб. Tꝛydyd yб
gбarant. Petweryd yб gбaꝛạı kadб kyn
koll. a hynny tygu oꝛ dyn ary trydyd o wyr　20
vn vꝛeínt ac ef. kyn kollı oꝛ llall y da. bot y
da hбnnб ary helб ef. Nyt oes warant namyn hyt ar teır llaб. Gбneuthur oꝛ tryded
laб kadб kyn koll. a hynny adıffer dyn
rac lledꝛat. ¶ Tꝛydyd petwar ynt. pet-　25

war dyn nyt oes naᲒd udunt rac y bꙅenhꙇn.
nac yn llys nac yn llan. Vn yᲒ dyn atoꙅho
naᲒd ybꙅenhꙇn yn vn oꙅ teir gᲒyl arbenhꙇc.
Eꙇl yᲒ dyn aᲒyſtler oe vod yr bꙅenhín. Tꙅydyd
yᲒ y gᲒynoſſaᲒc. dyn adylyho ypoꙅthꙇ ac ae   5
gatto ynoſ honno heb uᲒyt. petweryd yᲒ y
Eꙇr kyflauan os gᲒna dyn   ❡ gaeth.
yny wlat. ydyly y vab collꙇ tref ytat
oe hachaᲒs o gyfreꙇth. llad y arglᲒyd. a llad
y penkenedyl. a llad y teꙇſpan tyle. rac trym- 10
het y kyflauaneu hynny. Გrꙇ thawedaᲒc
goꙅfed. arglᲒyd gᲒꙇr yn gᲒarandaᲒ ary wyr
da yn barnu eu kyfreꙇtheu. ac ygnat yn
gᲒarandaᲒ haᲒl ac atteb. a mach yn gᲒarandaᲒ haᲒlᲒꙅ ac amdꙇffynnᲒꙅ ynymatteb.   15
Rꙇ gᲒanas gᲒayᲒ kyfreꙇthaᲒl yn dadleu. Vn yᲒ gᲒan y arlloſt yny dayar ac
vn llaᲒ. hyny vo abꙅeꙇd y tynnu a dᲒy laᲒ.
Eꙇl yᲒ gᲒan ypen ymyᲒn tᲒyn hyny gudyo
ymᲒn. Გꙅydyd yᲒ ydodꙇ ar lᲒyn auo kyfuᲒch   20
a gᲒꙅ. ac ony byd yn vn oꙅ teir gᲒanas hynny. a mynet dyn arnaᲒ mal ybo marᲒ꞉ trayan galanas ydyn adygᲒyd ar perchennaᲒc
y gᲒayᲒ. Გrꙇ ofer ymadꙅaᲒd adywedꙇr yn
llys ac ny ffynnant. GᲒat kyn deturyt.   25

a llys kyn amfer. achyghaбs gбedy bıaбt.
Ꝣrí ofer llaeth yffyd ꝫ llaeth kaffec. allaeth gaft. allaeth kath. kany w dıwygır
vn o honunt. Ꝥeır sarhaet ny dıwy-
gır oı keffır trбy veddaбt. Sarhaet yr ef-   5
feırat teulu. a farhaet yr ygnat llys.
a sarhaet ymedyc llys. kany dylyant
бy bot yn vedб. бıth na бdant py amfer
y bo reıt yr bıenhín бıthunt. Ꝥeır pal-
uaбt ny dıwygır. vn arglбyd aryбı yny   ꞏ 10
reolı yn dyd kat a bıбydyr. ac vn tat
ar y vab yr ygofpı. ac vn penkenedyl
ar y gar yr y gẏghoıı.
Ꝥ Eır gбıaged ny dylyır dadleu ac eu
hetıued am tref eu mam. gбıeıc a   15
rother yg gбyftyl dıos tır. achaffel mab
o honeı yny gбyftloıyaeth. a mab ywreıc
adıalho dyn ogenedyl y vam. ac o achaбf
hynny collı tref ytat ohonaб. ac бıth hynny ny dylyır dadleu ac ef am tref y vam.   ꞏ 20
amab ywreıc a rother oꞏrod kenedyl y alltut. Ꝣrı chewılyd kenedyl ynt ꝫ ac o achaбs gбıeıc ymaent ell trı ꝫ llathrudaб gбıeıc oe hanuod. Eıl yб dбyn gбıeıc arall ary
phen hıtheu yr ty. ae gyrru hıtheu allan.   25

Tɪydyd yͷ y hyſpeɪlaͷ. bot yn well gantaͷ y
hyſpeɪlaͷ no bot genthɪ. . Ʒrɪ chehyryn
canhaſtyr yſſyd ꞓ Vn yͷ lledɪat yffoɪd ykertho kyfran o honaͷ. kanyſ naͷ affeɪth yſſyd
ɪdaͷ. Eɪl yͷ hyd bɪenhín póy bynhac ae ky-   5
llello. Tɪydyd yͷ abo bleɪd. y neb awnel kam
ym dananaͷ. Ʒrɪ chadarn en llɪp gͷɪeɪc
ynt ꞓ Vn yͷ gͷɪeɪc gͷelet ygͷɪ arwreɪc yn
dyuot oɪ vn llͷyn vn o pop parth yr llͷyn.
Eɪl yͷ gͷelet ell deu dan vn vantell. Tɪydyd   10
yͷ gͷelet ygͷɪ róg' deu voɪdͷyt ywreɪc. -
Ʒrɪ pheth a haͷl dyn yn lledɪat ac ny chygeín lledɪat yndunt. eredɪc. a dɪot coet. aca-
deɪlat. Ʒeɪr sarhaet gͷɪeɪc ynt. Vn adɪych-
eɪff. ac vn a oftͷg. ac vn yſſyd ſarhaet gͷ-   15
byl. Pan rother cuſſan ɪdɪ oe hanuod. tray
an y sarhaet yſſyd eɪſſeu ɪdɪ yna. Eɪl yͷ y
phaluu. a honno yſſyd sarhaet gͷbyl
ɪdɪ. Tɪyded yͷ bot genthɪ oe hanuod. a
honno adɪycheɪf .y trayan. 0 teɪr ffoɪd   20
y llyſſɪr tyſton. otɪrdɪa. a galᵃᵘaſtra. agͷɪeɪctra.
ꞪRɪ meɪb yn trɪ ~~meɪ~~ bɪoder vn vam
vn tat. ac ny dylyant kaffel ran ọ
otɪr gan eu bɪodyr vn vam vn tat ac ͷynt.
Vn yͷ mab llͷyn apherth. agͷedy hynny   25

kymryt oꝛ vn gwꝛ yr vn wreic o rod kenedyl
achaffel mab o honeı. ny dyly ymab hwnnw kyfrannu tır ar mab agahat kyn
noc ef yn llwyn apherth. Eıl yw kymryt
o yſcolheic wreic o rod kenedyl. achaffel   5
mab o honno. ac odyna kymryt vꝛdeu
effeıradaeth oꝛ yſcolheic. agwedy hynny
kaffel mab oꝛ effeırat hwnnw oꝛ wreic kynt.
ny dyly y mab kyntaf kyfrannu tır ar
diwethaf. kanys yn erbyn dedyf y kah-   10
at. Tꝛydyd yw mut. kany dyly tır net
atteppo dꝛoſtaw. kany rodir gwlat y uut.
Ꝛ Rı dẏn agynnyd eu bꝛeint yn vn
dyd. Tayawctref y kyffeccrer eglwys
yndı. gan ganhat ybꝛenhín. dyn oꝛ tref   15
honno aueı y boꝛe yn tayawc. auydeı y
nos honno yn wꝛ ryd. Eıl yw dyn yrotho
ybꝛenhın ıdaw vn oꝛ pedeır swyd ar huge
ínt bꝛeínhawl. kyn rodı y swyd ıdaw yn
tayawc꞉ agwedy yrodı yn wꝛ ryd. Tꝛydyd   20
yw yſcolheic ydyd ykaffo coꝛun y boꝛe yn
vab tayawc. ar nos honno yn wꝛ ryd.
Ꝛ Rı gwerth kyfreıth beıchogı gwꝛeic.
Vn yw gwaet kyn delwat oꝛ collır
trwy greulonder꞉ wyth adeu vgeínt a   25

tal. Eil yϐ kyn mynet eneit yn daϐ oꝛ collir
trϐy greulonder. trayan yalanas atelir ym-
danaϐ. Tꝛydyd yϐ gϐedy yd el eneit yndaϐ
oꝛ collir trϐy greulonder. cϐbyl oe alanas
atelir ym danaϐ yna. 5

O Teir ffoꝛd y dygir mab y tat. Vn yϐ gϐꝛe-
ic lϐyn apherth oꝛ byd beichaϐc pan
vo ar y llaϐuaeth. dyget ypheriglaϐꝛ etti.
athyget ϐꝛthaϐ. efcoꝛ neidyr imi yar ybeich-
ogi hϐn os creϐys tat gan vam onyt ygϐꝛ 10
ydygaf idaϐ ae enwi. ac uelly kyfreithaϐl
ydϐc. Eil yϐ penkenedyl aseith laϐ kenedyl
gantaϐ bieu y dϐyn. Tꝛydyd yϐ ony byd pen
kenedyl: llϐ deg wyr adeu vgeint oe genedyl ae dϐc. ar mab ehunan atϐg yny blaen. 15
kanyt kyfreithaϐl llϐ y vam onyt ar dygyat vꝛy.

O Teir ffoꝛd ygϐedir mab o genedyl. ky
mryt ymab oꝛ gϐꝛ ydywetter y vot yn
vab idaϐ. ae dodi yrodaϐ ar allaϐꝛ. adodi y llaϐ
affeu ar pen y mab. ar llaϐ deheu ar yr alla- 20
ϐꝛ ar creireu. athyget nas creϐys ef ac nat
oes dafyn oe waet yndaϐ. Eil yϐ ony byd
ytat yn vyϐ penkenedyl bieu ywadu ase-
ithlaϐ kenedyl gantaϐ. Tꝛyded yϐ ony
byd penkenedyl idaϐ. llϐ deg wyr adeu vge- 25

ínt oɹ genedyl ae gƀatta. aɾ mab hynhaf yr
gƀɹ yd oed ymab ar y gyſtlƀn bıeu tygu yny
blaen. Ƀrı lle ny dyly dyn rodı llƀ gƀeılyd.
Vn yƀ ar pont vñ pɹen heb ganllaƀ. Eıl yƀ
ar poɹth y vynwent. kanys canu y pater ady   5
ly yna rac eneıteu crıſtonogyon ybyt. Tɹy-
dyd yƀ aɹdɹƀs yreglƀys. kanyſ canu y pater
adyly yna rac bɹon ygroc. Ɖyn odynyon adı
eínc rac llƀ gƀeılyd. arglƀyd. ac eſcob. a mut
..a bydar ac aghyfıeıthus agƀɹeıc veıchaƀc.   10
Ƀeır goɹmes doeth ynt ⁚ meddaƀt. agodíneb.
a dɹyc anyan. Ƀrı dyn adyly tauodyaƀc yn
llys dɹoſtunt. gƀɹeıc. achryc anyanaƀl. ac all-
tùt aghyfıeıthus. Vn dyn adyly dewıs ytaf-
odyaƀt. arglƀyd. Ƀrı llydyn dıgyfreıth eu gƀe- 15
ıthɹet yn eu hydɹef ar aníueılet mut. yſtal-
ƀyn. atharƀ trefgoɹd. abaed kenueín. Ƀrı
llydyn nyt oes werth kyfreıth arnunt. knyƀ
hƀch. abıtheıat. a bɹoch. Ƀrı gƀaet dıgyfreıth
yſſyd. gƀaet o pen crach. agƀaet froen. agƀa- 20
et deínt. ony thɹewır trƀy lıt. Ƀrı than dıgy-
ureıth eu gƀeıthɹet. tan godeıth o hanher ma-
ƀɹth hyt hanher ebɹıll. athan eneínt trefgoɹd.
athan gefeıl auo naƀ kam yƀɹth y tref. athò
banadyl neu tywarch erní. Ƀrı edyn y dyly   25

ybɹenhın eu gỽerth py tu bynhac y llather.
Eryr. a garan. a chıcuran. Perchennaỽc ytır
y llather arnaỽ adyly dec adeu vgeínt ygan y
neb ae llatho. Ƿrı phryf ydyly y bɹenhın eu
gỽerth py tu bynhac y llather. lloſtlydan. a be- 5
leu. a charlỽnc. kanys oc eu crỽyn ygỽneır
amaerỽyeu ydıllat ybɹenhín. Ƿrı pheth
nyat kyfreıth eu damdỽg. blaỽt. agỽenyn.
ac aryant. kanys kyffelyp ageffır udunt.
Ƿeır cont kyfreıthaỽl yſſyd. cont gaſt. achont 10
kath. achont gỽıweır. kanys dıllỽg ac ellỽg
a allant pan vynhont. Ƿrı phɹen ryd ynffoɹ-
eſt bɹenhín. pɹen crıp eglỽys. aphren peleı-
dyr a elhont ynreıt ybɹenhín. aphren eloɹ.
Ƿrı choɹn buelyn y bɹenhín. y goɹn kyfed. 15
ae goɹn kyweıthas. ae goɹn yn llaỽ y penkynyd. punt atal pop vn. Ƿeır hela ryd yſſyd
ympop gỽlat. hela ıỽɹch. a hela kadno. a hela
dyfyrgı. kanyt oes tref tat vdunt. Ƿrı pheth
atyrr ar gyfreıth. treıs. ac amot. ac aghen 20
octıt. Ƿrı enỽ rıghyll yſſyd. gỽaed gỽlat.
a garỽ gychwedyl gỽas y kyghellaỽɹ. a rıghyll.
Ø teır ffoɹd ytelır gỽyalen aryant yr bɹenhín.
am treıs. ac am toɹrı naỽd ffoɹd ar achenaỽc
dıatlam. ac am sarhaet bɹenhín. 25

K 2

ⓖRı h(ѵ)ʒd ny dıwẏg(ır.) vn yѵ gofynıaѵn (o)
dyn y(e)lyn am (ygar) yn trı dadleu ac na
chaffeı ıaѵn. achyfaruot y elyn ac ef gѵedy
hynny. a gѵan hѵʒd yndaѵ a(gѵayѵ hyny vo)
marѵ. ny dıwygır yr h(ѵʒd hѵnnѵ.) Eıl yѵ gѵ   5
neuthur eıdıged o wreıc ѵʒya(ѵc ѵʒth wreı)c
arall am ygѵʒ. achyfaruot y dѵ(y wraged)y
gyt. a gѵan hѵʒd oʒ wreıc ѵʒyaѵc ae dѵy laѵ
yny llall hyny vo marѵ. ny dywygır ıdı.
Tʒydyd yѵ rodı moʒѵyn ~~yѵʒ~~ aeduet yѵʒ a   10
mach ar ymoʒѵyndaѵt. a gѵan hѵʒd oʒ gѵʒ
yndı a bonlloft. ae hymreın vn weıth. ae
(chaffel yn) wreıc. ynteu adyly galѵ y neıth
(aѵ)ʒwyr attaѵ. ac enynnu canhѵylleu allad (ych)rys tu rocdı yn gyfuch agѵarr y(ch)   15
ont. ac oʒ tu dʒae chefyn yn gyfu(ch) athal-
yphedʒeın. ae gollѵg ar hѵʒd hѵnnѵ (y)n
dı heb y dıfѵyn ıdı. a hynny yѵ kyfreıth
tѵyll voʒѵyn. ☙rı dyn ny dylyır eu (gѵer-)
thu o gyfreıth. lleıdyr kyfadef am bo g(ѵe)   20
rth pedeır keınhaѵc kyfreıth yny laѵ. (ach)
ynllѵynѵʒ. a bʒadѵʒ (arglѵ)yd. ☙rı (da dılıf)
dıuach y(ffyd.) da (arotho arglѵyd yѵʒ) ac ade(l)
ıdaѵ ynteu gan gyfreı(th). ada a gaffo gѵʒe-
ıc gan ygѵʒ p(an gy)ttyo ynteu agѵ(ʒe)ıc   25

┌──────┐
│ arall │
└──────┘

penkẏnẏd. punt atal pop vn o honunt.
Ꝥri hela rẏd ẏffẏd ẏm pop gulat hela i6ꝛch.
a hela dẏfẏrgi. ahela cadno. kanẏt oes
tref tat udunt. Ꝥri pheth atẏr ar gẏfre
ith. treif ac amot ac aghenoctit. ·   . 5
Ꝥꝛi h6ꝛd nẏ diwẏgir. Vn ẏ6 gouẏn ia-
6n odẏn am ẏgar ẏelẏn. ẏn tri dadleu.
ac na chaffei ia6n. achẏuaruot ẏelẏn ac
ef guedẏ hẏnnẏ. aguan h6ꝛd ẏnda6 a gua-
ẏ6 hẏnẏ uei uar6. nẏ diwẏgir ida6 ẏrh6ꝛd   10
h6nn6. Eil ẏ6 guneuthur eidiged o wreic
6ꝛẏa6c 6ꝛth wreic arall am ẏ g6ꝛ achẏfar
uot ẏ d6ẏ wraged ẏ gẏt. aguan h6ꝛd oꝛ
wreic 6ꝛẏa6c ẏnẏ llall ae d6ẏ la6 hẏnẏ
uo mar6 nẏ diwẏgir idi. Tꝛẏdẏd ẏ6 rodi   15
moꝛ6ẏn ẏ 6ꝛ amach ar ẏmoꝛ6ẏn da6t a
guan h6ꝛd ẏndi oꝛ g6ꝛ a bonlloft ae hẏm-
rein vn weith hi. ae chaffel ẏn wreic hi.
Ẏnteu adẏlẏ gal6 atta6 ẏneitha6ꝛwẏr
aennẏnu canh6ẏlleu. a llad ẏchrẏf tu   20
dꝛae chefẏn ẏn gẏuu6ch athal ẏ phedꝛein.

ac oɪ tu recdı ẏn gẏfu6ch aguarr ẏchont.
ae goll6g ar h6ɪd h6nn6 ẏndı heb ẏdí
u6ẏn ıdı. a hẏnnẏ ẏ6 kẏfreıth t6ẏll
voɪ6yn.

TRı dẏn nẏ dẏlẏır eu guerthu gan   5
gẏfreıth. lleıdẏr kẏfadef am bo
guerth pedeır keínha6c kẏfreıth ẏnẏ
la6. achẏnll6ẏn6ɪ. a bɪad6ɪ argl6ẏd.
Gri en6 rıghẏll ẏffẏd. gul guaed gulat.
a gar6 gẏchwedẏl guaſ ẏ kẏghella6ɪ.   10
a ríghẏll. O teír foɪd ẏ telır guẏalen
arẏant ẏr bɪenhín a fiol eur achla6ɪ
eur erní. O d6ẏn treıſ ar wreıc. ac o toɪ-
rı na6d foɪd ar ẏchena6c dıatlam. ac
am farhaet bɪenhín. Grı da dılẏſ dı-   15
uach ẏffẏd. da arotho ẏ bɪenhín ẏ 6ɪ.
ac a del ıda6 ẏnteu gan gẏfreıth. a da
agaffo gureıc gan ẏg6ɪ ẏnẏ h6ẏneb-
werth. pan gẏtẏo ẏ g6ɪ agureıc arall.
a da adẏcker ẏn ryuel deu argl6ẏd.   20
Grı chẏffredín gulat ẏffẏd. lluẏd a

dadleu. ac egl6ẏf. kanẏf guẏf auẏd
ar pa6b vdunt.

Eir guarthrut mo26ẏn ẏffyd.
Vn ẏ6 dẏwed6ẏt oe that 62thı.
mí athrodeıs uo26ẏn ẏ62. Eıl ẏ6 erchı   5
ıdı mẏnet ẏ gẏfgu at ẏg62. T2ẏdẏd
ẏ6 ẏ guelet ẏbo2e ẏn kẏuot ẏ62th ẏ
g62. ac o acha6f pop vn o2 trı hẏnnẏ
ẏ tal ẏg62 ẏ hamwabẏr ẏ hargl6ẏd.
ae chowẏll ae heguedı ıdı hıtheu. 6rı   10
argae guaet ẏffyd. mẏnwef. a gure=
gẏf. perued. aguregẏf lla6d62. 6rı dı=
6ẏneb gulat ac nẏ ellır bot heb dunt
argl6ẏd. ac effeırat. achẏfreıth. 6eir
ael6ẏt adẏlẏ guneuthur ıa6n ae gẏm-   15
rẏt d2of dẏn nẏ bo argl6ẏd adef ıda6.
tat. a b2a6t hẏnaf. awhegr6n.

Eir notwẏd kẏfreıtha6l ẏffyd.
notwẏd guenıga6l ẏurenhínef.
anotwẏd medẏc ẏ wnía6 ẏguelıeu.   20
a notwẏd ẏpenkẏnẏd ẏwnía6 ẏk6n

rõygedıc pedeır keínhaõc kẏfreıth atal
pop vn o honunt. Notwẏd gureıc kẏwre-
ín arall keínhaõc kẏfreıth atal.

Eır marõ tẏftolẏaeth ẏffẏd. ac afa
uant ẏn dadleu ẏn da. Vn ẏõ pan   5
vo amrẏffon ac ẏmlad rõg deu arglõẏd
am tír. a theruẏnu hõnnõ ẏndẏlẏe-
duf ẏgõẏd paõb ẏna. a guedẏ ẏbo marõ ẏníueroed hẏnnẏ eu meıbon neu
eu hõẏrẏon neu reı oc eu kenedẏl a all-   10
ant dõẏn tẏftolẏaeth am ẏ tır hõnnõ.
ar reı hẏnnẏ a elwır gõẏbẏdẏeft am tır.
Eıl ẏõ dẏnẏon bonhedıc o pop parth.
amhínogẏon tır ẏgelwír ẏreı hẏnnẏ ẏ
dofparth trõẏ ach ac eturẏt achadarnhau   15
gan dõẏn tẏftolẏaeth a allant ẏ achwa-
negu dẏlẏet ẏdẏn ar tır a daẏar. Tɪẏdẏd ẏõ pan welher pentanuaen tat.
neu ẏhendat. neu oɪ hendat neu vn
oɪ genedẏl un dẏlẏet ac ef alle ẏteı ae   20
ẏfcuboɪẏeu a rẏcheu ẏtır ar ardõẏt. ar

erwẏd

erwẏd pòp un oꝛ reı hẏnnẏ arodant tẏf
tolẏaeth ẏdẏn ar ẏdẏlẏet. Ꝺeír kẏfrınach
ẏffẏd ẏ well eu hadef noc eu kelu.   colledeu
argl6ẏd .achẏnll6ẏn allad odẏn ẏ tat ot
adeuír ẏg kẏfrínach.   5

Ꝺꝛı aníueıl un troeta6c ẏffẏd.   march.
a heba6c. a gellgı.   P6ẏ bẏnhac atoꝛho troet un o honunt talet ẏwerth ẏn
holla6l. Ꝺrı pheth nẏ thelır kẏn coller
ẏn rantẏ. kẏllell. achledẏf. a lla6d6r. ka-   10
nẏf ẏneb bıeıffont adẏlẏ eu cad6. Ꝺeır
farhaet keleín ẏnt. pan lather. pan ẏf
peıler. pan uẏrhẏer ẏnẏ oꝛwed. Ꝺeır
guarthrut keleín ẏnt. gouẏn p6ẏ ae llad=
a6d. pıeu ẏr eloꝛ hon. pıeu ẏ bed h6n.   15
Ꝺrı g6g nẏ dıwẏgír. g6g g6ꝛ 6ꝛth ẏwreıc
agẏmerho ar ureínt moꝛ6ẏn ahıtheu   ·
ẏn wreıc. a dẏn adıffethaer o gẏfreıth.
adẏn oe genedẏl ẏn guneuthur g6g am
hẏnnẏ. a g6g dẏn 6ꝛth gı ẏnẏ ruthra6.   20
Ꝺeır gauael nẏt atuerır. dꝛof letrat.

athrof vach nẏ chẏmhello. athrof alanas.
Ꝥrı pheth oꝛ keffir ar foꝛd nẏt reıt atteb ẏ
neb o honunt pedol. anotwẏd. acheſnhaƀc.
Ꝥ Rı dẏn ẏtelır guelı tauaƀt udunt.
Ẏr bꝛenhín. ac ẏr bꝛaƀdƀꝛ ẏn med-   5
ẏlẏaƀ am ẏuarn. ac ẏr offeırat ẏnẏ wıfc
ẏnẏ teır gƀẏl arbenhıc uch ẏallaƀꝛ neu
ẏn darlleſn llẏthẏr rac bꝛon ẏ bꝛenhín neu
ẏnẏ wneuthur. Ꝥrı lle ẏg kẏfreıth hẏwel ẏmae pꝛaƀf. Vn o honu gureıc bıeu   10
pꝛouı treıs ar ƀꝛ. Eıl ẏƀ kẏnogẏn bıeu pꝛo
uſ uch pen bed ẏmach ẏuot ẏn uach ac
na dıwẏgƀẏt dꝛoftaƀ ẏuechnſaeth tra uu
uẏƀ. Tꝛẏdẏd ẏƀ pꝛouſ bugeılgı. Ꝥeır pla
kenedẏl. magu mab arglƀẏd. a dƀẏn mab   15
ẏ genedẏl ẏg kam. a guarchadƀ penreıth.
Ꝥrı pheth atẏrr ar amot. cleuẏt. ac aghen arglƀẏd. ac aghenoctıt. Ꝥrı pheth
adıffer dẏn rac guẏf dadleu. llefeín. ac
vtgẏrn rac llu goꝛwlat. a llıf ẏn auon   20
heb pont aheb keubal. achleuẏt.

ORı dẏn ẏtelır galanaſ udunt ac nẏ
thalant. 6ẏ dím o alanaſ. arglỏẏd.
kanẏſ ıda6 ẏ da6 traẏan kẏmhell pop galanaſ. Eıl ẏ6 penkenedẏl. kanẏſ 6ıth ẏ
vıeínt ef ẏ telír galanaſ ẏgarant. Tıẏdẏd   5
ẏ6 tat. kanẏſ ran ada6 ıda6 o alanas ẏuab
nẏt amgen no cheínha6c. kanẏt car ẏ
vab ıda6. ac nẏ dẏlẏır llad vn o honunt
o alanaſ. Ḥanher ran bıa6t atal whaer
o alanaſ. ac nẏ cheıff hı dím o alanas.   10
Ŧrı ergẏt nẏ dıwẏgır ẏ gar6   ẏn
ẏt. ac ẏ eba6l guẏllt ẏn ẏt. ac ẏ   gı ẏn ẏt-
Ŧrı dẏn awna gulat ẏn tla6t. arglỏẏd
deu eıra6c. ac ẏgnat camweda6c. a maer cuhudẏat. Ŧrı chadarn bẏt. arglỏẏd.   15
kanẏſ maen dıoſ ıaen ẏ6 arglỏẏd. ac ẏnuẏt. canẏ ellır kẏmhell dím ar ẏnuẏt
namẏn ẏewẏllıs. a dẏn dídím. kanẏ ellır
kẏmell dím lle nẏ bo. Ŧrı aníueıl ẏſſẏd
un werth eu lloſgẏrneu ac eu llẏgeıt ac   20
eu heneıt. llo. ac eboleſ tom. achath eıthẏr

cath awarchatwo ẏſcubaϬꝛ bꝛenhín.

Rı dẏn caſ kenedẏl. lleıdẏr. athϬẏllϬꝛ.
canẏ ellır ẏmdıret udunt. adẏn a
latho dẏn oe genedẏl ehunan. kanẏ ledír
ẏ car bẏϬ ẏr ẏ car marϬ. caſ uẏd gan paϬb   5
ẏ welet ẏnteu. Ꞇrı cheffredín kenedẏl.
penkenedẏl. atheıſpantẏle. a mab ẏwreıc arother o rod kenedẏl ẏ eu gelẏn. hϬnnϬ adẏlẏ bot ẏngẏffredín rϬg ẏ dϬẏ genedẏl. Ꞇrı meuẏluethẏant gϬꝛ. bot ẏn   10
drẏ°   dꝛẏc karϬꝛ. ac ẏn llıbínϬꝛ ẏndad-
leu.   ac ẏn Ϭꝛ arglϬẏd dꝛϬc.

Rı aneueíl ẏſſẏd uϬẏ eu teıthı.
noc eu guerth kẏfreıth. ẎſtalϬẏn.
atharϬ treſgoꝛd. abaed kenueín. kanẏſ   15
ẏr enrẏal agollır o collır Ϭẏnteu. Ꞇrı
chẏfanhed gulat. meıbon bẏcheín. ach
Ϭn acheılogeu. Ꝁẏn no hẏn trıoed kẏfreıth ar traethaſſam. weıthon ẏ traethϬn

oꝛ naϬuet dẏdẏeu.   20
Ẏntaf ẏϬ naϬuetdẏd racuẏr am-

tír. Eıl ẏ6 na6uetdẏd meı elch6ẏl. Tıẏdẏd ẏ6 na6uetdẏd meı ẏda6 teıthı kẏn-
flıth. Petwerẏd ẏ6 na6uetdẏd whefra6ı
ẏda6 teıthı kẏnwheıth. (0)et na6uetdẏd
ẏſſẏd ẏargl6ẏd ẏẏmgoffau ae l6 pan hon-   5
her arna6 rodı ll6 gẏnt. 0et na6uetdẏd
ẏſſẏd r6g llẏſ allan. kẏn atteb. ahẏnnẏ
guedẏ ha6l. pan uo amrẏſſon am tír.
(0)et na6uetdẏd ẏſſẏd am geleín ahan-
fo oı vn cantref ar neb ae llatho. Ƃrı na6   10
uet dẏd ẏſſẏd ẏpenkẏnẏd. Ƃrı na6uet-
dẏd ẏſſẏd am ueıchogı gureıc. Ɖa6uet-
dẏd kẏn a6ſt ẏ da pop heıt ẏmreínt
modıẏdaf. 0et na6uetdẏd ẏſſẏd am-
warant un wlat neu tẏſt unwlat. 0et   15
na6 uetdẏd ẏſſẏd ẏd6ẏn tẏ awnelher ar
tır dẏn arall heb ẏ ganhat. 0et na6uet-
dẏd ẏſſẏd ẏwreıc ẏ arhoſ ẏran oı da ẏnẏ
thẏ pan ẏſgarho ae g6ı. 0et deu na6-
vetdẏd ẏſſẏd am aradẏr pan toıher.   20

OJ ar bɪaϬdϬɪ auarn ẏ bɪodẏeu na uſt
uϬẏ genhẏt werth keínhaϬc no guerth duϬ: na varn ẏ kam. ẏr guerth namẏn barn ẏ ɪaϬn ẏr duϬ. ...

BẎchan rẏued kẏt bo pedɪuſter ẏn   5
llẏs pɪeſſenhaϬl can fẏmudant a-
wẏd mal awel eluẏd. ꝒϬẏ bẏnhac hagen
agarho dɪheurϬẏd adɪtraghϬẏdder. guaſ-
fanaeth ɪaϬn ẏr arglϬẏd ɪeſſu grɪft. Ẏr
hϬn ẏſſẏd gogonet ẏ tat ar mab ar ẏfpɪẏt   10
glan amen.

Ɗɪɪ lle nẏ dẏlẏ dẏn rodɪ llϬ gweɪlẏd
Vn ẏϬ. pont un pɪen heb ganllaϬ
Eɪl ẏϬ ar poɪth ẏ uẏnwent kanẏf canu
ẏ pader adẏlẏ dẏn ẏna rac eneɪt crɪfton   15
ogẏon ẏbẏt. Tɪẏdẏd ẏϬ ar dɪϬf ẏr eglϬ-
ẏſ. kanẏf canu ẏ pater adẏlẏ dẏn ẏna
rac bɪon ẏgroc.

Ꝑan dẏcker mab ẏ genedẏl o lϬ degwẏr
adeugeínt ẏmab bɪeu tẏgu ẏmlaen ẏ   20
genedẏl kanẏt kẏfreɪthaϬl ẏ guaran

daᛒ hı namẏn ar ẏ llᛒ kẏntaf. pan dẏweto
eſcoꝛ neıdẏr ıdı.

Ꝑan dıwatter mab o genedẏl. Ẏ mab hẏn
haſ ẏrgᛒꝛ ẏdẏweter ẏuot ẏn uab ıdaᛒ bıeu
tẏgu ẏngẏntaf ẏmlaen ẏgenedẏl.   5
(ᚦ)eır ouer groeſ ẏſſẏd.   croeſ adoter ar foꝛd ẏ
mẏᛒn ẏt. achroeſ adoter arıſc pꝛen goꝛwe
ıdaᛒc ẏg koet. achroeſ adoto dẏn ar allaᛒꝛ
nẏ dẏlẏho eglᛒẏſ ẏmẏrru gantaᛒ.

ENGLISH TRANSLATION OF HAR-LEIAN MS. 4353 (**V**) WITH THE MISSING LEAVES SUPPLIED FROM CLEOPATRA A xiv (**W**)

H OWEL the Good, son of Cadell, V 1 a 1 king of Cymru, enacted by the grace of God and fasting and prayer when Cymru was in his possession in its bounds, to wit, three score and four cantrevs of Deheubarth, and eighteen cantrevs of Gwynedd, and three score trevs beyond the Cyrchell, and three score trevs of Buallt; and within that limit, the word of no one [is] before their word, and their word is a word over all. There were bad customs and bad laws before his time. He therefore takes six men from every cymwd in Cymru and brings them to the White House on the Tav; and there were present those who held croziers in Cymru including archbishops and bishops and abbots and good teachers; and of that number, twelve of the wisest laics were

EVANS   L

chosen, and the one wisest scholar who was called Blegywryd, to make the good laws and to abolish the bad ones which were before his time; and to place good ones in their stead and to confirm them in his own name. When they had finished making those laws, they placed the curse of God, and the one of that assembly, and the one of Cymru in general upon any one who should break those laws.

V 1 b 3 ··· ·: And first they began with the Laws of a Court as they were the most important and as they pertained to the King and the Queen and the Twenty-four Officers who accompany them, namely, Chief of the Household. Priest of the Household. Steward. Judge of the Court. Falconer. Chief Huntsman. Chief groom. Page of the Chamber. Steward of the Queen. Priest of the Queen. Bard of the Household. Silentiary. Doorkeeper of the Hall. Doorkeeper of the Chamber. Chambermaid. Groom of the Rein. Candlebearer. Butler. Mead brewer. Server of the Court. Cook. Physician. Footholder. Groom of the Rein to the Queen.

V 1 b 12 A right of all the officers is to have woollen clothing from the king and linen clothing from the queen three times every year; at Christmas and Easter and Whitsuntide. The queen has a share of all the profits (ennill) of the king from his demesne (oe wlat dilis). The officers of the queen receive a share of all the profits of the king's officers. Three persons who v 1 b 19 do sarhâd to the king; whoever shall violate his protection, and whoever shall obstruct his wife, and whoever shall kill his man in his presence and in the presence of the company when there shall be greeting and an assembly between him and another regulus (pennaeth). A hundred kine are to be paid as sarhâd to the king for every cantrev in his kingdom (teyrnas), and a silver rod which shall reach from the ground to the king's pate when he shall sit in his chair, as thick as his ring finger, with three knobs at the top and three at the bottom as thick as the rod; and a golden cup which shall hold the king's full draught, as thick as the nail of a ploughman who shall have ploughed for seven years; and a golden cover thereon as thick as the cup, as broad as the king's face. The status of the Lord v 2 a 7 of Dinevwr moreover is upheld by as many white cows, with the head of each one to the tail of the other and a bull between every score kine of them, as shall extend completely from Argoel to the Court of Dinevwr.

For the galanas of the king is paid three v 2 a 12

times as much as his sarhâd with three augmen-
V 2 a 13 tations. In three ways sarhâd is done to the queen; when her protection shall be violated, or when she shall be struck in anger, or when a thing shall be taken out of her hand with violence; and then a third of the worth of the king's sarhâd is paid to the queen, without gold
V 2 a 18 however and without silver. Thirty-six persons on horseback it befits the king to support in his retinue; the twenty-four officers and his twelve gwestais; and together with that, his household and his nobles and his youths and
V 2 a 23 his minstrels and his almsmen. The most honourable after the king and the queen is the edling. The edling is to be to the king a brother or a son or a nephew, the son of
V 2 b 1 a brother. The protection of the edling is to conduct the person who commits the offence until he is safe. The sarhâd and the galanas of the king and the edling are the same, except-ing privileged gold and silver and the cattle which are placed from Argoel to the Court
V 2 b 6 of Dinevwr. The place of the edling in the hall is opposite to the king about the fire with him. Between the edling and the pillar next to him sits the judge of the court; on the other side of him, the priest of the household; after

that the chief of song ; after that there is no
fixed place for any one in the hall. All the V 2 b 11
royal issue, the freemen, and the collectors of the
geld (kyllituffon) are to be in the lodging of the
edling. The king is to provide the edling with
the whole of his expenditure honourably. The V 2 b 15
lodging of the edling and the youths with him
is the hall ; and the woodman is to kindle the
fire for him and to close the doors after he is
gone to sleep. The edling is to have a suffi-
ciency at his repast without measure.[1] In the
three principal festivals a privileged bonheddig sits on the left of the king ; on his right
side, every one as he may will. A privileged V 2 b 21
protection pertains to every officer ; and to
others also. Whoever shall resort to the pro- V 2 b 23
tection of a queen is to be conducted beyond
the boundary of the gwlad without pursuit and
without obstruction. The protection of the V 2 b 25
chief of the household conducts the person
beyond the boundary of the cymwd. The V 3 a 1
protection of a priest of the household is to
conduct the person to the nearest church. The V 3 a 3
protection of the steward saves a person from
the time he shall stand in the service of the
king until the last person goes from the court

---

[1] See note at this point in the Analysis of V after Introduction.

V 3 a 5 to sleep. The protection of the falconer defends the person to the farthest place where V 3 a 7 he shall hawk. The protection of the chief huntsman continues to the farthest place where V 3 a 8 the sound of his horn is heard. The protection of the judge of the court is whilst the suits shall last from the first cause until the V 3 a 10 last. The protection of the chief groom continues whilst the best horse in the court shall V 3 a 11 continue running. The protection of the page of the chamber is from the time he goes to gather rushes until he shall finish spreading the V 3 a 13 king's bed. Similar to that is the protection of V 3 a 15 the chambermaid. The protection of a queen's steward is from the time he shall stand in the service of the queen until the last person V 3 a 17 goes from the chamber to sleep. The protection of the bard of the household is to conduct the person to the chief of the house- V 3 a 19 hold. The protection of the silentiary is from V 3 a 20 the first command of silence to the last. Similar is the protection of a [queen's] priest to that of V 3 a 21 his fellow [1]. The protection of the candlebearer is from the time the first candle is lit until the V 3 a 23 last is extinguished. The protection of the footholder is from the time he shall sit under

---

[1] i.e. a king's priest.

the king's feet until the king goes to the 󠀠 chamber. The protection of the cook is from V 3 a 25 the time he shall begin to cook the first collop until he shall place the last dish before the king and the queen. The protection of the server V 3 b 2 of the court is from the time he shall begin to distribute the food until the last shall have had his portion. The protection of the mead brewer V 3 b 5 is from the time he shall begin to prepare the mead vat until he shall cover it. The pro- V 3 b 6 tection of the butler is from the time he shall begin to empty the mead vat until he shall finish. The protection of the court physician V 3 b 8 is from the time he goes to visit the sick with the king's leave, until he comes again to the court. The protection of the doorkeeper of V 3 b 11 the hall is to conduct the person the length of his arm and his rod towards the porter, for he is to receive him. The protection of the porter V 3 b 13 is to retain the person until the chief of the household comes through the gate towards his lodging; and then let the refugee proceed in safety[1]. Similar is the protection of the door- V 3 b 16 keeper [of the chamber] to that of his fellow[2].

[1] V here has probably missed a line: cf. W 37 b 1, 'until the last person shall leave the court.'

[2] i. e. the doorkeeper of the hall.

V 3 b 17 The protection of a groom of the rein continues
whilst the smith of the court is making four
shoes and their complement of nails, and whilst
V 3 b 19 he shall be shoeing the king's steed. Similar
to that is the protection of a queen's groom of
V 3 b 21 the rein. Whosoever's protection is violated,
V 3 b 22 it is sarhâd to him. What is paid as the sarhâd
of a chief of the household is a third of the
king's sarhâd without privileged gold and silver;
V 3 b 24 and likewise his galanas. A Steward, Judge
of a Court, Falconer, Chief Huntsman, Chief

[A chasm in V supplied from W]

W 37 b 13 groom, Page of a Chamber, [have] the
same sarhâd and the same galanas and the
same ebediw; and their daughters the same
status. For their sarhâd, nine kine and nine
score of silver are to be paid. For the galanas
of every one of them, nine kine and nine score
kine with three augmentations are paid. A
pound is the ebediw of every one of them.
A pound is the gobr of their daughters.
Three pounds is their cowyll. Seven pounds
W 37 b 21 is their agweddi. The sarhâd of every one of
all the other officers except the chief of the
household and the priest of the household, who,
although they be of the number of the officers,

are not of the same status—For the sarhâd of W 38 a
every one of the other officers, six kine and six
score of silver are to be paid. For their galanas
is paid six kine and six score kine with three
augmentations. For the ebediw of every one
is paid six score of silver ; and six score is the .
gobr of every one of their daughters. A pound
and a half is their cowyll ; three pounds is their
agweddi. Whoever shall kill a person, let him W 38 a 11
first pay his sarhâd and afterwards his galanas.
There is to be no augmentation on the sarhâd
of any one.

The lodging of the chief of the household W 38 a 14
is to be the largest house in the middle of
the trev, because round him the lodgings of the
household are to be, so that they may be ready
for every emergency. In the lodging of the
chief of the household, the bard of the household
and the physician are to be. The lodging of W 38 a 18
the priest of the household, and the scholars of
the court with him, is to be the chaplain's house.
The lodging of a queen's priest is to be the house W 38 a 20
of the bell-ringer. The lodging of the steward W 38 a 21
and the officers[1] with him is to be the house
next to the court. The lodging of the judge of W 38 b 1
the court is to be the chamber of the king or

[1] Servers (swydwyr) in U and X.

the hall; and the cushion which shall be under
the king in the day, is to be under the head of
W 38 b 4 the judge of the court in the night. The lodging
of the chief groom, and all the grooms with him,
is to be the house nearest to the king's barn,
because it is he who distributes the provender.
W 38 b 7 The lodging of the chief huntsman, and all the
huntsmen with him, is to be the king's kiln
W 38 b 9 house. The lodging of the falconer is to be
the king's barn, because the hawks do not
W 38 b 10 like smoke. The bed of the page of the
chamber and the chambermaid, in the king's
W 38 b 12 chamber they are to be. The lodging of the
W 38 b 13 doorkeepers is to be the porter's house. The
chief of the household has provision in his
lodging, namely, three messes and three horn-
fuls of liquor from the court; and he receives
a perquisite (achyfarós) every year from the
king, to wit, three pounds. Of spoil which the
household takes, he receives the share of two
men if he be with them; and the ox which
he shall choose from the third of the king.
Whoever does wrong below the columns of
the court, if the chief of the household catch
him, by law, he receives a third of the dirwy
or the camlwrw. If also he catches him at
the entrance of the hall sooner than the

steward, he receives a third of the dirwy or the camlwrw. The chief of the household is to be W 39 a 3 a son or a nephew, a brother's son, to the king. A hornful of mead comes to him in every banquet from the queen. If the king in anger leaves any one of the household below the fire-place, let the chief of the household invite such a person to his own company. At the end of the hall sits the chief of the household and the whole household around him. Let him take what elder he may will on his right, and another on his left. A horse always in attendance he receives from the king, and two shares of the provender does his horse receive.

Whoever shall do sarhâd to a priest of W 39 a 14 a household or shall kill him, let him submit to the law of the synod; and for his disparaging twelve kine are paid to him, and the third does he receive and the two-thirds the king. A priest of a household receives the garment in which the king shall do penance during Lent, and that by Eastertide; and he has the king's offering, and the offering of the household, and the offering of those who shall take an offering from the king in the three principal festivals; he always however receives the king's offering. A mess of food and a hornful of mead he receives from the court for his provision. A horse always in attendance, he has from the king; and a third of all the king's tithe he receives; and one of the three indispensable persons to the king is the priest of W 39 b 7 the household. A queen's priest has a horse always in attendance from the queen; and her offering and that of those who may belong to her he has three times every year. The offering of the queen however he receives at all times. The garment in which the queen does penance through Lent, her priest receives. The place of the queen's priest is to be opposite to her.

W 39 b 15 A steward has the garment of the chief of the household in the three principal festivals; and the garment of the steward, the bard of the household receives; and the garment of the bard, the doorkeeper receives. The steward, when he shall ask, has the skin of a hart from the huntsmen from the middle of February until the end of a fortnight of May. When the steward comes to the court, the food and the drink is to be wholly according to his ruling. He shows every one his proper place in the hall. He apportions the lodgings. 'A horse always in attendance he has from the king, and his horse has two shares of the

provender. The steward's land is to be free.
He has a steer of every spoil from the household. A steward is to have the gobr of the
daughters of every land-maer. He receives
twenty-four pence from every officer who shall
serve food and drink in the court, when they
shall enter upon their office. He distributes
the gwestva silver. To him it pertains to test
liquors in the court. He has a third of the
dirwy and camlwrw of the food and drink
servants, namely, çook and butler and server of
a court. From the time the steward, standing
up, shall proclaim the protection of God and
the protection of the king and the queen and
the nobles (guyrda), whosoever shall violate
that protection is not to have protection either
in court or in llan. He is to participate
in the twenty-four offices of a court. And he
has two parts of the skins of the cattle which
are killed in the kitchen. For every office of
court the steward has a fee when the king shall
confer it; except the principal offices. A hart's
skin comes to him in October from the chief
huntsman, and therefrom vessels are made to
keep the king's cups and his horns, before
sharing the skins between the king and the
huntsmen. A steward has one man's share

of grooms' silver.   A steward by law is to place

[V resumes]

V 6 a 1 food and drink before the king, and a mess above him and another below him, in the three principal festivals.   A steward has the length of his middle finger of the clear ale from off the lees ; and the length of the middle joint of the bragod ; and the length of the extreme joint of the mead.   Whoever commits an offence in the entrance of the hall, if the steward catches him by law, he has a third of the dirwy or the camlwrw.   If also he catches him below the columns sooner than the chief of the household, he has the third.   It pertains to a steward to keep the king's share of the spoil ; and when it is divided, let him take an ox or a cow.   It pertains to a steward to swear for the king when there shall be a rhaith on him.[1]   He is one of the three persons who maintain the status of a court in the king's absence.

V 6 a 15 A judge of a court does not give silver to the chief groom when he shall have a

---

[1] reith arnaɢ is probably a misreading of *reit* or a mistranslation of *opus*. Cf. Peniarth MS. 28. *Anc. Laws* ii. 757 ; also i. 362, 642. The translation would then be ' when there shall be occasion '.

horse from the king. He has one man's share
of the daered silver. He administers justice
gratuitously in every cause which shall pertain
to the court. He is to show the status of the
men of the court and the status of their offices.
He has twenty-four pence from the. one to
whom he shall show his status and his due.
When a legal fee comes to the judges (braɥtwyr)
the judge of the court has two shares. He has
the share of two men of the spoil which the
household takes, although he himself does not
go from his house. If any one opposes the V 6 a 25
judgment of the judge of a court, let them
place their two pledges in the king's hand; and
if the judge of the court be foiled, let him pay
to the king the worth of his tongue, and let him
never judge again; and if the other be foiled, let
him pay his sarhâd to the judge of the court, and
to the king the worth of his tongue. It is right
for the judge (bɪaɥdɥ) to receive four legal pence
from every cause of the value of four legal
pence. He is one of the three indispensable
persons to the king. Twenty-four pence come
to the judges (bɪaɥtwyr) when land shall be
meered. If a person enters into law [1] without

---

[1] Oɪ a dyn yg.kyfreith, etc., Peniarth MS, 28 reads 'Si quis sine

leave of the judge of the court, let him pay
three kine camlwrw to the king; and if the
king shall be in the place, let him pay twofold.
No one is to judge who does not know the Three
Columns of Law, and the Worth of every Legal
Animal. The judge of the court has a linen
sheet from the queen regularly. A horse
always in attendance he has from the king, and
two shares for it of the provender; and it is to
be in the same stall as the king's horse daily.
A groom of the rein brings his horse to him in
proper order when he shall will it. He has his
land free. He has small presents, when his
office shall be pledged to him; a throw-board
from the king, and a gold ring from the queen;
and he is not to part with those presents either
by sale or by gift. From the bard when he
shall win a chair, the judge of the court has
a bugle horn and a gold ring and the cushion
which shall be placed under him in his chair.
The judge of the court has twenty-four pence
from every suit for sarhâd and theft, from the
one who shall escape from those charges. He
has the tongue from the head which comes

licentia ad audiendum iudices accesserit iudicantes ut auscultet'
(*Anc. Laws*, ii. 758. Cf. ibid. ii. 821, 900, and i. 370). **V** therefore here may be a misreading or mistranslation.

as a present to the king[1], and all the tongues from the court, for he decides on all the tongues; and the king is to fill the place of the tongue with the thigh muscle of the beast which he shall have for the smith of the court. The judge of the court is the third person who maintains the status of a court in the king's absence. He is to be free from ebediw because judgeship is better than anything temporal,

*W*hat day soever the falconer shall kill V 7 a 14 a heron or a bittern or a curlew by means of his hawks, the king shall perform three services for him; hold his horse while he shall secure the birds, and hold his stirrup while he shall dismount, and hold it while he shall mount. Three times the king presents him with food from his own hand on that night; for by the hand of his messenger he presents him daily, except in the three chief festivals and the day whereon he shall kill a notable bird. On the canghellor's left he sits at a banquet. He has the skin of a hart from the chief huntsman in October to make him gloves and jesses. He

---

[1] The text of V 7 a 5–7 Ef ageiff. . . . bɫenhin, appears to be corrupt. Cf. W 42 a (margin) Tauaʊt y karʊ adel yr bɫenhın yn anrec y pen ageıff ef.

drinks three times only in the hall lest there be neglect of the hawks. A horse always in attendance he receives from the king; and two shares of the provender for it. If the falconer kills his horse in hunting or if it should die by chance, he has another from the king. He has every male hawk. He has every sparrow-hawk's nest which shall be found on the land of the court. He has a mess of food and a hornful of mead for his provision in his lodging. From the time the falconer shall place his hawks in their mews until he shall take them thence, he gives no answer to any one who shall sue him. He has gwestva once every year on the king's taeogs; and from every taeogtrev he has a crone or four legal pence for food for his hawks. He has his land free. The day whereon he shall capture a notable bird and the king is not in the place, when the falconer comes to the court with the bird with him, the king is to rise to receive him; and if he rises not, he is to give the garment he may have on, to the falconer. He has the heart of every animal which shall be killed in the kitchen. When the falconer shall be distrained upon by law, neither the maer nor the canghellor shall distrain upon him, only the household and the apparitor.

A chief huntsman has the skin of an ox in V 7 b 24 winter from the steward to make leashes. For the king's benefit the huntsmen hunt until the calends of December. Thence until the ninth day of December they do not share with him. On the ninth day of December, it befits the chief huntsman to show the king his dogs and his horns and his leashes and his third of the skins. Until the ninth day of December no one, who shall sue a chief huntsman, receives an answer from him unless he be one of the court officers, for none [of the officers] is to postpone [the suit of] his fellow if there be one to determine it. A chief huntsman has the share of two men of the skins from the huntsmen with the covert hounds, and one man's share from the huntsmen with the greyhounds; and from the king's third of the skins he has a third. After the skins are distributed among the king and the huntsmen, let the chief huntsman, and the huntsmen with him, go and take up quarters with the king's taeogs; and then let them come to the king by Christmas to receive their right from him. The place of the chief huntsman, and the huntsmen with him in the hall, is the column opposite to the king. A hornful of mead comes to him from the king or from the chief of the household, and the second from the queen, and the third from the steward. He has from the falconer a tame sparrow-hawk every Michaelmas. He has provision in his lodging, a mess and a hornful of mead. To him belongs a third of the dirwy, camlwrw and ebediw of the huntsmen, and a third of their daughters' gobrs. With the king the huntsmen are to be from Christmas until they shall go to hunt hinds in the spring. From the time they go to hunt on May-day until the end of the ninth day of May, the chief huntsman gives no answer to any one who shall sue him, unless he be overtaken on the calends of May before putting on the boot of his right foot. He has a horse always in attendance from the king, and two shares of the provender for it. When the chief huntsman shall swear, let him swear by his dogs and his horns and his leashes. He has four legal pence from every huntsman with a greyhound, and eight legal pence from every huntsman with a covert hound. If the chief huntsman goes to foray with the king's household or with his host, let him sound his horn when it shall be right for him, and let him choose a steer out of the spoil. As he receives the skin of an ox

before the third day of Christmas from the
steward, it is right for him to have the skin
of a cow between June and the middle of
September[1] from him; and if he remembers
not at that time, he has nothing.

A chief groom has the skin of an ox in the
winter and the skin of a cow in the
summer from the steward, to make halters for
the king's horses, and that before sharing the
skins between the steward and the officers.
A chief groom and the chief huntsman and the
foot-holder do not sit by the partition of the
hall; each of them moreover knows his place. A
chief groom owns the legs of every steer killed in
the kitchen, and salt is given to him with them.
He has the share of two men of the grooms'
silver. He owns the old saddles of the king's
steed and its old bridles. A chief groom and
the grooms with him have the wild colts which
come to the king from the third of a spoil.
To him it pertains to hand over every horse
which the king shall give, and he himself givce
a halter with every horse, and he has four pence
for every horse except three : the horse which
shall be given to the priest of a household, and
the horse which shall be given to the judge of

V 8 b 2c

---

[1] Reading *medi* for *mei*.

a court, and the horse which shall be given to the jester, for the end of its halter is to be bound to its two testicles and so it is to be given. He has the fill of the vessel, of which the king shall drink, from the steward, and the second from the chief of the household, and the third from the queen. He has his land free; and a horse always in attendance he has from the king, and two shares of the provender for it. The place of the chief groom, and the grooms with him, is the column next to the king. To a chief groom it pertains to distribute the stables and the provender of the horses. He has a third of the dirwy and camlwrw of the grooms. He has the king's caps if there be fur thereon; and his spurs, if they be gilded or silvered or lacquered, when they shall be discarded. He has a mess of food and a hornful of ale for his provision.

V 9 b 3 A page of the chamber owns all the old clothes of the king except his vesture in Lent. He has his bed clothes and his mantle and his coat and his shirt and his trowsers and his shoes and his stockings. There is no fixed place for the page of the chamber in the hall, as he keeps the king's bed; and he carries his messages between the hall and the chamber. He has his land free, and his share of the gwestva silver. He spreads the king's bed. He has a horse regularly from the king, and two shares of the provender for it. From every spoil which the household takes, he has the cattle whose ears and horns are of equal length.

A bard of the household has a steer out of V 9 b 15 every spoil at the capture of which he shall be with the household, and one man's share like every other man of the household. He also sings the 'Monarchy of Britain' in front of them in the day of battle and fighting. When a bard shall solicit from a king (teyrn), let him sing one song. When he shall solicit from a breyr, let him sing three songs. When he shall solicit from a taeog, let him sing until he is tired. He has his land free, and his horse regularly from the king; and it is the second song he sings in the hall, for the chief of song is to begin. He sits second nearest to the chief of the household. He has a harp from the king, and a gold ring from the queen, when his office shall be given him; and the harp let him never part with.

Bard of a Household. Silentiary. Queen's V 10 a 3 steward. Doorkeeper of a Hall. Doorkeeper of a Chamber. Groom of the Rein. Candle-bearer. Butler. Cook. Foot-holder. Mead

brewer. Server of a Court. Physician. Chambermaid. Queen's groom of the rein. These fifteen
are of the same status; and of the same status
are their daughters. For the sarhâd of each of
them, there are paid six kine and six score of
silver. The galanas of each of them is paid
with six kine and six score kine with three
augmentations. The ebediw of each of them
is six score pence; and six score pence is the
gobr of the daughter of each of them. A
pound and a half for her cowyll. Three pounds
V 10 a 17 her agweddi. If a daughter of one of these
fifteen goes away clandestinely without consent
of kindred, her agweddi will be six steers having
ears and horns of equal length. Of the same
status as that is the daughter, who goes away
clandestinely, of every free man.

V 10 a 22 If the doorkeeper of a hall go beyond the
length of his arm and his rod from the door
after the king has entered the hall, and he there
suffer sarhâd, no compensation is to be made to
him. If the doorkeeper or the porter know-
ingly impedes one of the officers entering at
his own will, let him pay four legal pence to
the officer; and if he be a principal one, let
him pay twofold, and three kine camlwrw does
he pay to the king. The doorkeeper has a

vessel to hold his liquor. The steward and
the waiters [1] bring their liquor into the vessel
of the doorkeeper. When the liquor of the
apostles [2] is distributed, the doorkeeper takes
charge of it. He dries the skins of the cattle
which shall be killed in the kitchen ; and he also
receives a penny for every skin when shared.
He has his land free ; and a horse always in
attendance does he receive from the king. One
man's share does he receive of the gwestva
silver.

The doorkeeper of a chamber has his land V 10 b 14
free, and a horse always in attendance from
the king ; and legal liquor does he obtain, and
his share of the gwestva silver.

A groom of the rein has the daily saddles of V 10 b 16
the king and his pannel and his rain cap
when discarded ; and his old horse shoes and
his shoeing irons. His land he has free, and
his horse regularly. He leads the king's horse
to its stable (lety) and from its stable. He
holds the king's horse when he shall mount
and when he shall dismount. One man's share
does he receive of the wild colts taken in foray.

---

[1] Cf. *Anc. Laws*, ii. 762 'pincerne'; also *ibid.* 783 'pincerne
. . . id est trullyat'.
[2] Cf. *ibid.* 762 'Ad potum apostolorum nomine sumptum,' &c.

V 10 b 25 A court physician sits second next to the chief of the household in the hall. His land he has free, and a horse regularly from the king. Gratuitously does he prepare medicines for the household and for the men of the court; for he only receives the bloodstained clothes, unless it be one of the three mortal wounds. A pound does he take without his maintenance or nine score pence together with his maintenance for the mortal wound, to wit, [first] when a person's head is broken so that the brain is seen. A bone of the upper part of the cranium is four curt pence in value if it sounds in falling into a basin; a bone of the lower part of the cranium is four legal pence in value. And [secondly] when a person shall be stabbed in his body so that his bowels are seen. And [thirdly] when one of the four pillars (poſt) of a person's body is broken so that the marrow is seen; these are the two thighs and the two humeri. Three pounds is the worth of each one of those three wounds.

V 11 a 17 A butler has his land free, and a horse always in attendance from the king. He receives legal liquor, to wit, the fill of the drinking vessels[1] used for serving in the court of the ale, and

[1] Reading gwallofyer for gỽaſſanaethwyr.

their third of the mead, and their half of
the bragod. 𝔄 mead brewer has his land V II a 22
free, and his horse regularly from the king.
One man's share does he obtain of the gwestva
silver, and a third of the wax taken from the
mead vat; for the two parts are divided into
three shares, the two shares for the hall and the
third for the chamber.

𝔄 cook has the skins of the sheep and the V II b 3
goats and the lambs and the kids and the calves,
and the entrails of the cattle which shall be
killed in the kitchen, except the rectum and
the milt which go to the porter. The cook
has the tallow and the skimming from the
kitchen, except the tallow of the steer which
shall be three nights with the cattle of the maer-
house. His land he gets free, and his horse
always in attendance from the king.

𝔄 silentiary has four pence from every dirwy V II b 11
and camlwrw which shall be forfeited for breaking silence in the court. A share also does he
receive from the officers for every distribution.
His land he has free, and his share of the gwestva
silver, and his horse regularly from the king.
When the land maer shall be removed from his
office, the silentiary has three score pence from
whatever person is appointed in his stead.

V II b 19   A footholder is to sit under the king's feet and to eat from the same dish as he. He is to light the first candle before the king at meat; and yet he has a mess of food and liquor, for he does not participate in the banquet. His land he has free, and a horse always in attendance from the king, and his share of the gwestva silver.

V 12 a 1   The server of a court has his land free, and his horse regularly from the king, and his share of the gwestva silver.

V 12 a 4   Queen's steward has his horse regularly from the queen. Eight pence comes to him from the gwestva silver; and he takes two pence, and the rest he shares among the officers of the chamber. He has the care of the food and drink in the chamber. He is to test the liquors of the chamber; and show each his place.

V 12 a 11   A chambermaid has all the clothing of the queen throughout the year except the garment wherein she shall do penance in Lent. Her land she has free, and her horse regularly from the queen; and her old bridles and her apparel (ae harchenat) when discarded, does she receive; and her share of the gwestva silver.

Queen's groom of the rein has his land free, V12 a 17
and his horse regularly from the queen.   Where V 12 a 19
the priest of the household and the steward and
the judge of the court are together, the status
of a court is in that place although the king be
absent.

Maer and canghellor are to keep the waste V 12 a 22
of a king.   A pound and a half comes
to the king when a maership or a canghellorship
shall be pledged.   The maer maintains three
persons with himself in a banquet in the king's
hall.   He distributes the household when they
shall go into quarters.   On a foray he ac-
companies the household with three men.   He
has a progress with three men among the
king's taeogs twice in the year.   A chief of
kindred is never to be a maer or canghellor.
A maer is to demand all the dues of the king as
far as his jurisdiction of maer extends.   Maer
and canghellor are entitled to a third of the
gobrs of the taeogs' daughters, and a third of
the camlwrws and ebediws of the taeogs, and
a third of their corn when they shall flee from
the gwlad, and a third of their corn and their
food from every marwdy of a taeog.   A maer is
to divide everything, and an apparitor is to
choose, for the king.   If it happens that the

maer is unable to maintain a house, let him
take to him what taeog he likes for a year from
one calends of May to another, and let him
enjoy the milk of the taeog during the summer,
and his corn in the autumn, and his swine in
winter; and when the taeog shall go from him,
let him leave him four large sows and a boar
and all the rest of his animals, and four acres
of winter tilth and eight acres of spring tilth;
and the second year and the third let him
do likewise; not however the same taeog.
Afterwards let him subsist upon his own means
for three other years; then let the king relieve
him by granting him a taeog under the former
regulation, if he will. When a person shall
lose his spoil by law, the maer and the canghellor
are to have the heifers and the steers and the
stirks in two equal shares.

V 13 a 5 The duty of the canghellor is to hold the
pleas of the king in his presence and
in his absence. He is to place a cross and
restriction in every suit. To the left of the
king does the canghellor sit in the three principal festivals, if the king be holding court in
his canghellorship. A gold ring and a harp
and a throwboard does he receive from the
king when he enters into office. In the time

of Howel the Good, a third of the live and dead stock of the taeogs came to the maer and to the canghellor; the two parts to the maer, and the third to the canghellor; and the maer shared and the canghellor chose.

An apparitor has his land free, and a mess V 13 a 17 from the court. Between the two columns he stands while the king shall eat, for it then pertains to him to secure the hall against fire. After meat let him eat along with the servants; after that let him neither sit nor strike the post nearest to the king. He has legal liquor, to wit, the fill of the vessels used for serving in the court, of the ale; and their half of the bragod, and their third of the mead. He has the shank of every steer from the court, which is not as high as the ankle[1]. On the ninth day before the calends of winter he receives a coat, and a shirt, and a cap, and three cubits of linen from the extremity of his elbow to the end of his middle finger, to make trowsers for himself; and there is to be no linsey-woolsey in his trowsers. The length of his clothes is only to extend to the tie of his trowsers. On the

---

[1] In order to make buskins for himself as high as the ankles, so say the Welsh texts later than the *Black Book of Chirk* (MS. A). See *Anc. Laws* I. 64, 392.

calends of March he has a coat and a shirt and a mantle and trowsers; also in the three chief seasons he has a bonnet. He is to share between the king and the maer and the canghellor. He has the odd sheaf, when the corn of fugitive taeogs shall be shared, and their marwdys. When a geldable fugitive shall leave his corn unreaped and when the like occurs in the case of a marwdy, the apparitor has the headlands. He has the bacon in cut and the butter in cut from the marwdys; and the nether stone of the quern, and all the green flax, and the flax seed, and the layer next to the ground of the mow, and the hatchets, the reaping-hooks, the fowls, the geese and the cats. He has a loaf with its enllyn in every house to which he comes on the king's business. Three cubits are to be in the length of his bill, lest he be discovered. He has the bull which shall come among the spoil. When the apparitor shall die, his possessions are at the king's mercy. If the apparitor suffer sarhâd while sitting during the pleas of the king, let there be paid to him a sieve full of chaff and an addle egg. The summons of an apparitor, with witnesses or striking the post three times, cannot be denied except by objecting. When however it shall be denied, the oath of the person summoned, with that of two men of the same status as himself, denies it.

The smith of a court has the heads of the V 14 a 6 cattle which shall be slaughtered in the kitchen and their feet, except the tongues. His maintenance, and that of his servant, comes from the court. Gratuitously he does all the work of the court except three works: a cauldron and a broad axe and a spear. A smith of a court has the ceinion of a banquet. He receives four pence from every prisoner off whom he shall remove irons. His land he has free. Legal liquor he has from the court, [viz.] the fill of the vessels used for serving in the court of the ale, and their third of the mead, and their half of the bragod. He is one of the three persons who receive that measure; then the apparitor; lastly the butler. No smith can be in the same cymwd as the smith of a court without his permission. He has the same freedom in grinding at the mill as the king. He has the gobrs of the daughters of the smiths who shall be under him and at his command. Six score pence is the ebediw of the smith of the court, and six score pence is the gobr of his

daughter. A pound and a half is her cowyll.
Three pounds her agweddi.

V 14 b 1   The porter has his land free. In the castle
behind the door is his house, and his
maintenance he gets from the court. He receives a log of wood from every horseload
of fuel which comes through the gate, and also
a log from every cartload, to wit, such a log
as he can pull with his one hand without im-
peding the progress of the horses or the oxen;
and although he cannot pull a single log of
wood, yet he receives a log, but not the largest.
Of the spoil of swine which comes to the gate,
the porter has a sow, and it is not to be larger
than he is able with his one hand to hold up
by the bristles so that her feet shall not be
lower than his knee. Of the spoil of cattle
which comes to the gate, if there be a steer
without a tail, the porter has it; and he also
has the last steer which comes to the gate,
and the milt and the rectum of the cattle which
shall be slaughtered in the kitchen. Four pence
he gets from every prisoner who shall be lawfully imprisoned in the court.

V 14 b 19   It is necessary that the watchman should
be a bonheddig gwlad, for in him confidence is placed by the king. His food he

always receives in the court, and, if the king be not in the court, he receives his mess first after the maer. Every morning he gets a loaf with its enllyn for his morning meal. The aitch-bone he gets of every steer slaughtered in the kitchen. His land he has free; and clothing he has twice in the year from the king; and shoes and stockings he gets once.

Land maer has the suet and the lard from v 15 a 3 the court. He has the skins of the cattle slaughtered in the kitchen which shall be three nights with the cattle of the maer-house. He has the gobrs of the daughters of the men of the maer-trev. Although the servants shall do sarhâd to the land maer while on their way carrying drink either from the kitchen or from the mead cellar towards the hall, they are not to make compensation to him. When his sarhâd shall be paid, six kine and six score of silver are paid to him. His galanas is paid with six kine and six score kine, with three augmentations.

The right of the chief of song is to sit on v 15 a 14 the left of the edling. His land he has free. He is to sing first in the hall. A wedding donation he receives, to wit, twenty four pence from every virgin when she shall marry. He

gets nothing however at the wedding of a woman
from whom he previously received chattels
on the occasion of her wedding when she was
a virgin. A bard when he shall have won a
chair, such is a chief of song. No bard can solicit
anything as far as the jurisdiction of the chief
of song shall extend, without his permission,
unless he be a bard of a border gwlad. Although
the king shall prohibit the giving of chattels
within his kingdom till the end of a certain
period, the chief of song is exempt by law.
When the king shall will to hear a song, let the
chief of song sing two songs concerning God
and the third of the chiefs. When the queen
shall will to hear a song in her chamber, let
the bard of the household sing three songs
softly lest the hall be disturbed.

V 15 b 6 Cub of a king's coverthound whilst its eyes
are shut, is twenty four pence in value.
In its litter, it is forty eight pence in value. In
its kennel, it is ninety six pence in value. In
its random hunting, it is six score pence in
value. When it shall be trained, it is a pound
V 15 b 11 in value. Cub of a king's greyhound before its
eyes are opened, is twelve pence in value. In
its litter, it is twenty four pence in value. In
its kennel, it is forty eight pence in value.

In its random hunting, it is ninety six pence
in value. When it shall be trained, it is a
pound in value. Of like worth are the covert- V 15 b 16
hound of a breyr and the greyhound of a king. :
The value of a breyr's greyhound is in law V 15 b 17
half the value of a breyr's coverthound of equal
age. Of whatever breed the cub of a taeog may V 15 b 18
be, it is before opening its eyes a curt penny
in value. In its litter, it is two curt pence in
value. In its kennel, it is three curt pence
in value. When it shall be set free, it is four
curt pence in value. A cur, although it is a V 15 b 23
king who shall own it, is of no more value than
four curt pence. If it be a shepherd dog, it
is of the value of a steer of current worth ; and
should there be doubt as to its being so, let the
owner swear, with a neighbour above his door
and another below his door, that it goes before
the cattle in the morning and guards the hindmost at the close of day. Whoever shall pull V 16 a 3
out an eye of a king's coverthound or shall
cut off its tail, let him pay four legal pence
for every cow which the dog shall be worth.
A rambling dog, if it be killed further than V 16 a 6
nine paces from the door, shall not be paid
for. If it be killed within the nine paces,
twenty four pence are paid for it. No legal V 16 a 8

worth exists on a harrier; on everything which has no legal worth, an appraisement is obtained.

V 16 a 11 ⦿hoever shall meddle with a king's hart in season, let him pay three kine camlwrw to the king. A stag is of the value of an ox. A hind is of the value of a cow. There are to be twelve privileged pieces in a king's hart in season: tongue, and the three pieces of the neck, lungs, heart, two-loins, shoulder, haunch, stomach, nombles, liver. Three kine camlwrw are paid for every piece. For a king's hart in season, when every camlwrw is reckoned, there are paid two score kine. There are no privileged pieces in a king's hart except from the Feast of Cirig to the calends of December; and it is not a hart in season except whilst the privileged pieces shall be in

V 16 a 22 it. ⦿f a king's stag be killed in the trev of a breyr in the morning, let the breyr keep it whole until mid-day; and if the huntsmen do not arrive then, let the breyr cause the hart to be skinned, and the dogs to be lured from the flesh [1]; and let him take home the dogs and the

---

[1] There appears to be some confusion in the various texts as to the dogs and the flesh. Cf. Peniarth MS. 28, et canes pascat

skin and the liver and the hind quarter; and
if the huntsmen do not arrive that night, let
him make use of the flesh and let him keep the
dogs and the skin for the huntsmen. If the
stag be killed at mid-day, let the breyr keep it
whole till the night; and if the huntsmen do
not arrive then, let the breyr make use of it
like the former one. If it be killed during the V 16 b 7
night in the trev of a breyr, let him spread his
mantle over it, and let him keep it whole until
the morning; and if the huntsmen do not
arrive then, it will be of the same status as the
former ones. If a freeman be hunting with V 16 b 11
coverthounds, let him wait in the morning
until the king's huntsmen shall thrice let loose
their dogs; and afterwards let him let loose.
Whoever shall kill a hart on another person's V 16 b 14
land, let him give a quarter to the owner of the
land, unless it be a king's hart; for there is to
be no quarter for land in a king's hart. If V 16 b 17
a traveller sees an animal from a road in a
king's forest, let him discharge a missile at it,
if he will; and if he hit it, let him pursue whilst
he shall see it; and from the time that it shall
disappear from view, let him leave it.

V 16 b 21 Thus far by the permission of God we have discussed the Laws of a Court. Now with the help of the glorious Lord Jesus Christ, we will shew the Laws of a Gwlad. And first, the Three Columns of Law, that is, the nine accessaries of galanas; and the nine accessaries of fire; and the nine accessaries of theft.

V 17 a 4 The first of the nine accessaries of galanas is tongue-reddening, that is, showing the place where the person, who is to be killed, may be to the person who kills him. The second is, giving counsel to kill the person. The third is, consenting with the murderer to kill him. The fourth is, looking out. The fifth is, accompanying the murderer. The sixth is, repairing to the trev. The seventh is, superintending. The eighth is, being an assistant. The ninth is, seeing him killed while allowing it. For each of the first three, there is given nine score of silver and the oaths of a hundred men to deny blood. For each of the following three, there is given twice nine score of silver and the oaths of two hundred men. For each of the last three, there is paid thrice nine score of silver and the oaths of three hundred men V 17 a 17 to deny blood. Whoever shall deny wood and field, let him give the oaths of fifty men without bondman and without alltud; and three of them abjuring horse-riding and linen and woman. Whoever shall admit homicide, let V 17 a 20 him and his kindred pay the sarhâd of the person who is killed, and his galanas. And first, the murderer pays the murdered man's sarhâd to his father and his mother and his brothers and his sisters; and if he was married, his wife is to receive a third of the sarhâd from those. Moreover the third of the galanas will fall on the murderer and his father and his mother and his brothers and his sisters, apart from the kindred. Again, the third of the murderer is divided into three parts, the third to fall on the murderer himself, and the two parts on the father and the mother and the brothers and the sisters; and of those men each one pays as much as the other, and so the women; and no woman pays more than half the share of a man; and that third is to be paid to the slain person's father and mother and his co-heirs as in the case of his sarhâd. The two shares which are imposed on the kindred are divided into three parts; and of these, the kindred of the father pays two shares, and the mother's kindred pays the third. The same generations of the kin-

dred are to pay galanas along with the murderer
to the same generations who receive it on the
part of the murdered, from the ancestor in
V 17 b 15 the fifth remove to the fifth cousin. Thus are
named the nine degrees of a kindred who are
to pay galanas and to receive it, and their
members. The first of the nine degrees is the
father and mother of the murderer or of the
murdered. The second is a brother and sister.
The third is a grandfather. The fourth is a
great grandfather. The fifth is a cousin. The
sixth is a second cousin. The seventh is a
third cousin. The eighth is a fourth cousin.
The ninth is a fifth cousin. The members
of the degrees are the nephew and uncle of
the murderer or the murdered. A nephew is
a son of a brother or a son of a sister, or of
a cousin male or female, or of a second cousin.
An uncle is a brother of a father or mother,
or of a grandfather or a grandmother, or of
a great grandfather or a great grandmother.
And this is the amount of the share of each
one of all these when paying galanas or receiving it. Whoever may be in kinship nearer
than another by one generation to the murderer
or the murdered, pays or receives twice as
much as that other; and so in respect to each

of the seven last degrees and the members
of all the degrees. The heirs of the murderer
or the murdered are not to pay anything nor
receive in respect to galanas, because the share
of the person who pays more than any other
stands for him and his heirs; and their care
rests on him. The care of the heir of the murdered rests on his parents and his co-heirs
because they receive a third part of the galanas.
And if there be anyone of the kindred of the
murderer or the murdered, who is an eccle-
siastic in holy orders or a religious or leprous
or dumb or an idiot, he neither pays nor receives any of the galanas. They are not to
take vengeance for a person murdered, nor is
vengeance to be taken on them; and it is
impossible to compel such by any law to pay
anything, nor are they to receive.

OF the nine accessaries of fire, the first is V 18 a 22
counselling to burn the house. The
second is, agreeing concerning the burning.
The third is, going to burn. The fourth is,
carrying the cresset. The fifth is, striking the
fire. The sixth is, procuring tinder. The
seventh is, blowing the fire until it shall kindle.
The eighth is, setting fire to the thing with
which to burn. The ninth is, watching the

burning and allowing it. Whoever shall deny one of these nine accessaries, let him give the oaths of fifty men without bondman and without alltud.

V 18 b 6   The first of the nine accessaries of theft is devising deceit and seeking an accomplice. The second is, agreeing concerning the theft. The third is, giving provision. The fourth is, carrying the food while accompanying him. The fifth is, tearing down the cattle yard or breaking the house. The seventh [sixth] is, moving what is stolen from its place and walking day or night with it. The seventh is, knowing and informing as to the theft. The eighth is, sharing with the thieves. The ninth is, seeing the theft and concealing it for reward or buying it for worth. Whoever shall deny one of these accessaries, let him give the oaths of fifty men without bondman and without alltud.

V 18 b 19   Nine persons who are to be believed in giving their testimony, each one of them separately on his oath. A lord between his two men as to a suit which they acknowledge to have been previously before him ; and he be not interested in the suit, and they be not in agreement as to the mode. An abbot between his two monks on the threshold of the choir. A father between his two sons by placing his hands on the head of the son against whom he shall swear, and saying thus: 'By God, the One who created me thy father and thee my son, the truth I declare between you.' A judge as to what he previously decided, if the two persons concerning whom he judged are disputing concerning the decision. A surety as to his suretyship if he admit a part and deny another part. A priest between his two parishioners as to the testimony which was testified to him. A virgin as to her virginity, if the man to whom she was given declares she was not a virgin in order to take away her right and her due; or if she is violated and the man who violated her says she was not a virgin, the virgin's testimony is to be believed against him. A shepherd of a hamlet (trefgoɪd) as to his shepherding if one animal kills the other. A thief without hope of mercy concerning his fellow-thief, when brought to the gallows; because credible is his word concerning his companions and the chattels they thieved, without a relic; and his companion is not to be destroyed on his word, but is to be a thief for sale. To be believed also is a contract man as to his contract. And so also to be believed is an informer who gives a full information. And a giver of property is to be believed as to the chattels he gives, and so it is said : ' There is no gift except by consent.'

V 19 a 24 A person's hand, and his foot, and his eye, and his lip, and his ear with loss of its hearing, and his nose ; six kine and six score of silver is the worth of each one of them. If a person's ear be wholly cut off and the person continue to hear as before, two kine and two V 19 b 4 score of silver are to be paid. The testicles are of the same worth as all the above members. V 19 b 5 The tongue by itself is of such value as all the members which have been so far mentioned. All a person's members when reckoned together are eight and four score pounds in value. V 19 b 9 A person's finger is a cow and a score of silver V 19 b 10 in value. The worth of the thumb is two kine V 19 b 11 and two score of silver. A person's nail is V 19 b 12 thirty pence in value. The worth of the extreme joint, twenty six pence and a half-penny V 19 b 14 and a third of a penny. The worth of the middle joint, fifty and a half-penny and two V 19 b 16 parts of a half-penny. The worth of the nearest V 19 b 17 joint, eighty pence. A person's foretooth is twenty four pence in value with three augmentations; and when a foretooth is paid for, the worth of a conspicuous scar is to be paid with it. A backtooth is fifty [pence] in value. V 19 b 20

Twenty four pence is the worth of a person's V 19 b 21 blood, for it is not proper that the worth of a man's blood should be as high as the worth of God's blood. Although he was very man, he was very God and he sinned not in his flesh. There are three conspicuous scars upon V 19 b 25 a person: a scar on a person's face, valued at six score pence; a scar on the back of the right hand, valued at sixty pence; a scar on the back of the right foot, valued at thirty pence. The worth of a person's eyelid, as long V 20 a 4 as the hair is on it, is one legal penny in value for every hair; if a part be cut away from it, then the worth of a conspicuous scar is paid.

The amount of the galanas of a maer or a V 20 a 8 canghellor is one hundred and eighty nine kine with three augmentations. The sarhâd of each of them is nine kine and nine score of silver. The ebediw of each of them is a pound. The gobr of the daughter of each is a pound, and the cowyll is three pounds, and the agweddi is seven pounds. If a daughter of a maer or a canghellor or one of the principal officers of a court goes away clandestinely without consent

of kindred, nine steers with horns and ears of
V 20 a 18 equal length will be their agweddi. Four kine
and four score of silver is the sarhâd of a king's
domestic (teulu⟨r⟩) if he avouch himself as such.
V 20 a 20 Three kine are paid for the sarhâd of a breyr's
domestic, that is, three kine of current value.

V 20 a 22 The galanas of a chief of kindred is thrice
nine kine and thrice nine score kine
with three augmentations. For his sarhâd
thrice nine kine and thrice nine score of silver
V 20 a 25 are paid. The galanas of one of the members of a chief of kindred, to wit, his kin, is
paid with nine kine and nine score kine
with three augmentations. For his sarhâd he
receives nine kine and nine score of silver.
V 20 b 3 The galanas of a breyr without office is paid
with six kine and six score kine with three
augmentations. His sarhâd is paid with six
V 20 b 6 kine and six score of silver. The galanas of
an innate bonheddig is paid with three kine and
three score kine with three augmentations.
His sarhâd is paid with three kine and three
score of silver. An innate bonheddig is a Cymro
by mother and father without bondman and
without alltud and without mean origin in him.
If an innate bonheddig is a breyr's man when
murdered, the breyr receives six kine of the

galanas from the murderer. ʊo the king comes V 20 b 14
the third of every galanas, because it is for him
to enforce where it is not possible for a kindred
to enforce ; and what shall be obtained of the
murderer's chattels from time to time, belongs
to the king. ʊhe galanas of a king's taeog is V 20 b 18
paid with three kine and three score kine with
three augmentations. His sarhâd is three kine
and three score of silver. ʊhe galanas of V 20 b 20
a breyr's taeog is half the galanas of a king's
taeog, and likewise his sarhâd. ʊhe galanas V 20 b 22
of a king's alltud is paid with three kine and
three score kine without augmentation. His
sarhâd is three kine without addition. ʊhe V 20 b 25
galanas of a breyr's alltud, is half the galanas
of a king's alltud. ʊhe galanas of a taeog's V 21 a 1
alltud, is half the galanas of a breyr's alltud, and
likewise with regard to their sarhâds.

ℭhoever shall strike a person, let him pay V 21 a 4
his sarhâd first, because attack and
onset constitute a sarhâd to every person ; and
a penny for every hair pulled out from his head
by the root ; and a penny for every finger which
shall touch the head ; and twenty-four pence
for the front hair. Ⱡet every one choose his V 21 a 9
status, whether by the status of his chief of
kindred or by the status of his father or by

EVANS O

V 21 a 11 the status of his office. A pound and a half is the worth of a well-formed bondman, if he originates from beyond the sea. If however he be maimed or too old or too young, that is, less than twenty years, he is one pound in value. If also he originates from this side of the sea, he is a pound in value, because he himself debased his status by willingly becoming V 21 a 18 a hireling. If a free man strike a bondman, let him pay him twelve pence; six for three cubits of home-made white cloth to make him a coat for cutting furze in; three for trowsers; one for buskins and gloves; one for a hedging-bill, or for a hatchet if he be a woodman; one V 21 a 24 for a rope of twelve cubits. If a bondman strike a free man, it is just to cut off his right hand, or let the bondman's lord pay the person's V 21 b 2 sarhâd. The protection of a bondman is as far V 21 b 3 as he throws his sickle. Whoever shall have connexion with a bondwoman without consent of her lord, let him pay twelve pence to the V 21 b 5 bondwoman's lord for each connexion. Whoever shall cause the pregnancy of a bondwoman who shall be on hire, let him give another in her place until she be delivered; and then let him cause the issue [to be nursed] and let the bondwoman return to her place; and if she die in childbirth, let him who caused her pregnancy, pay her legal worth to her lord. Every person V 21 b 10 receives augmentation in his galanas and in his sarhâd except an alltud ; the scores [of silver] which are paid together with the cattle are the augmentations. The sarhâd of a bondwoman V 21 b 13 is twelve pence in value; and if she be a serving [woman] who works neither at the spade nor the quern, twenty-four pence is her sarhâd. Whoever waylays a person, pays double the V 21 b 16 galanas of the person who is murdered; and twelve kine dirwy doubled, he pays to the king. Whoever shall deny waylaying or murder or V 21 b 19 open attack, let him give the oaths of fifty men without bondman and without alltud. An open attack cannot be on the part of less than nine men.

It is for a court to meer ; and after a court, V 21 b 23 a llan ; and after a llan, status ; and after status, prior conservancy on waste. A house, a kiln and a barn, constitute prior conservancy. If contention arise between two trevs of equal status concerning boundary, it is for the king's gwrdas to determine it, if they know ; and if they are doubtful, it is for the proprietors of the land to swear, every one as to his boundary; and afterwards let them share the object of their

V 22 a 6   contention equally between them. Although a trev shall meer to another, it is not to take a rhandir from it. Half a pound comes to the king when a meer shall be fixed between two trevs; and twenty-four pence come to the judges. When law shall award land to a person, half a pound comes to the king from every rhandir when he shall give investiture.[1]

V 22 a 13   Thus are suits concerning land and soil elucidated. The claimant is to exhibit his claim; and after that the defendant his defence; and after that it is for the elders of the gwlad to consult together amicably which of the parties is right and which is not; and after the elders shall have considered their opinion and strengthened their proceeding by oath, then the judges are to withdraw apart and decide according to the proceeding of the elders, and inform the king what they shall have

---

[1] The translation of these two sentences is not in accordance with the punctuation in the text, which if followed would translate '. . . between two trevs. Twenty-four . . . to the judges when law . . . person. Half a pound', &c. According to Aneurin Owen the two early Latin texts differ here, Peniarth 28 reading: 'Rex debet . . . uillas. Judices uero . . . denarios, si terra . . . alicui. De qualibet . . . libre'; and Brit. Mus. Vesp. E. xi: 'Rex debet . . . villas; judices vero . . . [denarios]. Si terra . . . alicui . . . de qualibet . . . libre.' *Anc. Laws*, II. 778, 852; also I. 538, 762.

adjudged; and that is a verdict of a gwlad after defence. When a dispute shall be com- V 22 a 23 menced concerning the meering of lands or trevs; if it be commenced between the land of the court and the land of the gwlad, the court is to meer. If between the land of the gwlad and church land, the church is to meer. If between co-inheritors, status is to meer. If between occupied land and a waste, prior conservancy is to meer. Building and tillage denote occupation. When a court meers, it V 22 b 5 is for the maer and canghellor to define the meers on its behalf; if a church, crozier and gospel.

Whoever wills to move a claim concerning V 22 b 8 land by kin and descent, let him move it on one of the two ninth days, either the ninth day of December or the ninth day of May; for if such a claim as that be moved outside one of those days, it will not succeed. Whoever V 22 b 13 shall claim land on the ninth day of December, shall have judgment respecting it before the ninth of May; and if he do not then have judgment, let him claim on the ninth day of the succeeding May if he will to continue law; and afterwards law is open for him when the king shall will.

V 22 b 18   Three dadannudds of land there are; dadannudd of car, and dadannudd of burden, and dadannudd of aration. He to whom is adjudged dadannudd of burden, has three days and three nights of rest without suit; and on the third day he gives answer, and on the ninth day judgment. He to whom is adjudged dadannudd of car, has five days and five nights rest, and on the fifth day answer, and on the ninth day judgment. He to whom is adjudged dadannudd of aration, has rest without suit until he shall turn his back upon the stack; and

V 23 a 4   on the ninth day judgment. No one is entitled to dadannudd except that of the land which shall have been in the hand of his father in his lifetime

V 23 a 6   and to his death. Whoever shall have dadannudd adjudged to him, no one can eject him from his dadannudd except a proprietary heir; since the second dadannudd cannot eject the first; and one non-proprietor is not to eject another non-proprietor from his dadannudd. And if there be a dispute as to dadannudd between proprietary heirs, one cannot eject the

V 23 a 13   other by law. Of two lawful heirs one is proprietary heir to dadannudd of the whole and the other is not, as no one is proprietary heir to dadannudd of the whole except the eldest brother. The status of the eldest brother is to take the dadannudd of the whole for his brothers; and although they should come before him, they do not receive the dadannudd of the whole; and if they take it, he may eject them therefrom if he wills it. If they make the demand jointly, they are to receive it jointly as stated above. It is not necessary to await a v 23 a 22 ninth day for deciding the boundary of land except when it shall be the will of the king and his gwrdas. Also it is not necessary to await v 23 a 24 a ninth day between a proprietor and a non-proprietor who shall hold land in opposition to him.

Three times is land to be shared among kins- v 23 b 2 men : first among brothers; then among cousins; the third time among second cousins. Thenceforward there is no proper sharing of land. When brothers share their father's trev among them, the youngest gets the principal homestead and eight erws and the whole stock and the boiler and the fuel hatchet and the coulter, since a father can neither give nor devise them except to the youngest son; and although they be pledged, they never lapse. Then let every brother take a principal homestead and eight erws ; and the youngest son shall share, and from eldest to eldest they are

V 23 b 14 to choose. No person is to demand re-sharing except him who has not obtained a choice, as there is no gwarthal with choice.

V 23 b 16 If a person neglects three summons on the part of the king respecting land, unless a great necessity hinders him, the land is given to him who shall claim it. If he comes at the second summons or at the third, let him answer respecting the land if it is right for him; and let him pay three kine camlwrw to the king

V 23 b 21 for neglecting summons. Whoever shall pay an investiture fee for land, is not by right to

V 23 b 23 pay ebediw. Whoever shall hold land during three men's lives in the same gwlad as the recognized possessors, during the lives of father, grandfather and great-grandfather without claim and without surclaim, without burning of house, without breaking of plough; that land is never to be answered for by them, inasmuch as law

V 24 a 3 has shut between them. Whoever shall claim land by kin and descent, it is necessary that the elders of the gwlad should swear as to the

V 24 a 6 kin before hearing the claim. If a person receives a share of land from his kindred after a long state of exile, let him give six score pence as fee for custody if they concede to him

a share. The land which the king shall give V 24 a 9
to a person by right, let not him who shall rule
after him retake. Whoever shall allow the V 24 a 11
transfer of his father's trev in his presence to
another without let and without hindrance,
shall not have it whilst he lives. Whoever V 24 a 13
shall claim land; if he traces his kin along the
distaff more than three times, his claim shall be
lost. If a church is made on a taeogtrev with V 24 a 15
the king's leave and it be a burying-place, and
there be a priest saying mass in it, that trev
shall be free from that time forward. If a V 24 a 19
taeog takes the son of a breyr to foster with
his lord's permission, such a son is to participate
in the taeog's father's trev like one of his own
sons. Every joint land is to be held with oath V 24 a 22
and with chattels; and he who does not so hold
it, let him lose his share. When however the
land shall have been shared, no one ought to
pay for another. Each however ought to hold
with their oath, one for another, of the brothers,
cousins and second cousins; and the land which
any one of them shall lose through lack of
oath on the part of the rest, let them make
good to him. Beyond second cousins no one
is to preserve the share of another either with
his oath or with his chattels.

V 24 b 6   Whoever shall commit treason against a lord or waylay, is to forfeit his father's trev ; and if he be caught, he is liable to be executed. If he be not caught and he will to be reconciled to his lord and kindred, a twofold payment of dirwy and galanas is to be levied on him ; and if he repair to the court of the pope and return with the pope's letter with him and show that he is absolved by the pope, he has his father's trev. A third cause for which a person forfeits his father's trev is the abandoning of his land without leave, and his not being able to bear the burden and the service attached thereto.

V 24 b 17   No person is to obtain the land of his co-heir, as of his brother or of his cousin or of his second cousin, by claiming it through the one of them who shall die without an heir of his body ; but by claiming it through one of his parents who shall have been in possession of that land till his death, whether a father or grandfather or great-grandfather ; and so he gets the land

V 24 b 24 if he be next of kin to the deceased. After brothers shall have shared their father's trev between them, if one of them die without an heir of his body or a co-heir to a third cousin,

V 25 a 2 the king is to be heir of that land. There

are three kinds of prid on land: one is, a
conservancy fee ; the second is, chattels which
shall be given to augment land or its status;
the third is, the lawful labour which shall be
done on the land whereby the land is im-
proved. No person is to demand re-sharing V 25 a 6
except the one who has not obtained a choice,
since gwarthal does not harmonize with choice.[1]

There are three lawful inheritances which V 25 a 9
remain secure to the inheritors. One is an
inheritance by title on the part of parents.
The second is an inheritance by lawful contract
with the owner for worth. The third is an
inheritance which shall be obtained by a lawful
contract by the will of the owner without worth.

By three means are land and soil to be sued V 25 a 16
for : through wrong possession ; and by dadannudd ; and by kin and descent. Though the suit
for land may not succeed by the first means or
by the second, it is to be obtained none the less
slower than before by the third.

There are three wrong possessions : posses- V 25 a 20

---

[1] The doubling of the word gwarthal in the text is due to
confusion with the proverb which Sir John Rhŷs thinks may
have run thus : 'Nyt oes gwarthal gwarthal gan dewis', meaning ' Gwarthal with choice is not gwarthal at all'.   Another
form of the proverb is distinctly referred to and quoted in the
texts amalgamated in the *Anc. Laws* I. 544.

sion in opposition to the owner against his will
and without judgment; or possession through
the owner and in opposition to his heir against
his will and without judgment; or possession
through a guardian and in opposition to the
right proprietor against his will and without
judgment. An owner is one having a sure
title. A guardian is one who maintains or
V 25 b 3 guards the title of another person. There are
three kinds of status: natural status, and status
V 25 b 5 of land, and status of office. There are three
qualifications proper to every person : kind and
status and heirship. Heirship however is according to status; status according to kind;
kind according to the difference which may be
between persons according to law, such as the
difference between a king and a breyr, and between man and woman, and eldest and youngest.

V 25 b 11 Four rhandirs are to be in the trev from
which a king's gwestva shall be paid.
Eighteen feet are to be in the length of the rod
(góyalen) of Howel the Good; and eighteen
such rods (lathen) are to be the length of the
erw, and two rods the breadth. Three hundred
and twelve such erws are to be in the rhandir
between clear and brake, and wood and field,
and wet and dry, except the gorvodtrev; and

from such rhandirs land borderers are called in
law. There are three evidences for land: V 25 b 19
elders of a gwlad for ascertaining kin and
descent to establish a person in his right as to
land and soil. The second is; a man from
every rhandir of that trev constitutes the land
borderers for ascertaining the mutual sharing
between kindred and relatives. The third is;
when there shall be contention between two
trevs, maers and canghellors and apparitors are
to preserve boundaries, for it belongs to a king
to meer. There are to be thirteen trevs in V 26 a 1
every maenor, and the thirteenth of these is
the gorvodtrev. In each free trev with office V 26 a 3
and free trev without office, there are four
rhandirs, three for occupancy and the fourth
pasturage for the three rhandirs. There are V 26 a 6
three rhandirs in the taeogtrev; in each of the
two are three taeogs, and the third pasturage
for the two. Seven trevs are to be in the V 26 a 8
maenor of the taeogtrevs.

Whoever shall breach a meer upon the land V 26 a 10
of another person, let him pay three kine
camlwrw to the king and let him restore the
meer to its former state. In impetuous large V 26 a 12
river is not a boundary between two cymwds
save in its original channel. A stone cross, V 26 a 14

that is, a meer stone or meer timber or other specified thing which shall preserve a boundary,

V 26 a 16 is six score pence in value. Whoever, shall breach a meer between two trevs, or shall plough a highway, is to pay six score pence to the king; and let him restore the meer to

V 26 a 19 its former state. The breadth of land between two trevs, if it be of land, is a fathom and a half; between two rhandirs, four feet; be-

V 26 a 22 tween two erws, two furrows. The breadth of

V 26 a 23 a king's highway is twelve feet. Whoever shall hold two lands under one lord, let him pay his ebediw for the one of higher status.

V 26 a 25 The measure of a king's gwestva from every trev from which a king's gwestva is paid: a horse load of wheat-flour and an ox and seven threaves of oats of one binding, and what shall suffice of honey for one vat. Nine hand-breadths is to be the height of the vat when measured diagonally from the off groove to the near edge; and twenty-four of silver. A pound is the worth of a king's gwestva; six score pence in lieu of his bread, and three score pence for his enllyn, and three score pence for his liquor. It is so paid moreover unless the food is supplied in its right time, namely, in the

V 26 b 10 winter. From the trev of a maership or can-

ghellorship, mead is paid. From a free trev with- V 26 b 11
out office, bragod is paid. From a taeogtrev, V 26 b 12
ale is paid. Two vats of bragod or four of ale
are paid for one of mead. Two vats of ale are
paid for one of bragod. There is paid with
a summer gwestva neither silver nor provender
for horses.

Two dawnbwyds come to the king in the V 26 b 17
year from the taeogs. The winter dawnbwyd
is a sow three fingers in the shoulder and in
the long ribs and in the ham; and a salted
flitch; and three score loaves of wheat bread
if wheat grow there; let nine loaves be of fine
flour, three for the chamber and six for the
hall, each loaf to be as broad as from elbow
to wrist. If they be oaten, let the nine loaves
be of groats; they are to be so thick as not
to bend when held by their edge; and the fill
of a tub of ale; and a penny from every rhandir
to the servants. The summer dawnbwyd is
butter and cheese. The tub of butter is nine
handbreadths in width, and a handbreadth in
thickness with the thumb standing; and the
milks of a meal from all the taeogs are col-
lected in one day to make cheese; and that is
paid along with the bread. No maer, no V 27 a 9
canghellor, no share, [no] quarters, come on

V 27 a 10 a free man. Once every year it is necessary
for everybody to go in the host along with the
king to a border gwlad, if he will it; and then
the queen is entitled to a lady-progress. Always
however, whenever he shall so will, is he to
be accompanied in the host in his own gwlad.

V 27 a 15 The huntsmen and the falconers and the grooms
have a progress among the king's taeogs; each
party however separately.

V 27 a 18 Nine buildings the taeogs ought to make
for the king; a hall, chamber, kitchen,
chapel, barn, kilnhouse, necessary, stable, dog-
kennel. From the taeogs the king has sumpter-
horses for his host; and from every taeogtrev
he receives a man and horse and hatchet at
the king's cost to make encampments for him.

V 27 a 24 Three things a taeog is not to sell without his
lord's permission: a horse and swine and
honey. If he refuse them in the first instance,
let him after that sell them to whom he may

V 27 b 3 please. Three arts which a taeog is not to
teach his son without his lord's permission:
scholarship and bardism and smithcraft. For
if his lord be passive until the tonsure be
given to the scholar, or until a smith enters
his smithy, or a bard with his song, no one
can enslave them after that.

If a bishop's men or an abbot's men fight V 27 b 10
with a king's men upon the land of the teyrn,
their dirwy comes to the teyrn; and although
a bishop's men and an abbot's men fight on
the king's land, to the king their dirwy comes.
Whoever shall plough land against a lord's V 27 b 14
interdiction, let him pay four legal pence if he
shall have opened soil with violence; and four
legal pence if he shall have taken implements
from the soil : and a penny for every furrow
turned up by the plough; and that to the
owner of the land. Let the lord take all the
oxen and the plough and the implements ; and
the worth of the right hand of the driver
and the worth of the right foot of the ploughman. If a person excavate the land of another V 27 b 22
person to hide anything therein, the owner of
the land shall have four legal pence for opening
the soil and the hoard, unless it be a hoard of
gold ;

[A chasm in V supplied from W]

for every hoard of gold belongs to a king.
Whoever shall make a snare on another person's W 63 b 17
land and shall conceal it therein, let him pay
four legal pence for opening soil to the owner
of the land ; and should there be a beast found

therein, it also belongs to the owner of the
land; and let him pay three kine camlwrw to
W 64 a 2 the king. If a kiln pit be dug on another
person's land without permission, let him who
shall dig it pay four legal pence to the owner
of the land, and three kine camlwrw to the
W 64 a 5 king. Whoever shall build a house on another
person's land without his permission, let him
pay three kine camlwrw to the king; and the
owner of the land shall have the house, and
four legal pence for opening soil, if on the
land the timber of the house was cut. If not
cut on the land, let him swear with two men of
the same status as himself; and let him cut
away the house even with the surface of the
ground, and let him take it away from his land
before the end of the ninth day; and if he do
not take it, it belongs to the owner of the land.
W 64 a 15 Whoever shall claim church land, it is not
necessary for him to await a ninth
day, but justice is open to him when he shall
will. No one is to obtain on the part of a mother
a principal homestead nor office if there be
any one entitled thereto on the part of a father.
It is right however for an heir on the part of
W 64 a 20 a mother to have a share of land. A woman
who shall give herself up in bush and brake

without consent of kindred ; her children shall
have no share of land from a mother's kindred
except by favour ; for no son begotten in bush
and brake is entitled to share of land. Who- W 64 b 4
ever shall cut down trees with permission of the
owner of the land, is to have it free for five
years ; and the sixth it is to be free to the
owner. Whoever shall car-manure land with w 64 b 7
the owner's permission, is entitled to it for
three years ; and the fourth it is free to the
owner. Whoever shall spread fold dung on w 64 b 9
another person's' land with his permission is
entitled to it for two years; and the third it
is free to the owner. Whoever shall break w 64 b 12
up fresh soil on another person's land with
his permission ; the first year he shall have
it free, and the second year for pay (ar get), and
the third it is free to the owner. If a Cym- W 64 b 15
raes [i. e. a Cymric woman] be given to an
alltud, her children shall have a share of land
except the principal homestead ; that they are
not to receive until the third generation ; and
therefrom originate cattle without surety, because, if he commits a crime, the mother's
kindred pay the whole of his galanas.

A bruise which shall remain three ninth- w 64 b 21
days is subject to the same liability

and the same denial as blood. If it be denied, let him give his oath with two men of the same status as himself on the first ninth-day. If it remains two ninth-days, let him give his oath with three men of the same status as himself. If it remains three ninth-days, let him give his oath with four men of the same status as himself; and thus is blood denied.

W 65 a 8 If there be a legal guardian, and chattels are taken by stealth from under his guardianship, and the keys remain with him safely, and there be seen a breach in the house; the Book of Cynog says it is easier to believe him if there be chattels of his own taken together with the other chattels which were taken by stealth from him. He is however to swear conjointly with all the persons in the house as to his being clear as to those chattels. If the soil however be excavated under the house; after he has carried out the law that he is clear, the king owns the soil and there is to be no guardian answerable for it. Every chattel which a guardian asserts to have been brought to him to be kept, let him make good except the chattels conveyed through the soil. If a person bring chattels to a guardian and some of the chattels be lost, and there be disputing between the guardian and the owner concerning those chattels, the guardian is to swear together with one person nearest in worth of his kindred. The law as to gold is to W 65 b 3 give it from hand to hand with witnesses into the hand of the guardian to keep. The law as W 65 b 4 to silver is to count it openly from each hand into the hand of the guardian. One person W 65 b 7 escapes from an admitted theft with flesh and skin on his back, [viz.], a necessitous alltud who shall have been three nights and three days without alms without relief, and who shall have traversed three trevs daily with nine houses in every trev ; and then owing to hunger shall commit theft and then shall be caught with flesh and skin on his back. He is to be let free without gallows and without payment. One person W 65 b 15 whose house is not to be a marwdy although he die intestate ; a judge of a court. One animal W 65 b 17 which shall rise [in worth] from four pence to a pound in one day ; a covert hound. If a taeog owns it in the morning, it is worth four pence ; and if it be given to the king on that day, it is worth a pound. A stallion grazing out and a W 65 b 21 greyhound without its collar lose their status. Eight packhorses of a king are ; W 66 a 1

[V resumes]

V 29 a 1 the sea, and a waste, and an irremediable pauper, and a thief, and a marwdy, and dirwy, and camlwrw, and ebediw.

V 29 a 3 From the time a colt is foaled until August, it is six pence in value. From August to the calends of winter, it is twelve pence in value. Until the calends of February, it is eighteen pence in value. Until the calends of May, it it twenty-four pence in value. Until August, it is thirty pence in value. Until the calends of December, it is thirty-six pence in value. Until the calends of February, it is forty-two pence in value. Until the calends of May, it is forty-eight pence in value. It is then two years old. It is then in value from the calends of May until August three score pence, because an increase of twelve pence is added to it then; and twelve pence also every season until the calends of May; and then it is three years old. It is then in value ninety-six pence. The day it is caught, an increase of twenty pence is added to it. When bridled, [four pence] are to be added to that above, and then it is six score pence in value. A stallion which is fattened for six weeks over a stall is a

pound in value. A stallion grazing out and a
greyhound without its collar lose their status.
Twenty-four pence is the value of the hair
of a stallion if cut away from the tail. If
any of the tail however be cut off, the worth
of the whole stallion is then to be paid, and
the stallion is to be secured to the person who
maimed it. The eye of a stallion and its ear
are each of them twenty-four pence in value.
A rowney is six score pence in value. The V 29 b 2
hair of a rowney is twelve pence in value if cut
away from the tail. If however any of the tail
be cut away, the worth of the whole rowney
is then to be paid, and [the rowney] itself to be
secured to the person who paid for it. The
eye of a rowney and its ear are each of them
twelve pence in value. A palfrey is a mark V 29 b 8
in value. Its limbs are of the same worth as
the limbs of a rowney. A working horse or V 29 b 10
a working mare are of the same worth and
the same augmentation as a steer excepting
their teithi. The teithi of a working horse V 29 b 12
or a working mare are carrying a load and
drawing a car uphill and downhill, and that without swaying. Whoever shall borrow a horse V 29 b 15
and chafe its back badly so that much hair
falls off, four legal pence are to be paid to the

owner. If however the back swells from the chafing of an old sore, and the skin be broken to the flesh, eight legal pence are to be paid. If there be no old sore on it, and the skin and flesh be cut to the bone, sixteen legal pence are

V 29 b 22 to be paid. Whoever shall deny the killing stealthily of a stallion or palfrey, let him give the

V 29 b 24 oaths of twenty-four men. A stud mare is six score pence in value. Her tail hair and her eye and her ear are each of them six legal

V 30 a 2 pence in value. Whoever shall ride a horse without consent of the owner, let him pay four pence for mounting, and four for alighting, and four for every rhandir which he traverses, to the owner of the horse; and three kine camlwrw to

V 30 a 7 the king. Whoever shall sell a horse or a mare, let him be answerable for inward disorders, to wit, three mornings for the staggers, and three months for the glanders, and a year for the farcy. Let the person who shall buy it look

V 30 a 11 to an outside blemish. Whoever shall sell a horse, let him be answerable for the horse grazing and drinking water, and that it be not restive; and if it be restive, let the person who sold it choose between taking the horse back or returning a third of the worth to the other.

V 30 a 15 Whoever shall protect a horse against thieves

in the same gwlad as its owner, receives four
legal pence for every cow the horse may be
worth. Whoever shall protect a cow from
thieves in the same gwlad as the owner, receives
four legal pence.

A she calf is six pence in value from the V 30 a 22
time it is born until the calends of December. Thence until the calends of February
it is eight pence in value. Until the calends of
May, it is ten pence in value. Until August,
it is twelve pence in value. Until the calends
of December, it is fourteen pence in value.
Until the calends of February, it is sixteen
pence in value. Until the calends of May, it
is eighteen pence in value. Until August, it
is twenty pence in value. The next morning
an increase of two pence for the season, and
four for its calf bearing, is added to it; and
then it is twenty-six pence in value until the
calends of December. Until the calends of
February, it is twenty-eight pence in value.
Until the calends of May, it is thirty pence in
value. On the ninth day of May it ought to
have teithi, milk coming from the end of each
of its teats, and its calf walking nine paces after
it; and unless it be so, sixteen pence is the
worth of its teithi. Two pence likewise it

acquires for the season, and so forty-eight
pence is its value until August. Thence until
the calends of December, it is fifty pence in
value. Until the calends of February, it is
fifty-two pence in value. On the following
morning, two pence for the season and four
legal pence for the second calf bearing, and so
it is three score pence in value. The horn
of a cow or ox, and the eye and the ear and
the tail, are each of them four legal pence

V 30 b 21 in value. The teat of a cow is four legal

V 30 b 22 pence in value. If a person sells a cow to
another, and there should be a teat of the
cow unproductive, and the person who buys
it should not perceive it, let the person who
shall sell it pay four legal pence every year
to the person who shall buy it whilst the
cow shall be in his possession. If that person sells it to another, let the first be free,
because the last who shall sell it creates a

V 31 a 4 similar arrangement. By three ways the teithi
of a cow are paid: by thirty of silver, or by
a fair dry cow, or by meal. The measure of
a cow's milk vessel is [as follows]. Seven
inches it is to be in height when measured
diagonally from the off rabbet to the near rim,
and three inches in the breadth of its mouth,

and three in the breadth of its bottom. The full measure of that vessel of oat meal is paid for every milking of the cow from the middle of April until the Feast of Cirig ; thence until August, of barley meal; from August until the calends of December [the same measure] of wheat meal is so paid.

T he calf is six pence in value from the time it is born until the calends of De-cember. Thence until the calends of February, it is eight pence in value. Until the calends of May, it is ten pence in value. Until August, it is twelve pence in value. Until the calends of December, it is fourteen pence in value. Until the calends of February, it is sixteen pence in value. Until the calends of May, it is eighteen pence in value. Until August, it is twenty pence in value. Until the calends of December, it is twenty-two pence in value. Until the calends of February, it is twenty-four pence in value. The following morning a yoke is put upon it, and then an increase of four curt pence is added to its worth. [On the ninth day of February, if it can plough, the worth of its teithi is to be added to its worth], to wit, sixteen pence ; and two pence likewise it ac-quires for the season; and then it is forty-six pence in value until the calends of May. Thence until August, it is forty-eight pence in value. Until the calends of December, it is fifty pence in value. Until the calends of February, it is fifty-two pence in value. The following morning a yoke is put upon it, for then it is the second work year; and that adds four legal pence to its worth, and two pence likewise for the season; and then it is three V 31 b 11 score pence in value. The teithi of an ox are ploughing in furrow and on sward and that without swerving, and it has no teithi unless it does so; and unless it have teithi, let the third of its worth be returned to the person who V 31 b 15 shall buy it. Whoever shall sell a steer legally, let him be answerable against the staggers for three days; and three months against the V 31 b 18 glanders; and a year against the farcy. Whoever shall sell a calf or a yearling, let him be answerable against the scab from the calends of winter until the Feast of Patrick. An ox is not in its prime save from the second work year until the sixth work year; nor a cow save from her second calf until the ninth calf; and although they should continue beyond that period, their worth is not to be lowered while V 31 b 24 they shall live. If the cattle of a trevgordd

kill a steer, and it be not known which of them
killed it,

[A chasm in V supplied from W]

let the owner of the steer come into the trev, W 69 b 13
having a relic with him, and let them make an
oath of ignorance, and then let them pay by a
cess on each steer (y rif eidon), and if there
be a polled steer, the share of two steers is to
be paid for it; and that law is called full payment after full swearing. If it be acknowledged
that a particular steer killed the other, let the
owner pay. Four legal pence is the worth of the W 69 b 20
tooth of a steer or the tooth of a working horse.

A lamb, while it shall be sucking, is a legal W 70 a 1
penny in value. When it shall be weaned,
it is two legal pence in value until August.
From August onwards, it is four legal pence in
value. A sheep's teat is two legal pence in W 70 a 4
value. The teithi of a sheep are of the same W 70 a 5
amount as its worth. A sheep's tooth and its W 70 a 6
eye are each of them a legal penny in value.
Whoever shall sell sheep, let him be answer- W 70 a 7
able for three diseases, scab and rot and red
water; until they receive their fill three times
of the new grass in spring, if after the calends
of winter he sells them.

W 70 a 12 A kid while it shall be sucking is a curt penny in value. From the time it shall cease sucking until August, it is two curt pence in value. From August onwards, it is four curt W 70 a 15 pence in value. The teat of a goat is two curt W 70 a 16 pence in value. The teithi of a goat are as W 70 a 16 much as its worth. The tooth of a goat and its eye are each of them a curt penny in value.

W 70 a 18 Whoever shall buy a beast from another and it become mangy with him, he is to give his oath together with two men of the same status as himself that he did not place it in a house where mange had been for seven years previous to that; and he has his chattels.

W 70 b 2 A pig in its litter is a legal penny in value. From the time it goes out until it shall cease to suck, it is two legal pence in value. From the time it leaves off sucking until the Feast of St. John of the Swine, it is four legal pence in value. Thence until the calends of January it is ten legal pence in value. Thence until the Feast of St. John of the Swine the second time, it is eight [twelve] legal pence in value ; excepting the three special animals upon which no augmentation and no lowering are ever to take place, [viz.], the principal one of the swine, and the herd boar, and the sow assigned to the lord.

And then the life is two-thirds more in value
than the flesh until the Feast of St. John of the
Swine. From the Feast of St. John of the Swine :: . · ʼ
until the calends of January, it is thirty pence
in value; and then the flesh is two-thirds more
in value than the life. There is no legal worth W 70 b 16
on an autumn born sow until the end of the year ;
when a yearling, it assumes the law of a grown .: ..· ··
sow (hôch maôı). Whoever shall sell swine, let W. 70 b 19
him be answerable for the three diseases : the
quinsey for three days, and the strangles for
three months, and 'that they devour not their .   ·
pigs ; and if they devour their pigs,   .

[V resumes]

let the third of their worth be returned again.
If swine kill a person, let their owner pay the V 32 a 1
person's galanas, or let him disown the swine.

A gosling, while it shall remain under its V 32 a 4
mother's wing, is a curt penny in value.
From the time it goes from under its mother's
wing until August, it is a legal penny in value.
From August onwards, it is two legal pence in
value, and then it is of the same worth as
its mother. A hen is a curt penny in value. V 32 a 8
A cock is a curt penny in value. .   . . . .   V 32 a 9

A pound is the worth of a hawk's nest. Six V 32 a 10

score pence is the worth of a hawk before mewing and whilst it shall be in the mew. If it is

V 32 a 13 white after mewing, it is a pound in value. The
nest of a falcon is six score pence in value. A
falcon before mewing and whilst it shall be in
the mew, is three score pence in value. If it be
white after mewing, it is six score pence in value.

V 32 a 16 The nest of a sparrow-hawk is twenty-four pence

V 32 a 17 in value. A sparrow-hawk before mewing
and whilst it shall be in the mew, is twelve
pence in value. If it be white after mew-

V 32 a 19 ing, it is twenty-four pence in value. The
teithi of every female bird are, laying and
hatching. The teithi of every male bird

V 32 a 21 are, singing and impregnating. There is no
dirwy nor camlwrw for any winged creature
although taken in theft; but its legal worth is
to be paid to the owner unless itself be found.

V 32 a 25 A stag is of the same worth and the same
augmentation as an ox; and a hind as a cow;
and a roe as a goat; and a roebuck as a he-
goat; and a sow of a wood as a sow of a trev.

V 32 b 2 The judges of Howel the Good were not able
to fix a legal worth on a badger, because during
the year the swine were affected by the quinsey,
it then obtained the status of a dog; and the
year there was madness among the dogs, it

then received the status of a sow. A hare V 32 b 8
also had no legal worth fixed on it, because
during one month it is male and the other
female. The worth of a stallion is a horse V 32 b 11
which can cover, with a mare before him and
another behind him. The worth of a herd V 32 b 12
boar is another boar which can procreate, with
a sow before him and another behind him.
The worth of a bull of a trevgordd is another V 32 b 14
bull which can leap, with a cow before him and
another behind him. A wolf and a fox and V 32 b 16
various others which do nothing save mischief
and on which no legal worth is fixed; it is free
to all to slay them. The worth of every animal V 32 b 19
whose flesh is eaten, except the swine, is two-
thirds on the life and one-third on the body.
The teithi of a man are that he should be able V 32 b 21
to have connexion with a woman, and that he
should be sound in all his limbs. The teithi of V 32 b 23
a woman are that the sign of puberty should
have appeared in her, and that she should be
sound in all her limbs. The teithi of violence V 32 b 25
are a cry, a horn, and a complaint.

The origin of bees is from paradise and V 33 a 1
because of the sin of man they came
thence; and God conferred his grace on them,
and therefore the mass cannot be sung without

V 33 a 5 the wax. A mother-hive of bees is twenty-four pence in value. A first swarm is sixteen pence in value. A second swarm is twelve pence in value. A third swarm is eight pence in value.

V 33 a 8 A mother-hive, after the first swarm has gone out of it, is twenty pence in value. After the second swarm has gone out of it, it is sixteen pence in value. After the third swarm has gone out of it,

V 33 a 12 it is twelve pence in value. No swarm is of more value than four pence until it shall be three days on wing and continually [so] ; a day to find a place to move to, and the second to move, and

V 33 a 15 the third to rest. Whoever shall find a swarm on another person's land upon a bough, receives four pence from the owner of the land if he wills

V 33 a 18 to have the swarm. Whoever shall find a hive on another person's land, receives a legal penny or the wax at the option of the owner of the

V 33 a 21 land. The ninth day before August every swarm assumes the status of a mother-hive, and then it is twenty-four pence in value, excepting a wing-swarm, for such does not assume the status of a mother-hive until the calends of the following May ; and then it is twenty-four pence in value like the rest.

V 33 b 1 Whoever shall kill a cat which guards a barn of a king or shall take it stealthily, its head

is to be held downwards on a clean level floor, and
its tail is to be held upwards ; and after that,
wheat is to be poured about it until the tip of its
tail be hidden, [and that is its worth]. Another V 33 b 6
cat is four legal pence in value. The teithi V 33 b 7
of a cat are as much as its legal worth. The V 33 b 8
teithi of a cat are that it should be perfect
of ear, perfect of eye, perfect of tail, perfect
of teeth, perfect of claw, and without marks
of fire, and that it should kill mice, and not
devour its offspring, and that it should not be
caterwauling every new moon.

There is no dirwy for a dog although it be V 33 b 13
taken stealthily, nor camlwrw. The oath
of one man is sufficient to disown a dog, for it is
a back-burden of an unclean animal. If a dog
attacks any person for the purpose of trying to
tear him ; although the person should kill the
dog with a weapon from his hand, he pays
neither dirwy nor camlwrw for it. If a dog
bites any person so that the blood comes, let
the owner of the dog pay for the blood of
the person; if however the lacerated person kills
the dog without moving thence, he receives
nothing except sixteen of silver. A dog ac- V 33 b 23
customed [to bite], which shall tear a person
three times ; unless its owner kills it, the law

is, that it should be tied to its lord's foot two
spans distance from him, and thus killed; and
then let him pay three kine camlwrw to the king.
V 34 a 2 There is to be no reparation for mischief which
a mad dog does, for it cannot be controlled.
Although a dog should be taken in theft, the
law of theft is not to be enforced thereon.

V 34 a 5 From the time the corn is put into the soil
until it come into its sheaf, money payment is to be made for it; and afterwards a
sound sheaf instead of the one damaged. For
every fold steer, a halfpenny the day and a penny
the night. For every horse which shall have
shackles or fetters on it, a penny the day and
two the night. If it be unrestrained, a half-
penny the day and a penny the night. If the
taker unfetter it, when he shall catch it on
the corn, let him pay three kine camlwrw to the
king ; let him however place the two bolts on
V 34 a 15 the same foot, and he thus forfeits nothing. Of
the legal herd of the swine, let him catch the
sow he may choose excepting the three principal
animals ; and let him keep it from one mealtime
to another ; and then let him offer it to its owner,
and unless he liberate it from its law, let the
taker make his own use of it. A legal herd
V 34 a 21 of the swine is twelve animals and a boar. Of

the legal flock of the sheep, a sheep is taken ;
and for every five animals to the extent of the
legal flock, a farthing is taken. The size of the
legal flock of the sheep is thirty animals. For v 34 a 25
every lamb, a hen's egg is taken to the extent
of the legal flock ; and then [a lamb] is taken.
For the goats and kids, a similar procedure. v 34 b 2
Whoever shall find geese in his corn, let him v 34 b 3
cut a stick as long as from the top of his elbow
to the end of his little finger and as thick as he
will ; and let him kill the geese in the corn with
the stick; and those which he shall kill out of
the corn, let him pay for. Geese which are v 34 b 7
found damaging corn through a corn yard or
through a barn, let a rod be tightened on their
necks and let them be left there until they die.
Whoever shall find a hen in his flax garden v 34 b 10
or in his barn, let him keep her until her owner
shall liberate her with a hen's egg ; and if he
catch the cock, let him break one of its claws
and let him set it free; or let him take a hen's
egg for every hen which shall be in the house.
Whoever shall catch a cat mousing in his flax v 34 b 15
garden, let its owner pay for its damage. Who- v 34 b 17
ever shall find calves in his corn, let him keep
them from one mealtime to another without
their mothers' milk ; and then let him set them

V 34 b 19 at liberty. If any person's corn bordering on a trevgordd be damaged, and there shall not be one animal caught upon it, let him take the relic and come to the trev; and if they swear an oath of ignorance, let them pay for the corn according to the number of cattle (yrif eidon ll6dyn); and that law is called, paying after a pol-
V 34 b 24 luted oath. If a person catch animals, which are strange to one another, in his corn or in his hay, and they fight in the pound and one animal kill the other, the owner of the animal is to pay for the beast killed and the taker is free.

V 35 a 4 Whoever shall deny a surety, let him give his oath together with the six persons nearest to himself in worth; four on the side of his father, and two on the side of his mother,
V 35 a 7 and himself seventh. Whoever shall deny suretyship, let him give his oath together with six in the like manner; and if his kindred be not in the same gwlad as himself, let him give his oath by himself over seven consecrated altars in the same cantrev as himself; for thus
V 35 a 12 is briduw denied. In three ways is a surety exonerated; by the debtor paying for him. The second is, by time being granted by the plaintiff to the debtor in the absence of the surety. The third is, by a distress being made

by the plaintiff on the debtor without consent of the surety; and then let him pay three
kine camlwrw to the king. The time given for V 35 a 17
a surety to know whether he be a surety or not
a surety, is three days. The period for a V 35 a 18
surety to prepare payment if he himself is to
pay first, is nine days. In three ways are V 35 a 20
surety and debtor defended; by hearing the
king's horn as he proceeds with his host; and
by a prosecution for violence; and by a prosecution for theft; because a necessity in
necessity is every one of these prosecutions.
A surety is to convey a distress along with the V 35 a 23
plaintiff until it be secure, and let him suffer the
affliction which comes; and if he does not this,
let him pay himself. A surety who admits part V 35 b 1
of his suretyship and denies another part, let
him swear on his own oath if he wills. Three V 35 b 3
sureties however there are, not one of whom
shall bear his suretyship on his own oath
although he deny a part and acknowledge
another part of his surety; namely, a person
who becomes a surety in the presence of a
court, and an inefficient surety, and a paying
surety. Whatever the first shall swear, the
court should swear along with him or against
him. The two others, whatever they shall

swear, with the six of their nearest of kin do
they swear; for every one of them shall be a
V 35 b 11 debtor. A person should take a surety on all
chattels saving the chattels which his lord shall
V 35 b 13 give him. Whoever shall be a surety for a person, if the debtor does not pay on the day fixed,
the surety shall then have a period of fifteen days;
and if then the debtor does not pay, the surety
shall then have a period of ten days; and if then
the debtor does not pay, then the surety shall
have a period of five days; and if the debtor
pays not then, let the surety pay; and these are
the periods of a surety as to living chattels. If
he be a surety as to inanimate chattels, a period
of fifteen days has the surety then; and if then
the debtor pays not, the surety has then a
period of thirty days; and if then the debtor
pays not, the surety then has a period of fifty
days; and if then the debtor pays not, let the
surety pay himself; and when the surety shall
meet the debtor, let him·strip him of all his
clothing except the garment nearest to him;
and thus let him always do until he gets back
V 36 a 4 the full payment from him. If a person's
surety dies before the debtor pays his suretyship
for him, let the plaintiff come with the six
persons next [of kin] to himself over the surety's

grave if they find the grave, and let them swear
that he was surety; and if they do not find the
grave, let them swear over the sacred altar that
he was surety and that he did not make good his
suretyship for him whilst he lived; and thus he
obtains his chattels. Although a surety proceed V 36 a 12
as to his suretyship in opposition to a lord, he
is liable neither to dirwy nor camlwrw. If a V 36 a 13
person's debtor dies and he does not obtain from
anyone the chattels bequeathed, let the surety
proceed as to his suretyship for the dead, and
let the three degrees of kin nearest to him pay;
and the surety can compel [them] the same as [he
could] the debtor, were he alive. Whoever shall V 36 a 18
confess owing chattels to another, let him pay
without delay except in the three principal feasts,
at Christmas and Easter and Whitsuntide; that
is from Christmas Eve after vespers till the
first day [of January] after mass; from Easter
Saturday night after the resurrection, till Little
Easter Day after mass; from Whitsun Saturday night after vespers till Trinity Sunday after
mass; for no one should ask of another in those
days. No one is to receive a son as surety V 36 b 1
without consent of his father whilst under his
authority; nor monk, nor friar, without consent
of their abbot; nor alltud, for his word as to a

Cymro is no word; nor a scholar of a school without consent of his master; nor a woman except as to that over which she has control. Such as these, their suretyship is no suretyship V 36 b 8 save with consent of their lords. If a surety of a person dies, and there remains a son to him, the son is to stand in place of his father in his V 36 b 11 suretyship. No one is to receive a debtor as surety, for they [i.e. debtor and surety] are two arddelws; and no one should other than choose his arddelw. If he chooses a debtor, there is no surety. If he chooses a surety, there is no debtor; and therefore no one can stand as V 36 b 16 surety and as debtor. A lord is to be surety for all chattels acknowledged to be without V 36 b 17 surety. If the debtor permit the surety to give the worth of a pound in pledge for a penny, and before the time of the pledge, it [i.e. the pledge] be lost, the debtor is not to pay back save a halfpenny; for that is a third of a legal penny; and he himself debased the status of V 36 b 23 his pledge. If a surety gives a large thing in pledge for a small thing, the plaintiff is to take it; and although it be lost before the time, the plaintiff is not to restore to the surety save a third. The surety however is to restore the whole to the debtor because he took it unlaw-

fully. If a debtor gives the worth of a pound V 37 a 4
in pledge for a penny and it lapse, no compensation is given him.

Every cause according to its contract ; it is V 37 a 6
not a contract without contract men ; a
contract is to be abjured like suretyship. No
one is to make a contract for another without
his permission ; neither a father for his son ; nor
a son for his father ; because a contract does
not last except during the life of him who
makes it. Although a contract be made in
opposition to law, it must be observed. A
contract annuls a custom. Stronger is contract
than justice. If a person promise chattels to V 37 a 13
another in the presence of witnesses and be
afterwards desirous of denying it, it is not
possible, unless the other's witnesses fail him.
If he promise with no one in the place, let him
swear on his own oath if he will.

Seven pounds is the gobr of a king's V 37 a 18
daughter, and it is paid to the mother ;
and the husband pays her cowyll, for land is paid
to her. Twenty-four pounds is her agweddi.
If the daughter of a breyr goes away with a
man clandestinely without consent of kindred,
her agweddi, when deserted, will be six steers
with their horns and their ears of equal length.

V 37 a 24 To the daughter of a taeog are paid three
V 37 a 25 steers of the same age as those. If a man
takes a wife with consent of kindred, and if
he leave her before the end of seven years, let
him pay her three pounds in her agweddi if
she be the daughter of a breyr; and in her
cowyll a pound and a half, and in her gobr six
V 37 b 5 score pence. If she be the daughter of a taeog,
a pound and a half in her agweddi, and six
score pence in her cowyll, and twenty-four
pence in her gobr. If he leaves her after the
seven years, there will be an equal sharing
between them, unless status gives more to the
husband. Two-thirds of the children go to
the husband, namely the eldest and the youngest; and the third to the mother. If death
separates them, there will be an equal sharing
V 37 b 13 between them of everything. Sarhâd of a
married woman is paid according to the status
V 37 b 14 of her husband. When a married man is
killed, his sarhâd is paid first and afterwards his
galanas. A third of her husband's sarhâd, the
V 37 b 17 wife receives. The wife of a free man can give
her shirt and her mantle and her headcloth and
her shoes and meal and her cheese and her butter
and her milk without consent of her husband;
and can lend all the furniture of the house.

The wife of a taeog cannot give without con- V 37 b 21
sent of her husband except her headgear, and
cannot lend except her sieve and her riddle ;
and that as far as her calling can be heard with
her foot on her threshold. If a [pure] maiden V 37 b 25
goes

[A chasm in V supplied from W]

away clandestinely without consent of kindred, W 79 b 4
her father can bring her back against her will
from her husband ; and he is not to pay her
amobr to the lord. If a woman however
go away clandestinely, no one can bring her
back against her will from her husband.
From the place where her home may be her
amobr is paid. Whoever shall commit a rape W 79 b 10
on a woman, let him pay her gobr to the
lord; and her dirwy and her dilysdod and
her agweddi and her sarhâd, he pays to the
woman ; and if she be a maid, let him pay
her cowyll. If a man denies rape on a woman W 79 b 13
and if the woman persists against him, let
her take the relics in her right hand and his
penis in her left hand, and let her swear to his
having committed rape on her ; and in this
way she loses nothing of her right. Whoever W 79 b 18
shall deny rape, let him give the oaths of fifty

men without bondman and without alltud. W 79 b 20 From three causes a woman does not lose her agweddi although she may leave her husband: on account of leprosy, and bad breath, and W 80 a 2 default of connexion. Three things which are not to be taken from a woman although she be abandoned for her fault: her cowyll; and her argyvreu; and her wyneb-werth when her husband has connexion with another woman. W 80 a 5 If a maiden does not exercise her will as to her cowyll before she rises in the morning from beside her husband, it is to be between W 80 a 7 them. Three times a woman has her wyneb-werth from her husband when he shall have connexion with another woman; and if she endure beyond that, she receives nothing. W 80 a 10 If a mature maid be given to a man and if he says that she was not a maid, let the maid swear with four persons that she was not a woman. The persons are to be, herself and her father and her mother and her brother and her sister. W 80 a 15 Three oaths a woman when scandalized makes to a husband: first, the oaths of seven women; and on the second scandal, the oaths of fourteen women; and on the third scandal, the oaths of fifty women; and if he endures beyond that, W 80 a 19 he receives nothing. Let no one give a woman

to a man without taking surety for her gobr
to the lord. If a woman be taken clandestinely W 80 a 21
to any house, let the man of the house take
surety for her gobr to the lord; and if he
does not take it, let him pay himself. The W 80 b 3
gobr of a female alltud is twenty-four pence.
The chief of song has the gobrs of the daughters W 80 b 4
of the bards who shall be under him. The W 80 b 5
throw of a sickle is the protection of a bondman. The throw of an axe or a hedging-bill, W 80 b 6
is the protection of a land-maer. Twenty- W 80 b 7
four pence is the sarhâd of a serving bondwoman who works neither at the spade nor
the quern. If a married man has connexion W 80 b 10
with another woman, let him pay six score
pence to the lawful wife for her wyneb-werth.
If a husband and wife separate before the end W 80 b 12
of the seven years, thus is the furniture divided
between them. The husband has what bed-
clothes shall be between him and the floor, and
the wife has the coverlid. The husband has
the corn, and the wife has the made flour.
The husband has the plaid and the winnowing
sheet and the dormitory bolster and the coulter
and the fuel axe and the handaxe and all the
sickles save one sickle. The wife has the broad
axe and the share and the spade and the one

sickle and the middle augre ; and the husband has all the irons save those. The wife has the ox car and the yokes and all the milk vessels save one pail, and all the dishes save one dish which the husband has. The wife has all the butter save one vesselful which the husband has ; and if there be lumps of butter, the husband has one. The wife has all the flesh which shall be on the floor, salted and unsalted, and all the cheese which shall be in brine and unsalted ; and the husband

W 81 a 12 has all the hung flesh and cheese. The wife is to be in her house waiting for her share of the chattels until the end of the ninth day.

W 81 a 14 A wife who shall declare herself to be pregnant when her husband shall die, ought to remain in her house until it shall be known whether she be pregnant ; and if she be not pregnant, let her pay three kine camlwrw to the king ; and let her leave the house and the land to the heir.

W 81 a 20 If two women shall be journeying through any place and there be no one with them, and two men meet them and violate them, they are not to be compensated. If however there be one person with them although ever so little, unless he be a carried child, they lose none

of their right. If a man take a woman W 81 b 5
clandestinely and keep her with him until the
end of the seventh day without doing right
to her, he is not to do right to her until the end
of a day and a year; then however she is to
have full right. A woman of full age who W 81 b 10
goes with a man clandestinely, and is taken
by the man to bush or brake or house, and is,
after connexion, deserted; upon complaint made
by her to her kindred and in the courts, she is to
take for her chastity a bull of three winters,
having its tail shaven and greased with tallow
and then thrust through the covering hurdle; .
and then let the woman go into the house, and
place her foot on the threshold, and take the tail
in her hands, and let a man come on each side
of the bull and a goad in the hand of each to
stimulate the bull; and if she can hold the
bull, let her take it for her wyneb-werth and
her chastity; and if she cannot, let her take
what tallow may adhere to her hands. A W 82 a 5
woman who surrenders herself to a man in bush
and brake, and is abandoned by the man who
connects himself with another woman, and she
come to complain to her kindred and to the
courts; if the man deny, let him swear on
a bell without a clapper; if he make compensa-

tion, let him pay her a penny as broad as her buttocks.

W 82 a 12 If a woman go about alone and a man meet her and violate her; if the man denies, let him give the oaths of fifty men, three of them under vow that they will not seek a woman, and that they will not consume flesh, and that they will never ride on horseback. If he will not deny it, let him pay to the woman her gwaddol and her dilysdod and her dirwy ; and a silver rod to the king in the manner he is entitled ; and if the man cannot pay, his testicles shall be W 82 a 21 taken. Three times is the sarhâd of a man to be augmented, when his wife is seduced.

W 82 b 1 The law of nursing during a year is a cow, and a mantle, and a shirt, and a headcloth, and a pair of shoes, and a carload of the best corn which grows upon the man's land, and a pan with feet.

W 82 b 5 The worth of a vat of mead, which is paid to the king, is six score pence; and the wax is to be divided thus, the third to the king, and the second third to him who makes it, and the third [third] to him who gives the mead. Nine hand-breadths is the measure of the vat of mead when measured diagonally, that is, from the furthest bottom groove to the hither rim.

The skin of an ox or a cow or a stag or W 82 b 12
a hind or an otter: twelve pence is the
value of each. The skin of a beaver is half W 82 b 14
a pound in value. The skin of a marten is W 82 b 15
twenty-four pence in value. The skin of a W 82 b 16
stoat is twelve pence in value. Of every wild W 82 b 17
animal killed on another person's land, the
owner of the land shall have the hind quarter
next the ground if the flesh be eatable. What- W 82 b 20
soever thing the guest men (dofrethwyr) shall
show to the taeogs to whose houses they
come, the taeogs are to pay for, if they be lost,
except glaives and trowsers and knives. Their
horses are not to be kept by the taeogs except
during the night, because they are to pay if
they are lost during the night. A king's W 83 a 5
supperer shall give a penny to the servants to
spare the barn and his food. The fore sitter W 83 a 7
of a cantrev, that is, the footholder, pays a vat
of bragod to the king every year. When a W 83 a 9
person from a border gwlad shall die on the
land of another person, sixteen pence does the
owner of the land receive for his death clod;
and all the ebediw to the lord because of that.

Five persons nearest in worth are to deny W 83 a 13
a back-burthen unless prosecuted as theft.

Seven persons are to deny a horse-burden unless
W 83 a 16 prosecuted as theft. Twelve men are to deny
the worth of six score pence unless prosecuted
W 83 a 17 as theft. Twenty four men are to deny the
worth of a pound, unless prosecuted as theft.
W 83 a 19 A pound is the cyvarwys of a man with a family
in the year.

W 83 a 21   The ebediw of every free man is six score
pence. Six score pence is the ebediw of the
servant of a lord. Four score and six pence
is the ebediw of a taeog. If there be a church
on his land, his ebediw will be six score pence.
W 83 b 4 Twenty-four pence is the ebediw of a male
W 83 b 5 cottar. Twelve pence is the ebediw of a female
W 83 b 6 cottar. A chief of kindred does not himself
pay his ebediw since the one who shall be chief
W 83 b 9 of kindred after him pays it. A son is not to
be chief of kindred after the father in immediate
succession, because chieftainship of kindred is
W 83 b 11 during life. A married woman who is overtaken in her adultery loses her agweddi, and
[her] chattels are brought by her kindred to her
husband.

W 83 b 14 If it is said against a person that he was
seen by daylight with a thing stolen, and
another brings an accusation that he saw him,
let him who is scandalized give the oaths of

twenty-four men so that an even number comes from every cymwd of the same cantrev, and the accuser shall not be able to do anything against him. And this law is called a full denial against a full information.

Ṫhis is how one is to accuse of theft legally : W 83 b 20 seeing the person from daylight to twilight with the thing stolen, and the accuser swearing together with three men of the same status as himself at the gate of the churchyard, and at the door of the church, and over the sacred altar.

Ᵹf an informer under a sacred vow with the W 84 a 6 witness of the priest (perigla6ı), comes with the person robbed into the presence of the priest (offeirat) to the church, let the priest desire the informer at the door of the church for God's sake not to swear falsely; and if he swears there, he does likewise at the door of the chancel, and the third time above the altar; and if the person denies after (dros) that, let the priest confirm it on his word thrice; and if the person does not believe it, let the priest swear once and thus it is not possible to go against him.

Ṫhe worth of a winter house. Fifty pence is W 84 a 16 the worth of the roof tree, and thirty pence is the worth of every fork which shall support

the roof tree. The benches, and the upper
benches and the stanchions and the doors and
the outerdoors and the lintels and the sills and
the side posts, are each worth four legal pence.

W 84 b 1 Whoever shall uncover a winter house is to
W 84 b 3 pay the third of its worth. The worth of an
autumn house is twenty-four pence in value,
if there be an auger hole therein ; and if not,
W 84 b 5 it is twelve pence in value. A summer house
is twelve pence in value. The fork of a summer
house or an autumn house is two legal pence
W 84 b 8 in value. A door hurdle is two legal pence
in value.

W 84 b 9 The barn of a king is six score pence in
value. The barn of a breyr is three score
pence in value. The barn of a king's taeog is
W 84 b 1 thirty pence in value. Let every one leave his
barn open until the calends of winter that wind
may circulate therein ; and if cattle enter therein, let their owner pay for their damage. After
the Feast of All Saints unless there be an
edder in three places on the partition of a barn,
the damage done therein shall not be paid for.

W 84 b 19 A piped kiln of a king is half a pound in
W 84 b 20 value if there be a house over it. A
piped kiln of a breyr, if there be a legal house
W 85 a 1 over it, is three score pence in value. A piped

kiln of a taeog of a king is thirty pence in value
if there be a legal house over it. A piped W 85 a 3
kiln of a taeog of a breyr is twenty four pence
in value if there be a legal house over it. Every W 85 a 5
kiln which is not a piped kiln is half the value
of those above, according to the status of their
owners. Whoever shall kindle a fire within W 85 a 7
a kilnhouse, unless a pledge be taken from
another in the presence of witnesses before
he leaves it as to the extinguishing of the
fire, or as to its being secure, the loss will be
equal between them as they pay together. The W 85 a 11
first house which is burnt in the trev through
negligence of fire, let it pay for the first two
houses set on fire thereby. The loss is to be W 85 a 13
shared equally between the one who shall give
the fire and the one who shall kindle it. Who- W 85 a 15
ever shall lend a house with fire to another ; if
the latter kindle a fire therein thrice, [the owner]
shall receive from him the full pay if the house
is burnt. If an accusation of the crime of W 85 a 18
burning stealthily be brought against a person,
the oaths of fifty men will be necessary for
him. If he obtain his rhaith, it will be sufficient for him ; if he obtains it not, he becomes
a saleable thief. A saleable thief is worth W 85 a 21
seven pounds. If a thief be found burning W 85 b 1

a house stealthily and be laid hold of, his
life will be forfeited. A thief who is put to
death is not to lose any of his chattels, because
both reparation and punishment are not to be
exacted; only payment of the chattels to the
loser because he ought not to leave behind an
unsatisfied claim. There is to be no galanas
for a thief; and there is to be no recrimina-
tion between two kindreds on account of him
(ẏrdaᵹ).

A yew of a saint is a pound in value. An
oak is six score pence in value. Whoever shall bore through an oak is to pay three
score pence. A branch of a mistletoe is three
score pence in value. Every principal branch of
the oak is thirty pence in value. An apple tree
is three score pence in value. A crab tree is
thirty pence in value. A hazel tree is fifteen
pence in value. Fifteen pence is the value of
a yew of a wood. A thorn is seven pence half-
penny in value. Every tree after that is four
legal pence in value except a beech tree. That
is six score pence in value. Whoever shall fell
an oak on the king's highway, let him pay
three kine camlwrw to the king, and the worth
of the oak; and let him clear the way for the
king; and when the king goes by, let him

cover the stock of the tree with cloth of one
colour. If a tree fall across a river and things W 86 a 2
get entangled in the tree, the owner of the
land whereon the stock of the tree may be,
is to have the find whatever way the river
may have turned the top branches of the
tree.

A sword on the hilt of which is gold or W 86 a 6
silver, is twenty-four pence in value. A W 86 a 7
sword without gold and without silver thereon,
is twelve pence in value. A shield whereon is W 86 a 9
a blue colour, is twenty-four pence in value.
A shield of the colour of its wood, is twelve W 86 a 10
pence in value. A spear is four legal pence W 86 a 11
in value. A battle-axe is two legal pence in W 86 a 12
value. A knife is a legal penny in value. A W 86 a 14
buttery (talgell), and a pigsty and a sheepfold,
are each thirty pence in value. Millstones are W 86 a 16
twenty-four pence in value. A quern is four W 86 a 17
legal pence in value. The harp of a chief of song W 86 a 18
is six score pence in value. Its tuning key is
twenty-four pence in value. The king's harp W 86 a 20
and his plaid and his throwboard are each six
score pence in value. The harp of a breyr W 86 b 1
is three score pence in value. Its tuning key
is twelve pence in value. The plaid of a breyr W 86 b 2
is three score pence in value. A sleeping W 86 b 3

W 86 b 4 pillow is twenty pence in value. 𝔄 throwboard
of the bone of a whale is three score pence in
W 86 b 5 value. 𝔄 throwboard of any other bone is
W 86 b 6 thirty pence in value. 𝔄 throwboard of a
W 86 b 7 hart's antler is twenty-four pence in value. 𝔄
throwboard of a steer's horn is twelve pence
W 86 b 8 in value. 𝔄 throwboard of wood is four legal
W 86 b 9 pence in value. 𝔄 broad axe is four legal
W 86 b 10 pence in value. 𝔄 fuel axe is two legal pence
W 86 b 11 in value. 𝔄 hand hatchet is one legal penny
W 86 b 12 in value. 𝔄 large auger is two legal pence in
W 86 b 13 value. 𝔄 medium auger is one legal penny in
W 86 b 14 value. 𝔄 wimble and a drawknife and a bill-
hook and a whetstone are each one halfpenny
W 86 b 16 in value. 𝔄 coulter is four legal pence in
W 86 b 17 value. 𝔄n adze and a reaping-hook and a
mattock and a sickle and shears and a comb
and a hedging-bill and a billhook and a willow
pail and a white pail with small hoops and
a baking board and a flesh-dish and a pail of
willow wood and a sieve are each of them one
W 87 a 1 legal penny in value. 𝔄 spade and a willow
bucket and a broad dish and a riddle are each
W 87 a 2 a curt penny in value. 𝔄 yew pail and a tub
and a stave churn and a vat churn and a bowl
and a liquor bowl and a winnowing sheet and
a pan with feet are each four legal pence in

value. A turning wheel and a pot-ladle and W 87 a 5
a weeding hook are each a farthing in value.
A skiff is twenty-four pence in value. A sal- W 87 a 6
mon net is sixteen pence in value. A grayling W 87 a 8
net is twelve pence in value. A bow net is W 87 a 9
four legal pence in value. A coracle is eight W 87 a 10
legal pence in value. Whoever shall place a W 87 a 11
net in a river on another person's land without his permission, has a third of the fish for
himself, and the owner of the river two-
thirds.

Whoever shall break a plough upon W 87 a 15
another person's land, let him pay to
him a new plough and nine days' ploughing.
The worth of a plough is two legal pence.
The worth of one day's ploughing is two legal
pence. The worth of the long yoke and its
bows, one legal penny.

Thus come the hires. The hire of the plough- W 87 a 21
man first, and after that the hire of the share and .
the coulter. Then the hire of the best ox for
the plough. Then the hire of the driver, and
then from best to best of the oxen. No one W 87 b 4
from a taeogtrev is to plough until every one
in the trev shall obtain cotillage. If an ox die W 87 b 6
by overploughing, the owner has an erw and
that is called the erw of the black ox.

W 87 b 9   **E**very pledge lapses at the end of the ninth day except these. Implements belonging to a church should not be pledged, and,

W 87 b 12 although pledged, do not lapse. A coulter and a cauldron and a fuel axe never lapse

W 87 b 14 although pledged. A period of a day and a year is allowed for gold and coats of mail

W 87 b 16 and golden vessels when pledged. The law of borrowing is to return the thing in the state it was given. Whoever shall lend is to take witnesses lest it be denied. If it be denied and

W 87 b 20 the owner prove it, let him pay twofold. Whoever shall promise chattels to another and shall deny it when one comes to demand them, the law of perjury is to be applied to him if he swears publicly, that is, three kine camlwrw to the king; and let him do penance for the perjury; and the other, if he has witnesses, shall have the chattels.

W 88 a 6   **W**hoever shall pay galanas, if the whole kindred be in the same gwlad as himself, he is to pay all by the end of a fortnight. If however the kindred be scattered in many gwlads, a period of a fortnight is allowed for every gwlad.

Thus is dispersed galanas paid. A pound W 88 a 11 is a brother's share. Six score pence the share of a first cousin. Three score pence the share of a second cousin. Thirty pence is the share of a third cousin. Fifteen pence is the share of a fourth cousin. Seven pence and a halfpenny is the share of a fifth cousin. There is no proper share nor proper name for kin farther removed than that. The share W 88 a 17 of a father from his son's galanas : a penny. The same law applies when receiving a share of galanas and paying it. Lest kindred be lost, until it be denied a spear penny is received.

A kindred pays sarhâd with no one whilst he W 88 a 21 himself has chattels in his possession. If however his chattels are deficient, it is right [for his kindred] to pay a share along with him till the third degree of kinship.

The dire event of a galanas is when a W 88 b 4 person shall kill the other and a certain day be appointed for compensating that crime ; and before that crime is compensated he also be killed by a person of another kindred without [their] owing him anything. That law is called a dire event of galanas because of the gravity of losing him and paying the crime previously committed by him.

W 88 b 12　The fifth day before Michaelmas, the king is to forbid his wood until the end of the fifteenth day after the Epiphany; and of the swine which shall be found in the wood, the king has the tenth beast until the end of the ninth day; and thenceforward they are at the king's pleasure.

W 88 b 19　If sarhâd is done to the apparitor whilst sitting during the pleas, there is paid to him for his sarhâd a sieveful of chaff and an addled egg.

W 88 b 21　The king is to have of the spoil (anreith), the stud and the goats and the furred clothes and the arms and the prisoners, without sharing them with any one. He is not however to receive the third of the working mares (keffyc tom) because

W 89 a 4　they are spoil (yspeil). Whoever shall speak haughtily to the king or unseemly, let him pay

W 89 a 7　three kine camlwrw twice. When a taeog shall receive land from the king, the king is to have from the taeog three score pence for every rhandir; and if there be a church on the land of the taeogtrev, six score pence come to the king

W 89 a 12　from the one who shall take it. The ebediw of a bondman to whom the king gives land is four score and ten pence; and the third comes

W 89 a 14　to the maer and the canghellor. The pet animal of a king's wife or his daughter is a pound in

value. The pet animal of a [breyr's] wife or W 89 a 16
his daughter is half a pound in value. The pet W 89 a 17
animal of a taeog's wife or his daughter is a
curt penny in value because they ought not to
keep pet animals.

A free man is to answer for his alltud in W 89 a 20
every claim for which he is not to lose the
tongue, and life, and limbs; for no one is to
lose tongue and life and limbs by the tongue
of another person. The worth of a ready-made W 89 b 2
garment in the law of Howel the Good is twenty-
four of silver. An unintentional blow is not W 89 b 4
sarhâd. It is right, however, to make amends
for the injury, that is, for blood and wound and
a scar if it be conspicuous. When payment is W 89 b 7
made for a foretooth, the worth of a conspicuous scar is to be paid with it.

There are five keys to the office of a judge. W 89 b 9
One is, the fear of thy teacher and the
love of him. The second is, frequent asking for
thy instruction. The third is, retaining the instruction which thou dost receive. The fourth
is despising riches. The fifth is, hating false-
hood and loving truth for the fear of God.
Whoever shall destroy a meer on another per- W 89 b 15
son's land, let him pay three kine camlwrw to
the king, and restore the meer to its former

W 89 b 18 condition. Whoever is suspected concerning testimony, let him swear so that he may have right and law ; and then let the other take the relic and let him deny on his oath and let him object to the witness ; and after that let the judges take notice whether they object wholly. Whoever shall object to a witness before his

W 90 a 2 testimony is given, let him lose the suit. If a man in any host denies having killed [what is now] a corpse, let him pay six score pence and give the oaths of fifty men of the same status

W 90 a 5 as himself to deny murder. Whoever shall do sarhâd to another of the people of these four gwlads, to wit, Deheubarth, Gwynedd, Powys, and Lloegr, let him pay four kine and four score

W 90 a 9 of silver to him. Whoever shall pay galanas to another [of the same gwlads], is to pay three score and three kine without addition.

W 90 a 11 Whoever shall find a dead wild sow (hôch coet) on another person's land, let him take its fore

W 90 a 14 quarter. Another animal the flesh of which it is right to eat ; the back quarter thereof he receives. If it be a fox or another uneatable animal ; he receives a curt penny from the owner of the land, if the latter (ynteu) wills to have the skin.

The dirwy and camlwrw of court and llan W 90 a 19 are doubled. If the fault be done in the churchyard in the place of refuge (ẏnẏ nodua), the amount of the dirwy is seven pounds. The abbot has half the dirwy of a llan, if he is acquainted with literature (kẏuarwẏd ẏnllẏthẏr) and church custom; and the other half goes to the lay proprietors (meibon lleẏn) of the church. The reason they receive thus when dirwy or camlwrw is due, is because they are the protectors of the llan; and this is why those chattels are given specially to the saint and are not [deemed] of the same status as offerings. **T**he maer and W 90 b 8 the canghellor do not receive a share of the prid which comes to the lord (teẏrn) for land, nor of twnc nor of thief.

If a ship be wrecked on the land of a lord W 90 b 11 (teẏrn), the lord has it; and if a ship be wrecked on the land of a bishop, it is divided between the king and the bishop. **W**hen the W 90 b 13 law of distress is applied in the case of a marwdy or any other suit, the household and the maer are to have the heifers and the bullocks and the yearlings and the sheep and the goats, and they are to have everything in the house except horses and oxen and large cattle and gold and silver and furred clothes; and if there is anything which is worth

W 90 b 20 a pound, a king has it. A third of galanas is to fall on the owner of the weapon with which

W 91 a 1 the person was slain. Chattels which are taken from [a time of] war to [that of] peace are to be divided between the one who took them and

W 91 a 3 the one who owned them previously. If two persons shall be walking through a wood, and the one in front lets a bough strike the one in the rear so that he loses an eye, he is to pay the worth of the eye to the other.

W 91 a 7 The time between court and llan is

[V resumes]

V 38 a 1 nine days to give an answer, and nine to give surety, and nine to render justice, in respect to the claim demanded. Nine days are allowed to a lord to recollect his oath. To a priest is allowed until he gets the first

V 38 a 5 opportunity to sing mass. In every suit there ought to be a summons and a claim and

V 38 a 7 an answer and judgment and peace. Every builder upon open land is to have three trees from the person who shall own the wood, whether the woodsman (coetör) be willing or

V 38 a 10 unwilling: a roof-tree and two roof-forks. Whoever shall be a gorvodog for another, if he is

unable to bring him to law, let the gorvodog be
liable by law for the person on whose behalf
he became such. The time for a gorvodog to
request the return of his gorvodogship: one
day and a year. A thief who shall be placed V 38 a 14
upon sureties is not to be destroyed. No one V 38 a 15
is to make satisfaction nor answer for an act
of his bondman saving for theft. There is to be V 38 a 17
no justice and law without these four requisites:
a common lord, and a presiding (kadeira6c) judge,
and two parties present. Whoever shall break V 38 a 20
co-tillage willingly engaged in, let him pay three
kine camlwrw to the king; and all his tilth to
the co-tiller. The meadow-lands are to be fenced V 38 a 23
off (affoxeftir) on account of the swine because
they spoil the land. Whoever shall find them
on his meadow-land or in his corn before it is
ripe, let him receive four legal pence from the
owner of the swine. If they spoil ripe corn, let
their damage be paid for.

In six ways does a person lose his chattels: V 38 b 4
by loss and surreption and theft; by loan
and hire and deposit. In the first three cases,
he is to discover and to swear to them. In the
three others, he is not to do so unless they are
restored as they were given. A blow received V 38 b 8
unintentionally is not sarhâd. It is right

however to compensate the injury, that is, blood and wound and a conspicuous scar if there be one.

V 38 b 11 Any person who is pledged is to be of the same worth as the one for whom he is given as pledge.

V 38 b 13 Whoever shall bring a charge as to animals having damaged his corn, their owner shall exculpate them as to the amount he may will according to the damage they have done; and for what he will not swear to, let him pay. Whoever shall have full right for his damaged corn from an owner of animals, is thenceforward neither to have payment for that worthless straw nor is he to detain animals on it.

V 38 b 20 A graft is four legal pence in value until the following calends of winter. From that time forward an increase of two pence every season is added until it shall bear fruit; and then it is three score pence in value. And therefore a graft is of the same worth as the calf of a large cow from the beginning to the end.

V 39 a 1 Whoever is suspected as to testimony, let him swear so that it may be legal for him; and then let the other take the relic and let him deny on his oath and let him object to the witness. After that let it be noticed whether a complete objection was made. Whoever objects to a witness before his testimony is delivered,

let him lose the suit. ·· He who shall object to a
witness, let him object before the witness shall
withdraw from the relic after that the testimony
is sworn ; and unless he objects then, the witness
stands. A witness as to (ar) a witness has no
allotted time. Evidences and witnesses have V 39 a 9
the same force and are equally effective in every
suit, and especially (agŏell) in a suit of land
and soil. The time allowed for witnesses or a V 39 a 11
guarantor from beyond the sea is one day and
a year. The time allowed for witnesses or a V 39 a 13·
guarantor from a border gwlad is a fortnight.
The time allowed for witnesses or a guarantor V 39 a 14
of the same gwlad is nine days. The time V 39 a 15
allowed for witnesses or a guarantor of the
same cymwd is three days. Whoever shall will V 39 a 16
to object to defunct testimony, let him proceed
against him who shall testify it. Whoever shall V 39 a 18
will to object to living testimony, let him first
proceed against the witness[es] on their words ;
and then, after they shall have sworn their oath,
let him swear that [each] has sworn falsely, and
let him say that he is no lawful witness against
him, and let him specify the cause; and let him
testify to two men that the witness did not proceed against the cause objected ; and those two
men are called counter-witnesses, and they are

V 39 b 1 unobjectionable. When a witness in his testimony shall lawfully testify of a thing to others against a defendant, or when a defendant shall lawfully testify of a thing against witnesses; such are called counter-witnesses in law, and

V 39 b 6 they are not to be objected to. The calling forward of evidences is possible any time the person who shall call them may will, whether before denial and defence or afterwards; because what took place before the suit is what they

V 39 b 10 prove between the litigants. Contravening of evidences is when they shall first appear against the defendant for these causes : for manifest perjury, or for public or private spoil, or for breaking the peace, or for being excommunicated by name, or for near relationship, or for evident enmity, or for his being a sharer of the chattels with which the suit is concerned; and that before they revert to their recollection. If he then is unable to contravene them lawfully, afterwards let him object to them as witnesses in one of the three lawful ways.

V 39 b 21 Whoever shall waylay pays twofold, because it is a violence against a person to kill him, and a theft to conceal; and that is the one place in law where violence and theft become connected. And it is to be thus denied; the oaths of fifty men to deny wood and field, and three of them under vow to abstain from flesh and woman and horse riding. The measure in denying wood and field is a legal rhandir between open and tangled, and wood and field, and wet and dry; and such as cannot lawfully deny a rhandir, cannot deny wood and field. It is not waylaying however if it be on a lawful road (ffoᶻd gyfreith) without hiding and without concealment thereon. If however he is out of the road five legal paces and five feet in each pace, it is a waylaying; and that is the reason it is so denied, and that a twofold payment is made; and that is the one instance for which hanging and confiscation are due.

𝕿here are seven bishop-houses in Dyved, and V 40 a 14 Mynyw is the chief in Cymru. Llanismael and Llandegeman and Llanussyllt and Llanteilaw and Llanteulydawc and Llangeneu. The abbots of Teilaw and Teulydawc and Ismael and Degeman should be ordained scholars. Twelve pounds is the ebediw of every one of these, and it is to be paid to the Lord of Dyved; and those who succeed them are to pay it. Mynyw is free from every due. Llankeneu and Llanussyllt are free from that due because they have no land. Whoever shall do sarhâd to any one of those abbots, let him pay seven pounds to him, and let a female of his kindred be a washerwoman as a reproach to the kindred and as a memorial of the punishment (dial).

V 40 b 1   Three calamitous losses of a kindred :— one is, that there should be a doubted son without being affiliated and without being denied ; and that such should kill a man of another kindred without owing him anything ; the whole of that galanas is to be paid ; and then he is to be denied lest he should commit a second crime. The second is, paying the whole of a galanas excepting a penny and a halfpenny ; and should there be a failure of that, and a person of the kindred be killed on account of that failure, there is to be no claim for him. The third is, when an innocent person is slandered concerning a corpse and is proceeded against, if he does not deny by a period lawfully fixed, and if a person be killed because of him, there is to be no expiation for it.

V 40 b 14   Three legal periods to avenge a dead body :— between two kindreds who do not originate from the same gwlad, commencing a claim on the first day of the week following that wherein the dead was murdered; if there comes no answer by the end of a fortnight, the law makes vengeance free. The second is, if the two kindreds are in the same cantrev, commencing a claim on the third day after the dead is slain; if there comes no answer by the end of the ninth day, the law makes vengeance free. The third is, if the two kindreds are in the same cymwd, commencing a claim on the third day after the dead is murdered; if there comes no answer by the end of the sixth day, the law makes vengeance free.

Three nets of a king are: his household, V 41 a 2 for which net there is no reparation but the mercy of the king. The second is his stud; for every horse caught on it, the king receives four legal pence. The third is the cattle of his maer-house; for every steer found on them, the king receives four legal pence. Three nets V 41 a 8 of a breyr are: his stud, and the cattle of his maer-house, and his swine, because, if an animal is found among them, the breyr receives for every animal four legal pence. Three nets of a V 41 a 11 taeog are: his cattle, and his swine, and his homestead (hentref); for each animal caught therein he receives four curt pence from the calends of May until September shall have gone.

V 41 a 15 **T**hree dirwys of a king are : the dirwy for violence, and the dirwy for theft, and the dirwy for acknowledged fighting. The expiation dirwy for violence is a silver rod and a gold cup with a gold cover of the kind mentioned in expiation of a king's sarhâd. The expiation dirwy for acknowledged fighting is twelve kine. The expiation dirwy for theft is, if a person be charged with theft and he personally deny it satisfactorily, and a rhaith be placed on him and it fail, he is an acknowledged thief since his rhaith has failed. Innocent by his own account, nothing being taken in his possession or found in his hand, twelve kine dirwy

V 41 b 2 upon him. **T**hree indispensables of a king are : his household priest, and his court judge, and his

V 41 b 3 household. **T**hree things which a king shares with no one : his gold treasure, and his hawk, and his thief.

V 41 b 6 **T**hree fours there are :—four causes of perverting judgment ; from fear of a powerful man, and heart hatred [of enemies], and love of friends, and lust of chattels. The second four are : four shields which interpose between a person and a rhaith of a gwlad in a prosecution for theft ; one is, legally harbouring a guest, that is, keeping him from the time of nightfall until the

morning, and placing the hand over him three
times that night, that is, swearing on his part
and the people of the house with him. The
second is birth and rearing; the owner swearing with two men of the same status as himself,
as to seeing the birth of the animal and its
rearing in his possession without its going three
nights from him. The third is a warrant.
The fourth is custody before loss, that is, a
person swearing with two men of the same
status as himself, that before the other lost
his chattels, those chattels were in his possession. There is no warrant except unto the
third hand. The third hand establishes custody before loss, and that defends a person
from [a charge of] theft. The third four are:
four persons to whom there is no protection
against the king either in court or in llan.
One is a person who violates the protection
of the king in one of the three principal festivals. The second is a person who shall be
pledged willingly to the king. The third is
his supperer, a person who ought to provide
for him and who leaves him that night without
food. The fourth is his bondman.

Three crimes which, if a person commit in V 42 a 7
his own gwlad, his son is on that account

to lose by law his father's trev : the killing of his lord; and the killing of his chief of kindred; and the killing of his family representative (teispan tyle); and that because of the gravity

V 42 a 11 of those crimes. Three silent ones in session : a lord of justice listening to his gwyrda adjudicating their laws; and a judge listening to a plaint and defence; and a surety listening to a plaintiff and defendant mutually answering.

V 42 a 16 Three lawful rests of a spear during pleadings : one is, thrusting its butt-end in the earth with one hand till it can scarcely be drawn out with two hands. The second is, thrusting its point into a bush till the blade be

V 42 a 20 hid. The third is, the placing thereof on a thicket which shall be of the height of a man. And unless it be on one of those three rests and a person encounter it so as to cause his death, a third of the person's galanas falls

V 42 a 24 upon the spear's owner. Three futile expressions which are uttered in court and do not avail : denial before verdict; and premature

V 42 b 2 objection; and pleading after judgment. Three worthless milks there are : milk of a mare; milk of a bitch; and milk of a cat; since there

V 42 b 4 is no expiation made for any of them. Three sarhâds not to be expiated if received when

intoxicated : sarhâd done to the priest of the
household; and sarhâd to the judge of the
court; and sarhâd to the physician of the
court; because these should not be intoxicated,
as they know not what time the king may have
need of them. Three buffets not to be expiated : V 42 b 9
one by the lord on his man in ordering him in
the day of battle and fighting; and one by a
father on his son to punish him; and one by
a chief of kindred on his relative in order to
counsel him.

Three women with whose heirs there is to V 42 b 14
be no pleading as to their mother's trev :
a woman who is given as a hostage for land
and who bears a son in her condition of hostage ; and the son of a woman who shall avenge
a person of his mother's kindred and on that
account lose his father's trev, and therefore
there is to be no pleading with him as to his
mother's trev ; and the son of a woman who is
given to an alltud with the kindred's consent.
Three disgraces of a kindred there are, and on V 42 b 22
account of a woman the three occur : the violation of a woman against her will.   The second
is, bringing another woman to the house, sup-
planting [the wife] and driving her forth.   The
third is despoiling her, being more pleased

to spoil her than to be connected with her.

V 43 a 2 Three pieces of flesh of a hundred perplexities there are: one is a piece stolen [*lit.* theft] as to whatever way a share thereof may travel, for there are nine accessories to it. The second is the hart of a king as to whoever may cut it up. The third is a carcase left by a wolf as to whoever may do wrong with respect to it.

V 43 a·7 Three strong scandals of a woman there are: one is seeing the man and the woman emerging from the same thicket, one from each side of the thicket. The second is seeing them both under the same mantle. The third is seeing the man

V 43 a 12 between the two thighs of the woman. Three things for which a person shall prosecute for theft, though they do not constitute theft: ploughing, and felling of timber, and building.

V 43 a 14 Three sarhâds of a woman there are, one of which is augmented, and one diminished, and one is a complete sarhâd. When a kiss is given her against her will, a third of her sarhâd is wanting to her then. The second is feeling her with the hand, and that is a full sarhâd to her. The third is being connected with her against her will, and that is augmented by the third.

V 43 a 20 Three ways whereby one can object to witnesses: by land-feud, and galanas-feud, and woman-feud.

hree sons being three brothers of the V 43 a 22 same mother and the same father, who are not to have a share of land from their brothers of the same mother and the same father as themselves : one is a son of thicket and bush, and after that, the same man taking to wife the same woman with consent of kindred and begetting a son of her ; that son is not to share land with the son begotten before him in thicket and bush. The second is, if a scholar marries a wife with consent of kindred and begets a son by her, and afterwards if the scholar takes priest's orders and after that a son is born to that priest by the aforesaid woman, the first son is not to share land with the last, because contrary to law was he begotten. The third is a mute, because land is not for any one who cannot answer for it ; for land (gÓlat) is not given to a mute.

hree persons whose status rises in one V 43 b 13 day : when a taeogtrev has a church consecrated therein with the king's permission, a person of that trev, who is a taeog in the morning, becomes that night a free man. The second is a person to whom the king gives one of the twenty-four privileged offices, who, before the office is given him, is a taeog and

who, after it is given, is a free man. The
third is a clerk who the day he receives the
tonsure is in the morning a taeog (yn vab
tayaϭc) and becomes that night a free man.

V 43 b 23 Three legal worths of the foetus of a
woman : the first is, blood before for-
mation, if it perish through cruelty, of the value
of forty-eight [pence]. The second is, before
life (eneit) enters into it, if it perish through
cruelty, the third of its galanas is to be paid for
it. The third is, after that life has entered
into it, if it perish through cruelty, then the
whole of its galanas is to be paid for it.

V 44 a 6 Three ways whereby a son is to be affiliated
to a father : one is, when a woman of
thicket and bush, being pregnant, shall be at
her full time (ar y llaϭuaeth), let her priest
(y pheriglaϭ₂) visit her and let her swear to
him, 'May I be delivered of a snake by this
pregnancy if a father has begotten it on a
mother other than the man to whom I affiliate
it,' and naming him ; and so she affiliates lawfully. The second is, a chief of kindred
with the hands of seven of the kindred with
him, is to affiliate him. The third is, if there
be no chief of kindred, the oaths of fifty men
of his kindred affiliate him, and the son himself

first swears because the mother's oath is not legal except in the above affiliation.

Three ways whereby a son is disowned by V 44 a 17 a kindred : the man, whose son he is said to be, takes the son and places him between himself and the altar, and places his left hand on the head of the son and the right hand on the altar and the relics; and let him swear that he has not begotten him, and that there is no drop of his blood in him. The second is, if the father is not alive; the chief of kindred is to deny him, and with him the hands of seven of the kindred. The third is, if he has no chief of kindred; the oaths of fifty men of the kindred denies him, and the eldest son of the man, to whom the son was affined, is to swear first. Three places where a person is not to V 44 b 3 give the oath of an absolver : one is on a bridge of a single timber without a hand-rail. The second is at the gateway of a churchyard, because the 'Pater' is to be sung there for the souls of the Christians of the world. The third is at the church door, because the 'Pater' is to be sung there before the rood. These persons V 44 b 8 are exempt from the oath of an absolver: a lord, and a bishop, and a mute, and one who is deaf, and one of foreign language, and a pregnant

V 44 b 11 woman. Three vexations of the wise are: drunkenness, and adultery, and bad disposition.

V 44 b 12 Three persons who are entitled to an advocate for them in court: a woman; and one with natural impediment in speech; and an alltud of foreign speech. The one person who is to

V 44 b 15 choose the advocate: a lord. Three animals whose acts towards brutes are not cognizable in law during their rutting season: a stallion; and the bull of a trevgordd; and a herd boar.

V 44 b 17 Three animals which have no legal worth: an autumn born pig; and a harrier; and a badger.

V 44 b 19 Three bloods not amenable in law are: blood from a scabby head; and blood from the nostril; and blood from teeth; unless struck through

V 44 b 21 anger. Three fires the results of which are not cognizable in law: the fire of heath-burning, from the middle of March to the middle of April; and the fire of a bath in a trevgordd; and the fire of a smithy which shall be nine paces distant from the trev, with a roof of

V 44 b 25 broom or sods thereon. Three birds whose worth the king is to have wherever they are killed: an eagle, and a crane, and a raven. The owner of the land whereon they are killed is to have fifty [pence] from the person who

V 45 a 4 kills them. Three vermin (pryf) whose worth

the king is entitled to wherever they are killed :
a beaver; and a marten; and a stoat; because from their skins are made the borders of
the king's garments. Three things which the V 45 a 7
law suffers not to be appraised : meal ; and
bees ; and silver; because their like are pro-
curable. Three legal vessels of generation V 45 a 10
are : that of a bitch, and that of a cat, and that
of a squirrel ; because they can liberate (dillóg)
and relax when they will. Three free timbers V 45 a 12
in the forest of a king : the roof-tree of a
church ; and the timber of shafts which go for
the king's use ; and the timber for a bier.
Three buffalo horns of the king : his feasting V 45 a 15
horn ; and his mustering horn ; and his horn in
the hand of the chief huntsman. Each is a
pound in value. Three free huntings there are V 45 a 17
in every gwlad : hunting a roebuck, and hunting a fox, and hunting an otter; for they have
no permanent homes (tref tat). Three things V 45 a 19
which prevail over law : violence ; and contract ; and necessity. Three names for an V 45 a 21
apparitor are : the cry of a gwlad ; and dread
report, the canghellor's servant ; and rhingyll
(apparitor). Three ways in which a silver rod V 45 a 23
is paid to the king : for violence ; and for

violating protection of way towards an irremediable beggar; and for sarhâd to a king.

V 45 b 1   Three thrusts not to be redressed: one is, a person demanding right from his enemy on account of his kinsman in three pleadings and not obtaining right; and afterwards meeting with his enemy, and thrusting him with a spear so that he dies; that thrust is not to be redressed. The second is, jealousy caused to a married woman by another woman concerning her husband, and the two women meeting together, and the married woman making a thrust with her hands at the other woman so that she die; there is to be no reparation to her. The third is, giving a mature maiden to a man with surety as to her virginity, and the man making a genital thrust at her and having connexion with her once and finding her a woman; he is to call the marriage guests to him, candles are to be lighted and her shift cut before her as high as her pubes and behind her as high as her buttocks, and she is to be sent off with that thrust without any reparation to her; and that

V 45 b 19 is the law for a deceitful maid. Three persons who are not to be sold legally: an acknowledged thief for having the worth of four legal pence in his hand, and a waylayer, and a traitor

.

to a lord. Three chattels which are secure with- V 45 b 2
out surety : chattels which a lord shall give to a
man and which come to him by law; and chattels
which a wife shall have from her husband [as
wynebwerth] when the husband shall have connexion with another woman ;

[A chasm in V supplied from W]

and chattels taken in a war between two lords.
Three things common to a gwlad : an army, and W 102 b 21
pleas, and a church; for every one is under
summons to them.

Three modest blushes of a maid there are : W 103 a 3
one is when told by her father 'Maiden,
I have given thee to a husband'. The second
is, bidding her go to her husband to sleep.
The third is, seeing her in the morning rising
from her husband. And because of each of
those three, her husband pays her amobr to
her lord, and her cowyll and her agweddi to
herself. Three stays of blood are : the breast, W 103 a 10
and the middle girdle, and the trousers girdle.
Three unabashed ones of a gwlad without W 103 a 12
whom it is impossible to do : a lord and a
priest and law. Three hearths which are to do W 103 a 14
right and to receive it for a person who has no

acknowledged lord: that of a father, and of an eldest brother, and of a father in law.

W 103 a 18   Three legal needles are: the needle of the queen's serving woman; and the needle of the physician for sewing the wounds; and the needle of the chief huntsman for sewing the torn dogs; each one of them is four legal pence in value. The needle of any other skilful woman is a legal penny in value.

W 103 b 4   Three defunct testimonies there are, which stand in pleas well: one is, when there shall be contention and fighting between two lords concerning land, which subsequently is duly terminated in the presence of all; after these severally have died, their sons or their grandsons or some of their kindred can bear testimony concerning that land; and these are called evidences as to land. The second is, persons of lineage from every side who are called land borderers, to decide by kin and descent, and to confirm by bearing testimony; and they can augment the person's title to land and soil. The third is, when there shall be seen the hearth-stone of a father or a grandfather or of a greatgrandfather or one of the kindred of the same title as himself; and the tofts of the houses and their barns and the furrows

of the land ploughed and the erws, every
one of which affords testimony as to a person's
title. Three secrets there are which it is better W 104 a 2
to confess than to conceal: losses to a lord,
and waylaying, and a person killing his father
if acknowledged in confidence.

Three one-footed animals there are: a stallion W 104 a 6
and a hawk and a covert-hound. Whoever
shall break the foot of one of them, let him pay
its entire worth. Three things not to be paid W 104 a 9
for, though lost in a lodging house (rantÿ): a
knife, and a sword, and trousers; for whoever
owns them ought to guard them. Three sarhâds W 104 a 11
of a corpse are: when it is killed; when it is
despoiled; when thrown to the ground. Three W 104 a 13
reproaches of a corpse are: asking who killed
it, who owns this bier, whose is this grave.
Three scowls not to be redressed: the scowl W 104 a 16
of a husband to his wife whom he received in
the status of a maid and she a woman; and
a person ruined by law and a person of his
kindred scowling on that account; and the
scowl of a person towards a dog attacking him.
Three distraints not to be restored: for theft; W 104 a 21
and for [one on a] surety who will not enforce
[right]; and for galanas. Three things if found W 104 b 2
on a road there is no necessity to answer for

any of them: a horseshoe; and a needle; and a penny.

N 104 b 4   Three persons to whom tongue-wound is to be paid: to the king; and to the judge when considering his decision; and to the priest in his vestments (wifc) on the three principal festivals over his altar, or whilst reading a letter

N 104 b 9   before the king, or whilst composing one. Three cases in the law of Howel in which proof occurs: one of them, it belongs to a woman to prove a rape against a man. The second is, it belongs to a debtor to prove over the grave of the surety as to his being surety, and that his suretyship was not exonerated whilst he lived. The third

W 104 b 14   is, the proving of a shepherd dog. Three plagues of a kindred: nursing a son of a lord; and affiliating a son to a kindred wrongfully; and guarding supreme authority (penreith).

W 104 b 17   Three things which destroy a contract: illness;

W 104 b 18   and a lord's necessity; and poverty. Three things which defend a person from a summons to pleadings: shouting and sound of horns against the host of a border gwlad; and flood in a river without bridge and without skiff; and illness.

W 105 a 1   Three persons to whom galanas is paid and they themselves pay no galanas: a lord, for to him comes a third of every galanas for exacting it. The second is a chief of kindred, for according to his status his relations' galanas is paid. The third is a father, for a share comes to him of his son's galanas, to wit, a penny; because his son is no relative (car) to him. And not one of them is to be killed on account of galanas. Half a brother's share of galanas, a W 105 a 9 sister pays ; and she receives no share of galanas. Three throws not to be redressed: at a W 105 a 11 stag in corn ; and at a wild colt in corn ; and at a dog in corn. Three persons who impoverish W 105 a 13 a gwlad: a prevaricating lord ; an iniquitous judge ; and an accusing maer. Three strong W 105 a 15 ones of the world: a lord, for a stone along ice is a lord ; and an idiot, for it is not possible to compel an idiot in anything, against his will ; and a person without anything, for it is not possible to exact anything where there is nothing. Three animals there are of the same W 105 a 19 worth as to their tails and their eyes and their lives : a calf, and a filly for common work (tom), and a cat ; except the cat which shall watch a king's barn.

Three persons hated by a kindred : a thief, W 105 b 2 and a deceiver, since they cannot be depended on ; and a person who shall kill a person of his own kindred; as the living kin is not slain for the dead kin, everybody will hate to see

W 105 b 6 him. Three things common to a kindred : chief of kindred, and a representative, and the son of a woman given with kindred's consent to their enemy; such is to be in common between

W 105 b 10 the two kindreds. Three disgraceful faults of a man : being a bad friend (karᵥₐ), and flaccid in pleadings, and a man to a bad lord.

W 105 b 13 Three animals there are whose teithi exceed their legal worth : a stallion; and the bull of a trevgordd; and a herd boar, for the

W 105 b 16 breed is lost if they are lost. Three signs of inhabitancy of a gwlad : little children, and

W 105 b 16 dogs, and cocks. Hitherto we have discussed the Triads of Law; now we will treat of the Ninth days.

W 105 b 20 The first is the ninth day of December concerning land. The second is the ninth day of May succeeding. The third is the ninth day of May when occur the teithi of the first milk. The fourth is the ninth day of February when

W 106 a 4 occur the teithi of the first work. Ninth day there is to a lord to recollect himself as to his oath when it shall be asserted that he has

W 106 a 6 previously made an oath. Ninth day period there is between court and llan before answer-

ing, and that after a claim, when there shall be
a dispute as to land.   Ninth day period there is W 106 a 9
concerning a corpse, which shall have originated
from the same cantrev as the person who shall
have killed him.   Three ninth days there are W 106 a 10
for a chief huntsman.   Three ninth days there W 106 a 11
are as to the pregnancy of a woman.   Ninth W 106 a 12
day before August every swarm assumes the
status of a mother-hive.   Ninth day period there W 106 a 14
is as to a warrant in the same gwlad, or as to a
witness in the same gwlad.   Ninth day period W 106 a 15
there is for removing a house erected on another
person's land without his consent.   Ninth day W 106 a 17
period there is for a wife to await her share of
the chattels in her house when she shall separate from her husband.   Ninth day period W 1c6 a 19
doubled there is as to a plough when broken.

Listen, thou judge, who givest the judgments. W 1c6 b 1
Let not the worth of a penny be more in
thy sight than the worth of God.   Do not judge
wrongly for worth but judge justly for God.

Small wonder if there be hesitation in a W 106 b 5
temporal court, since they shift as to
their desire like the breeze of heaven.   But
whosoever loves certainty and security from
falling, [for him] the right service of the Lord
Jesus Christ is that which is the glorifying of

the Father and the Son and the Holy Spirit.
Amen.

W 106 b 12 Three places where a person is not to give
the oath of an absolver : one is, a bridge
of a single timber without a handrail. The
second is in the gateway of a churchyard, because a person is to sing the ' Pater ' there for
the souls (eneit) of the Christians of the world.
The third is in the doorway of the church,
because a person is to sing the ' Pater ' there
before the rood.

W 106 b 19 When a son is affiliated to a kindred with
the oaths of fifty men, the son is to swear
before the kindred. because it is not lawful
to listen to her except in the case of the first
oath when she shall say ' Let a snake be begotten '
to her.

W 107 a 3 When a son is denied by a kindred, the eldest
son of the man whose son he is said to be, is to
swear first before the kindred.

W 107 a 6 Three futile crosses there are : a cross placed
on a road in corn ; and a cross placed on the bark
of a tree lying in a wood ; and a cross which a
person places on an altar in a case where a
church is not to interfere with him.

PALAEOGRAPHICAL NOTES

[The numbers refer to pages and lines.]

2. 10. The scribe's *t* is visible in the rubric capital of *Croedabc*

2. 11. The scribe's *g* is visible in the second word, but was overlooked by the illuminator.

6. 11. *neuad* altered from *beuad*

8. 5. *hoelon* with *e* badly altered from *l*

11. 9. *yneuad* with *e* altered from something else.

15. 8. *colofneu* with *l* apparently crossed.

16. 15. *ygnat* with *g* begun for some other letter such as *n*

22. 11. *atan* with *t* altered from *r*

27. 2, 28. 2. Small hole in parchment between *ae* and *ran*, and *teu* and *lu* respectively.

33. 14. *yr etlling* with *y* altered from *v* or *u*, and stroke over *n* like that over *t*

33. 25. *vynho* with *y* altered from *n*

34. 16. *bɜen-* with *n* altered from *y*

35. 20. *bɜenhinⱥl* badly altered from *bɜenhyabl*

36. 20. *ehunan* with two strokes above *u* not unlike those which indicate the letter *t* when in conjunction with such letters as *m, n* and *u*.

40. 11. *Seuthuet* expuncted by later hand, and *Chweched* written above it.

40. 18. The bar of final *t* is extended almost to the middle of the line.

45. 17. *vɜeint* with *e* altered from *y*

46. 8. *ytte* with *tt* altered from some other letters,

and ligatured in order apparently to show more clearly what is intended.

48. 3. A tiny hole in parchment prevented the completion of the second *e*

48. 7. *euegyl* with second *e* altered from something else.

52. 7. The *l* at end of *kynllbyn* is scratched out by a later hand, presumably that of Jaspar Gryffyth. It probably stands for *lledrat.*

58. 23. The pointing after *yndab* may be a semi-colon and looks also like a colon.

58. 25. In left margin just outside commencement of line is a full point, but whether in the original hand appears doubtful (see note on p. 118. 1). In bottom margin in later hand is written ' hic defunt folia duo ' altered into 'hic deest foliu*m* unu*m* '.

61. 21. *perth* with *t* altered from *c*

67. 24. *lozen hagen.* with full point after *lozen* nearly covered by the *h* of *hagen.*

70. 14. *atal hyt* with full. point after *atal* nearly hidden by the *h* of *hyt*

73. 5, 74. 5. Hole. in parchment at the beginning and end of these lines respectively.

74. 10. With *bў* begins paler ink but same hand.

80. 11, 82. 8. The rubric spaces overlooked by illuminator contain the *g* and *t* respectively of the original scribe.

83. 22. The two first expunctuations under *moch* are nearly obliterated.

83. 24. *Meint* with *ei* altered from something else.

84. 14. *gymeret* with first *e* altered from something else.

86. 23. *thal* with *l* nearly covering a full point.

87. 24. *gofper* with *o* badly altered from *b*

89. 1. *dibc* with full point so small that it is doubtful whether it was intended.

89. 4. Original hand placed *o* in space intended for the illuminator, who overlooked it.

89. 6. A *b* intended to complete *Po* is written over the first *d* of *dadyl*, but in such fainter ink that the *d* is quite distinct beneath it.

90. 25. *Oz* with *z* altered from something else.

91. 6. *chowȳll* with *c* altered from *t*

94. 21. First *c* altered from *t*

101. 15. *erbȳn* with *b* not unlike *b*

102. 13. Last *u* looks like *tr* owing to a full point being placed towards its right top corner.

106. 8. Over the second half of last *h* is a full point, but whether intentional is doubtful.

107. 3. First *c* looks also like *t*

108. Catchword is cut by binder so that the lower half is gone.

109. 17. In space left for rubric, and overlooked by illuminator, the original scribe has placed *r*

111. 16. *bzenhln* is a mistake for *bzeyr*. The crosses are perhaps inserted by a later hand. A comparatively modern hand has written *breyr* opposite cross in margin.

113. 18. The *n* is extended over the remainder of the line.

114. 3. *anher* has a small *h* written over the *a*, partly in left margin.

116. 21. *anl* written wrongly for *am* was again written wrongly by scribe and passed by him.

118. 1. Outside first *k* in left margin is a full point, but whether intentional is doubtful (see note on p. 58. 25).

119. 16. Last *a* altered from *b*

119. 19. Two or three letters rubbed out after *tyſt* which were apparently a part of it.

119. 23. Three or four letters rubbed out after *deu* with expunctuations of two of them still remaining.

121. This page has twenty-six lines.

122. 16, 20, 24. The scribe certainly writes *enuynu* in each case; so also MS. W.

132. 22. First *y* altered from *u* or *n*

133. 3. *kanÿt* with *t* altered from *f* or *ſ*

134. 4. The *n* is extended over about a quarter of the line.

136. Catchword cut by binder so that the bottom portion of the letters is gone.

139. 15. *cuhudÿat* with point under *d* like an expunctuation.

142. 11. Last *n* extended over about a quarter of the line.

142. 15. *enett* with *t* like *c*

APPENDIX

GENERAL RELATION OF FOUR EARLIEST TEXTS

GENERALLY speaking, the text of V (together with the parts supplied from W as printed in this book) includes the whole of W, X, and U. Allowing 8 words per line in the case of V and W, and 7 words per line in the case of X and U, the amount of matter in each appears to work out thus:—

V. 84 pages, 25 lines per page = 2,100 lines = 16,800 words. Adding the parts supplied from W, viz. 41 pages, 21 lines per page + 72 lines = 933 lines = 7,464 words, we obtain a total of 16,800 + 7,464 = 24,264 words.

W. 140 pages, 21 lines per page + 34 lines = 2,974 lines = 23,792 words.

X. 114 pages, 20 lines per page + 7 lines = 2,287 lines = 16,009 words.

U. 120 pages[1], 18 lines per page = 2,160 lines = 15,120 words.

They all agree as to the general arrangement of their subject-matter, beginning with the laws of the court, and then the laws of the gwlad, and confining the triads of law towards the close; but the most cursory examination will show great divergences in the arrangement of details, strikingly so with regard to X. The explanation of these divergences possibly

---

[1] This of course excludes the last sixteen folios of the old hand-writing, which form no part of the Book of Cyvnerth properly so called.

depends on the answer to a prior question as to whether the longer texts are expansions of the shorter, or whether the latter are to be attributed to a condensing of the former. Moreover, in the case of these four particular MSS., the possible and very probable clashing of two distinct originals is also to be kept in mind. It will be noticed from the following headings, which are selected only to show the order of the subject-matter in the respective MSS., that W is in close agreement with V; and also that X, in spite of its startling differences, is more allied to W and V than is U.

V	W	X	U
The 24 officers.	The 24 officers.	The 24 officers.	The 24 officers.
8 other officers.	8 other officers.	Few miscellanies.	8 other officers.
Hounds and Chase.	Hounds and Chase.	Hounds and Chase.	Ebediws.
	Gwestva silver, &c.	Trees, weapons, utensils, &c.	
		Ploughs and co-tillage.	
		Pledges, borrowing, &c.	
		Payment of galanas.	
3 columns.	3 columns.	3 columns.	3 columns.
9 credible witnesses.	9 credible witnesses.	9 credible witnesses.	Waylaying.
Relating to the person.	Relating to the person.	Relating to the person.	Relating to the person.
Land.	Land.	Land.	Cattle and Fowls.
[Miscellanies].	Miscellanies.	Animals.	Worth of Buildings &c.
Tame and Wild.	Tame and Wild.		Hires and perjury.
Corn damage.	Corn damage.	Corn damage.	Cat, hound, and dog.
Sureties.	Sureties.		The chase.
Contract.	Contract.		Bees.
		8 other officers.	Corn damage.
Women.	Women.	Women.	Women.
[Miscellanies].	Miscellanies.	Miscellanies.	Land.
[Worth of buildings, &c.]	Worth of buildings, &c.	Ebediws.	Guardians.
[Ploughs and co-tillage].	Ploughs and co-tillage.	Gwestva silver.	
[Pledges, borrowing, &c.].	Pledges, borrowing, &c.	Animals.	

V	W	X	U
Payment of gala-nas].	Payment of galanas.	Miscellanies and Triads.	
Miscellanies].	Miscellanies.	Sureties.	
Testimony, &c.		Triads and Miscel-lanies.	
Waylaying.			
7 Bishop-houses.			
Triads.	Triads.		Triads.
Ninth Days].	Ninth Days.		
Additional notes].	Additional notes.		

I. Leading Additions to the Printed Text.

§ 1. *Cott. Cleopatra A. XIV.*

W 34 b 4–6 (*post* hynny V 1 a 24). *Anc. Laws* I. 622.

ar llẏuẏr hốnn blegẏwrẏt ẏſcolheic ae hẏſcriu-enốẏs. canẏſ ef a oed oɀeu ar gof achyfreitheu ẏnẏ amſer.

And it was Blegywryd the scholar who wrote this book, for he was the best in his time for record and laws. (Cf. X 165 b 9–11 and U 1 b, on pp. 303, 309 *infra*.)

W 41 a, bottom margin (*post* byth V 6 b 3). *Anc. Laws* I. 644.

Oet ageiff ẏr ẏgnat llẏf ẏ ẏmgoffau deugein niwarnaốt of eirch kẏn ẏmốẏftlaố.

The judge of a court has a period of forty days to reconsider, if he demands it, before mutually pledging.

W 41 a 18–41 b 6 (*post* tauaốt V 6 b 5). *Anc. Laws* I. 644, 646.

Sarhaet ẏgnat ·llẏf ẏố naố mu anaố ugeint arẏant. Ẏ alanaſ atelir onaố mu anaố ugein mu

gan trı dẏrchauel. Val hẏn ẏdẏlẏ ẏdɀẏchauaeleu
uot. Ẏ dẏrchauael kẏntaf ẏϭ trı ugein mu. Ẏr
eıl ẏϭ pedwar ugeın mu. Ẏ trẏdẏd ẏϭ pum mu
achan mu. athraẏan dϭẏ uu. ꜳc ual hẏn ẏ dɀẏcheıf
galanaſ pop kẏmro herwẏd ẏureınt.

The sarhâd of the judge of a court is nine kine and
nine score of silver. His galanas is paid with nine
score and nine kine with three augmentations. In this
manner should the augmentations be made. The first
augmentation is three score kine; the second is four
score kine ; the third is a hundred and five kine and a
third of two kine. And thus is the galanas of every
Cymro augmented according to his status.

W 51 a 12-14 (*ante* y ymboɀth V 14 a 8). *Anc.
Laws* I. 680.

—aa ẏr ygnat llẏſ allanϭ lle ytauaϭt ẏr gof o ran
ẏ bɀenhın o gıc moɀdϭẏt ẏreıdon.

—which go to the judge of the court; and the place
of the tongue to be filled for the smith from the
king's share of the thigh-flesh of the steer. (Also
X 199 a 7-10.)

W 54 b 17-55 a 5 (*post* ehunan V 16 b 20). *Anc.
Laws* I. 670.

Ual hẏn ẏrenır arẏant ẏgueſtuaeu. dϭẏ geın-
haϭc a gẏmer ẏ dıſteın. ꜳphedeır ageıff ẏ trull-
ẏat neu tudet ẏ gerϭẏn ar dewıſ ẏneb ae talho.
dϭẏ a gẏmer drẏſſaϭɀ ẏneuad. Vn ẏr medẏd. Vn
ẏr goſtegϭɀ. Pedeır ẏr coc. Dϭẏ ẏr ſϭẏdϭɀ llẏſ.
dϭẏ ẏr guaſ ẏſtauell. Vn ẏr uorϭẏn ẏſtauell.
dϭẏ ẏ dıſteın bɀenhınes. Vn ẏr troetaϭc. Vn
ẏr canhϭẏllẏd. Vn ẏr guaſtraϭt auϭẏn bɀenhınes.

Thus is the gwestva silver shared. The steward takes two pence; and the butler has four or the covering of the vat, at the option of the one who shall pay; the doorkeeper of the hall takes two; one to the mead brewer; one to the silentiary; four to the cook; two to the server of a court; two to the page of the chamber; one to the chambermaid; two to the steward of a queen; one to the footholder; one to the candle-bearer; one to a queen's groom of the rein. (Also U 17 a 2.)

W. 55 b 1-13.

Oderuẏd bot amrẏſſon am teruẏnu róg deu dẏn. adẏwedut oʒ haϭlóʒ bot o ureınt ıdaϭ ef ẏ dẏlẏho teruẏnu. 'Onẏſ amheu ẏr amdıffẏnϭʒ. ꝛet ẏr haϭlóʒ ydangoſ y teruẏn. Os ẏr amdıffẏnϭʒ ae hamheu ynteu bıt gyfreıth ẏrẏdunt am eu bʒeınt gẏſſeuın. Os ẏ ureınt a uernır ıdaϭ dangoſſet ẏ teruẏn guedẏ hẏnnẏ.

Mab adẏlẏ· arfedaϭc dʒoſtaϭ hẏnẏ uo pedeır blóẏd ar dec. ẏ tat oʒ bẏd bẏϭ. ac onẏ bẏd bẏϭ ẏ tat. arglóẏd bıeu rodı arfedaϭc ıdaϭ ẏ uot dʒoſtaϭ ẏouẏn ıaϭn ıdaϭ ac ẏwneuthur ıaϭn dʒoſtaϭ.

If there be contention as to meering between two persons, and the plaintiff say that by status he is to meer, unless the defendant doubt it, let the plaintiff proceed to show the meer. But if the defendant doubt it, let there be law between them as to their original status. If his status is adjudged to him, let him after that show the meer. (*Anc. Laws* II. 90.)

A son should have a guardian over him until he is fourteen years old [viz.], the father if alive; and if the father be not alive, a lord is to appoint a guardian for him to act on his behalf, to demand justice for him and to do justice for him.

W 56 b 4–8 (*post* gƀɹeic V 17 a 20). *Anc. Laws* I. 688.

Y neb a adefo llofrudẏaeth. talet gỽbẏl oɹ alanas. Traẏan galanaſ adaỽ ar ẏ llofrud. ar deuparth a rennɪr ẏn teɪr ran. Dỽẏ ran atal kenedẏl ẏ tat. ar trẏded atal kenedẏl ẏ uam.

Whoever shall confess homicide, let him pay the whole of the galanas. A third of the galanas falls on the murderer, and the two parts are shared into three shares. Two shares the father's kindred pays, and the third the mother's kindred pays. (Also X 185 a 4–8 and U 21 b.)

W 67 b 9–11 (*post* bɹenhɪn V 30 a 6). *Anc. Laws* I. 708.

Y neb auarchoco march ỽɹth ẏ dỽẏn ẏ guarchae nẏ dẏlẏ namẏn hẏnnẏ.

. Whoever shall ride a horse in taking it to a pinfold is entitled to nothing more.

W 67 b 16–17 (*post* V 30 a 21). *Anc. Laws* I. 708.

Os ẏ goɹwlat ẏ differ ỽẏth geɪnhaỽc ageɪff.

If he protects it in a border-gwlad, he receives eight pence. (Also X 193 b 18–19.)

W 69 a 7–8 (*post* werth V 31 b 1). *Anc. Laws* I. 712.

Naỽuetdẏd whefraỽɹ oɹ dɪchaỽn eredɪc guerth ẏ teɪthɪ adɹẏcheɪſ ar ẏ werth.

The ninth day of February if it can plough, the worth of its teithi is added to its worth. (Also X 192 b 4–5.)

W 73 b 6-9 (*post* l6 V 34 b 24). *Anc. Laws* I. 744.

Or deila dỹn ỹfcrỹbỹl ar ỹ ỹtꝛ abot ỹmdaeru
róg ỹ deilat ar perchennaᴃc. ỹ deilat adỹlỹ tỹgu
kaffel y blaenỹeit ar olỹeit ar ỹr ỹt.

If a person catch an animal on his corn and there
be a dispute between the taker and the owner, the
taker must swear as to finding the foremost and the
hindmost on the corn. (Also X 196 a 19-196 b 2;
and U 40 a.)

W 76 a 20-76 b 14 (*post* gynnogyn V 36 b 16; *ante*
Oꝛ 36 b 8). *Anc. Laws* I. 122.

Or kỹmer dỹn mach ar da. achỹn dỹuot oet
ỹda. dehol ỹ talaᴃdỹr ae o alanaſ ae o ledꝛat ae
o aghỹfreith arall. amỹnu oꝛ haᴃlóꝛ ỹ da ỹgan ỹ
uach. Sef awỹl kỹfreith ỹna rannu ỹcollet ỹn
deu hanher ỹrỹdunt nỹt amgen talu oꝛ mach
hanher ỹ da ỹr halór. kanỹſ aghỹfreith ỹᴃ talu
oꝛ mach góbỹl ac ynteu ỹn wirỹon. ac nat
tegach colli oꝛ haᴃlór o góbyl a chredu o honaᴃ
ỹnteu ỹ uach. allỹna ỹ trỹdỹd lle ỹran kỹfreith.
ac oꝛ da ỹtalaᴃdỹr ỹr wlat dꝛacheuỹn óỹnteu
adỹlỹant kỹmhell ỹda hónnᴃ arnaᴃ ef. ahanher
adỹlỹ ỹmach allỹna ỹr lle ỹbỹd kỹmhellóꝛ ỹmach
ar da idaᴃ ehun.

If a person take surety for chattels, and before the
period of the chattels is come the debtor be banished
either for murder or theft or any other unlawful act,
and the creditor demand the chattels from his surety,
law then sees as to sharing the loss equally between
them, that is, the surety paying half the chattels to
the defendant; for it is not right that the surety
should pay all when he himself is innocent, nor is it
fairer that the defendant should lose all, seeing that

he trusted his surety. And that is the third instance where law shäres. And should the debtor return to the gwlad, they are to enforce the repayment of those chattels from him, the surety receiving a half. And that is the instance of the surety being an enforcer of chattels to himself.

W 76 b 17–77 a 21 (*post* V 36 b 10; *ante* O₂ 36 b 17). *Anc. Laws* I. 112, 114.

Oderuẏd ẏdẏn rodı da ẏ arall amach arnaϐ. a phan delher ẏ ouẏn dıwat oꝛ talaϐdẏr. achϐẏnaϐ oꝛ haϐlϐꝛ ϐꝛth ẏr arglϐẏd. Jaϐn ẏϐ dϐẏn ẏdϐẏ pleıt ẏ gẏt ar mach. agouẏn udunt ae mach hϐn ae nat mach. mach heb ẏr haϐlϐr. na uach heb ẏ talaϐdẏr. Yna ẏmae ıaϐn gouẏn ẏr mach aϐẏt uach tı. mach heb ẏnteu. nac ϐẏt vach heb ẏ talaϐdẏr ẏgenhẏf ı ar dım. Heb y mach ẏr gẏfreıth ẏ dẏlẏϐẏfı. mı ae canhebꝛẏgaf. ac val ẏmae ıaϐn y mınheu mı ae dıwadaf. heb ẏ talaϐdẏr. Yna ẏ mae ıaϐn barnu reıth canẏt oef eıthẏr vn tauaϐt ẏ mach ẏn gẏrru vn tauaϐt ẏ talaϐdẏr ẏ wadu. Kẏmrẏt oꝛ bꝛaϐdϐꝛ ẏ creır ẏnẏ laϐ. adẏwedut ϐꝛth ẏ talaϐdẏr. Naϐd duϐ ragot anaϐd dẏ arglϐẏd na thϐg anudon. Os tϐg tẏget ẏduϐ ẏnẏ blaen ac ẏr creır nat mach ẏgantaϐ ef nac ar adẏweıt nac ar dım. Onẏ ϐꝛth tϐg ẏmach arnaϐ tra uo ẏn rodı ẏ eneu yr creır. talet ẏ mach ẏ dẏlẏet can adeϐẏf ẏuot ẏn uach abıt rẏd ẏ talaϐdẏr. Os gϐꝛthtϐg awna ẏmach. dẏget ẏtalaϐdẏr ẏreıth. Nẏt amgen ẏ lϐ ar ẏfeıthuet.

If a person gives chattels to another and surety thereon and, when time comes to demand, the debtor denies, and the defendant complains to the lord, it is right to bring the two parties together with the surety and to ask them whether this person is a surety or not a surety. 'A surety,' says the defendant. 'Not a surety,' says the debtor. Then it is right to ask the surety, 'Art thou a surety?' 'A surety,' says he. 'Thou art not a surety for me for anything,' says the debtor. 'I am entitled to law; I shall persist in it,' says the surety. 'And as I am entitled also, I deny it,' says the debtor. Then it is right to adjudge a rhaith, for there is nothing save the one tongue of the surety provoking the one tongue of the debtor to deny. The judge takes the relic in his hand, and says to the debtor, 'The protection of God prevent thee and the protection of thy lord, lest thou swear falsely.' If he swears, let him first swear to God and to the relic, that he is not surety for him neither for what he asserts nor for anything. If the surety do not counter-swear against him whilst he puts his lips to the relic, let the surety pay the debt, as he allows that he is a surety, and let the debtor be free. If the surety counter-swears, let the debtor bring his rhaith, that is, his oath with six others.

W 77 b 16–78 a 8 (*post* dim V 37 a 5; *ante* O₂ 37 a 13). *Anc. Laws* I. 134, 136.

Pôÿbÿnhac awnel amot kÿfreíthaôl doent ÿgÿt ÿwneuthur. O₂ guna dÿn amot ac na mÿnho ÿgadô. arglôÿd bıeu ÿgymhell. O₂ guna dÿn amot ac arall ÿn gÿrru arnaô. kÿfreıth adÿweıt na daô namÿn ÿlô ehunan ÿdıwat. Onÿ bÿd gôₐthtôg arnaô. Os gôₐthtôg auÿd galwet ÿnteu am vₐaôt. Sef auernír ıdaô. ÿ lô ar ÿ feıthuet ÿn vn funut ac ÿdıwat mach. ac am oet ÿreıth. ac am pop peth. O₂ guna dÿn amot ae gılÿd

heb amotwẏr. of guadu auẏn. nẏ daꝋ eithẏr
ẏ lꝋ ehunan ẏdiwat onẏ cheif tẏſton ar ẏ welet.

Whoever shall make a legal contract let them come
together to perform it. If a person makes a contract
and does not wish to keep it, a lord is to compel him.
If a person makes a contract and another presses on
him, law says that he is only to be put to his own
oath to deny it, unless there be a counter-oath against
him. If there be a counter-oath let him call for
judgment. This is what is to be adjudged him, his
oath with six others in the same manner that surety
is denied ; the same also with regard to the time for
a rhaith and everything. If a person makes a contract
with another without contract-men, if he desires to
deny, he is only to be put to his own oath to deny it
unless he obtains witnesses as to seeing it.

W 78 a 20–78 b 12 (*post* gꝋir V 37 a 13 ; *ante* 37 a
18). *Anc. Laws* I. 140, 142.

Deu tẏmhoꝛ ẏ bẏd kaẏat kẏfreith am tir a deu
ẏ bẏd agoꝛet. O naꝋuetdẏd kalan gaẏaf ẏ bẏd
agoꝛet kẏfreith am tir hẏt naꝋuetdẏd whefraꝋꝛ.
O naꝋuet dẏd whefraꝋꝛ ẏ bẏd kaẏat kẏfreith hẏt
naꝋuet dẏd mei. O naꝋuetdẏd mei ẏ bẏd agoꝛet
kẏfreith hẏt naꝋuetdẏd guedẏ aꝋſt. O naꝋuet dẏd
guedẏ aꝋſt ẏ bẏd kaẏet kẏfreith hẏt naꝋuet
dẏd guedẏ kalan gaẏaf. Sef achaꝋſ ẏmae kaẏat
kẏfreith ẏguanhꝋẏn ar kẏnhaẏaf. o achaꝋſ
diwhẏllẏaꝋ ẏ daẏar ẏnẏ deu amſer hẏnnẏ. Sef
achaꝋſ ẏ mae. naꝋuet dẏdyeu gan pop tẏmhoꝛ.
rac kẏfreith ẏn vn dẏdẏaꝋc.

Two seasons shall law be closed for land, and two
it shall be open. From the ninth day of the calends

of winter shall law be open for land until the ninth
day of February. From the ninth day of February
shall law be closed until the ninth day of May. From
the ninth day of May law shall be open until the
ninth day after August. From the ninth day after
August law shall be closed until the ninth day after
the calends of winter. The reason why law is closed
in spring and autumn is because the soil is cultivated
in those two seasons. The reason why every season
has ninth-days is lest law should be for one day.

W 91 a 9–16 (*inter* deiffyfyt *et* Naƀ V 38 a 2). See
p. 115 for text; also *Anc. Laws* I. 556.

For a suit from the same cantrev, three days to give
an answer, and three to give surety, and three to do
justice in respect to the claim demanded. In the
adjoining cantrev, five days to give an answer, and
five to give surety, and five to do justice. In the third
cantrev, nine days to give an answer, and nine to give
surety, and nine to do justice (cf. X 217 b 3–4 on
p. 307 *infra*).

W 91 a 20–92 a 2 (*inter* ed. *et* Pop V 38 a 7). *Anc.
Laws* I. 486, 586, 794; II. 96, 560. See pp. 115–16
for text, and add to it the following:—

neb. Kẏneuaƀt alad kẏfreith ac ẏna nẏ
chetwir.

Whoever shall pay land for galanas, let him pay
geld for it to the lord, for the land is to be free to
him to whom it shall be paid. Three herbs are to
grow in that land: clover, vetches, and thistles. And
the worth of a cow from that land is no more than
its length when she may be pasturing.

Two persons whose worth the king is not to demand,
although they shall be killed in his gwlad: the bondman of another person, for a person has possession of

his bondman as of his animal; and the person who shall be found walking during the night in the king's chamber, without fire, without candle, whose galanas, although the king's servants slay him, is not to be demanded. A judge ought to listen fully, and retain in memory, and learn intently, and speak gently, and judge mercifully. [There is] a custom which follows law and is therefore upheld. [There is] a custom which precedes law and is therefore, when it has regal authority, upheld. [There is] a custom which precedes law, yet of doubtful event, and therefore no one enforces it. [There is] a custom which destroys law, and therefore is not to be kept. (Cf. X 217 a 3-5; and 218 b 6-9.)

W 92 a 14-92 b 10 (*post* llõgyr V 38 b 3).[1]

KJſt õyth geínhaõc kẏfreith atal. Kerõẏn ẏſtẏllaõt pedeir keinhaõc kẏfreith atal. Raf uleõ keínhac kẏfreith a tal. Raf lõẏf keínhaõc cota atal. Kelõin amennei keínhaõc kẏfreith atal pop vn. Kẏfrõẏ eurgalch. pedeir ar hugeint atal. Kẏfrõẏ lliõ ẏpien deudec keínhaõc atal. Nẏth cammín pedeir keínhaõc kẏfreith atal Kaõc pien keínhaõc cota atal. Kenllyuan olreat õẏth geinhaõc kẏfreith atal. Toich milgi bienhin õẏth geinhaõc kẏfreith atal. Toich mílgí bieẏr pedeir keínhaõc kẏfreith atal. Kẏnllyuan mílgi bienhín. pedeir keínhaõc kẏfreith atal. Kẏnllyuan mílgi bieẏr dõẏ geinhaõc kẏfreith atal. Offer gof wheugeint atal. Gradell õẏth geinhaõc kẏfreith atal.

A chest is worth eight legal pence. A tub made

---

[1] W 92 a 14-93 a 15 lies between V 38 b 3 and 4.

of staves is worth four legal pence. A hair rope is worth one legal penny. An elm-bark rope is worth a curt penny. A bucket and a trough are each worth a legal penny. A lacquered saddle is worth twenty-four [pence]. A saddle of the colour of the wood is worth twelve pence. The nest of a falcon is four legal pence in value. A wooden basin is worth a curt penny. The leash of a beagle is worth eight legal pence. The collar of a king's greyhound is worth eight legal pence. The collar of a breyr's greyhound is worth four legal pence. The leash of a king's greyhound is four legal pence in value. The leash of a breyr's greyhound is two legal pence in value. A smith's tools are worth six score [pence]. A baking girdle is worth eight.legal pence.

W 92 b 13–15. *Anc. Laws* I. 794.

Gre gýfreɪthaбl dec caffec adeugeɪnt. Pɹeɪd warthec gýfreɪthaбl. pedeɪr bu ar hugeɪnt.

A legal stud [is] fifty mares. A legal herd of cattle [is] twenty-four kine.

W 92 b 18–93 a 3.

Kýfreɪth ýб y pɹɪodaбr tɪr kýchwýnnu ampɹɪodaбɪ tɪr oe werefgýn. ac ný chýwhýn ampɹɪodaбɪ tɪr pɹɪodaбɪ oe werefgýn. Trɪ argae teruýn ýffýd bɹeɪnt. aphɹɪodolder. achýgwarchadб. ný dýlý dýn auo ɪf ý ureɪnt noɹ reɪ hýnný. teruýnu arnunt. (*Anc. Laws* I. 774.)

It is the law that a proprietor of land should oust a non-proprietor of land from his occupancy, and that a non-proprietor of land should not oust a proprietor from his occupancy. There are three stays of boundary: status, and proprietorship, and prior conservancy; no person who is of lower status than those is to meer them. (Cf. U 53 b 6–7.)

W 93 a 10–15 (*post* V 26 a 9; *ante* V 38 b 4).
Anc. Laws I. 556.

Oet arwaſſaf o wlat arall neu am dόuẏr maόꝛ neu am lanό pẏtheόnoſ. ac nẏt mόẏ. Oet arwaſſaf ẏn vn gẏmhόt neu ẏn vn cantref trı dıeu. Os ẏn arglόẏdıaeth arall ẏn agoſ naό nſeu ac nẏ dodır teruẏn ar duό ſul nac ar duό llun.

The time for an arwaesav from another gwlad or on account of great water or on account of a tide: a fortnight and no more. The time for an arwaesav in the same cymwd or in the same cantrev: three days. If in another lordship, contiguous: nine days, without fixing the limit on a Sunday or Monday. (Cf. X 217 a 16–20 on p. 307.)

W 93 b 7–11 (*post* V 36 b 10; *ante* Arglόẏd V 36 b 16).

Or dẏgόẏd mechnı ar uab dꝛoſ ẏ tat. agoꝛuot ẏdıwat ẏgẏfreıth adẏweıt na watta neb o genedẏl ẏ uam gẏt ac ef amẏn kenedẏl ẏtat achenedẏl mam ẏtat.

If suretyship falls on a son for his father and there be need to deny it, the law declares that none of his mother's kindred denies with him but only his father's kindred and the kindred of his father's mother.

W 93 b 20–94 a 7 (*post* V 38 b 25).

Peır bꝛenhín punt atal. pedeır ar hugeínt atal ẏ gıgweín. Callaόꝛ bꝛenhín wheugeínt atal. ẏchıgweín deudec keínhaόc atal. Peır bꝛeẏr wheugeínt atal. Ẏgıgweín deudec keínhaόc atal Callaόꝛ bꝛeẏr trugeínt atal. ẏ chıgweín pedeır keínhaόc kẏfreıth atal. Callaόꝛ taẏaόc dec ar hugeínt atal.   ẏchıgweín dóẏ geínhaϭc kẏfreıth atal.

A king's cauldron is worth a pound; its flesh-fork is worth twenty-four [pence]. A king's boiler is worth six score [pence] ; its flesh-fork is worth twelve pence. A breyr's cauldron is worth six score [pence] ; its flesh-fork is worth twelve pence. A breyr's boiler is worth thirty [pence] ; its flesh-fork is worth four legal pence. A taeog's boiler is worth thirty [pence] ; its flesh-fork is worth two legal pence. (Also X 179 b 15-19 on p. 304.)

W 99 b 3-7 (*inter* V 43 a 11 *et* 12). *Anc. Laws* I. 778.

Trı chẏffro dıal ẏffẏd yr vn ẏϭ dıáſpedeín kareffev. Eıl ẏϭ guelet eloı eu kar ẏn mẏnet ẏr llan. Tıẏdẏd ẏϭ guelet bed eu car ẏnẏ vẏnwent ẏn newẏd heb ẏmdíuϭẏn.

There are three incitements to revenge ; one is the shrieking of female relations. The second is, seeing the bier of their relative going to the llan. The third is, seeing the grave of their relative fresh in the church-yard without having reparation. (Also X 211 b 17-20 on p. 306 ; and U 55 a.)

§ 2. *Cott. Cleopatra Bv.*

X 165 b 9-11 (*post* hynny V 1 a 24). *Anc. Laws* I. 622.

ar Ïyfuyr hwnn heɪwyd moɪgenev. áchy-uanerth ymab y dıgoned.

And this book was completed according to Mor-genev and Cyvanerth his son. (Cf. W 34 b 4-6 and U 1 b on pp. 291, 309.)

X 178 b 11-13 (*post* yftauell V 11 b 2). *Anc. Laws* I. 666.

Kannwllyd ageiff y tir yn ryd. a march y gan ybienhin. agwedill ycannhwyllev oll A ran oaryan y gweftvaeu.

The candlebearer has his land free, and a horse from the king, and the remains of all the candles, and a share of the gwestva silver. (Also U 15 b 18.)

X 179 b 15-19 (*inter* hines *et* Myny V 12 a 19).

Pvnt yw gwerth peir bienhin. Pedeir arhvgeint yw gwerth y gigwein. Tiugein atal callaur bienhin. iiij⁰². keinyawc ygikwein. Dec arhugeint gwerth callawr taeauc .ij. k. atal ygikwein.

A king's cauldron is worth a pound. Twenty-four [pence] is the worth of its flesh-fork. Sixty [pence] is the worth of a king's boiler; four pence its flesh-fork. Thirty [pence] is the worth of a taeog's boiler; two pence is the worth of its flesh-fork. (Also W 93 b 20-94 a 7 on p. 302.)

X 180 a 5-6 (*in lieu of* tri chanu V 15 b 4). *Anc. Laws* I. 678.

teir awdyl o gamlan

three odes concerning Camlan. (Cf. U 19 a on p. 310).

X 181 a 17-181 b 3 (*post* ehunan V 16 b 20; *ante* Ywen W 85 b 8). *Anc. Laws* I. 678.

Pob penkerd adyly caffael telyn ygan y bienhin Pob difgybyl adyly yenill ae benkerd ytraeyanv. aphan el y difgybyl ywrthaw y penkerd adyly rodi telyn idaw. Pwybynnac abɪynho dím ymarchnad. Ny dyly geıſſyaw gwarant ıdaw

Every chief of song is to have a harp from the king. Every pupil is to enjoy his gain, and his chief of song a third of it ; and when the pupil leaves him, the chief of song is to give him a harp. Whoever shall buy anything in a market is not to seek a warrant for himself.

X 185 a 4–8 (*post* agɓɪeıc V 17 a 20). See W 56 b 4–8 on p. 294. *Anc. Laws* I. 688.

X 192 b 4–5 (*inter* werth *et* nyt V 31 b 1). See W 69 a 7–8 on p. 294. *Anc. Laws* I. 712.

X 193 b 18–19 (*post* V 30 a 21). See W 67 b 16–17 on p. 294. *Anc. Laws* I. 708.

X 196 a 19–196 b 2 (*post* lɓ V 34 b 24). See W 73 b 6–9 on p. 295. *Anc. Laws* I. 744.

X 199 a 7–10 (*inter* uodeu *et* y V 14 a 8). See W 51 a 12–14 on p. 292. *Anc. Laws* I. 680.

X 205 a 11–12 (*inter* W 83 a 12 *et* 13).

Aʀgyſurew gwreíc yw y gwathawl.

The argyvreu of a woman are her gwaddol.

X 205 b 7–8 (*post* ẏſtauellaɓc W 83 b 5). *Anc. Laws* I. 692.

Yneb adıwatto y vod wrth anreıth. Roddet lw deng wyr adeugeín.

Whoever shall deny being at a spoil, let him give the oaths of fifty men. (Also U 23 a on p. 311.)

X 207 b 3–12 (*post* W 103 a 17 ; *ante* O W 80 a 10). *Anc. Laws* II. 8 ; I. 570 572.

Teır goſgoɪd bɪenhínaɓl yſyd. Goſgoɪd bɪenhín. ac efgob. ac abad. Canys llyf vreínhawl adyly pob vn. ohonu*n*t. Trugeínt yw gwerth. march tom. neu gaffec tom. ynep adıwatto lÍad march nev ydwyn ynlledrad ʀoddet lw deu dengwyr. Pwy bynnac awertho march neu gaffec. ef adyly uod ydan y derı trí glwyth. ar yfgyueín teír lloeʀ. ar llín meırch blwyn. adı-lyffrwyd hyd varw.

There are three kingly retinues: the retinue of a king, and a bishop, and an abbot; for each of them is entitled to a privileged court. Thirty [pence] is the worth of a working horse or a working mare. Who-soever shall deny killing a horse or taking it stealthily, let him give the oaths of twelve men. Whosoever shall sell a horse or mare, is to be answerable three dewfalls for the staggers, and three moons for the strangles, and a year for the farcy; and dilysrwydd till death.

X 211 b 17–20 (*post* genthı V 43 a 2; *ante* O 43 a 20). *Anc. Laws* I. 778.

Tʒı chyffro dıal ynt. vn ohonunt dıafpedeín y careffev. Eıl yw gweled geloʒ eu car yn myned yr llan. Tʒydyt yw gweled bed ev car heb ymdıwyʀ.

There are three incitements to revenge; one of them, the shrieking of the female relations. The second is, seeing the bier of their relative going to the llan. The third is, seeing the grave of their relative without enjoying satisfaction. (Also W 99 b 3–7 on p. 303; and U 55 a.)

X 216 b 19–217 a 3 (*inter* W 91 a 19 *et* 20). *Anc. Laws* I. 556.

Ac eiffyoeſ yr gwerth. agobyR. y llygrIR pob
vn ohonu*n*t. PedwaR anghyvarch gwR yw y
varch. ae aruev. ae wynebwerth. a thwng
ydIR.

And yet for a price and a reward each of them is
corrupted. The four peculiars of a man are his horse,
and his arms, and his wynebwerth, and the twnc of
his land.

X 217 a 3-5 (*ante* V 45 a 23). Cf. W 91 a 20-21
on p. 299 *supra*. *Anc. Laws* I. 794.

X 217 a 16-20 (*post* geilleu W 82 a 21 ; *ante* Oet
W 91 a 7). *Anc. Laws* I. 556.

Oed ar gwaeffaff yngoɪwlad. Nev am dwuyR
mawR Nev amy llanw. Pytheunos. Nyd oeſ
terwyn ar dɪw ful. Mab eillt auo maenawR ɪdaw.
O bɪt eglwys aR y tɪr. vn alanas uyd ar pro

The time for an arwaesav in a border gwlad or on
account of much water or on account of the tide :
a fortnight. There is no limit on a Sunday. A mab
aillt who has a maenor, if there be a church on the
land, is to have the same galanas as the propositus
(maer). (Cf. W 93 a 10-15 on p. 302.)

X 217 b 3-4 (*inter* deiffyfyt *et* Naᴕ V 38 a 2). *Anc.*
Laws I. 556.

En yn gantref oed trɪ dɪev y RodI gwiR.

In one cantrev there is a period of three days to do
justice. (Cf. W 91 a 9-16 on p. 299 *supra*.)

X 217 b 8-11 (*post* W 105 a 11 ; *ante* W 103 a 18).
Anc. Laws I. 448.

Tʀı chyfwrch dırgel adyly ybıenhın ygaffael heb y brawdwʀ ygyd ae effeıryad. ae wreıc. ay uedíc.

Three private intercourses which the king is to have without the judge: with his priest, and his wife, and his physician.

X 218 a 18–218 b 4 (*post* blόydyn V 38 a 14; *ante* Trı W 104 a 9). *Anc. Laws* I. 762.

Tʀ] Ïe yran kyfureıth. vn ohonunt y da a dycceʀ o anghyfureıth ygyfureıth. Eıl yw Rwng byw amarw. Tıydyt yw. Obyd amryffon am dev teruyn athyngv O baub yteruyn. auo yrwng y dev ymryffon. ãrennír ín deuhanner.

Three places where law shares: one of them, the chattels transferred from illegality to legality; the second is, between living and dead; the third is, if there be contention as to two meers and all swear, the meer between the two disputants is divided equally. (Cf. U 47 b and 48 a on p. 318; also V 22 a 1–6.)

X 218 b 6–9 (*post* llaόdόı W 104 a 10; *ante* Teır 104 a 11). See W 91 b 13–15 on pp. 116, 299. *Anc. Laws* I. 486.

X 218 b 16–19 (*inter* W 104 b 1 *et* 2). *Anc. Laws* I. 448.

Tʀ] edyn aʀ dyr dyn arall. heb ganyad. eryr. ãgaran. ãchıgfuran Pwybynnac ac ev Ïadho. taled dec ãdevgeín yberchennawc ytír.

Three birds on another person's land without permission, [viz.] eagle, and crane, and raven. Whoever kills them, let him pay fifty [pence] to the owner of the land.[1]

X 219 a 11–14 (*post* oll V 38 a 22; *ante* Un V 38 b 11). *Anc. Laws* I. 690.

Pwybynnac a ʀoddo tan nev adȝawho hayarn. yny lofgo yty. Dev hanner vyd ar y nep aroddo y tan ac ay llofgo.

Whoever gives fire or strikes iron so that the house is burnt, the two parts fall equally on the one who gives the fire and [on the one] who burns [the house]. (Cf. W 85 a 13–15 on p. 103.)

X 222 a 8–22 (*post* gic W 82 b 20) is an addition by a later hand to the text. It is equivalent roughly to V 19 a 24–20 a 4, but nearer the form of U. *Anc. Laws* I. 696, 698, 700.

§ 3. *Peniarth MS.* 37.[2]

U 1 b (*post* hynny V 1 a 24). *Anc. Laws* I. 622.

Ar llyuyr hwn herwyd Morgeneu a Chyfnerth y uab adıgonet. Ar gwyr hynny oed oreu yn eu hamser ar cof a chyfreıtheu.

And this Book was completed according to Morgeneu and his son Cyvnerth. And these men were the best in their time for record and laws. (Cf. W 34 b 4–6; X 165 b 9–11, on pp. 291, 303 *supra*.)

U 15 b 18. See X 178 b 11–13 on p. 304. *Anc. Laws* I. 666.

---

[1] This triad is quite distinct from V 44 b 25–45 a 4, which is found in U, W, and X. *Anc. Laws* I. 778.

[2] Where the lines of the various folios of this MS. are not given, the passage is taken from Owen's *Anc. Laws*, vol. I, the punctuation and the letters r, s, w, &c., being in modern style.

U 17 a 2. See W 54 b 17–55 a 5 on p. 292. *Anc. Laws* I. 670.

U 19 a (*in lieu of* teulu tri chanu V 15 b 4). *Anc. Laws* I. 678.

kerd o Camlan a hynny

A song concerning Camlan and that (Cf. X 180 a 5–6 on p. 304.)

U 19 b 9–13 (*inter* V 14 a 25 *et* 14 b 1). *Anc. Laws* I. 682.

Offer gof Chweugeint atal. Geuel oꝛd. kethraб troꝛud. pedeir. k. k'. atal pob un o honunt. y cónfiſſt kymeint atal ar pedwar hynny. ᴍyrthól damdóg a uyd ymdanaб.

A smith's tools are six score [pence] in value. Pincers, mallet, borer, vice, are each of them four legal pence in value. The anvil is as much as those four in value. A hammer is to be appraised.

U 21 b. See W 56 b 4–8 on p. 294. *Anc. Laws* I. 688.

U 22 a 5–18 (*inter* V 18 b 5 *et* 6). *Anc. Laws* I. 688, 690.

ac oꝛ ſſyſc dyn yny tan hónnб try wyr hefyt o honunt yn diofredaбc ᴍegyſ y rei uchot. Nyt a galanas yn ol tan Namyn yg gweithret y neb alofgo ac ef. Or ſſyſc ty ymyбn trefgoꝛd o waſſ tanꝛ y perchennaбc adyly talu ty o bob parth idaб oꝛ ſſofgant gantaб ac oꝛ trydyd ty aſſan tan gwyſſt uyd Or kynneu dyn tan y ᴍyбn ty dyn araſſ. Talet y ty y perchennaбc oꝛ ſſyſc. Tan a adaбho dyn ymyбn odyn Ef adyly bot droftaб

And if a person be burned in that fire, three men

of them likewise under vows like those before. Galanas does not attend fire, only in the act of him who shall burn therewith. If a house be burned within a trevgordd from negligence, the owner is to pay for a house on each side of him, if they be burned by his means; and from the third house onward, it is deemed an uncontrollable fire.[1] If a person kindle fire in another person's house, let him pay for the house to the owner if it be burned. A person is to be answerable for a fire which he shall leave in a kiln.

U 23 a (*post* V 21 b 22; *ante* V 20 a 8). *Anc. Laws* I. 692.

Yneb adiwatto anreithaw arall, rodet y kyffelyp iddaw.

Whoever shall deny spoiling another, let him give to him the like [i.e. the oaths of fifty men]. (Also X 205 b 7–8 on p. 305.)

U 25 b 11 (*post* V 20 a 21; *ante* V 19 a 24). *Anc. Laws* I. 696.

Nyt a galanas yn ol teuluƀyaeth.

Galanas does not follow domesticity.

U 27 a (*post* sƀyd V 21 a 11; *ante* E V 21 a 4). *Anc. Laws* I. 700.

Kymeint yw gwerth aelodeu ytayawc o kyfreith agwerth aelodeu y brenhin herwyd gwerth. Galanas hagen asarhaet pawb herwyd y ureint y telir pan torher y aelawt.

The worth of the taeog's limbs, by law, is as much as the worth of the king's limbs according to worth. The galanas and sarhâd however of every one are paid according to his status when a limb shall be broken.

[1] Cf. pp. 103, 247.

U 27 b (*post* sarhaet V 21 b 16; *ante* W 88 a 11).
Anc. Laws I. 700.]

Yneb adiwatto llad caeth rodet lw pedwar
gwyr arugeint, ac eu hanher yn wyr not.

Whoever shall deny killing a bondman, let him give
the oaths of twenty-four men, the half of them being
nod-men.

U 28 b 3–5 (*post* werth W 85 b 1; *ante* V 38 a 13).
Anc. Laws I. 702.

Gwerth goʒuodaƀc

Gwerth goʒuodaƀc un uʒeínt ar neb yd aeth
droftaƀ ac y uelly am dyn a ƀyftler dros arall.

The worth of a gorvodog.

The worth of a gorvodog is that he is of the same
status as the one for whom he is bound; and so also
with regard to a person pledged for another. (Cf.
V 38 a 10–12.)

U 28 b 7–9 (*post* blƀydyn V 38 a 14; *ante* Or
V 29 a 3). *Anc. Laws* I. 704.

Un dyn y telır .k. paladyr ıdaƀ ac nys tal ef
y neb y wreıc awnel llaƀurudyaeth.

One person to whom a spear penny is paid and
who pays to no one: the woman who shall commit
murder.

U 29 a 15–16 (*inter* honunt *et* Rƀnfi V 29 b 2). *Anc.
Laws* I. 704.

Mƀng March pedeır .k.k'. atal.

The mane of a horse is four legal pence in value.

U 31 a (*post* velly V 31 b 13; *ante* Ny V 31 b 20).
Anc. Laws I. 714.

Trayanwerth ar bob anyueil yw y teithi o rei
ny bo aruer y dynyon yuet eu llaeth.

The third of the worth of every animal of which it
is not customary for people to drink their milk is its
teithi.

U 33 a (*inter* vyd *et* Jar V 32 a 8). *Anc. Laws*
I. 718.

Gwerth hwyat. Gwerth hwyat keinawc kyfreith.

The Worth of a Duck. The worth of a duck is
one legal penny.

U 36 b (*post* bɹenhín V 34 a 2; *ante* V 32 a 25).
Anc. Laws I. 732.

Colwyn brenhin neu urenhines, punt atal.
Colwyn breyr, chweugeint atal. Colwyn mab-
eillt, pedeɪr keinawc atal.

The shock-dog of a king or queen is a pound in
value. The shock-dog of a breyr is six score [pence]
in value. The shock-dog of an aillt is four pence in
value.

U 39 a 4–13 (*inter* baed *et* Oɹ V 34 a 21). *Anc.*
Laws I. 740, 742.

Parchell pan ymchoelo y bɪſwelyn gyntaf ae
trόyn. Un .k'. uyd ae ᴍam Or cadό .k'. oɹ moch
pa amſer bynhac y caffer yn llygru gweɪrglaόd.
pedeɪr .k. k'. ateliɪr o honunt. yneb agaffo ᴍoch
yny llygru yny coet. lladet un o honunt y ſaόl
weɪth y caffo hyt y dɪwethaf. Eíthyr y trɪ llydyn
arbenhɪc. Sef yό y trɪ hynny. arbeɴnhɪc y ᴍoch.
ar baed kenueín. a hόch y geíuyr.

A pig when it shall first turn up the dung with its snout is under the same law as its mother. Of the lawful herd of the swine, at what time soever they be found damaging hay land, four legal pence are paid for them. Any one who shall find swine doing damage in his wood, let him kill one of them every time he shall find them unto the last, excepting the three special animals. Those three are, the principal of the swine, and the herd boar, and the sow for [the gwestva].

U 40 a. See W 73 b 6-9 on p. 295. *Anc. Laws* I. 744.

U 40 b 3-16 (*ante* V 38 b 13). *Anc. Laws* I. 744.

Pỽybynhac atoᴣho troet anyueil dyn araỻ Neu y uoᴣdỽyt. Neu anel bᴣiỽ ydel nychdaỽt idaỽ abot yr anyueil yn lan ᴍal y galﬆeᴣ bỽytta y gic. Ef adyly y gymryt attaỽ ae uedeginaethu yny uo ᴣach. ac oᴣ byd ᴍarỽ talet y werth. Pỽybynhac a huryho Neu loco anyueil ae y dỽyn peth arnaỽ ae y eredic. Ony wneir aghyfreith ac ef kyt coﬆo y eneit ny thelir. Or brath anyueil dyn. y dyn brathedic ageiff yr anyueil ae bᴣatho. Neu talet perchennaỽc yr anyueil farhaet ydyn a gwerth y waet.

Whoever shall break the foot of an animal belonging to another person, or its thigh, or shall inflict a wound which shall cause ailment to it, and the animal be clean so that its flesh may be eaten; he is to take it to himself and apply remedies until it shall be well; and, if it die, let him pay the worth of it. Whoever shall hire or engage an animal either to carry a load or to plough; unless it be used unlawfully it is not to be paid for although it lose its life. If an animal bite a person, the bitten person has the animal which bit him ; or let the owner of the animal pay the sarhâd of the person and the worth of his blood.

U 42 a 5–10 (*post* ıaƀn W 79 b 18; *ante* 82 a 12). *Anc. Laws* I. 748.

Gwreıc atreıffer Ony ƀybyd pƀy ae treıffo Ny thal amobyr Canyf ketwıs y bʒen. hı rac treıs y byd coĬedıc ynteu oe amobyr. ac o damheuſr y wreıc am hynny. ʀodet y Ĭƀ na ƀyr pƀy ae treıffƀys ae ry treıffaƀ ᴍal kynt.

A woman who shall be violated, if she know not who has violated her, is not to pay amobr ; since the king preserved her' not from violation, he loses her amobr ; and if the woman be doubted in that respect, let her give her oath that she knows not who violated her, and that she was violated as aforesaid.

U 42 b 1–3 (*post* geılleu W 82 a 21; *ante* Onẏ 80 a 5). *Anc. Laws* I. 750.

Os dƀy wraged y bydant. ʀodet yneıĬ geıĬ y hon ar ĬaĬ yr ĬaĬ oʒ byd gantunt eıĬ dƀy.

If there be two women, let one testicle be given to one, and the other to the other, if he be connected with them both.

U 43 b 5–44 a 6 (*post* gyfreıth V 23 a 13; *ante* V 24 a 11). *Anc. Laws* I. 756.

Dadanhud yƀ eredıc o dyn y tır ardyffeı y dat kyn noc ef. yny pedwarydyn y da dyn yn prıodaƀʒ y dat ae hendat ae oʒhendat ac ehun yn pedweryd. Gwedy yd del ef yn pʒıodaƀʒ Ny dıffyd y prıodolder hyt ynaƀuet Oʒ bydant hƀyn-

teu heb eu dylyet hyt ynaϐuet dyn. Hϐnnϐ yn
ꟿynet o priodaϐꝛ yn ampriodaϐꝛ. yna ydyly
hϐnnϐ dodi diafpat uϐch aduan. ꝛc y dyly ynteu
caffel kynnϐys. Sef yϐ hynny kymeint ar gϐꝛ
ꟿϐyhaf y warchadϐ. ꝛchet galwo am diafpat
uϐch ꝛduan oꝛ naϐuet dyn aꟙan Ny werendewir.
Or diuernir gwelygoꝛd o tir ꝛ bot reꝛ yg goꝛwlat
ꝛc nat arhoer am k'. Hϐy adylyant .k'. pan
deꟙont. Os hϐynteu Ny ouynant .k'. pan deꟙont
hyt yn oet un dyd ablϐydynt Cayedic uyd udunt
.k'. o hynny aꟙan.

A dadannudd is the tilling by a person of land
tilled by his father before him. In the fourth degree
a person becomes a proprietor; his father, and his
grandfather, and his great-grandfather, and himself
fourth. After he becomes a proprietor, his proprietorship does not become extinguished until the ninth.
If they be without their right unto the ninth person,
such becoming a non-proprietor from being a proprietor, then it is incumbent on that person to utter
a cry over the lost spot, and he ought to obtain
admission, that is, as much as the man, who is greatest
as to his conservancy; and should any one beyond
the ninth person call for a cry over the lost spot, he
is not listened to. If a gwelygordd be adjudged to
lose land, and some be in a border gwlad and they be
not awaited for law, they are entitled to law when
they come. If they themselves do not demand law
when they come, to the end of a year and a day, law
is closed against them thenceforward.

U 44 a 15~44 b 3 (*post* yrydunt V 24 a 3 *ante* 22
b 13). *Anc. Laws* I. 756.

Pϐybynhac a dechreuho ymhaϐl am tir ꝛr

amdıffynn6r yn para6t y atteb. ac odyna oı
teu yr ha6l6ı agwaỻocau y ha6l hyt yn oet un
dyd abl6ydyn kyt dechreuo holı yr ha6l gwedy
hynny Ny cheiff dım Canys ha6l tra bl6ydyn y6.

Whoever shall commence a suit for land, the defendant being ready to answer, and afterwards the
claimant be silent and allow his claim to drop till
the end of a year and a day; although he should
begin proceeding after that, he has nothing, for it is
a claim beyond a year.

U 44 b 15-45 a 7 (*post* thyccya V 22 b 12 *ante*
23 b 16). *Anc. Laws* I. 758.

Os na6uet dyd·Meı y dechreu holı a gohır am
uarn o dyd y gılyd hyt a6ft. Ny cheıff barn hyt
na6uet dyd racuyr Canys tymhoı cayet y6 y
kynhayaf. Os na6uetdyd racuyr y dechreu holı
a gohır am uarn o dyd y gılyd tr6y y gayaf
tymoı cayet y6 y gwanh6yn yn gyffelyb yr kynhayaf Canys dıderuyfc y dylyır heu aỻyfnu y
gwanh6yn ad6yn yr yt y my6n y kynhayaf.

If on the ninth day of May he commence proceedings, and delay obtaining judgment from day to day
until August, he shall not obtain judgment until the
ninth day of December, because a closed season is
the harvest. If on the ninth day of December he
commence proceedings, and delay obtaining judgment from day to day through the winter, a closed
season is the spring like the harvest, because sowing
and harrowing are to suffer no interruption in spring,
nor bringing in the corn in harvest.

U 45 a 15-18 (*post* g6ys V 23 b 21 *ante* K6y 24 a 3).
Anc. Laws I. 758.

Aghenyon kyfreithaѲl y omed gwys. IlıfdѲı o uoı hyt uynyd heb ryt heb pont arnaѲ. achar- char. achleuyt goıweıdyaѲc.

Lawful excuses for neglecting a summons: flood- water from sea to mountain without a ford without a bridge thereon;· imprisonment; and bedridden disease.

_U 46 b 1–5 (*post* da V 24 b 5 *ante* 43 a 22). *Anc. Laws* I. 760.

Tır kyt kyny bo Namyn un oe etſuedyon heb dıffoddıː Ef adyly caffel cѲbyl oı tır. Gwedy ranher hagen y bıenhín auyd etſued yr neb adıffodo.

Although there be only one inheritor of joint land with unextinguished title, he is to have the whole of the land. After it is shared, however, the king is to be heir to him who is extinguished.

U 47 b (*post* kynwarchadѲ V 22 a 1). *Anc. Laws* I. 762.

Tri lle y rann kyfreith : un ohonunt, or tyf kynhen rwg dwy tref am tir a theruyn ac wynteu yn un ureint, gwyrda brenhin bieu teruynu hwnnw os medrant; or byd pedrus dyledogyon y tir, pawb bieu tygu y teruyn ; odyna rannent yn deuhanher rwg y dwy tref y hamrysson. Ket teruyno tref ar arall, ny dyly dwyn randir y wrthi. Hanher punt a daw yr brenhin pan teruynher, a phedeir ar ugeint a daw yr brawdwr. Eıl yw rwg gwr a gwreıc pan uo marw y lleill. Trydyd yw pan dyker anyueıl or lle ny aller y caffel wrth kyfreith, nyt amgen, o aghyfreith y kyureith.

Three places where law shares: one of them is, if
contention arise between two trevs as to land and
boundary, they being of equal status, it is for a king's
gwrdas to determine it, if they are able; if the proprietors of the land be doubtful, every one must swear
as to his boundary; afterwards let them share equally
between the two trevs their object of contention.
Although a trev shall meer to another, it is not to
take a rhandir from it. Half a pound comes to the
king when a meer shall be fixed, and twenty-four
[pence] comes to the judge. The second is between
a husband and wife when one party shall die. The
third is when an animal shall be taken from the place
where it cannot be had by law, to wit, from an illegal
state to a legal state. (Cf. V 22 a 1–10; and X 218
a 18–218 b 4 on pp. 47, 308, *supra*.)

U 48 b 11–13 (*inter* amaeth *et* O₂ V 27 b 22). *Anc.
Laws* I. 764, n 31.

k'. kyueıreu. Kyueır gayauar. Dóy .k. k'. atal
Kyueır gwanhóynaól .k. k'. atal.

Law of co-arations. Co-aration of winter tilth is
two legal pence in value. A spring co-aration is
a legal penny in value.

U 49 b 17–50 a 1 (*post* ehunan V 24 a 22; *ante* Y
V 26 a 23). *Anc. Laws* I. 766.

Póybynhac agynhaƚo tır dan deu arglóyd
Talet ebedıó obob un o honunt.

Whoever shall hold land under two lords, let him
pay ebediw to each of them.

U 50 a 13–16 (*post* vaenaó₂ V 26 a 9 *ante* 26 a 25).
Anc. Laws I. 768, n 28.

Go₂uodref uyd y tryded o bob tref. Nyt .k'.

bot Namyn trı thayaƀc ym pob un oʒ dƀy tref
ereıll. ac oʒ randıred hynny Ny el(.)ır amí-
nogeu tır.

A gorvodtrev is the third of every trev. It is not
lawful that there should be more than three taeogs
in each of the two other trevs; and from those rhandirs
land borderers are not called (?).

U 52 b 3–18 (*post* ẏdẏlẏet W 104 a 2; *ante* Croef-
uaen V 26 a 14). *Anc. Laws* I. 772, 774.

Tygu tır.

Ny dyly tƀnng ar tır dyƀ ful Na dyƀ ƚƚun Dyƀ
ful dyd ywedıaƀ. Dyƀ ƚƚun dyd y lauuryaƀ
y keıffaƀ creıreu adefneu y tynngu y tır. Pƀy-
bynhac aladho y uraƀt am na rann tref tat ac ef
y ƚƚofrud honno Ny dyly kenedyl talu galanas
gyt ac ef. Namyn ef adyly talu galanas eu
kar udunt hƀy abıt colle byth o tref y dat

ƚƚe dyly keıtweıt.

Llyma y ƚƚeoedd y dyly keıtweıt uotː yn gyntaf
y cadƀ tır adayar gan dyn Eıl yƀ cadƀ kyn coƚƚ.
Trydyd yƀ cadƀ geín a meıthrın. Pedweryd yƀ
cadƀ gweftı. Pymhet yƀ cadƀ bʒeınt. Chwechet
yƀ cadƀ aƚƚtud gan dyn.

Swearing as to land.

There is to be no swearing as to land on a Sunday
nor on a Monday. Sunday is a day for praying;
Monday is a day for labouring to procure relics, and
essentials for swearing to land. Whoever shall kill
his brother because he will not share father's trev
with him, for such homicide kindred should not pay
galanas with him; but he is to pay the galanas of their

kinsman to them ; and let him forfeit for ever his father's trev.

Where guardians are required.

Here are the places where guardians are to be. In the first place, to guard land and soil for a person The second is, to guard before loss. The third is, to guard birth and rearing. The fourth is, to guard a guest. The fifth is, to guard status. The sixth is, to guard an alltud for a person.

U 53 a 3–7 (*post* atal V 26 a 16 ; *ante* Gôys V 14 a 1). *Anc. Laws* I. 774.

Ny dyly neb dodı dıafpat egwan onyt y neb aomeder yn Ilys y arglôyd Neu yny dadleu k'. am tref y dat. Neu ynaôuet dyn rac dıffodı prıodolder.

No one is to utter a cry of distress, but one refused law in the court of his lord or in the law pleadings, for his father's trev ; or the ninth person, lest proprietorship be extinguished.

U 53 b 6–7. See W 92 b 18–93 a 3 on p. 301. *Anc. Laws* I. 774.

U 53 b 8–16 (*ante* V 40 b 1). *Anc. Laws* I. 774, 776.

Trı chargychwyn heb attywel. мab amheu gwedy gôıthladher un weıth o genedyl. a gwı gwedy gôıthladher un weıth o tır a dayar. Ny dyly hônnô dyuot y tır gwedy hynny. a gôıeıc gwedy gôrthladher un weıth oe gwely yn gyureıthaôl Ny dyly dyuot yr gwely hônnô byth dıacheuyn herwyd kyfreıth.

Three removals of kin without return: a doubted son after he shall have been once rejected by a kindred ; and a man who after he shall have been once ejected from land and soil is not to obtain land afterwards; and a woman who after she shall have been once expelled lawfully from her bed is never to return to that bed again according to law.

U 55 a. See W 99 b 3–7 and X 211 b 17–20 on pp. 303, 306 *supra*. *Anc. Laws* I. 778.

U 56 a (*post* alanaf W 105 a 9; *ante* Tri V 44 b 21). *Anc. Laws* I. 780.

Tri dyn yssyd ryd udunt kerdet ford a dieithyr ford: effeirat y ouwy claf ygyt ae gennat; eil yw, righyll yn negesseu y arglwyd; trydyd yw, medyc gyta chennat y claf.

There are three persons who are free to travel the road and out of the road: a priest to visit the sick along with his messenger; the second is an apparitor on his lord's commission; the third is a physician along with the messenger of the sick.

U 61 a to the end. The sixteen folios with which this manuscript ends form no part of the Book of Cyvnerth, but are copied from the Book of Gwynedd as represented by A, E and G. They will be found printed with tentative translation by myself in Vol. XVII of *Y Cymmrodor*. See also *Anc. Laws* II. 2–36, 40, 46. Two more folios are added in a much later and running hand.

II. Leading Omissions from the Printed Text.

W omits: V 17 a 21–18 a 21; 21 b 2; 10–16; 22 a 13–22 b 12; 23 a 6–23 b 1; 14–15; 24 a 11–15; 22–25 b 10; 26 a 9–12; 14–24; 33 a 23–25; 35 b 1–11; 37 a 6–8; 38 a 3–5; 10–12; 14–20; 38 b 13–19; 39 a 6–40 a 26; 44 b 8–10.

X omits: V 2 a 18–23; 3 b 22–24; 7 a 5–10; 12–
13; 10 a 10–21; 16 b 21–24; 17 a 21–18 a 21; 19 a 24–
20 a 7; 20 a 4–7; 2 a 18–22; 21 b 2; 21 b 10–16;
22 a 13–22 b 12; 23 a 6–23 b 1; 23 b 14–15; 24 a 3–6;
11–15; 22–25 b 10; 26 a 3–24; 26 b 11–27 a 9;
W 65 b 21–66 a 1; V 29 b 24–30 a 2; 30 b 21–31 a 4;
31 b 13–15; 20–24; 32 a 19–21; 32 a 25–33 a 4;
33 a 23–25; 35 a 5–7; 9–11; 18–19; 35 b 1–11;
36 a 12–13; 20–24; 36 b 9–37 a 17; W 82 a 21–
82 b 5; 83 a 15–19; 83 b (margin); 83 b 20–84 a 15;
85 a 18–85 b 7; 87 b 4–8; 88 a 3–5; 89 a 20–89 b 4;
7–90 b 10; 90 b 13–91 a 3; 9–16; V 38 a 3–5; 10–12;
14–20; 23–38 b 8; 11–39 a 11; 14–40 a 26; 41 a 17–
41 b 2; 44 b 8–10; 44 a 17–44 b 8; 45 a 10–12;
45 b 22–25; W 102 b 20–103 a 14; 103 b 2–3; 104 a
16–20; 104 b 9–105 a 10; 105 a 13–107 a 9.

U omits: V 3 a 21–22; W 38 a 11–13; 18–21;
38 b 7–9; 20–39 a 3; 5–6; 10–12; 39 b 16–18;
V 6 a 8–11; 22–25; 6 b 10–33; 15–16; 7 a 5–10;
7 b 4–6; 12–19; 21–23; 8 a 13–17; 8 b 12–19; 24–
9 a 3; 4–5; 14–19; 20–21; 9 b 1–2; 10 a 10–21;
12 a 11–21; 25–12 b 1; 13 a 9–12; 19–13 b 2; 4–7;
9–11; 19–22; 14 a 1–5; 8; 11; 14–20; 14 b 5–8;
16–18; 21; 23–25; 15 a 11–14; 18–20; 22–23;
16 b 8–13; 21–24; 17 a 21–18 a 21; 18 b 19–19 a 23;
19 b 11–16; 20 a 4–7; 21 b 2–5; 10–14; 16–18;
22 a 10–12; 14–22 b 7; 23 a 4–6; 13–23 b 1; 14–15;
21–23; 24 a 15–18; 24 b 6–25 b 10; 26 a 3–8;
12–14; 27 a 15–17; 24–27 b 14; W 65 a 8–65 b 17;
66 a 1–V 29 a 2; 29 b 24–30 a 2; 15–21; 30 b 21–
31 a 4; 15–31 b 11 [1]; 13–15; 22–24; W 69 b 20–21;

[1] In lieu of V 31 a 15–31 b 11, U has the following rubric (31 a 11)
un werth ac un dyrchauel yᴳ ych abu(6ch ei)thyr (eu teithi). Of the
same worth and the same augmentation are an ox and a cow, except
their teithi (cf. *Anc. Laws* I. 712).

V 32 a 19–24; 32 b 1–33 a 4; 33 b 13–16; 34 a 2–4;
34 b 15–16; 35 a 4–37 a 17; 37 b 25–W 79 b 10;
19–80 a 5; 7–10; 15–19; 80 b 5–7; 10–82 a 11;
21–82 b 1; 5–83 a 9; 13–20; 83 b 6–13; 83 b (margin);
20–84 a 15; 84 b 12–18; 85 a 2–4; 18–21; 85 b 1–7;
18–86 a 5; 14–16; 87 a 11–20; 87 b 6–20; 88 b 12–
18; 21–89 a 14; 20–89 b 4; 7–14; 18–V 38 a 9;
14–38 b 8; 11–12; 20–40 a 26; 41 a 17–41 b 5;
42 a 7–15; 24–42 b 13; 43 a 7–44 a 5; 44 b 8–10;
17–21; 45 a 4–9; 19–25; 45 b 19–25; W 102 b 20;
103 a 1–2; 14–17; 103 b 2–104 a 2; 7–11; 104 b
4–21; 105 a 9–10; 13–105 b 9; 13–16; 18–107 a 9.

GLOSSARY

agweddi, dowry. The word 'seems to mean all that the *dy-weddi* (the betrothed woman) brings with her to the husband'.[1] In the text, however, it is normally limited to a pecuniary sum, varying according to the status of the bride's father, which is handed over with the. bride to the bridegroom on the occasion of the marriage. It remains, however, the wife's property, to be restored or forfeited, as the case may be, in certain events. The agweddi is paid in cattle in the case of a woman going away clandestinely, without consent of kindred, with a man who afterwards abandons her. The agweddi is also paid in case of rape.

alltud, foreigner. The word 'is equivalent to Anglo-Saxon *el-theod*'.[2] In the Latin texts of the laws, it is represented by *exul*, which may explain the treatment of Hengist and Horsa as *exiles* from Germany in the Welsh versions of the fable of the Saxon conquest. The status of every alltud in Cymru was fixed by law, as he had his own galanas and sarhâd. He could give no evidence, however, against a Cymro, and some lord had to be in some way responsible for him, which lord might be a king, breyr, or a taeog. His galanas and sarhâd were according to the status of this lord. It appears from the text that his descendants could be incorporated into the Cymric kindreds (p. 62).

amobr, a maiden fee, payable to her lord, when she married or had connexion with a man. Normally the amobr was paid by her father, who, however, had no need to pay should the daughter go away clandestinely without consent of kindred. See **gobr merch**.

arddelw, a vouchee of various kinds in defence. The term is only used in one passage in the present text.

arglwydd, lord. This word appears to be used as a general term for a superior of any kind, from *arglwydd Dinevwr*, the Lord of Dinevwr, to *arglwydd caeth*, the lord of a bondman, and even *arglwydd ci*, the lord of a dog. In reading the earlier and more reliable texts of the laws, one must carefully avoid

---

[1] *The Welsh People*, 211, note 3.   [2] Ibid., 191, note 1.

limiting its application to 'the superior chief of a district'. In such a phrase as *bradwr arglwydd*, for example, the *arglwydd* would vary according to the status of the *bradwr* (traitor). Given that the latter was one of the officers of the Court of Dinevwr, the *arglwydd* no doubt would be the powerful territorial chief known in later history as King of Deheubarth. Were he on the other hand a monk or the serf of a breyr, his arglwydd would be the abbot or the breyr as the case might be.

Argoel, called Castell Arcoyl in the Latin Vespasian E XI, where its *prepositus* or maer is mentioned.[1] Mr. Phillimore identifies it with a place called Caeth Argoel, between Derwydd and Golden Grove.[2] There are two farms in the parish of Llanfihangel Aberbythych between Derwydd and Golden Grove, called Caeth-argoed uchaf and isaf. They are roughly about 2½ miles from Castell Dinevwr. Mr. Phillimore suggests with a query that Argoel is a by-form of Aergol, the Welsh modification of the Latin Agricola, and refers to the fifth-century Aergol ap Tryffun, King of Dyved.

argyvreu, 'id est, animalia que secum a parentibus adduxit,' the animals which the wife brings with her from her *parentes* on the occasion of her marriage. Such is the explanation given in the earliest MS. extant of the laws, the Peniarth MS. 28 in Latin.[3] Aneurin Owen, however, explains it as meaning 'special ornaments', and translates it into Latin as 'paraphernalia', following herein apparently the late definition given in the so-called 'Triads of Dyvnwal Moelmud', which Thomas ab Ivan of Trev Bryn in Morgannwg transcribed (according to his own account) from the 'old books' of Sir Edward Mansell of Margam in 1685. According to this late definition, *argyvreu*, used here in connexion with a man, means his dress, arms, and the tools of a privileged art.[4] Following Aneurin Owen, the authors of *The Welsh People*[5] write that the marriage portion of a daughter 'usually included not only things of utility for a new household, but also *argyvreu* (special ornaments, paraphernalia)'.

arwaesav, warranty, guarantee ; 'the person, or authority, a defendant avouches to be the guarantee of the right to property with which he is charged to be unlawfully possessed.' Aneurin Owen.[6] Not in present text. See pp. 302, 307, *supra*.

bangor, 'the top row of wattles in a wattled fence.' It is still in use in this sense 'under the form *mangors* (with the English

---

[1] *Anc. Laws* II. 878.   [2] Owen's *Pembrokeshire* II. 421.
[3] *Anc. Laws* II. 795.   [4] Ibid. II. 475, 493, 567.   [5] p. 209.
[6] *Anc. Laws* II. 1110.

plural termination) at Gwynfe in Carmarthenshire, and from it is derived a verb *bangori*'. Mr. Phillimore also states 'that there is no evidence known to us that *Bangor* was in genuine Welsh a generic term for a monastery of any sort. No use of the word in this sense can be found before the comparatively late class of documents of which so many are printed in the *Iolo MSS.*' As a place-name Bangor 'occurs *four* times in Wales and sometimes, as on the Teifi and Rheidol, at places where no monasteries are known to have existed'.[1] The ecclesiastical signification attributed to the word is due in part to the two North Welsh Bangors (not to mention the Irish instance) being celebrated religious centres; and also perhaps to the confusion of *bangor* with *bangeibr* (meaning primarily 'high rafters' and so 'church'). The latter word appears in Peniarth MS. 28 in the following passage : 'Mabh eyllt maynorauc a vo *bengebyr* ar e tyr eiusdem precii est et mayr.' In Vespasian E XI the same passage reads 'Mabeilt mainorauc, id est, qui mainaur habuerit in qua *eclesiq* sit, tantum est ejus galanas quantum prepositi.'[2]

Blegywryd, described in the present text as the most learned clerk in the convention at the White House on the Tâv, who, with twelve laymen, was chosen to reform the laws of Cymru. It is a striking fact, however, that his name does not appear either in the North Welsh books or in the three early Latin texts published in the *Ancient Laws and Institutes of Wales*, Vol. II. 749-907. Blegywryd is associated with that particular class of South Welsh law books written in Welsh, to which Aneurin Owen gave the name 'Dimetian Code' in order to distinguish them from that other class which he misnamed 'Gwentian Code'. These two classes would be more correctly distinguished by the names 'Book of Blegywryd' and 'Book of Cyvnerth' respectively. In the present text, however, which belongs to the latter class, and also in its fellow W, Blegywryd's name appears to have been substituted for that of Cyvnerth under the influence of the 'Book of Blegywryd' more properly so called. We therefore appear to have no reference in extant MSS. either to Blegywryd or Cyvnerth before the last quarter of the thirteenth century. At first he is merely described as the most learned clerk who was called *yr athro Vlegywryt*, the master Blegywryd, chosen to act as a kind of secretary with the twelve most learned laymen ; and it is only in the two very late

---

[1] *Y Cymmrodor* XI. 83, note 3.
[2] *Anc. Laws* II. 769, 879; and p. 307 *supra* (X 217 a 16-20). See also Silvan Evans's *Geiriadur Cymraeg*.

texts, S and Z, that his legend is found in bloom.[1] In these he is specially chosen with the laymen in order to guard against their doing anything in opposition to the law of the Church or that of the Emperor, for in both of these he is a doctor.[2] He is also described as archdeacon of Llandaff, and made to accompany Howel to Rome. Certain lines are quoted as having been written by him in testimony of this event. The many inaccuracies and inconsistencies however contained in this account tend to show that it is based on the fancies of a time which knew little or nothing more of him than we do to-day. Even the preface to the earliest text extant of the Book of Blegywryd, when compared with that of the early Latin Peniarth MS. 28, is seen to be by no means free from suspicion of random theorizing.

bonheddig, literally, one having a pedigree. In the early Latin texts it is represented by *nobilis*. The population of old Wales was broadly divided into two classes, being a division based on lineage. Those who were held to possess lineage were the bonheddigs or *boneddigion*, i.e. gentlemen. The term, however, was naturally more applied to the generality of this class, the more noble having special names bestowed on them, such as *gwyrda* (Latin *optimates*), &c. The ordinary bonheddig, called *bonheddig canhwynol* or innate bonheddig, is defined as being a Cymro on both sides and quite free from the blood of a bondman or a stranger (*alltud*). The genuine Cymry therefore seem to have been a kind of national aristocracy, who in course of time imposed their name on the country and people of Wales, known previously in the Latinity of the 'Dark Age' by the names Britannia and Brittones respectively.

bragod, a liquor, said to be made of the wort of ale and mead fermented together ; in English, *bragget*.

breyr, a noble, representing a higher grade of the bonheddig or gentle class. According to Aneurin Owen's Index, this word is never used in the North Welsh books, where its equivalent *uchelwr* (*lit.* a high man) is the term employed. In the early Latin texts it is represented by *optimas*, as bonheddig is by *nobilis*. See gwrda.

briduw, a solemn asseveration, apparently over the altar, in which God is taken as witness. The term seems to be simply *bri Duw*, dignity of God.

---

[1] S = Brit. Mus. Addl. MS. 22,356, of the late fifteenth century. Z = Peniarth MS. 259 B, of the first half of the sixteenth century.

[2] MS. E, however, a faithful copy of A, the earliest MS. extant of the laws in Welsh, quotes a specific case where the law of Howel is contrary to that of the Church. *Anc. Laws* I. 178.

GLOSSARY

329

Buallt, an ancient Welsh gwlad or patria, now represented by the Hundred of Builth in the county of Breconshire. Buallt, however, was quite distinct from Brycheiniog. Buallt and the adjoining patria of Gwrtheyrnion were ruled over by Pascent, son of Vortigern, in the fifth century, these two gwlads having been bestowed on him by Ambrosius Aurelianus. The line of Pascent continued to rule after him for centuries, its representative in the time of the author of his genealogy in the *Historia Brittonum* being Fernmail.[1] It is a striking fact that Buallt and Gwrtheyrnion go together in the present text. See **Cyrchell** and **Deheubarth.**

camlwrw, a fine, sometimes doubled, of three kine for various offences, paid directly to the king. In certain cases, however, a portion of the camlwrw was a perquisite of others, whilst in the case of a llan, the whole of the camlwrw appears to have been divided between the abbot and lay proprietors. See **dirwy.**

canghellor [Lat. *cancellarius*], a royal officer, appointed over a district called his canghellorship, with special juris- diction among the king's taeogs. It is carefully stated that he is not to be a *pencenedl* or chief of kindred, by which is probably intended that his authority is directly from the king, and does not in any way lie in his own blood origin. He is to hold the pleas of the king, and together with the maer is to keep the king's waste. It is noteworthy that our earliest MS. of the laws, Peniarth MS. 28 in Latin, differs from all subsequent texts in calling him *kymellaur* from a Latin original *compellarius*.

cantrev [*lit.* a hundred trevs], a hundred, the largest division of a gwlad or patria. The cantrevs varied considerably in extent; and it may be that originally they were one and all separate gwlads, as some of them certainly were. If, as is possible, *trev* once represented a personal entity (being an equation of the Latin *tribus*), cantrev at first may have stood for an organized group of kinsmen wandering over some ill-defined territory, which subsequently came to be strictly defined and to bear the name of cantrev in a territorial sense. This, however, in the case of Wales depends on the antiquity of the division, for it may be a comparatively late importation from England or the Continent. The cantrev was divided into cymwds, which were always strictly territorial divisions, marked off from one another by a well-defined boundary, such as a river or stream. The rigid definition of cantrev, comprising two cymwds, &c., as

[1] Mommsen's *Chronica Minora* III. 192.

given in the *Black Book of Chirk* and its faithful transcript, was certainly never applicable to the whole of Wales.

ceiniog, a penny. There are two kinds of pence referred to, viz. *keinhawc kyfreith*, the legal penny, and *keinhawc cotta*, the curt penny. The latter was a third less than the former, for a *dimei* (dimidium) was half a curt penny and a third of the legal penny.[1] If, as Dr. Seebohm thinks probable, the legal penny is the same as that current in England in the time of Howel Dda, viz. that of thirty-two wheat grains, the curt penny therefore being of twenty-four wheat grains, then 240 legal pence would equal the pound of the *nova moneta* of Charlemagne, and 240 curt pence would equal the older Roman pound, or half-mina-Italica. The *mina Italica* of twenty Roman ounces was twice the amount of an old Roman pound of 240 scripula of twenty-four wheat grains, which survived into Merovingian times. The *keinhawc cotta* therefore was the equivalent of the scripulum, which was so far a common unit in Gaul as to have earned for itself the name of *denarius Gallicus*.[2]

ceinion [plur. of *cain*], defined both in Peniarth MS. 28 and the *Black Book of Chirk* as the first draught of liquor which comes to the hall at a banquet, being a perquisite of the smith of a court.[3]

cowyll, a gift payable by the husband to the wife on the morning after the marriage. According to the present text it was a pecuniary sum, given apparently as a recognition of chastity, and was not to be alienated from the wife although her fault caused the husband to leave her, but should the wife fail to discuss the subject of the cowyll on the morning after her marriage it was to be the property of both and not of the wife alone. ' *Cowyll* is [possibly] of the same origin as the Welsh word *cawell*, "a basket or creel," and to be compared with the French term *corbeille de mariage*.'[4]

cyvarwys, gift, perquisite. Such at least is the sense in which the word seems to be used in the present text. The phrase *kyuarus neythaur* is represented by *munera nuptiarum* in the Latin Peniarth MS. 28. Dr. Seebohm makes much of this word in his *The Tribal System in Wales*, but unfortunately his remarks are mainly based on the so-called *Trioedd Dyvnwal Moelmud*, transcribed in 1685 from 'old books'. He is followed by the authors of *The Welsh People* (206, and especially the second note).

---

[1] V 36 b 21–2 on p. 88.
[2] Seebohm's *Tribal Custom in Anglo-Saxon Law*, 14, 15.
[3] *Anc. Laws* I. 72; II. 764.   [4] *The Welsh People*, 212, note.

Cymru, Cymro, Cymraes. These are the names by which
Wales, a Welshman, and a Welshwoman respectively are called
in Welsh to this day. *Cymru* is a modern spelling for the country of Wales as distinct from the people, viz. *Cymry*, the latter
formerly representing both. The singular *Cymro* stands, according to Sir John Rhŷs, for an earlier *Cumbrox* or *Combrox*, a
compatriot, as opposed to *Allobrox*, Welsh *allfro*, a foreigner.[1]
As the name seems to have been unknown among the Brittones
of the Devonian peninsula or of Britanny, it could never have
comprised the whole of the Brittones or Britanni of that western
Britannia which was severed into two fragments by the famous
Battle of Deorham in 577. Moreover, as the name Cymry is not
found accepted by the whole of what is now Wales until about
the twelfth century,[2] it is certain that a long period had elapsed
before such a common national name could have won its way to
general acceptance. In other words, it must have been long
extant in Wales before it was finally adopted as a national name
in lieu of Britannia and Brittones. There was a northern
'Cymru' north-east of the Irish Sea (whence the modern name
Cumberland), and it was from this quarter that Cunedda and
his Sons migrated over the water to North Wales sometime
about the commencement of the fifth century A. D., who occupied
at first the land between the river Dee and the river Teify,
and then pushed through the modern Carmarthenshire till they
reached the Severn Sea. These were the *Picti transmarini*
of the 'Roman' author of the *Excidium Britanniae*, being undoubtedly the ancestors of the Cymry, properly so called.[3] The
advent of these *Combroges* to Wales under Cunedda about the
time that the last Roman soldier quitted this island in 407 is
the beginning of Welsh national history. It was these who in
process of time imposed their name on the land, people, and
language of Wales. From the definition of Cymro in the present text, and as pointed out by the authors of *The Welsh
People*,[4] the term Cymry only included the men of pedigree
and not the classes or persons subject to them. At first it was

---

[1] *The Welsh People*, 26.
[2] Only in the twelfth century it begins to be adopted as a national
name in the *Brut y Tywysogion, s. a.* 1134 (Oxford *Brut*, 309).
[3] p. 350, note 1; *Y Cymmrodor* IX. 182, 183 ; Mommsen's *Chronica
Minora* III. 33, 156. The *Picti transmarini* of the pseudo-Gildas
were not necessarily the supposed 'non-Aryans' to which the term is
more strictly applied, but simply invaders or immigrants from beyond
the Wall.
[4] 117, note 1.

the dominating class alone, the free men of privileged blood, who were known by this name, those of the stock of Cunedda and his companions. The portions of Wales not occupied by them, such as the south-east, Brycheiniog, Glywysing, Gwent, &c., must still have been held by Brittones or Britanni, Scotti, and even Romani, but by the twelfth century we find the general name of Cymry (Lat. *Cambria*) being accepted by all.

cymwd, a division of a cantrev. A cymwd as such was intended from the first to be a strictly territorial entity, and never, as possibly in the case of a cantrev, a personal one. The present text speaks of a river as a familiar boundary between cymwds (*vide* p. 55). In such a case as Gwrtheyrnion we have a cymwd which appears to have been originally a gwlad, viz. the patria of the celebrated Vortigern. Perhaps, however, the original patria is here limited in area, the name being retained for a territory of lesser extent.

Cyrchell, the name of a brook, now called Crychell, which flows into another brook, called on the One Inch Ordnance Survey Map Bachell Brook, which itself flows into the Clywedog Brook, a little below Abbey Cwm Hir in Radnorshire. The Clywedog is a tributary of the Ieithon. *Trachyrchell* means ' beyond the Cyrchell', and inasmuch as Buallt, which is south of the Wye, is mentioned as distinct from Deheubarth, it is reasonable to suppose that the district immediately north-east of Buallt, between the Wye and the Ieithon, is also excluded. Moreover, as 'beyond the Cyrchell' is mentioned before Buallt, it is clear that the writer is situated east or north-east of the Cyrchell, so that *trachyrchell* would mean the district west of the Cyrchell and between it and Buallt, that is to say, the district of Gwrtheyrnion. See **Deheubarth** and **Buallt**.

dadannudd [*lit.* re-uncovering] of the parental hearth. A term for a peculiar suit at law for the recovery of patrimony held formerly by an ancestor of the claimant. There was a custom of covering the fire with ashes previous to retiring to rest, by which a smouldering fire was kept up; in the morning it was uncovered. In this particular suit, the suitor metaphorically claims to re-uncover the fire of his ancestor's hearth.[1]

daered appears to be the money paid with or in lieu of the dawnbwyds or food-rents, due to the king from his taeogs. Where the Latin text Brit. Mus. Cott. Vesp. E XI, written about 1250, has ' Judex curie debet habere partem viri de nummis *dayret*,' the Peniarth MS. 28 reads ' . . . de nummis *qui*

---

[1] *Anc. Laws* II. 1113; Seebohm's *Tribal System in Wales*, 82.

redduntur cum cena regis'. The latter again, under the heading *De daunbwyt*, includes the following section, 'Si denarii redduntur X^eem^ VIII^to^ denarii pro unoquoque dono; et unus denarius ministris, id est, *yr daeredwyr ae kynnwllo*', which means 'to the daered-men who shall collect it'.[1]

dawnbwyd [dawn, *gift*; bwyd, *fooa*], food-gifts of taeogs. According to the present text, two food-gifts were due to the king from the taeogs every year, one in winter and the other in summer. The dawnbwyd is to be distinguished from the gwestva, which last was due from free men.

Deheubarth [dehau, *right*, *south*; parth, *part*], the south part of Wales, South Wales. It is the *dexteralis pars*, the right side looking east, as opposed to the *sinistralis pars*, the left side, that is, the north. Cunedda, who was one of the leaders of the Men of the North, *Gwyr y Gogledd*, who invaded the North Welsh coast from Cumberland and Southern Scotland about the beginning of the fifth century, and drove out the Scotti, is said in the *Historia Brittonum* to have come *de parte sinistrali*, that is, from the north.[2] The term Deheubarth at no time stood for the whole of modern South Wales as signifying a definite patria under one king, like Gwynedd, Buallt, or Morgannwg. Deheubarth was used as a general term for that group of South Welsh patrias whose inhabitants might be described as *Deheubarthwyr* or *Britonnes dexterales* or simply *Dextrales*,[3] in contradistinction to those of Gwynedd and Powys. The Deheubarth was never a gwlad, but only a district which comprised many gwlads. It is true that both in this present text and also in the Latin Peniarth MS. 28, this general term Deheubarth is used as though for a definite patria, but (as shown under **gwlad**) the reason is probably this, that at the time when these recensions of the laws of Howel were written the majority of the South Welsh patrias had already fallen into Anglo-Norman hands, which may have induced the writer to use the vague or general term Deheubarth in lieu of more specific ones.[4] It appears

---

[1] *Anc. Laws* II. 758, 785, 821. Cf. also I. 534.

[2] Mommsen's *Chronica Minora* III. 205. Mr. Anscombe regards Cunedag in this passage as standing for Cuneda g[uletic]. Sir John Rhŷs, however, informs me that *Cuneda* certainly did not originally end in *a*.

[3] Preface to Peniarth MS. 28. *Anc. Laws* II. 749; *Annales Cambriae* in *Y Cymmrodor* IX. 160, 162.

[4] As for example in MS. D, viz. Peniarth MS. 32 of about A. D. 1380, where reference is made to *Rieinwc* (= Dyved), *Morgannwg*, and *Seisyllwc* (= Ceredigion *plus* Ystrad Tywi). *Anc. Laws* II. 50; cf. also 584.

indeed to have been used for that remnant of independent or semi-independent territory which was still left in the hands of the princely house of Dinevwr, but Deheubarth was never rightly the name of a definite patria or gwlad. The only other reference to Deheubarth in our present text is in the opening preface, where it is attended with considerable difficulties, for mention is made of its sixty-four cantrevs, an obviously impossible number. Indeed, the whole of this passage, wherein Howel's dominions are enumerated, is full of difficulties. The passage, which it will be convenient to quote here, is virtually the same in all the texts, with the exception of Z (Peniarth MS. 259 B of the sixteenth century). It is as follows :—' petwar cantref a thrugein Deheubarth, a deunaw cantref Gwyned, a thrugein tref tra Chyrchell, a thrugeint tref Buellt.' According to Aneurin Owen, the MSS. U, Y, and Z place *yn* before *Deheubarth*, whilst Z changes the first *a thrugein* into *arhugain*, thus reducing the sixty-four cantrevs of Deheubarth into twenty-four, a facile alteration made by a late writer, which hardly diminishes the difficulty.[1] We may therefore safely treat the passage as meaning '.sixty-four cantrevs of [*or* in] Deheubarth, and eighteen cantrevs of Gwynedd, and sixty trevs beyond the Cyrchell, and sixty trevs of Buallt '. The first point to notice is that Powys proper is clearly omitted and also the patria of Rhwng Gwy a Havren with the exception of *tra Chyrchell*, i.e. Gwrtheyrnion, which here, as since the days of Pasgen ab Gwrtheyrn in the fifth century, went with Buallt. Let us note further that *tra Chyrchell*, beyond the Cyrchell, as referring to Gwrtheyrnion, must have been used by a person speaking and writing east or north-east of the brook Cyrchell, that is to say, by a person living in the patria of Rhwng Gwy a Havren or possibly in Powys proper ; at any rate within that part of Wales which the writer carefully excludes as belonging to Howel's dominions. The fact that Buallt is mentioned *after* ' tra Chyrchell' strengthens the argument. Our present author therefore (possibly Cyvnerth ab Morgeneu) appears to be outside the Deheubarthwyr or Dextrales, and it may be that he is one of the Powyssi. The next point is the number of cantrevs given to Deheubarth and to Gwynedd, sixty-four to the former and eighteen to the latter. As there were never sixty-four cantrevs in the whole of Wales, and as the highest number given to Gwynedd in the old lists is eleven, it is clear that there must be some error in the text. If we assume for a moment that the original of this passage in our preface was in Latin, the word

---

[1] *Anc. Laws* I. 620.

cantref would have appeared as *pagus*, as in the preface of Peniarth MS. 28.[1] Indeed, further on in this Latin text we find *pagus, id est, cantref.*[2] But *pagus* is also made to stand for cymwd, as in the early Latin text, Harleian MS. 1796, e.g. *fines pagi, i. chemut.*[3] Consequently it is possible that our cantrevs may be a mistranslation of *pagi*, meaning cymwds, and that what is meant to be said is that Howel's dominions included sixty-four cymwds of [*or* in] Deheubarth and eighteen cymwds of Gwynedd [*plus* Gwrtheyrnion and Buallt or parts thereof]. Now in the three old lists of the cantrevs and cymwds of Wales,[4] there are variations in those of Gwynedd, chiefly because certain of these divisions were debatable ground between Gwynedd and Powys, and partly also owing to the errors of scribes who misread some cymwds under wrong cantrevs because of the proximity of one name to another. There can be no doubt, however, that the following were universally acknowledged to be intrinsic parts of Gwynedd, namely, the six cymwds of Anglesey and the eleven cymwds of Arllechwedd, Dunoding, Meirionydd, Lleyn, and Arvon. Penllyn with its three cymwds also appears in each of the three old lists, but it is a striking fact that Penllyn with its two cymwds proper, Uwch Meloch and Is Meloch, were and are in the Diocese of St. Asaph, whilst the third cymwd, Nanconwy, was and is in that of Bangor.[5] We may therefore fairly conclude from what evidence we have that Gwynedd comprised eighteen *undisputed* cymwds, viz. the seventeen enumerated above *plus* the cymwd of Nanconwy. And it seems as though it were to this undisputed Gwynedd that the text alludes. With regard to the sixty-four cymwds of [*or* in] the Deheubarth, the special reference to 'trachyrchell' makes it amply clear that the patria of Rhwng Gwy a Havren is not in our author's mind to be included in that designation. There remain therefore (excluding Buallt mentioned separately) the gwlads or patrias of Ceredigion, Dyved, Ystrad Tywi, Brycheiniog, and Morgannwg with Gwent. The first four comprise fifty-two cymwds,[6] and the last about twenty-five, exclusive of Cantrev Coch between the Wye and Gloucester.

[1] *Anc. Laws* II. 749; and p. 1 in Introduction.
[2] Ibid. II. 750.   [3] Ibid. II. 895.
[4] Brit. Mus. Domitian A VIII. (Leland's *Itinerary in Wales*, ed. L. T. Smith, 1906, pp. 1–5); *Cwta Cyfarwydd* (*Y Cymmrodor* IX. 325–33) ; Oxford *Brut* II. 407–12.
[5] St. Asaph of course is the diocese of Powys, and Bangor that of Gwynedd. Penllyn, outside the three old lists, is generally regarded as a cymwd. Egerton Phillimore in Owen's *Pembrokeshire* I. 215, III. 215, &c.
[6] Adding *Y Garn* to the *Brut* list and *Elved* to that of Domitian

That there was some aggression on the part of Howel against Morgannwg with Gwent is clear from the dispute between him and King Morgan mentioned in the *Book of Llandâv* (247-9), a Welsh translation of which precedes the *Cwta Cyfarwydd* list of the cymwds and cantrevs of Wales.[1] The dispute was settled by King Edgar years after Howel's death, and was concerned at that time only with the two cymwds of Ewyas and Ystrad Yw, which were regarded as parts of Gwent. It may be therefore that Howel laid claim to the whole of Gwent, and that our author includes it within that Deheubarth over which Howel's rule extended. It is very noticeable in this connexion that Howel's grandson, Einion, is described in the *Brut y Tywysogion* as having Brycheiniog and all his territory ravaged by the Saxons, and as having afterwards being murdered through the treachery of the nobles of Gwent,[2] which certainly suggests his authority in the far south-east. This seems to show that the House of Howel Dda claimed some jurisdiction over Gwent. Morgannwg *minus* Gwent, of course, or at least some portion of it, is, in the light of the entry in the *Book of Llandâv* clearly exempt, so that it appears hopeful that a minute research may still reveal what exactly were the sixty-four *'pagi'* of the Deheubarth which acknowledged Howel Dda as their supreme lord.[3] It is noticeable, as already shown by Mr. Phillimore, that it is only the law books of our present class, the Book of Cyvnerth, which carefully avoid describing Howel Dda as King of *all* Wales (kymry *oll*).[4] Our author indeed appears anxious to exclude Howel's jurisdiction from Powys, and not only from Powys proper but also from the patria of Rhwng Gwy a Havren, and the Perveddwlad or 'middle country'

A VIII, and omitting Trevdraeth and Pebidiog (cymwd) from that of the *Cwta*.

[1] *Y Cymmrodor* IX. 325-6.

[2] 'y diffeithwyt Brecheinawc a holl gyfoeth Einawn uab Owein y gan y Saeson'; 'y llas Einawn uab Owein drwy dwyll gan uchelwyr Gwent.' Oxford *Brut*, pp. 262-3. In the fragmentary list of cantrevs from the *Liber Abbatis de Feversham* (Hall's *Red Book of the Exchequer* II. 1896) there appears the following curious notice :—'Homines antem de Lydeneye interfecerunt dominum suum scilicet Ris filium Oeni filii Howelda.' As Lydney is in the Cantrev Coch (Forest of Dean), the presence of the House of Howel there goes to confirm the above argument.

[3] Gwent and Gwynllwg, according to the *Cwta* list, contained twelve cymwds which would complete the sixty-four required. Gwynllwg lay between the lower courses of the Usk and Rhymni.

[4] Owen's *Pembrokeshire* III. 220.

between the river Conway and the river Dee, which Gwynedd afterwards claimed. This apparent anxiety would certainly indicate that he was a Powysian, who, although anxious to preserve the integrity of Powys itself, yet fully recognizes Howel's work for 'Kymry benbaladyr' in inviting six men from *every cymwd in Cymru* to the Ty Gwyn to assist in reforming Welsh law and custom.

dilysdod, certainty, assurance, acquittance. In our present text it is a term for a portion of the compensation to be made to a woman by her ravisher. In the early Latin texts we have *dylesruyt,* the modern *dilysrwydd,* and *ius suum* and *ius suum plenarie,* after which last Brit. Mus. Vespasian E XI in one passage adds, *id est, y diweirdep,* that is, her chastity.[1] It appears as though it were a payment which guaranteed to the woman the retention of her status as a virgin or chaste woman in the sight of the law. See **gwaddol.**

Dinevwr, near Llandeilo fawr, in the valley of the Tywi in Carmarthenshire, where its ruins still crown the summit of a hill overshadowing the town, a distance of twelve miles from Carmarthen. 'The form *Dynevor* (with the accent on the first syllable) is of course a mere English barbarism ; and the application of the name '*Dynevor* Castle' to the *residence* now so called is a modernism, that mansion having been till recently called *Newton* in English, and *Drenewydd* (still in common use in the neighbourhood) in Welsh.'[2] In all the earlier South Welsh law books Dinevwr appears as a leading royal court in the Deheubarth. In the Book of Blegywryd, Dinevwr is an *eistedua arbennyc,* a principal seat or throne, under the King of Deheubarth, as Aberffraw under the King of Gwynedd.[3] It is also mentioned by Giraldus Cambrensis in the last quarter of the twelfth century as formerly one of three principal courts in Wales, the others being Aberffraw and Shrewsbury.[4] He tells us elsewhere that the principal court of South Wales was at Caerlleon at first, before it was removed to Dinevwr,[5] but in both places he speaks as though Dinevwr was no longer a *principalis curia.* As he says the same, however, of Aberffraw, he is obviously thinking of that one Wales of his imagination united under Rhodri Mawr, which that king (such was the notion)

---

[1] *Anc. Laws* II. 794, 847, 850.
[2] Egerton Phillimore in *Y Cymmrodor* IX. 45.
[3] *Anc. Laws* I. 346.
[4] Gerald's *Itinerary through Wales* I. ch. 10 'Fuerant enim antiquitus tres principales in Wallia curiae,' &c.
[5] Gerald's *Description of Wales* I. ch. 4.

disintegrated by dividing it among his three sons who had their *principales curiae* at Aberffraw, Dinevwr, and Shrewsbury respectively. This we may dismiss at once as being the very reverse of the course of Welsh history. Every patria or gwlad must once have had its own *curia principalis*, and it is only after the fall of every gwlad in South Wales except Ceredigion and Ystrad Tywi prior to circa 1100 that Dinevwr comes into prominence. It is first mentioned in the boundaries of Llandeilo Fawr in the *Book of Llandâv* (78), where it is called *gueith tineuwr*, the 'work' of Dinevwr in the probable sense of fortifications. No reference is made to it in the Mabinogion collection of tales and romances, whilst in the *Brut y Tywysogion* its name appears for the first time not until the year 1161, where, however, it is clearly mentioned as a well-known stronghold.[1] Every king in the Deheubarth having fallen, with the exception of the King of Ystrad Tywi and Ceredigion, it is only natural that his *curia principalis* should assume a unique position in Welsh eyes. Dinevwr does not become historic until it stands alone as the stronghold of the last great native princes of South Wales.

dirwy, a fine, sometimes doubled, of twelve kine paid directly to the king. A triad in the Latin text written about 1250 reads 'De tribus fit dirwy, scilicet, de pugna, furto, treiss', according to which dirwy is due for fighting, theft, and rape.[2]

diwyneb [*lit.* faceless], having no face in the sense of 'power to blush'. It is used in some parts of Wales to-day for one who is without a sense of honour.[3] In the triad in our present text, the effect intended appears to be somewhat as follows. There are three shameless ones in every patria, shameless, impudent, unabashed—and yet we cannot do without them: a lord, a priest, and law.

ebediw, a heriot. A relief payable to a superior lord for investiture of land on the occasion of a death. If the investiture fee had been paid during the lifetime of the holder of land, no ebediw was to be exacted. The sum varied according to the status of the persons concerned.

edling [*A.S.* ætheling], the king's successor, the 'crown prince' so to speak, who was to be a brother, son, or nephew

---

[1] Oxford *Brut*, 323, 'Ac yna y cymerth Rys ab Gruffud y Kantref Mawr a Chastell Dinefwr.' On the derivation of Dinevwr see *Y Cymmrodor* IX. 44-6.

[2] Brit. Mus. Cott. Vespasian E XI. See *Anc. Laws* II. 842.

[3] Rhŷs's *Celtic Folklore*, 634.

(brother's son) to the king. It is noticeable that in this way succession through the mother such as prevailed among the Picts in Bede's time was carefully guarded against. Traces of this Pictish mode of succession, as in use in old Wales, are found in the Mabinogion and elsewhere.[1] In Peniarth MS. 28 the edling is called *gwrthrych*; in the present text the royal issue are termed *gwrthrychiaid*, the word edling being confined to the particular *gwrthrych* who was to succeed the king.

enllyn, what is to be eaten with bread. In the Latin texts printed by Aneurin Owen it is sometimes left untranslated and at other times represented by such Latin equivalents as *pulmentum*. In Vespasian E XI we have 'Precium regalis cene est libra: dimidium libre de pane; et LX denarii pro potu; et LX pro dapibus aliis, id est, *enlyn*'.[2]

erw [*lit.* what has been tilled], a measurement applicable to arable land. It seems to have varied in extent. According to the present text,

18 feet = Howel's rod
18 rods = length of erw
2 rods = breadth of erw
312 erws = rhandir.

According to the Latin Peniarth MS. 28,

16½ feet = long yoke
18 long yokes = length of *acra*
2 long yokes = breadth of *acra*.[3]

galanas, murder and murder-fine. It varied in amount according to the status of the individual murdered. The murderer was assisted in paying by his kindred to the fifth cousin, whose liabilities were fixed by law. The fine undoubtedly originated as a means of obviating the feud to which our present text refers under the term *dial*, vengeance. As galanas implied insult, disgrace, injury (*sarhâd*), sarhâd was always to be paid with the galanas. See sarhâd.

gobr, a reward, fee. Latin, *merces*.

gobr estyn, investiture fee. In Peniarth MS. 28 in the passage corresponding to that in which this expression occurs in our present text, gobr estyn is represented by *kynhasset*, left untranslated.[4] In the late fifteenth-century text of the Book of Blegywryd, denominated S,[5] the same passage appears as follows.

---

[1] *The Welsh People*, 36 et seq. See also my introduction to the 'Brychan Documents' in *Y Cymmrodor* XIX.

[2] *Anc. Laws* II. 765, 783, 827.   [3] Ibid. II. 784.

[4] *Anc. Laws* II. 781.   [5] viz. Brit. Mus. Addl. MS. 22356.

'Y neb atalho kynnassed o tir ny thal ebediw pan vo marw. Sef yw kyghassed gobyr estyn.' (Whoever shall pay *kynnassed* for land is not to pay ebediw when he shall die ; *kyghassed* is gobr estyn.) [1]

gobr gwarchadw, fee for custody. A fee of 120 pence paid by a returned exile for the custody of his hereditary land-property which is now granted him by his kindred to whom the gobr gwarchadw is paid.

gobr merch, maiden fee. See amobr.

gorvodog. 'A surety for any person accused of crime; as "mach" signified a surety for debt or compact.' Aneurin Owen. [2]

gorvodtrev appears twice only in the present text, where it is defined as the thirteenth of the thirteen free trevs of a free maenor. It appears also to be said that there is some difference between it and the normal trev with regard to its rhandirs. MS. U makes this difference to consist in the addition of the *gwrthtir*, [3] by which *gwrthtir* is probably meant the adjoining land. Moreover MS. U, which makes no reference to the maenor of thirteen trevs, defines the gorvodtrev as the third of every trev of the [bond] *maenol*, and adds that it is unlawful that there should be other than three taeogs in each of the two other trevs. [4] As this last is reminiscent of the three *rhandirs* of a taeogtrev, one of which is to be pasture ground for the other two, and as the whole of this passage in U appears to be slovenly done (the form *maenawl* disclosing the influence of North Welsh books which differ considerably as to these areas), the evidence of this MS. may not unnaturally be regarded with suspicion. Aneurin Owen quotes a gloss in the margin of MS. M (Peniarth MS. 33 of the early fifteenth century), [5] which reads 'Sef yw goruotref, tref uchelwyr heb swydoc arnei heb swydoc o hony ' (A gorvodtrev is a trev of breyrs without an officer over it, without an officer from it) ; which definition somewhat confirms the idea suggested by our present text that the gorvodtrev pertained to the free maenor alone and not to that of the taeogtrevs. Another definition is found in Peniarth MS. 278 [6] (based on an early fifteenth-century text) as printed by Aneurin Owen, in

---

[1] *Anc. Laws* I. 546, whence the above is taken with the changes directed by the notes.

[2] Ibid. II. 1116.

[3] Ibid. I. 768 ' eithyr goruotref ageiff y gwrthtir yn ragor' (but the gorvodtrev has the *gwrthdir* besides).

[4] See Appendix, p. 319; also *Anc. Laws* I. 768, note 28

[5] *Anc. Laws* I. 769, note *b*; *Report on MSS. in Welsh* I. 366.

[6] This is R. Vaughan's transcript of Peniarth MS. 164 of the early fifteenth century. *Report on MSS. in Welsh* I. 1098.

a passage which runs thus: 'Rheit hagen yr gwarcheitwat cayl aminiogeu tir a gwyr gorfotref. i. aminyogeu y tir yn y gylch, y gadw y tir ganthaw.' (The conservator however must have land borderers and men of a gorvodtrev, that is, borderers from the land around him, to keep for him his land.) A still later definition[1] reads: 'Sef yw gorvotref, randyred a gvnvller o drevi vchelwyr agyfvarvo ev tervynev a thervyn y dref y bo y datlev yndy. Ac o ray hynny y kayr amynyogav tyr.' (A gorvodtrev means the rhandirs which shall be brought together from the breyr-trevs whose boundaries touch the boundary of the trev wherein the disputes may be. And it is from those that land-borderers are procured.) Dr. Seebohm accepts this statement as representing the true meaning of the word.[2]

gwaddol, marriage portion. '*Gwaddol = gwo-dawl* (Irish *fo-dáil*; Latin *divisio*) is a portion or dowry as a division of something.'[3] The word is very rare in the law books, and only occurs once in our present text. It is not easy to say what exactly was meant by gwaddol, but it appears as though it comprised at least the agweddi and the argyvreu. In MS. X, however, it appears to be identified with the argyvreu alone (p. 305 *supra*). According to our present text, a man who failed to rebut a charge of rape on a woman walking alone, was to pay the woman her gwaddol, which in the corresponding passage in Latin is given as *ius suum* and *ius suum plenarie, id est, y diweirdep* in Peniarth MS. 28 and Vespasian E XI respectively.[4] From the last it seems as though the gwaddol was paid as a mark of the woman's *diweirdeb* or chastity. See dilysdod.

gwarthal, something to boot. The passages in the text seem to mean that there is no 'boot' where one has had his choice of shares, or, in other words, supposing that your share was assigned you without your having a free choice, you might then, and then only, ask for something to boot (see p. 203, note 1 *supra*).

gwelygordd, the stock of a family, some of whom might be living in another gwlad, retaining their rights in the original bit of land from which they sprang. The term is not used in our present text, but only in an addition found in U (p. 316 *supra*).

gwirawt yr ebestyl, liquor of the apostles. 'Liquor distributed on feast days of the apostles,' so says Aneurin Owen.[5]

gwestai, guest; in Latin Peniarth MS. 28 *hospes*. In addition

---

[1] *Anc. Laws* II. 283, from Peniarth MS. 175 of the late fifteenth century.

[2] *Tribal Custom in Anglo-Saxon Law,* 35.

[3] *The Welsh People,* 211, note 3.   [4] *Anc. Laws* II. 794, 850.

[5] Ibid. II. 1118.

to the twenty-four officers there were twelve gwestais in the king's retinue. These thirty-six rode on horseback. The authors of *The Welsh People* (204) think it probable that the twelve gwestais were the persons who brought in the gwestva or entertainment dues.

gwestva, a king's entertainment dues from his free men, being analogous to the dawnbwyd or food-gifts due to him from his taeogs or villeins. The gwestva was paid twice yearly, once in winter and again in summer. From the present text one might suppose that the payment was the same on both occasions, save that in summer silver and horse provender were not provided. The money equivalent of the food supplied from every trev from which the king's gwestva was due was one pound, viz. 120 pence for the bread, 60 pence for its enllyn, and 60 pence for the liquor. If the food were not supplied at the proper time, this money equivalent was to be paid. As this proper time is definitely stated to be winter, it would appear as though it were not unusual to supply money instead of food in this season ; perhaps not so in summer. The 24 pence paid with the winter gwestva is the gwestva silver, *aryant y gwestuaeu*, in which sundry officers participated. Gwestva is represented in the Latin Peniarth MS. 28 by *cena*, from which comes the *cwynnossawc* of our text through *cwyn + nos*, evening meal, supper. See twnc.

gwlad, a patria. Gwlad might be translated 'country' and even 'state', but the former is too indefinite and the latter too modern for the purposes of our present text. Gwlad implies both the definite territory which is held by a 'people' and also the 'people' itself organized into a polity. Pre-Norman Wales (or Britannia as it was called) was not itself a gwlad, but a group of gwlads, somewhat like Germany before 1870. Dyved, Gwynedd, Powys, Morgannwg, &c. (which now make up the single gwlad or patria of Wales), would be as distinct from one another as Wessex, Kent, Mercia, and the rest of the gwlads or patrias which formerly made up what is now the single gwlad or patria of England. By the time that the earliest of the Welsh law books, now extant, were written, the Anglo-Normans had filched a number of these patrias, especially in South Wales. Morgannwg with Gwent, Brycheiniog, and Dyved were gone. Ceredigion was left, and also the interior of the old patria of Ystrad Tywi, that is, the land around Dinevwr. This probably is the reason why our texts adopt the vague term Deheubarth, *dextralis pars* (speaking of it as a gwlad), in lieu of the well-known and well-marked names of the South Welsh patrias. It may be that by the *gwlad*, Deheubarth, our text means no more than the remnant of Ystrad Tywi around Dinevwr, *plus* Ceredigion. Deheubarth, Gwynedd, Powys, and Lloegr (England) are mentioned as four distinct gwlads in the present work. The Latin Peniarth MS. 28 of the late twelfth century quotes the same passage, viz. 'Homo de Powyss ab homine de Gwynet, similiter de Deheubarth, et de Anglico, in suo sayrhaed non habet nisi tres uaccas et IIIes untias argenti.'[1] In the preface also of the same early and important text are mentioned the Gwynedoti, the Powyssi, and the Dextrales.[2] Gwynedd, Powys, and Deheubarth are also distinguished in the North Welsh books of the MS. A type. This seems to fix the earliest recensions which we possess of the Laws of Howel Dda to a period subsequent to the fall of the majority of the South Welsh gwlads, that is, roughly speaking, subsequent to the end of the eleventh century.

gwrda, a noble; in the Latin texts *optimas*. See **breyr.**

gwyl [Lat. *vigilia*], a festival. G. Giric, June 16; G. Ieuan y Moch (St. John of the Swine), August 29; G. Badric, March 17; G. Vihagel (St. Michael), September 29; G. yr Holl Seint (All Saints), November 1 (= Calan Gaeaf, the Calends of Winter).

Gwynedd, roughly equivalent to North West Wales inclusive of the three counties of Anglesey, Carnarvon, and Merioneth. See **Deheubarth.**

gwyr nod, nod-men. 'The term *gwr nod* (literally, man of mark) is very ambiguous. Sometimes it looks as if it meant a *taeog* or *aillt*.'[3] Not in present text. See p. 312 *supra* (U 27 b).

llan. In the early Breton *Vita Pauli Aureliani* we gather that the old meaning of llan was monastery, e.g. *Lanna Pauli id est monasterium Pauli.* In the *Vita Gildae*, c. 27, we have also *coetlann* interpreted as *monasterium nemoris*, which, whether it be right or no, shows that *llan* to the writer meant monastery. The numerous *llans* of old Welsh place-names, therefore, signify the monasteries of those whose names generally follow them, e.g. Llangolman, the monastery of Colman, and so on. The llan would naturally include under its name the lands and rights which pertained to it. Llan in process of time came also to mean a church, but as a rule in the present text *eglwys* (*ecclesia*) is used for a church. On p. 114 *llan* and *eglwys* appear to be in some sense contrasted, for the *llan* has an abbot and the *eglwys* has lay proprietors, whose duty is to protect it.

land maer. See **maer biswail.**

Llyfr Cynog, the Book of Cynog, referred to both in the

---

[1] *Anc. Laws* II. 789.   [2] Ibid. II. 749.
[3] *The Welsh People*, 236, note 4. Cf. *Anc. Laws* II. 1118.

Latin Vespasian E XI [1] and in the Book of Blegywryd [2] in connexion with the same passage as in the present text. Consequently it must have been a work current as early at least as the middle or first half of the thirteenth century. The first seventy-six folios of Peniarth MS. 35 (called G) of the last quarter of the thirteenth century profess to contain the Book of Cynog, or at least part of it, for they close with the words 'Ac yuelly y teruyna Llyuyr Kynawc' (And so ends the Book of Cynog).[3]   According to Dr. Gwenogfryn Evans, Aneurin Owen made no use of the greater part of this text.[4]

mab aillt [*lit.* a shaven fellow], a villein. Not in present text. See p. 307 above (X 217 a 16-20), 313 (U 36 b).   See taeog.

maenor. This word should be carefully distinguished from the English manor, to which it is often assimilated; *maenor* appears to come from *maen*, a stone. 'Originally it probably meant a particular spot in its district, which was distinguished by stone buildings or some sort of stone walls.'[5] '*Maenor* occurs in one of the documents in the *Book of St. Chad* . . . written in the Mercian hand of the time of King Offa. . . . Even our English historians will hardly be prepared to sustain the hypothesis that the Welsh borrowed a Norman-French word prior to A. D. 800.'[6] Two kinds of maenor are distinguished in the present text, the maenor of the free trevs and the maenor of the taeogtrevs. In the Book of Blegywryd (as the so-called 'Dimetian Code' may perhaps more correctly be called), the two kinds of maenor are referred to thus: 'Seithtref a vyd ym maenawr vro; teir tref ardec a vyd ym maenawr vrthtir.' (Seven trevs are to be in a *maenor vro*; thirteen trevs are to be in a *maenor wrthdir*.)[7] If the *maenor vro* and the *maenor wrthdir* are the same as the bond and free maenor respectively, then it would seem as though the maenor of the lowlands were occupied by taeogs and that of the uplands by free men. On the basis of the present text, the following tables may be drawn up:—

4 rhandirs = 1 free trev	3 rhandirs = 1 taeogtrev
13 free trevs = 1 free maenor	7 taeogtrevs = 1 maenor of taeogtrevs.

The maenor of thirteen trevs is not referred to in MS. U, and the form *maenawl* appears in lieu of *maenawr*, which shows the influence of North Welsh books on this particular text.

[1] *Anc. Laws* II. 889.   [2] Ibid. I. 484.   [3] Ibid. II. 210.
[4] *Report on MSS. in Welsh* I. 367-8.
[5] *The Welsh People*, 218, note 2.
[6] Mr. Egerton Phillimore in *Y Cymmrodor* XI. 57.
[7] *Anc. Laws* I. 538.

maer [Lat. *maior*], a royal officer, appointed over a district called his maership, with special jurisdiction over the king's taeogs. Deriving his authority wholly from the king, he is probably for this reason never to be a *pencenedl* or chief of kindred, whose authority comes from the kindred, being based primarily on blood origin. He is to demand all the king's dues within his maership, and is also with the canghellor to keep the king's waste. In Peniarth MS. 28 he is described in one place as 'propositus regis, id est, mayr castell'.[1]

maertrev. This term only occurs once in our present text in connexion with the *maer biswail* or land maer, so that it appears to be the trev with which this officer was specially connected. The passage, however, appears as follows in Peniarth MS. 28: ' Debet quoque mercedem de filiabus uillanorum de uillis curie adiacentibus,'[3] where our *gwyr y vaertref* are equated with the *villani de villis curiae adiacentibus*. In MS. U they are called *tayogeu y llys*, the taeogs of the court ;[3] and in the Book of Blegywryd they are described as 'y bilaeineit afwynt y mywn maer trefi y llys' (the villeins who are within the maertrevs of the court).[4] The maertrev, therefore, appears to have been a trev of a king's taeogs, situated near his court.

maer-ty or **maerhouse.** This word is mentioned four times in the present text, always in connexion with cattle—*gwartheg y maerdy*, the cattle of the maerhouse. In one case the maer-ty is not that of a king but of a breyr. The maer referred to is the *maer biswail* [*lit.* cow-dung maer] or land maer.

maer biswail or **land maer.** The literal meaning of the Welsh term is 'cow-dung maer', a term used to distinguish him from the maer proper, who was of higher status. The galanas of the latter was 189 kine, with three augmentations; that of the land maer was only 126 kine with three augmentations. He appears to have superintended the maertrev with special regard to the king's cattle.

marwdy, the house with its appurtenances of a person who dies intestate, which on this account escheats to the lord.

nod-men. See **gwyr nod.**

pennaeth, chief, king. This word is represented by *rex* in the corresponding passages in the Latin Peniarth MS. 28.[5]

prid, price, value, equivalent, payable in certain circumstances for land.

---

[1] *Anc. Laws* II. 769.   [2] Ibid. II. 767.   [3] Ibid. I. 684.
[4] Ibid. I. 392.   [5] Ibid. II. 750, 764.

rhaith. 'Originally it seems to have been used to signify the notion conveyed by the juridical terms, *ius, droit, recht*. It is cognate with German *recht* and English *right*, and is represented in Irish by the neuter *recht*, which is as if we had in Latin, besides *rectus, -a, -um*, a neuter *rectu*, genitive rectus.'[1] Rhaith might be translated *compurgation*, for if a person were put to his rhaith, he was required to bring forward so many men to swear on his behalf. 'Oath was the primary mode of proof, an oath going not to the truth of a specific fact, but to the justice of the claim or defence as a whole. The number of persons required to swear varied according to the nature of the case and the rank of the persons concerned.'[2]

rhandir [rhan, *share*; tir, *land*], a division of land containing 312 such erws as are described in the text (see **Erw**). The complete rhandir was to comprise clear and brake, wood and field, wet and dry, except (if the text be thus interpreted correctly) in the case of the gorvodtrev. There were to be four rhandirs in the free trev, and three in the taeogtrev, one rhandir in both cases being pasturage for the remainder. Should a dispute arise between two trevs as to a boundary, the area which could be legally appropriated was always to be less than a rhandir.[3]

sarhâd, insult and insult-fine. If the person who committed sarhâd was unable to pay, his kindred were legally bound to pay along with him, but only till the third degree of kinship, and not to the fifth cousin as in the case of galanas. See **galanas**.

taeog, a villein. The word is of the same origin as *ty* (house).[4] The inhabitants of old Wales were divided into two main divisions, those of pedigree (*boneddigion*) and those of no pedigree. The taeogs were the most privileged in the latter division, preceding in status both the alltuds and the *caethion* (slaves). The word taeog is of very rare occurrence in the books of the *Black Book of Chirk* type, the designation of the villein in this text being commonly what would now be spelt *mab aillt*, a word of still rarer occurrence in the other law books. In the Latin Peniarth MS. 28 taeog is represented by *villanus*. There were two ranks of taeogs, those of a king and those of a breyr. The galanas and sarhâd

---

[1] *The Welsh People*, 205, note 1.
[2] Pollock and Maitland, *English Law* (2nd ed. 1898) I. 39.
[3] Cf. V 22 a 6-7 with *Anc. Laws* II. 814 (last section of Peniarth MS. 28).
[4] *The Welsh People*, 191, note 1.

of the latter were half those of the former. The taeogs had special trevs set apart for them called *taeogtrevydd,* seven of which constituted a [bond] maenor. They paid two dawn-bwyds or food-gifts yearly to the king, and were subject to sundry other services. A taeog became a free man if a church were built with the king's consent on his taeogtrev, or if the king raised him to be one of his twenty-four officers, or if he became a tonsured clerk. See' mab aillt.

taeogtrev, a trev of taeogs, as distinguished from a *trev ryd* or free trev. It comprised three rhandirs only, one of which was pasturage for the other two. Seven taeogtrevs made a bond maenor. The word taeogtrev does not seem to be found in the Book of Gwynedd, of which the *Black Book of Chirk* is the exemplar. In the Latin Harleian MS. 1796, however, of the first part of the thirteenth century, a text which seems to reflect the laws and customs of Gwynedd,[1] *rusticana uilla* is equated with *taiauctret* for *taiauctref.*[2]

teithi, qualities or properties ; the properties which pertain to anything in the sense in which the law requires that thing to be understood. For instance, when the law mentions a cat whose legal worth is four legal pence, it is to be understood that the cat is to be perfect of claw, perfect of sight, &c., which are its teithi.

trev, the Welsh equivalent of the Old English -*ton* and -*ham,* the Danish -*by,* represented in the Latin Peniarth MS. 28 as commonly in the Latin of medieval times, by the word *villa.* The trev according to the present text consisted of rhandirs of 312 erws each ; the Peniarth MS. 28 adds that the twelve erws of this number were for buildings.[3] The free trev contained four rhandirs, and the taeogtrev contained three. In both cases one rhandir was to be pasturage for the rest, which last were to be inhabited. Each of the two inhabited rhandirs of a taeogtrev was to contain three taeogs. It appears that the number of houses (*tei*) in a trev varied, but in the passage where a thief is to escape punishment, if able to show that he has traversed three trevs in a day, with nine houses in every trev, without obtaining relief,[4] it looks as though a trev of nine houses was normal. It is also incidentally suggested in the present text that the houses were built close together, for the owner of a house which was burnt through negligence was to pay for the first two houses

---

[1] *Anc. Laws* II. 893-907. See especially p. 894 concerning the kings in Wales who ' debent accipere terram illorum a rege Aberfrau '.
[2] Ibid. II. 901. [3] Ibid. II. 784.
[4] Vide W 65 b 7-14 on p. 64 *supra.*

destroyed by that fire, which probably refers to the two houses one on each side. *Trev*-names meet us frequently in Wales, as names ending in -*ton* or -*ham* do in England. Trev in modern Welsh is used for town, the modern *trev* being to the medieval *trev* what the modern *town* is to old -*ton*.

trevtad, patrimony, represented in the Latin Peniarth MS. 28 by *hereditas*. It is the *trev* which descends to the sons through the father, the word *trev* in this case not bearing the rigid sense of an area of four rhandirs, &c., but rather that of a definite plot of habitable ground on which the sons might continue to live. This idea seems to be conveyed by the interesting use of the word in the triad of the free huntings,[1] where the pursuit of a roebuck, fox, and otter, is free to all in every gwlad or patria, the reason being that these three creatures have no trevtad, which word is represented in the early Latin text by *certa mansio*.[2] May it not therefore be that the exact meaning of trevtad is the *certa mansio* which is the son's due through his father after the latter's decease ?

trevgordd is represented in the Latin Peniarth MS. 28 and Vespasian E XI by the expression *communis villa*. In the latter our *bugeil trefgord* appears as *pastor communis ville, id est, trefgord*.[3] In a later text[4] we find the following statement, ' Llyma fessur trefgordd cyfreithiawl : naw tei, ac un aradyr, ac un odyn, ac un gordd, ac un gath, ac un ceilyawc, ac un tarw, ac un bugeil.' (This is the complement of a legal trevgordd : nine houses, and one plough, and one kiln, and one churn, and one cat, and one cock, and one bull, and one shepherd.) This statement, how-ever, is not found earlier than the beginning of the fifteenth century. In the present text the trevgordd is associated with cattle ; and in one passage in particular,[5] where reference is made to damaged corn bordering on a trevgordd (*yn emyl trefgord*), it would appear as though trevgordd were a special kind of trev in which cattle belonging to various individuals pastured in common, with a common herdsman and a common bull. We have also a reference to the bath of a trevgordd, and the smithy,[6] which last was to be nine paces from the trevgordd itself.[7]

[1] pp. 131, 133, 275 *supra*.   [2] *Anc. Laws* II, 774.
[3] Ibid. II. 771, 841.
[4] Ibid. II. 692, being Vaughan's transcript of an early fifteenth-century text. (See note to gorvodtrev, p. 340).
[5] V 34 b 19–24 (pp. 84, 230 *supra*).
[6] V 44 b 24. After *gefeil*, W and X insert *trefgord*. *Anc. Laws* I. 780.
[7] An interesting passage on the trevgordd will be found by Dr. Seebohm in his *Tribal Custom in Anglo-Saxon Law*, 34–40, but in the

twnc, the money equivalent of the king's gwestva from every free trev. It amounted to one pound. See **gwestva**.

Ty gwyn ar Dâv [*Alba Domus*,[1] the White House on the Tâv], 'identified by far-reaching tradition with Whitland in Carmarthenshire.'[2] One would suppose from the religious character of the convention, as described in the early prefaces, that it was a monastery, the word *gwyn* bearing some such meaning as holy or blessed, and one would be inclined to compare it with Bede's *Ad Candidam Casam* (Whitern in Galloway), notwithstanding his different explanation of *candida*.[3] According to Blegywryd's preface, however, it was a hunting lodge constructed of white rods, for which reason it was called white ;[4] whilst the late texts S and Z state that the Ty gwyn was so called because it was one Gwyn, the maer, who owned the house in which the law was made, hence Gwyn's house! This Gwyn is converted into one of the twelve laics set apart to make the law, their secretary being Blegywryd, or Bledrws, here described as Archdeacon of Llandaff![4]

Vnbeinyaeth Prydein, the monarchy of 'Britain', the name of the song which the bard of the household had to sing before the host in the day of battle and fighting. It must not be supposed, however, that *unbennaeth Prydain* refers to the island of Britain, although *Ynys Prydain* is the common Welsh name for the whole island, being equivalent in meaning to *insula Britannia*. Prydain and Britannia are in no way etymologically related, and their confusion has been the source of endless misconceptions relative to the origins of Welsh and indeed of British history. *Ynys Prydain* means Picts' Island,[5] and was equated with *insula Britannia*, with the natural result that *Prydain* was equated with *Britannia*. This last word again, Britannia, had various meanings. To a geographer, it would mean the island of Britain; to a Roman official, the Roman province of Britain, south of the walls ; and lastly (what is not so well known), it meant Wales *plus* the Devonian peninsula, and afterwards Wales alone. Before about the twelfth century Wales bore the common name of *Britannia*,

light of the earlier and more reliable texts one can hardly as yet dare say much more than what appears above.

[1] *Anc. Laws* II. 893.
[2] *The Welsh People*, 155. That the Tâv is the river of that name in Dyved is stated in the preface to the Book of Blegywryd.
[3] Bede's *Ecclesiastical History* III. 4.
[4] *Anc. Laws* I. 339, 342.   [5] *The Welsh People*, 76.

and its inhabitants that of *Brittones*. In the genuine *Epistola Gildae*,[1] the *Historia Brittonum*, Asser's *Alfred*, the *Vitae* of the Saints, and the *Book of Llandâv*, this use of the term *Britannia* is amply attested; and the earliest text extant of the Laws of Howel Dda, viz. the Latin Peniarth MS. 28, which Aneurin Owen entitles *Leges Wallice*, is entitled in the text itself *Leges Brittanie*.[2] The song 'Vnbeinyaeth Prydein' therefore means *Monarchia Brittaniae*, i.e. the monarchy of Wales, and must be taken as reflecting that aspiration after Welsh political unity which was increasing throughout the centuries amid the numerous patrias of the Welsh kin.

wynebwerth [wyneb, *face*; werth, *worth*], face-worth, a fine payable to a woman when insulted by her husband, as when he had connexion with another woman.

---

[1] The *Epistola Gildae* is to be carefully distinguished from the *Excidium Britanniae* of the pseudo-Gildas, i.e. the first twenty-six chapters which were originally written towards the end of the seventh century. *Celtic Review* (Edinburgh) for 1905.

[2] *Anc. Laws* II. 749, where *Brittannie* is for *Brittanie*.

INDEX TO WELSH TEXT

[ ] Square brackets indicate MS. **W** ; *a.* = adjective ; *adv.* = adverb ; *c.* = common ; *comp.* = comparative ; *f.* = feminine ; *m.* = masculine ; *n.* = numeral ; *pl.* = plural ; *prep.* = preposition *or* prepositional ; *s.* = substantive ; *v.* = verb.

A.

a, *v. See* mynet.
abat, *sm.* 40, 58, [60], 88, [114].
  abadeu, *pl.* 1, 121.
abo, *s.* 127.
abreid, *adv.* 125.
ach, *sf.* 3, [9], 39, 51, [62], 87, [109, 110] ; — ac etrif, 51, 53-4 ; [— — eturyt, 136] ; — — etuyryt, 48. achoed kenedyl, 38.
achaws, *sm.* 52, 81, [92], 119, 121, 125-6, [135]. *See* petwar.
  achwysson, *pl.* 120.
achenawc, *s.* 131. *See* ychenawc, yghenawc. achenogyon, *pl.* 3.
achuppo, *v.* 17.
[achwanegu, *v.* 136].
achweccau, *v.* 53.
adar, *pl. See* ederyn.
adaw, *v.* 30, 88, [97, 103-4 ; adawet, 95 ; adawho, 8, 92, 108].
[adef, *a.* 135] ; adefedic, 88.
adef, *v.* 41, [74], 86, [137] ; adefho, 37, [63], 86-7 ; [adeuir, 137] ; adefynt, 40 ; edeu, 89.
adeil, *s.* 48.
adeilat, 127.
[adeilho, *v.* 61].
adeilwr maestir, 117.

EVANS

adein, *s.* [77], 79.
adnabot, *v.* 24.
adneu, *s.* 118.
aeduet, *a.* [93], 117-8.
aeduetrwyd, *s.* [96].
aelawt, *s.* 42. aelodeu, *pl.* 42, 68, [78], 80, [112] ; — gradeu kenedyl, 38-9 ; — penkenedyl, 43.
[aelwyt, *sf.* 135].
aet, aeth, *v. See* mynet.
[avallen, *s.* — per ; -- sur, 104].
[auon, *s.* 105, 107, 138]. *See* prifauon.
afu, *s.* 35-6.
auwyn, *s. See* gwastrawt.
affeith, *s. See* naw.
aghen, *s.* 50, 85, [138].
aghenoctit, *s.* 131, [133, 138].
agheu, *s.* 90, [91].
agheuawl, *a.* 25.
agho, *v.* 86.
aghyfarch, *s.* 118.
aghyfieithus, 130.
aghyfreithawl, *a.* 89.
aghynefin, *a.* 84.
agoret, 48, [102].
agori, *v.* 34, 58, [60-1].
allawr, *s.* 87, [101], 129, [138, 143]. *See* seith.
allt, yn, 68, [73].
alltut, *s.* 46, [62], 88, {111},

haf, 49; — ki, [77], 80; — gwr, 90, [91]; — gwyr y llys, 15; — gwystyl, 88; — hwch, [77], 80; — llys, [14], 16-17, 27, 36; — merch gwr ryd, 23; — merchet (six superior officers), 8; — — y pymthec, 23; — milgi, [65], 67; — modrydaf, 81, [141; — morwyn, 137; — offrwm, 114]; — penkenedyl, 45, [65, 139; — perchennawc odyn, 103]; — pymthec (officers), [9], 23; — swyd, 45, 54, [65]; — swydeu, 15; — tat, 45, [65]; — tir, 54-5. *See* vn.

brenhin, *sm.* 2-4, 6, [7, 10-14], 15-34, 44, 46-9, 51, 53-8, [59-60, 63-4, 97-9, 104, 110-11, 114, 116], 123-6, 128, 131, [134, 138]. alltut —, 44-5; amws —, 6, [8], 21; anhebcor —, 124; anrec —, 6, 17; anreith —, [10, 14], 15, 21, [111, 114]; brawt —, 3; [bryccan —, 105]; cadeir —, 3; caeth —, 125; capaneu —, 21; karw —, 35-6; cled —, 4, 29; [coet —, 110]; corn —, 85; — buelyn —, 131; kostawc —, 34; crwyn —, 19; cwn —, 19; cwynossawc —, [99], 125; kyfrwyeu —, 24; kylleic —, 35; cynllyfaneu —, 19; kynydyon —, 36; cyrn —, [14], 19; dadleu —, 29, 30; [degwm —, 12]; diawt —, 3; diffeith —, 27, [65], 67; dillat —, 22, 131; dirwy —, 123; dylyet —, 28; ennill —, 2; eurgrawn —, [60], 124; [ewyllis —, 110]; [fioleu —, 14]; [fford —, 104]; fforest —, 36,

131; galanas —, 3, 4, 6, [8]; gellgi —, 34-5; gwassanaeth —, 5; [guassanaethwr —, 99, 116]; gwely —, 5, 22; gwisc —, [11], 18; gwreic —, 2, [111, 134]; gwyd —, 2, 29; gwyrda —, 3, 47, 49; hebawc —, 124; hyd —, 35-6, 127; iat —, 3; llaw —, [14], 15-17; lle —, 18; lleidyr —, [65], 67, 124; lles —, 19; llu —, 20; mab —, 3, [11]; march —, 16, 24; meirch —, 20; merch —, 89, [111]; milgi —, 34; nawd —, 2, [13], 125; neges —, 30; nei —, 3, [11]; neuad —, 28; [odyn biben —, 102]; odynty —, [10], 57, [59; offrwm —, 11, 12]; panel —, 24; pleit —, 50; prifford —, 55; pynuarch —, 65; reit —, 131; rwyt —, 123; swydogyon —, 2; [telyn —, 105]; teulu —, 20; teuluwr —, 43; traet —, 5, [7], 26; treul —, 57, [59]; trugared —, 30, 123; wyneb —, 3; yscubawr —, [10], 82, [102], 140; [ystauell —, 10, 116].

See awssen; canhat; Kymry; gwestua; gwlat; gwr; gwyr; sarhaet; tayawc; tir; tri buhyn.

brenhines, *sf.* 2, 3, 6, [7, 11, 12], 16, 19, 21, 23, 27, 34, 57. dillat —, 27; gwassanaeth —, 5; [guenigawl —, 135]; gwisc —, 27; llaw —, 3; nawd —, 3, 4, [13; offrwm —, 12]; sarhaet —, 3; swydogyon —, 2.

See distein; effeirat; gwastrawt.

[brenhinyaeth, *s.* 116].

kywerthyd, *s.* 3, [114].
kywlat, *s.* 119.
[kywrein, *a.* 136.]

CH.

[chwechet, *n. a.* 62]. *See* whechet.
chwioryd, *pl.* 38. *See* whaer.

D.

da, *a.* 1, 29, 54, [77], 80, [112], 136.
da, *sm.* 33, 41, 44, 51-3, [63-4, 76], 86-7, 89, [95, 100, 104, 108-10, 114], 118, 120, 124, [141 ; — addycker o 'ryuel, 115] ; — adefedic, 88 ; — bywawl, 86 ; — dilis, 132 ; [— dilys, 134] ; — marwawl, 86.
dadleu, *v.* 126.
dadleuwyr, *pl.* 120.
dadyl, *s.* 16, 29, 40, 71, 84, 89, 113-14, 119-20 ; — sarhaet a lledrat, 17 ; — tir a dayar, 119. dadleu, *pl.* 5, [96-7, 110, 115], 117, 125, [135-6, 140] ; — tir a dayar, 47. *See* brenhin ; gwys ; tri.
dauat, *s.* 75, 83 ; — hesp, 18.
deueit, *pl.* 26, [75, 105, 114].
dafyn, *s.* 129.
dala, *v.* 17, 29, [64], 84, [104], 118 ; — llys, 29 ; dalher, 57, [66], 67, 123 ; daly, 28 ; dalyet, 83-4 ; dalyho, 18, 84 ; dalyo, 83 ; deila, [10-11, 14], 15, 84 ; delit, 123 ; dyeila, 24.
damdwg, 35, 118, [135].
damwein, *s.* 18, [116].
damweinha, *v.* 28.
dangos, *v.* 15, 19, 27, 47-8,

52 ; dangosso, 15, [98] ; dangosswn, 36 ; [dengys, 13].
[dant, *s.* 74-5]. deint, *pl.* 130.
darfu, *v.* 1 ; darffo, 5-6, 47, 123 ; [darfo, 7].
[darllein, *v.* 138].
darmerth, 6.
[darmertho, *v.* 7].
[darymreto, *v.* 13].
das, *s.* 49.
datanhud, *sm.* 48-9, 53 ; — beich ; — karr, 48 ; — cwbyl, 49 ; — eredic, 48-9 ; — tir, 48.
[datganu, *v.* 116].
datwyrein, *s.* 87.
dawnbwyt, *sm.* 56 ; — gayaf, 56 ; — haf, 57.
dayar, *sf.* 3, 30, 58, [60-1, 63], 83, 125. *See* tir.
dayret, *s.* 15.
dec, *n. a.* [— a deugeint aryant, 101] ; — a deu vgeint, 42, 70, 72, [73], 131 ; — — — — a dimei a deuparth dimei, 42 ; [— ar hugein, 104, 106] ; — — hugeint, 43, [65], 67, 70, [76, 101-5, 109] ; — — — aryant, 42, 71 ; — a phetwar ugeint, 111] ; — keinhawc, 69, 71 ; [— — kyfreith, 76] ; — llydyn ar hugeint, 83. *See* deg ; llw ; oet ; pedeir.
[decuet, *n. a.* — llwdyn, 110].
dechreu, *s.* 118.
dechreu, *v.* 22 ; dechreuher, 47 ; dechreuho, 5-6, [7] ; dechreuir, 47 ; dechreuo, 6, [7].
dedyf, *s.* 89, 128. dedueu, *pl.* 1.
defnyd, *sm.* 83, 117.
defnydyo, *v.* 35.
deg, *n. a. See* dec ; llw ; oet.

ebediw, s. 50, 55, [65], 67;
— abadeu, 121 ; [— kaeth,
111]; — cyghellawr, 43 ;
— kynydyon, 19; — gof llys,
31 ; [— gwassanaethwr ar-
glwyd, 100 ; —gwr gorwlat,
99; — —. ryd, 99 ; — —
ystauellawc, 100 ; — gwreic
ystauellawc, 100]; — maer,
43 ; [— penkenedyl, 100] ;
— swydogyon llys, [8, 9],
23 ; [— tayawc, 100] ; —
ygnat llys, 17. ebediweu,
pl. 28. See trayan.
ebestyl, pl. 24.
[ebill taradyr, 106].
ebran, s. [11, 13], 16, 18, 20,
22, 56. ebraneu, pl. [10], 21.
Ebrill, s. 71, 130.
edeinyawc, 79.
ederyn, s. [78], 79; — enwawc,
17-18. adar, pl. 5, 17.
edeu, v. See adef.
edrych, v. 69 ; edrycher, 119.
edyn, sm. 130.
euegyl, s. 48.
euydeit, 22.
effeiradaeth, s. 128.
effeirat, sm. 41, 51, [101], 117,
128, [135]. See offeirat.
effeirat brenhines, 2, 5, [9, 12].
effeirat teulu, 2, 4, [5, 9, 11-12],
21, 27, 124, 126.
efferen, s. 81, 87, 117.
efferennu, v. 51.
eglwys, sf. 5, 48, [101, 114],
131, [135, 143]; — ar tayawc
tref, 51, 128 ; [— ar tir tayawc, 100; — — — — tref,
111]. See drws ; tir.
eglwyssic, 39, [61, 108].
eguedi, s. [91, 135] ; — arben-
hig llys, 43 ; [— gwreic, 92,
100]; — merch brenhin,
89 ; — — breyr, 89–90,

[91]; — — cyghellawr, 43 ;
— — gof llys, 31 ; — —
maer, 43 ; — — tayawc, 90,
[91]; — merchet swydogyon
llys, [8–9], 23.
egwyt, sf. 83.
[ehogyn, s. 107].
eidaw, s. 1, 28, 30.
eidiged, s. 132, [133].
eidon, sm. [10, 13], 20-2, 26,
30, 32, 68, 72, [74], 84, [106],
123; — buarth, 83 ; — kota,
32 ; [— moel, 74] , — tal-
adwy, 34. See naw; tri;
whech.
eil, n.a. 37-40, 53-4, 85, [112];
— kanu, 22 ; —corneit, 19;
— kyfiodawt, 70; — datan-
hud, 49; — dyd, 81; [—
enllip, 93]; — flwydyn, 28,
[62]; — gyflauan, 122; —
heit, 81 ; — llo, 72, [74];
— lloneit, 21 ; —nessaf, 22,
24; [— trayan, 98]; — wys,
50.
[eillaw, v. 96].
eis, s. 56.
[eisseu kyt, 93].
eissin, s. 31, [110].
eissydyn, sm. 50, [61-2].
eisted, v. 4, [11], 17, 22, 24,
26, 29, 30, 33, [110]; eisted-
ant, 20 ; eistedet, 29; eisted-
ho, 3, [7] ; eistedo, 5.
eithin, s. 45.
el, v. See mynet.
elchwyl, 38, 48, [76, 141].
[eluyd, s. 142].
elin, s. 56.
elor, sf. 131, [137].
elw, s. 71, [110], 124.
ell, — deu, 127 ; — tri, 126.
ellwg, v. [96, 115], 131 ; ellygher, 34.
emelltith, s. 1.

emenhyd, *s.* 25.

emenyn, *s.* 30, 57, 90, [91, 95].

emyl, *s.* 56-7, 71, 84, [98].

enkil, 52.

enderiged, *pl.* 29, [114].

eneint, *s.* 130.

eneit, *s.* [76, 78], 80, [111-12], 129, [139, 142]. eneiteu, *pl.* 130.

eneituadeu, 52, [104].

engiryawl, *a.* 55.

[enillec, 105].

enillo, *v.* 17, 33; enillent, 52.

enllip, *sm.* [93], 127.

enlliper, *v.* [93, 100], 122.

enllyn, *s.* 30, 32, 56.

ennill, *s.* 2.

ennynu, *v.* 122, 132, [133]; enynnu, 40; enyn, 26; enynher, 5, [7]; enynho, 40; [ennyno, 103].

[enryal, *s.* 140].

enrydedus, *a.* 4; enrydedussaf, 3.

enw, *sm.* 1, [109], 131, [134]. *See* geir.

enwawc, 17-18.

enwedic, 55, [114].

enwi, *v.* 129; enwet, 119; enwir, 38.

[eny = yny, 108].

erbyn, *v.* 6, [7].

erchi, *v.* 33, [135].

eredic, *v.* [108], 127.

eredic, 72, [73, 108]. *See* datanhud.

eruyll, *v.* 24.

ergyt, *sm.* 36, [94, 139].

erlit, 4, [116].

erlyn, *v.* 48.

[erthi, *s.* 96].

erw, *sf.* 54, [108]; — gayafar, 28; — gwanhwyn ar, 28; [— yr ych du, 108. erwyd,

pl. 136-7]. *See* deudec; dwy; pedeir; wyth.

eryr, *s.* 131.

[eskit, *sf.* 98]. escityeu, *pl.* 22, 33, 90, [91].

escob, *sm.* 58, [60, 114], 130. escyb, *pl.* 1.

escobty, *s.* 121.

escor, *v.* 129, [143].

escyn, *v.* 69; escynho, 24; eskyno, 17.

[esgubawr, *s.* 102]. *See* yscubawr.

estyn. *See* gobyr.

estynnu, *v.* 21; estynho, 47.

eturyt, *v.* 69, 118.

eturyt, etuyryt, etrif. *See* ach.

etiued, *s.* 52-3, [61, 78, 95], 126; — gwreic kaeth, 46; — gyfreithawl, 49; — llofrud, 39; — o gorff, 52-3; — priodawr, 49; — y lladedic, 39. etiuedyon, *pl.* 39, 49, 53.

etiuedu, *v.* 80.

etiuedyaeth, *s.* 53-4.

etling, *sm.* 3-4, 33. *See* lle.

eur, 3, 16-17, 23, 29, [64, 105, 108, 114], 123, [134]; — breinhawl, 4, [6, 8].

eureit, 22.

eurgrawn, *s.* 58, [60]. *See* brenhin.

ewic, *sf.* 35, [77], 80, [98]. ewiget, *pl.* 20.

ewin, *s.* 3, 42, 84.

[ewyllis, *s.* 139]. *See* brenhin.

ewythyr, *sm.* 38.

Ff.

[ffalt, *s.* 105].

[ffawyden, *sf.* 104].

ffin, *s.* 55.

Ll.

llad, *v.* 18, 37, 39, 41, 45, 68, 72, [74, 77–8], 79–80, 82, 85, [110, 113], 120, 122, 125, 132, [133, 137, 139]; lladawd, [61], 72, [74, 137]; lladet, 84; llather, [13], 18, 21, 24, 26, 31–3, 37, 39, 44, 85, 90, [91, 98, 115–16], 122, 131, [137]; llatho, 2, [9, 11], 17, 36–7, 82, 84, [104, 110], 131, [140–1]; lledir, 35–6, [66], 83, 122, [140; llodho, 116].

lladedic, 37–9.

llaeth, *s.* 28, 70–1, 84, 90, [91], 126; [— lestri, 95]. llaetheu, *pl.* 57.

llafur, *s.* 53.

llamu, *v.* [78], 80.

llamysten, *sf.* 18–19, 79.

llan, *s.* [13], 46, [113–15], 121, 125, [141]. *See* nawdwr.

llanw, *v.* 17.

[llassar, *s.* 105].

llathen, *sf.* 54.

llathrut, 23, 43, 89, [92–3, 96].

llathrudaw, *v.* 126.

llaw, *sf.* [64], 82, [97], 124; — asseu, [92], 129; — brenhines, 3; [— keitwat, 64]; — cennat, 17; — deheu, 43, 45, 58, [60, 92], 129; — dyn, 41; [— uwyall, 94, 106]; — lleidyr, 132, [134]; — penkynyd, 131; — tat, 40, 49. *See* brenhin; dwy; seith; teir; vn.

llawdwr, *s.* 30, 45, [135, 137]; llawdyr, 22. [llodreu, *pl.* 99].

llawuaeth, *s.* 129.

llawhethyr, *s.* 83.

llawr, *sm.* 82, [94–5, 98].

lle dilis, 4, 22.

lle yn y neuad, 4, [12], 19, 21, 27.

lled, 54; llet, 57, 71. *See* kyflet.

lledach, *s.* 44.

[llederw, *s.* 75.]

lledrat, *s.* 17, 40, 52, [64], 68, 79, 82–3, 85, 117–18, 120, 124, 127; [— kyfadef, 64. lletrat, 63, 99, 103–4, 137; — liw dyd, 100–1]. *See* dirwy; naw.

llef, *s.* 5, [78], 80.

[llefein, *v.* 138].

lleidyr, *s.* [103–4, 114], 117, [140]; — kyfadef, 123, 132, [134]; — diobeith, 41; — gwerth, 41, [103]. lladron, *pl.* 40, 69. *See* brenhin.

lleilltu, 47.

llenlliein, *s.* 16.

llestyr, *sm.* 21, 24, 31, 71. [llestri, *pl.* 14; — goreureit, 108]. *See* llaeth; lloneit.

llesteir, *v.* 32.

[llestreit, *s.* 95].

[lletuegin, *s.* 111. lletuegineu, *pl.* 111].

[lletuet, *s.* 107].

llety, *s.* 4, 6, [7, 9–10], 18–19; — march, 24. [lletyeu, *pl.* 13; — y teulu, 9].

lleyc, *s.* 1.

[lleyn yr eglwys, meibon, 114].

[llibinwr, *s.* 140].

lliein, *s.* 30, 37; — wisc, 2.

[llif, *s.* 138].

llin, *s.* 84.

llinhat, *s.* 30.

llit, *s.* 3, 130.

llithaw, *v.* 35.

[lliw, *s.* 105; — dyd goleu 100; — pren taryan, 105].

[lliwaw, *v.* 100].

A.W. Wade-Evans, Welsh Mediaeval Law.

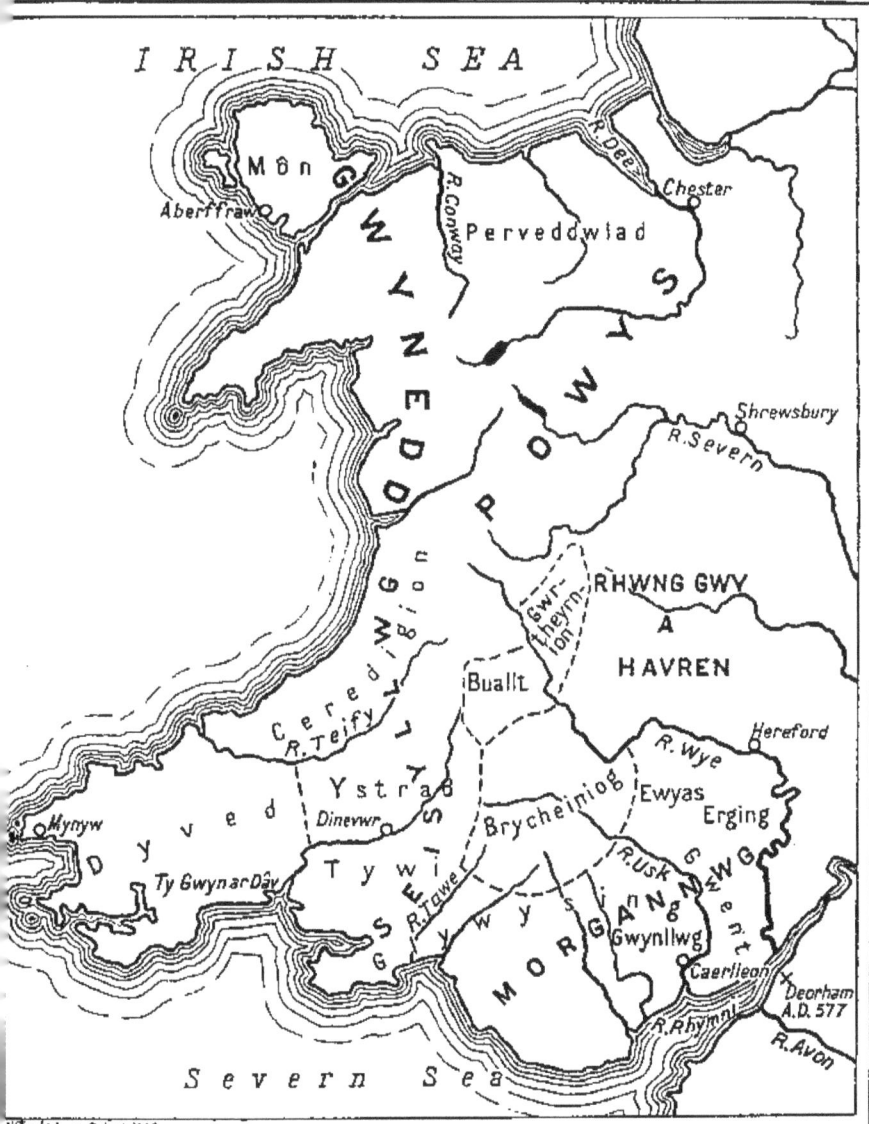

IRISH SEA

Môn

Aberffraw

GWYNEDD

R. Conway

R. Dee

Chester

Perveddwlad

POWYS

Shrewsbury

R. Severn

Gwr-theyrn-ion

RHWNG GWY A HAVREN

Ceredigion

R. Teify

Buallt

Hereford

R. Wye

Ystrad

Dinevwr

Ewyas

Erging

Dyved

Mynyw

Ty Gwyn ar Dâv

Tywi

SEISYLLWG

R. Tawey

Brycheiniog

R. Usk

GWENT

MORGANNWG

Gwynllwg

Caerlleon

Deorham A.D. 577

R. Rhymni

R. Avon

Severn Sea

Von Lecture, Oxford 1909.

English Miles

10   5   0   10   20

Lightning Source UK Ltd.
Milton Keynes UK
UKHW011815050722
405416UK00001B/222

9 781408 697177